THE FIRST SPRING

Wadah Khanfar

The First Spring: Political and Strategic Praxis of the Prophet of Islam (ﷺ)
Originally published in Arabic as *al-Rabīʿ al-Awwal: Qirāʾah Siyāsīyyah wa Istarātījīyyah fī al-Sīrah al-Nabawīyyah*

Translated by: **Aslam Farouk-Alli**

United Kingdom
60 Blakes Quay
Gas Works Road
RG1 3EN
Reading
United Kingdom
info@dararab.co.uk
www.dararab.co.uk

First Edition 2024
ISBN 978-1-78871-103-6

دار عرب للنشر والترجمة
DAR ARAB FOR PUBLISHING & TRANSLATION

Subjects: Prophetic Biography (Sīrah); Politics; History.

Text Edited: Na'eem Jeenah & Marcia Lynx Qualey
Text & Cover Design: Nasser Al Badri

WADAH KHANFAR

THE FIRST SPRING

POLITICAL & STRATEGIC PRAXIS OF THE PROPHET OF ISLAM (ﷺ)

TRANSLATED BY ASLAM FAROUK-ALLI

daraab

I dedicate this work…

to all who dream of a just and merciful world.

Table of Contents

Prologue: The final act....9

Preface to the Arabic edition....13

Preface to the English Edition....19

Translator's Preface....23

Introduction....29

CHAPTER ONE

Makkah's location and status....47

CHAPTER TWO

The world surrounding Makkah....67

CHAPTER THREE

Makkah – From periphery to centre....107

CHAPTER FOUR

Qurayshi exceptionalism....125

CHAPTER FIVE

Makkah contends with the future....153

CHAPTER SIX

Migration towards the future....199

CHAPTER SEVEN

The Prophetic strategy in Madinah....233

CHAPTER EIGHT

Leadership crisis in Makkah....245

CHAPTER NINE

The decisive moment....251

CHAPTER TEN

Abū Sufyān's tenure 275

CHAPTER ELEVEN

Uḥud – Lessons in crisis management....................283

CHAPTER TWELVE

Preparing for the final confrontation 311

CHAPTER THIRTEEN

Upheaval....................325

CHAPTER FOURTEEN

A strategic coup 339

CHAPTER FIFTEEN

Emergence of the Islamic nation....................351

CHAPTER SIXTEEN

Khaybar – The last citadel 383

CHAPTER SEVENTEEN

The Madinah Pact 389

CHAPTER EIGHTEEN

Addressing the new world 403

CHAPTER NINETEEN

The Great Conquest 421

CONCLUSION

A new beginning, a brighter future 457

Glossary....................471

References

Arabic Sources....................475

Non-Arabic Sources....................478

Prologue: The final act

Time: Morning of 13 Ramaḍān 8 AH / 4 December 629 CE.

Place: Makkah, in front of Dār al-Nadwah (the House of Assembly).

They come in sluggish droves on a cold morning, gathering before the leader of Quraysh and Kinānah, staring at the grim individual standing before them, their looks troubled.

Abū Sufyān is wrapped in a thick damascene mantle. A black dishevelled silk turban has been wound around his head in haste, and he leans on his staff, his back stooped. He is exhausted, staring at the ground, lost in contemplation.

The crowd finally gathered; people wait in anticipation. Abū Sufyān lifts his head and looks upon them with a nervous stare. He clears his throat and, with a trembling voice, proclaims:

"O people of Quraysh, here comes Muḥammad at the head of 10,000 armed men. He comes to you with a force never seen before, a force that you have no chance of overcoming."

Time freezes. Abū Sufyān's words sink in. Deep breaths are inhaled and passions flare, not because the crowd is unaware that the army that lies in wait at the gates of Makkah is Muḥammad's (ﷺ) army, but because they had hoped the Qurayshi delegation that had visited the Muslim encampment the previous night would have agreed on terms with him. They now realise that the delegation has failed to prevent the fall of Makkah and that their only option is to surrender.

The ominous silence is pierced by the shrieking voice of Hind, daughter of 'Utbah: "People of Makkah! Kill this useless glutton, a shame to our leaders."

Abū Sufyān responds to his wife's insult by addressing the people, raising his voice in a decisive tone: "Woe unto you! People of Quraysh, do not be swayed by this woman."

A mocking voice from the crowd cuts him short: "May Allah bring shame upon you, gatherer of this crowd!"

Abū Sufyān continues speaking, ignoring the heckler: "O People of Quraysh, woe unto you! I have seen what you have not; I have seen men and steeds and weapons that none of you can overpower. He has come with the likes of that which you have never seen before, and so whosoever enters the home of Abū Sufyān has amnesty."

An angry voice interrupts: "May Allah bring shame upon you. Of what use is your home to us?"

Abū Sufyān ignores the man and continues: "Whoever shuts his door has amnesty; whoever enters the mosque has amnesty; and whoever surrenders his weapons has amnesty."

He then withdraws, mumbling to himself and dragging his robes behind him. He passes through the crowd as he heads for his house, carefully avoiding meeting the eyes of the people.

An incoherent mix of words and mutterings rises from the gathering; people are divided between those affirming what was said and those rejecting it, between those utterly confused and those just astounded. Some try to be positive, while others break down, seized with fear. Between these two groups, there are some simply overcome by silence.

Confusion is widespread; emotions and tensions run high; voices intermingle. The people cannot wrest control of their senses. Suddenly, screams echo across Makkah: "Muḥammad's army has reached Dhi Ṭuwa!"

The crowd disperses more quickly than it had gathered. Most people enter their homes and shut the doors behind them. The city's nobility takes to the hills while others sit in front of the Ka'bah. A small group gathers around Ṣafwān ibn Umayyah, 'Ikrimah ibn Abī Jahl, and Suhayl ibn ‘Amr, vowing that Muḥammad (ﷺ) will not enter Makkah by force.

Hours pass…

The scene reaches its climax when the Prophet (ﷺ) emerges from the Ka‘bah door and stands before the crowd of people gathered in front of the sanctuary, on their knees, awaiting their fate, with only one question on every pair of lips: “What will he do to us?”

They listen in earnest as he speaks: “There is no deity except Allah, the One and Only, and He has no partner. He has fulfilled His promise and has made His servant victorious, and has defeated the confederates all by Himself.”

“Why does he insist on attributing everything to his Lord?

“And what will Muḥammad do to us? Will he treat us in the same way that we treated him? Will he exact his revenge? Will he confiscate our wealth just as we confiscated the wealth of his companions when they migrated with him to Madinah, or will he build his kingdom on the remains of our legacy and culture? Has the authority of the Quraysh finally come to an end after none was able to best it before? Will it become a vassal of a victorious king who will exercise full authority over Makkah for himself and his people, from providing water for the pilgrims to custodianship of the sanctuary around the Ka‘bah? What is to stop him from doing so?”

Muḥammad (ﷺ) continues to address them, and they listen intently: “Indeed, every glorious deed or claim on wealth or act of retribution lies under my two feet, except for the custodianship of the sanctuary and the provision of water for the pilgrims.”

The crowd lets out a sigh of relief.

“This is not the logic of a vanquishing king, so what does Muḥammad truly want? And what novelty will he offer us in exchange for our old ways?”

He continues: “O People of Quraysh. Allah has indeed stripped you of the arrogance of the time of ignorance and of the veneration of your forefathers. All people are from Adam and Adam is from clay."

He then recites a verse of the Qur'ān (49:13): "O People! We have created you from a male and a female, and made you into nations and tribes that you may know one another. Verily the most honourable of you by [the standards of] Allah is the one who is most conscious [of Allah]. And Allah has full knowledge and is well-acquainted [with all things]."

"People are from Adam and Adam is from clay!"

"People, all people, including us? We who expelled him and showed him only enmity?"

"Or will he exclude those who expelled him from the Holy Mosque and fought against him?"

Then came the question that the onlookers had anticipated: "O People of Quraysh, what do you think I will do to you?"

As soon as the question is posed, heads rise with dejected gazes, staring at the conqueror at the door of the Ka'bah, its handgrips in his firm grasp and, along with it, the fate of the Quraysh, the future of Makkah, and the future of the Arabs. They look on with hope and humility, wishing that he will show compassion. Some speak with trembling voices: "A gracious brother and the son of a gracious brother!"

They hold their breath as they search the expression on his face, hoping to detect their fate before his lips pronounce it. His face beams with satisfaction as the light of a new era in Makkah shines upon their faces and the glad tidings are pronounced: "I say what my brother [the Prophet] Yūsuf said before me: 'No blame is there upon you this day. Go forth, for you are free!'"

Preface to the Arabic edition

History is replete with the stories of exceptional individuals from different civilisations and ethnicities, people who redrew the global map and tipped the strategic balances of power. The list includes emperors, conquerors, leaders, and revolutionaries; they share similar traits but are differentiated by their aims and objectives. History has immortalised them because their actions led to the transformation of nations, and sometimes, of the world.

Such exceptional personalities necessarily occupy an important symbolic status in the lives of the nations they are a part of, occupying a position at the centre of the national identity and collective heritage of their people. Their biographies are invoked in political and cultural discourse, statues are erected in their honour, buildings are named after them, and their life stories are studied in national curricula. This is because every nation has a perennial need to know itself, and such symbols are often important means by which to entrench national identity.

Not too long ago, I was following the crisis between Greece and Macedonia, which emerged from a dispute over history and became a political tussle. Alexander the Great lay at the heart of this dispute. He is the pride of Greece and is regarded as the symbol of their national identity; they therefore reject any other country's claims of ownership over him.

According to the current national borders, Macedonia, from which Alexander hails, lies in northern Greece. The Republic of Macedonia, which declared its independence under this name after the collapse of Yugoslavia, was not the historical Macedonia, but only a portion of it. Greece thus regarded this latter name to be a violation of Greek history and patrimony, at the forefront of which lies the greatest Greek symbol of all: Alexander.

The Republic of Macedonia, for its part, also claimed Alexander as part of its heritage, and erected a huge statue of him in the centre of its capital city, Skopje. This provoked a strong reaction from Greece, and its parliament banned the recognition of Macedonian passports until the country changed its name. Greece also blocked Macedonia's accession to the European Union and NATO. The political crisis escalated until the two sides reached an agreement through international mediation; the Republic of Macedonia was renamed the Republic of North Macedonia.

Nations need extraordinary historical symbols to entrench their national identity, and they feel provoked when others lay claim to their historical right to a particular symbol. Many historical personalities are identified by their national affiliations: Darius is Persian, Alexander is Macedonian, Julius Caesar is Roman, Justinian is Byzantine, and so on.

Another common characteristic among these personalities is that many left their mark on history through military accomplishments. Some had great architectural, legislative, and economic accomplishments as well, but these were also a result of the military conquests that granted them legitimacy and the necessary wealth to entrench their authority and status. Most strategic historical transformations have resulted from contestations over authority and wealth. This is evident in the biographies of many exceptional historical figures.

Darius I, also known as Darius the Great, reigned from 521 BCE to 486 BCE, and was the greatest monarch of the Persian Achaemenid Empire. He made important architectural and administrative contributions, but his reign was distinguished by his military conquests and victories against Egypt, Athens, Macedonia, and Central Asia.

Ruling from 336 BCE to 323 BCE, Alexander the Macedonian, also known as Alexander the Great, established the greatest empire known to the ancient world before the age of thirty. This followed an illustrious military career marked by great victories over the Persians and by conquests in India, Central Asia, and Egypt.

Julius Caesar, who reigned from 49 BCE to 44 BCE, also left his mark on Roman history only after he had achieved numerous military victories in the Gaul region, expanding the territory of the Roman

Empire. This enabled him to forcefully argue his own terms before the Roman legislature and to impose himself as Dictator of the Republic. The result was the suspension of the republican era after Caesar's death, and the birth of the Roman Empire.

Similarly, Justinian I, or Justinian the Great, who reigned from 527 to 565, increased the domain of the Byzantine empire by a series of military confrontations. He regained control of Rome and most of the territory that the Western Roman Empire had lost to the Germanic tribes. He also successfully suppressed a popular rebellion in Constantinople in 532, in which 30,000 citizens were killed. He is credited with undertaking the most important legislative reforms in the Byzantine Empire.

What captures our attention when we ponder the achievements of these four extraordinary individuals is that they were able to redraw the strategic map of the world and to radically change the balance of power. In so doing, they employed a comprehensive approach, based on military action, which led to the strengthening of their authority and the growth of their wealth; yet they remained firmly attached to nation or empire.

From a strategic perspective, the Prophet Muḥammad (ﷺ) achieved a radical and speedy global coup, but he differed fundamentally from these other individuals. His strategic approach is not rooted in the centrality of power and a monopoly on wealth; he was neither driven by a nationalistic logic nor did he aspire to create an empire. One can grasp the uniqueness of the prophetic strategic praxis only from this perspective.

In this book, we will uncover the Prophet's (ﷺ) strategic and political methodology by examining his strategies, tactics, and the actions that led up to and included the conquest of Makkah. We will consider his various actions and pronouncements, which occurred in the context of interactions with authorities, tribes, and various individuals. These include engagements; correspondence; alliances; military expeditions, including both raids and battles; relations between Madinah and regional and global political powers; as well as attitudes toward various Arab tribes and alliances or disputes with them. It will also consider the publicity campaigns launched by the Prophet (ﷺ) and his companions. This includes pronouncements by the Prophet (ﷺ) himself, his messengers, his military leaders, and those who composed panegyric or defamatory poetry on Madinah's behalf, such as Ḥassān ibn Thābit, 'Abdallah ibn Rawāḥah and Ka'b ibn Mālik.

We will begin by tracing the strategic contours of Makkah, examining its geographic location, status, politics, and economy. We will examine its cross-border agreements and pacts, its tribal structure, and its internal tensions. After that, we will trace the strategic economic map of the world around Makkah, followed by a presentation of the regional and global balance of power just prior to the prophetic mission. This will be followed by an examination of the situation on the Arabian Peninsula at the close of the sixth century and an interrogation of its social and religious structures.

Thereafter, we will explore the emergence of the Prophet's (ﷺ) strategic methodology in the first years of his mission. We will examine his attempts to find a support base, a task that took him to Yathrib, and consider how that village, torn apart by internecine strife, was transformed into a city characterised by order and initiative, and driven by a brave strategic vision that was able, in only a few years, to establish a new social contract that challenged Makkah's obsolete one.

Our assessment will then proceed to examine—first theoretically, then practically—how the Prophet's (ﷺ) strategic method guided his military confrontations and political alliances, and how it established the psyche required for his future struggles. We will see how this strategy was characterised by clear priorities, comprehensive and systematic coordination, precise assessments of the balance of forces, and a highly developed capacity to plan for the future.

Through this process, we will realise that the Prophet's (ﷺ) message was at the heart of every move he made. It was, in fact, this message—through its engagement with the political and strategic realities that it encountered—that birthed a new approach, different from the methodologies common before that time. We will see clearly how this unique method was able to achieve stunning success in a world characterised by turmoil, degradation, and loss of purpose. Muḥammad's (ﷺ) message offered an Islamic universalism that ushered in a new era for the liberation of human beings and shattered the shackles of oppression, domination, and monopolistic control.

Today, the world is again witnessing major transformations that touch on every aspect of life, with strategic and political changes at the forefront. While humanity tries to sketch the future that we desire, and while we seek an approach that might steer us to safety, I present this work, which is the culmination of intense reflection on the sīrah[1] of the Prophet (ﷺ) from political and strategic perspectives. This is a humble beginning, and it is my hope that this task will be taken up and continued by other researchers and people interested in learning the lessons from, and developing a paradigm based on, the life of the Prophet (ﷺ).

I thank all the friends who honoured me by reviewing earlier drafts of this book, and who enriched it with their opinions, comments, and corrections. I pay tribute to them and am truly grateful to them all.

All praise is due to Allah, firstly and ultimately, for He alone guides us along the straight path.

28 May 2019 / 23 Ramaḍān 1440 AH

Doha, Qatar

---

1. In the Islamic sciences, al-Sīrah al-Nabawīyyah, commonly abbreviated to sīrah, refers to the biography of the Prophet (ﷺ). From the root word which means to travel (sārah), it refers to the journey of the Prophet's (ﷺ) life. The sīrah is generally regarded by Muslims as not just a historical or biographical account but as normative and, therefore, a model for emulation.

Preface to the English Edition

Our world is experiencing what is perhaps the most complex transformation in recent memory. Profound, multifaceted, and all-encompassing changes are taking place simultaneously. A shift in the balance of forces is recalibrating the international order, and the consequent polarisation threatens to descend into a destructive global conflict. Fundamental changes have been effected by modern technology, starting with the information and communication technologies (ICT) revolution and culminating in the artificial intelligence (AI) revolution, with its seemingly unlimited applications. This has already had—and continues to have—an effect on patterns of consciousness and human behaviour, and it impacts our psychological makeup and social order. In addition, our world has begun to pay the price for the encroachment and insatiable greed of capitalism and its neoliberal manifestations, which have caused massive economic imbalances between nations and a widening gap between rich and poor. Capitalist predation has also led to the destruction of the environment and almost irreversible change in the climate, with all its devastating consequences.

In this era of unpredictability and rapid change, humanity is in dire need of a new philosophical vision and a fresh start. The western hegemony that has dominated the global stage for the past three centuries is rapidly eroding; it has reached a point of bankruptcy, where it can no longer offer creative solutions that might guarantee a secure future for humanity. In any case, the future is far too expansive to be dominated by a single civilisation. The world's civilisational and cultural heritage is rich and diverse, encompassing much wisdom and collective experience that has been accumulated over many millennia. Our present malaise demands that we study this enormous human capital and draw lessons from it so that we might devise solutions for the future that are inspired by a multiplicity of sources, including Islam.

Islamic history is replete with profound and rich experiences, the most important of which was arguably the greatest strategic upset in history. The period between 630 and 642 ushered in an era in which the entrenched but aging global bipolar order finally collapsed and was replaced by a new power, the ascendance of which no one could have predicted. The Muslim Arabs, relatively unknown at the time, burst forth from the global periphery and advanced with lightning speed. They overran the entire Persian Empire and half of the Byzantine Empire. Their sphere of influence widened even further thereafter, reaching the borders of China in the east and the shores of the Atlantic Ocean in the west.

Unique in its approach, the programme of Islamic conquests carried a universal message. Its aim was not to centralise power and wealth in the hands of the conquerors or to make one people subjugate another. Nor did it seek to wipe out its enemies, as was the case with previous imperial expansionism. Rather, Islam was offered as a liberating force and gave its subjects the choice to maintain their religions and cultures, thereby constructing and establishing a global civilisation and economy whose builders were from a diversity of ethnicities and religions.

The roots of this major global transition lay in a small settlement in the western Arabian Peninsula that is hardly noticeable on the maps of the ancient world. The remote hamlet of Makkah, whose inhabitants were regarded as inconsequential to geopolitical conflicts of the time, did not attract the attention of regional and international powers. It was no more than a crossing point for caravans traversing the desert, carrying Chinese and Indian merchandise from the ports of Yemen to the Levant and Iraq. However, from the early seventh century onwards, the intense struggle between the two global powers, the Persians and the Byzantines, *was* of concern to Makkah's inhabitants. Their attention was drawn particularly to the impact of this enduring war on the safety of their trade routes and caravans.

Within this frantic and dangerous global crucible, the message of Islam emerged from the shadow of the Ancient Sanctuary in Makkah, which was venerated by the Arabs. In 611, Muḥammad ibn ʻAbdallah proclaimed that he was Allah's Messenger and that he had been sent for the guidance of all humanity. He invited others to the belief in one God and a return to the principles of the religion propagated by the Prophet Ibrāhīm (Abraham). He proclaimed that all people were equal and that there were no differences between them except in piety and good deeds; neither race, ethnicity, language, social class nor gender was relevant to God. In their arrogance, however, the majority of his people rejected this message and, after thirteen years of his inviting them to Islam, he was forced to migrate with a small number of his companions to another, even more remote settlement, Yathrib. There, he was able to spread his message with greater freedom and to establish a new strategic and political centre. From Yathrib—which was renamed Madinah after his arrival—he brought about a radical change in people, society, and the Arab and regional political reality. He also mentored a unique generation of his companions, who carried his message to the world after his death in 632.

This book examines the political and strategic trajectory pursued by the Prophet Muḥammad (ﷺ) during a mission that spanned twenty-three years, and it carefully considers the regional and international contexts within which the Prophet's (ﷺ) life played out. From an examination of his biography, it seeks out the fundamentals and principles of the new methodology that resulted in the greatest-ever strategic upset and historic transformation of the international system. The Prophet's (ﷺ) biography is replete with lessons for individuals, communities, and nations. I have, however, chosen to focus on an under-studied area of his life: its political and strategic dimensions.

This book, originally published in Arabic, owes a great debt to a great many people. For this English edition, I would like, in particular, to thank my friends Aslam Farouk-Alli, who undertook the translation from the original Arabic with much care, and Na'eem Jeenah, who edited the translated text. The immense effort expended by Aslam and Na'eem resulted in the work as it now appears in its final form. Translation, especially to English, is not an easy task because language—any language—is a civilisational repository and an embodiment of a culture, having its own unique spirit. The translation of the Arabic text into English thus required a great deal of effort, for which I am grateful.

I hope that this book is the first step in an enduring dialogue on our history and our future. All praise is due to Allah, Lord of the worlds.

20 April 2023 / 29 Ramaḍān 1444

Doha, Qatar

Translator's Preface

This book is a culmination of the author's lengthy and intense reflection on the Sīrah, the life-story of the Prophet of Islam, Muḥammad ibn 'Abdallah (ﷺ). Sīrah Studies is an established discipline in the Islamic sciences and, like numerous other works in this field of inquiry, *The First Spring* engages the Prophet's biography as a normative framework that provides devout Muslims with a model for praxis. However, the unique approach adopted by the author marks a clear departure from earlier studies and represents an important methodological turn in the genre. By breaking new ground, the book makes an important contribution to Sīrah Studies and deserves a wide, diverse, and critical audience. It therefore gives me great pleasure to present this work to an English readership.

Most recent English works of Sīrah published by Muslim scholars have sought to provide a faithful portrait of the Prophet Muḥammad (ﷺ) as captured in the primary Arabic sources. The now-classic studies by Muhammad Husayn Haykal[2] and Martin Lings (Abū Bakr Sirāj ad-Dīn)[3] enjoy great popularity, as does the more recent biography by Adil Salahi.[4]

For contemporary Sīrah works in Arabic, the question of the authenticity of the primary source material has been an abiding concern; these studies have been more attentive to filtering out spurious narrations prevalent in many pre-modern biographies. The Sudanese historian Mahdī Rizqallah made an important contribution with his account of the Prophet's (ﷺ) life;[5] it draws exclusively on source material that meets the exacting standards of authenticity established by Islamic scholarship.

2. Muhammad Husayn Haykal, *The Life of Muhammad*, trans. Isma'il Ragi A. al Faruqi (Oak Brook, USA: American Trust Publications, 1976).
3. Martin Lings, *Muhammad: His Life Based on the Earliest Sources* (Cambridge: The Islamic Texts Society, 1983).
4. Adil Salahi, *Muhammad: Man and Prophet* (Leicestershire: The Islamic Foundation, 2002).
5. Mahdī Rizqallah Aḥmad, *al-Sīrah al-Nabawīyyah fī Daw al-Maṣādir al-Aslīyyah: Dirāsah Taḥlīlīyah* (Riyadh: Markaz Malik Fayṣal li al-Buḥūth wa al-Dirāsāt al-Islāmīyyah, 1992).

While these works strive to present an authentic biographical narrative and to affirm the normative framework of the Sīrah, they do not explicitly aim to extrapolate lessons from the Prophet's (ﷺ) biography. This has been the primary focus of contemporary Islamic reformist scholars, as seen in the works of Muṣṭafa al-Sibā'ī,[6] Muḥammad al-Ghazālī,[7] and Sa'īd Ramaḍān al-Būṭī,[8] which have attracted a large readership. They examine and interrogate events in the life of the Prophet (ﷺ) while also deliberately drawing lessons and extracting principles from them. These reformist scholars attempt to demonstrate that the Sīrah is an important source from which to learn about Islam, its doctrines, legal precepts, and ethical principles, all of which contribute to the development of the character of a Muslim. These studies do not, however, venture far from the Islamic context and are more akin to a dialogue within the tradition itself.

By contrast, *The First Spring* focuses not only on the nascent Muslim community in the Arabian Peninsula, but also on that of the world of the great powers around it. In this way, it draws the Sīrah into a conversation with its own context and with interlocutors beyond it. In pursuing this dialogue, the author does not limit himself to invoking classical Islamic and western historical sources; his methodological toolbox draws liberally from the contemporary social sciences, and he invokes the academic disciplines of Political Studies, International Relations, Security Studies, and Strategic Studies, among others.

While the book is clearly directed at a Muslim audience, its broad methodological scope is sure to attract the interest of a western academic audience as well. Unfortunately, Orientalist Sīrah scholarship has generally not been able to traverse its self-imposed boundaries of religious polemic and scepticism.[9] While earlier Orientalist scholarship focused on the theme of Muḥammad (ﷺ) as a false prophet,[10] recent

6. Muṣṭafa al-Sibā'ī, *al-Sīrah al-Nabawīyyah: Durūs wa 'Ibar* (Beirut: al-Maktab al-Islāmī, 1985).
7. Muḥammad al-Ghazālī, *Fiqh al-Sīrah* (Cairo: Dār al-Shurūq, 2000).
8. Muḥammad Sa'īd Ramaḍān al-Būṭī, *Fiqh al-Sīrah al-Nabawīyyah* (Damascus: Dār al-Fikr, 1991).
9. For an overview of the Orientalist literature on the Sīrah, see Andreas Görke, "Prospects and limits in the study of the historical Muḥammad", in Nicolet Boekhoff van der Voort, Kees Versteegh, and Joas Wagemakers (eds.), *The Transmission and Dynamics of the Textual Sources of Islam: Essays in Honour of Harald Motzki* (Leiden and Boston: Brill, 2011).
10. Norman Daniel's classic study on the formation and development of Western attitudes about Islam from medieval times to the present gives a detailed account of anti-Islamic polemics in

scholarship is dominated by the question of Islamic origins and the veracity of Islamic sources and methodology. This sceptical trend was given traction by Crone and Cook in their 1977 book, *Hagarism*, where they argue that Islam was actually a late version of apocalyptical Judaism in which the Arabs of the Hejaz had rediscovered their Abrahamic roots and sought to retake the Holy Land of Palestine.[11] More recently, Fred Donner pursued a line of thought on the nascent Muslim community in which he argues that it was only later transformed into Islam by historical processes.[12] Reviewing the literature on Islamic origins, Jonathan Brown has concluded that perhaps the only novel contribution by the Revisionist approach is the sheer scale of its scepticism.[13]

In its most extreme manifestation, Orientalist scholarship has impudently questioned the very existence of the historical Muḥammad (ﷺ).[14] Nonetheless, the positive contributions on source methodology made especially in German Orientalist scholarship must be acknowledged; the notable contributions of Harald Motzki,[15] Gregor Schoeler,[16] and Andreas Görke[17] deserve study and reflection. In addition to these studies, Sean Anthony's book on the Sīrah is also worthy of mention.[18] While Anthony pays tribute to the work of

the West and its portrayal of Muḥammad as a false prophet; see: Norman Daniel, *Islam and the West: The Making of an Image* (Oxford: Oneworld, 1993). John Tolan's more recent study is a necessary compliment to Daniel's work. See John Tolan, *Saracens: Islam in the Medieval European Imagination* (New York: Columbia University Press, 2002).

11. Patricia Crone and Michael Cook, *Hagarism: The Making of the Islamic World* (Cambridge: Cambridge University Press, 1977).

12. Fred M. Donner, *Muhammad and the Believers: At the Origins of Islam* (Cambridge, Massachusetts: Harvard University Press, 2010).

13. Jonathan A. C. Brown, *Hadith: Muhammad's Legacy in the Medieval and Modern World* (Oxford: Oneworld, 2009), pp. 220-224.

14. In this regard, see: Yehuda D. Nevo and Judith Koren, *Crossroads to Islam: The Origins of the Arab Religion and the Arab State* (Amherst: Prometheus Books, 2003).

15. See, for example, his edited volume: Harald Motzki (ed.), *The Biography of Muḥammad: The Issue of the Sources* (Leiden: Brill, 2000).

16. See: Gregor Schoeler, *The Biography of Muḥammad: Nature and Authenticity*, trans. Uwe Vagelpohl, ed. James E. Montgomery (London and New York: Routledge, 2011).

17. In addition to several published works on the primary sources, Görke has engaged in fruitful collaborations with Gregor Schoeler and Harald Motzki in re-examining the primary sources and prevalent Orientalist scholarship on the topic. See, for example: Andreas Görke and Gregor Schoeler, "Reconstructing the earliest *sīra* texts: The Hiğra in the corpus of 'Urwa b. al-Zubayr", *Der Islam* (vol. 82, no. 2, 2005), 209-220; Andreas Görke, Harald Motzki, and Gregor Schoeler, "First Century Sources for the Life of Muḥammad? A Debate", *Der Islam* (vol. 89, no. 2, 2012) 2-59.

18. Sean William Anthony, *Muhammad and the Empires of Faith: The Making of the Prophet of Islam* (Oakland, California: University of California Press, 2020). Anthony's translation of one of

Patricia Crone, who was one of his teachers, he does not shy away from challenging many of the claims of the early sceptics. It is however Görke and Schoeler who sound the death knell for Crone's 'Hagarism' thesis, in the revised and expanded English translation of their German-language study that focuses on the 'Urwa ibn al-Zubayr Corpus and the earliest non-Muslim sources on the life of the Prophet (ﷺ).[19] In spite of their tremendous erudition and painstaking research, all of these works are still limited by an extremely narrow focus and offer little in terms of engaging in the kind of reading attempted in *The First Spring*. Thus, this book may well provide the impetus for broadening the parameters of the debate on the Prophet's (ﷺ) life within western academia as well as in Muslim confessional thought.

It has been a daunting task to render into English this multifaceted and multidisciplinary work, which resonates in both classical and contemporary Arabic registers by drawing on a considerable number of primary sources. As such, a few words on the technical aspects of the translation are merited. I opted to use a standard transliteration convention for Arabic names and places, with a few exceptions for commonplace names that enjoy wide usage in English. In translating Qur'anic verses, I consulted and utilised several excellent English renditions of the Holy Book, including those of Abdullah Yusuf Ali, Muhammad Muhsin Khan and Taqi al-Din Hilali, Marmaduke Pickthall, Muhammad Abdel-Haleem, and the Saheeh International translation by Emily Assami, Mary Kennedy, and Amatullah Bantley. I have on rare occasions modified these translations in a manner that I deemed more reflective of the original meaning. Translations of all prophetic sayings are my own, as are the lengthy passages from the primary Sīrah sources utilised by the author, namely, the works of Ibn Isḥāq and al-Wāqidī, which are available in English translation.[20]

---

the earliest works of Sīrah is also an important contribution to the field; see: Ma'mar ibn Rāshid, *The Expeditions: An Early Biography of Muḥammad*, edited and translated by Sean W. Anthony (New York and London: New York University Press, 2014).

19. See: Andreas Görke and Gregor Schoeler, *The Earliest Writings on the Life of Muhammad: The 'Urwa Corpus and the Non-Muslim Sources* (Berlin: Gerlach Press, 2024).

20. See: Alfred Guillaume, *The Life of Muhammad: A Translation of Ibn Isḥāq's Sīrat Rasūl Allāh* (Oxford: Oxford University Press, 1955); Rizwi Faizer (ed.), *The Life of Muḥammad: Al-Wāqidī's Kitāb al-Maghāzī*, trans. Rizwi Faizer, Amal Ismail and AbdulKader Tayob (London and New York: Routledge, 2011).

I would not have been able to complete this work without the support and assistance of a few outstanding individuals. The author, Wadah Khanfar, made time to revise the translation and offered valuable advice and suggestions. Ahmed Vall Ould Dine generously brought his Arabic expertise to bear in unraveling difficult passages and expressions in the primary sources. Osama El-Mourabit undertook the unenviable task of checking and correcting all the references and did so with consummate professionalism. My biggest debt is, nevertheless, owed to Na'eem Jeenah, the editor of the English translation. Na'eem not only revised the text, but also subjected it to a rigorous fact-check. He also compared my translation of passages from the classical sources with extant translations published elsewhere, undertaking all of this with great industry and humour. I am grateful to him for all that I have learnt in the process. While I have no doubt that this collaborative effort has made the English rendition of *The First Spring* much better, I alone assume responsibility for whatever infelicities remain.

Aslam Farouk-Alli

Ankara, Türkiye

07 April 2023 / 16 Ramaḍān 1444

Introduction

Message and methodology

The divine mandate entrusted to Muḥammad ibn ʻAbdallah (ﷺ) was unique. It was the last and final mandate in which there was a direct relationship between God's revelation and humankind. Muḥammad (ﷺ) was the final prophet sent to all creation; there is no prophet after him. Importantly, he was a prophet sent not only to his people, but to all of humanity.

This mandate has several implications. Most importantly, it was a divine affirmation that human beings had reached a moment of distinguished maturity that enabled them to bear the message in its fully articulated and final manifestation, and for their future to unfold without the need for further revelation from the heavens. It also affirmed that humanity had begun moving toward a universalism that transcended nation, tribe, gender, or colour, and therefore needed a universal discourse that was not limited to one group over another.

In essence, Muḥammad's (ﷺ) message bears glad tidings for all humanity. It announced the beginning of the phase of human maturity and universalism. The ascension of humanity to a level of collective consciousness and universal understanding made it possible for human beings to be addressed by a universal message that transcends the limitations of place and time. Place is transcended by going beyond linguistic, ethnic, and national categories, while time is transcended because the message is not constrained by the necessities of a specific era.

Say: "O People, I am the Messenger of Allah to you all, [from Him] to Whom belongs the dominion of the heavens and the earth. There is no god but Him; He gives life and death, so believe in Allah and His Messenger, the unlettered Prophet who believes in Allah and His words, and follow him so that you may be guided. (Qur'ān 7:158).

This divine address, directed to all people, did not simply announce the sending of a prophet like the prophets sent before him. The prophets before Muḥammad (ﷺ) had been sent specifically to their communities, and their messages addressed the circumstances of the people in those eras. Allah, the Sublime, would send a prophet and, after a period, would send another to renew the covenant and to correct any deviations and shortcomings. History proceeded in this manner until humanity reached a level of interaction and integration, having developed mutual dependence in terms of thinking, modes of living, and well-being. It had thus become difficult for them to be divided into opposing and closed civilisational centres, with each claiming to possess absolute truth and dismissing those outside their circle as barbarians and savages. There arose a need for a new universal discourse that would enable humanity to move into the future in peace and security, safeguarded by the perfect religion, interacting with it, and guided along the path it mapped out without the need for further divine intervention through the deployment of more prophets.

At the beginning of the seventh century, humanity was heavily burdened by conflict that caused destruction, terror, and subjugation. It was clear that, "Corruption has appeared on land and sea because of what the hands of humankind have earned." (Qur'ān 30:41). For humanity to find a balance and again grow and develop, there was a need for a new philosophy of being and a methodology capable of sparking a global transformation in thinking and conduct, while maintaining relevance for humanity across time. It therefore became necessary to change the thinking, methodology, and spirit of the world, and for humanity to be liberated from its chains and limitations, to enable the initiation and spread of a new global revolution. This spirit was illustrated in the response by one of the Prophet's companions, Rabi' ibn 'Amr, when the Persian general, Rustum, asked him: "Why did you come to our land?"

Rabi' ibn 'Amr responded: "Allah has sent us to deliver whichever of his servants desire [such deliverance] from the narrowness of this world to its wide expanse, and from the oppression of religions to the justice of Islam. Allah has sent us with His religion to His creation and whoever accepts it will be accepted by us."[21]

21. 'Alī 'Izz al-Dīn Ibn al-Athīr, *Al-Kāmil fī al-Tārīkh* (Beirut: Dār al-Kitāb al-'Arabī, 1997), vol. 2, 298.

This was the conjuncture for the final divine message to be delivered, as a natural and organic evolution that was neither strange nor unforeseen. This message was not an unprecedented innovation, but one whose essence was known to humankind, a message from which people had strayed with the passage of time. It was part of the psyche and collective memory of human beings, a memory that had been suppressed by time, self-interest, and vain desire.

The message of Islam is not a deviation from humanity's religious heritage; it is, rather, the legitimate heir of previous divine messages, which had all been Islamic messages, but had been confined to particular times and places. The message of Muḥammad ibn 'Abdallah (ﷺ) thus came as the final instalment that completed the earlier messages. It consolidated the teachings and legislation that had come before it, since they had been only partial manifestations suited to particular phases of human development. Islam, in the form conveyed by Muḥammad (ﷺ), is the perfect religion delivered after human consciousness had developed fully and was suited and ready to bear the complete message. "This day have I perfected your religion for you, completed My favour upon you, and have chosen for you Islam as your religion" (Qur'ān 5:3).

Allah, the Glorious and Sublime, assured us that the prophets before Muḥammad (ﷺ) had taught their people the major principles of Islam, from belief in Allah to belief in the day of reckoning, and that they had been given laws that suited their needs and level of maturity. Muḥammad (ﷺ), however, conveyed the complete Islam, in terms of principles, values, and legislation, an Islam that coalesced with human consciousness, beginning from a fixed moment in a specific place, and progressing toward a universalism that transcends borders and is open to the future. Its principles did not need any amendment, correction, or supplementation.

The novel aspect of this message is that it takes people back to their origin, to their affiliation to Adam, which encompasses all of humanity and affirms that Adam originated from clay. This concept of humanity goes beyond narrow affiliations and rises above the bigoted prejudices that have led to conflict and destruction on earth. This message elevates religious, political, and cultural frameworks above the notion of inevitable conflict that controls the evolution of empires, nations, and groups, replacing it with a universal system, the essence of which is the belief in one God, and the foundations of which are ethical.

Another new characteristic of this message is that it extends to the end of time. Allah informed His Prophet Muḥammad (ﷺ) that he was the final prophet and messenger, that there would be no prophet after him, and that his message would be the final revelation from Allah to His creation. This message will not deteriorate with the passing of time and will remain vital and relevant for all future generations. From this perspective, Islam inhabits the future and has, therefore, to be in continuous development, constantly in touch with current realities and oriented toward tomorrow. Islam is equipped with a unique trait that gives it internal momentum, steering it through time along the path of human destiny. This trait is the continuous interaction between the fixed foundation of revelation and the evolving human intellect, between the fixed text and evolving interpretation, which generates the vital thinking that is in harmony with the movement through time. Islam is, therefore, a constantly developing, living entity that never fails to provide solutions to the problems that humanity may face at any future conjuncture. Therefore, if we ever feel that Islam is in crisis, this would be an indication that the ongoing and necessary interaction between the foundation and the intellect had been disrupted. Since the foundation is pristine and perfect, the intellect that is responsible for interpreting and conveying the message must therefore be in crisis.

Model for emulation

A reader of the sīrah will find a clear consistency and symmetry between the Prophet's (ﷺ) actions and his leadership. This is obvious in his grasp of priorities, his constant consideration of the balance of forces, his deep comprehension of the details of political thinking and activity, and his knowledge of the historical background and ancestral memory of tribes and societies. He also possessed piercing insight, was able to see the strategic gaps within various groups, and exhibited a highly developed capacity to use these abilities to forge alliances and form coalitions.

In addition to being fully cognisant of the political and strategic realities of the Quraysh and other Arabs across the peninsula, the Prophet (ﷺ) was also familiar with the balance of forces in the region surrounding him, whether between regional powers—like the kingdoms on the periphery of the Arabian Peninsula that included the Ghassanids, the Manādhirah, the Yemenites and the Abyssinians—or international powers like the Persians and Byzantine Romans.

It is therefore unsurprising that the prophetic strategy resulted in stunningly profound changes in the Arabian Peninsula and transmitted global shockwaves that destabilised the international centres of power that had remained unshakeable for eight centuries. The Islamic strategic coup played out over the very short period of two decades, making it the swiftest and most important transformation in the history of international strategy.

Books on the Prophet's (ﷺ) life offer richly textured narratives on his battles, alliances, and pronouncements, but this is only raw material that requires examination and verification, and it needs to be assessed within the framework of a general methodology that ties together various incidents so that they can be read within their specific contexts. Only then can we have a comprehensive and coherent narrative that stands on a firm foundation. Only after such an exercise would we be able to extract a deeper understanding of the fundamentals of the Prophet's (ﷺ) strategic praxis.

Four authoritative reference points

Adopting this approach, I decided to engage particularly with those sīrah texts that have a strategic dimension, and to interrogate them within the framework of four authoritative points of reference.

The first of these points of reference is the Noble Qur'ān, a text whose authenticity has been validated with absolute certainty. The Qur'ān addresses numerous events that occurred during the Prophet's (ﷺ) mission. These are of the highest value in the study of the Prophet's (ﷺ)

life and are clearly articulated in the Qur'ān. It is therefore necessary to link narrations of specific events in the sīrah to the verses revealed to him at that time and place. Since the divine message coincides with the stages and unfolding events of the prophetic mission, evoking the verses of the Qur'ān based on the order and occasion of their revelation provides us with a rich base of knowledge for understanding the sīrah and for grasping the contexts within which it played out. Furthermore, the divine message was also a discourse that addressed popular opinion, with elements directed at the Prophet (ﷺ) and the Muslim public, and with messages to others as well. Thus, if we evoke the specific message revealed at a particular time and consider the political and strategic responses provoked by that Qur'ānic address, we are able to grasp the general context within which the Qur'ān was revealed, and are able to see the strategic horizons that directed the Prophet's (ﷺ) actions at that particular moment. In our present context, this is similar to interrogating and analysing official statements and national security discourse emanating from the highest authorities of states and governments, to understand the priorities, strategic security vision, and political postures of those countries, and to grasp their international relations' positioning. On this basis, we may determine the future balance of international relations.

The second point of reference is arrived at by counterposing the sīrah presented in Islamic reference works against the history of other nations in the same period, such as that of the Persians, Romans, Abyssinians (the Aksum kingdom), Himyarites, and others. Many events with a strategic dimension that have been dealt with in the sīrah are also mentioned in the historical writings of these nations, especially in Roman history. The Byzantines were meticulous about recording the history of their emperors, especially their wars, many of which occurred in regions under Byzantine control. These histories also recorded relations with other empires, and they assist in giving us an understanding of the regional and international environment in the period coinciding with specific events in the Prophet's (ﷺ) lifetime. There are also several Himyarite histories recorded in the ancient South Arabian Musnad script that were produced in Yemen in the southern Arabian Peninsula between the tenth and ninth centuries BCE. They include four records of the battles and wars of Dhū Nuwās al-Ḥimyarī against the Christians, two of which bear his signature. There are also Byzantine narratives and records of delegations and envoys from this period.

The third point of reference is derived from reading isolated events within a broader context, drawing on the notion in politics that dependence exclusively on information—even if it is accurate—may not lead to an understanding of an event or its implications, since information without context is not necessarily enlightening. I agree with the adage that information is often no more than accurate lies, because information that is bereft of its motives, foundations, and sources is not helpful for understanding events, and could, in fact, be confusing and misleading, especially if deliberately manipulated. Historians and chroniclers are, after all, human beings with their own inclinations, interests, political and religious affiliations, and biases. A source or a historian may transmit an event accurately, and yet may relate it in a manner that suggests a meaning that he favors, allowing that narration to then be utilised in a manner that is far removed from what the event really suggested.

Therefore, to understand a historical experience and to extract lessons from it, we need to read whatever information and accounts we have at our disposal within the framework of a complex methodology. Such a methodology should allow us to glean the overall objectives of the actors, and to make an accurate evaluation of the balance of forces and alliances, as well as an assessment of the event that considers the vested interests of the various parties involved at the time it occurred, while also taking into account the weaknesses, strengths, opportunities, and risks relating to the actors at the time.

The methodology that we have adopted is one where a single event is considered as part of a greater whole, giving the event a life and meaning while protecting it from isolation and exploitation. In this way, we can transform information into knowledge, and historical narratives are thereby liberated from their literal prisons and descriptive import, as well as from their political projections. They then become comprehensive accounts consistent with an inclusive understanding of the spirit of the sīrah and its higher objectives, and in harmony with the norms of life and its challenges.

The fourth point of reference is the adoption of a comprehensive view of the strategic context. A strategic balance of forces is not created solely by armies and alliances; it is the result of a complex process comprising of several elements in which the political integrates with the economic, the social with the religious, and the regional with the international. Therefore, in our attempt to map out the context in which the prophetic strategy was born and took shape, we will broaden our field of vision and examine the situation in all its complexity. Our reading of the sīrah is a comprehensive interrogation of many of these elements. It is, therefore, a reading that encompasses the events in the life of the Prophet (ﷺ) as historians have narrated them, but one that also transcends these accounts in search of the strategic, economic, and religious contexts that defined this region and the world over three centuries.

Principles of the Prophetic strategic methodology

The divine mandate descended on the Noble Prophet (ﷺ) from the heavens in a fixed time and place: in the year 610, in Makkah. From the very first revelation, the Qur'ānic directives mapped out the terms of his mandate, explaining that he was sent as a messenger to all humankind until the final hour, and that his message was intended to be a mercy for all creation. Since these two dimensions were deeply entrenched in the very nature of the divine mandate, the Prophet (ﷺ) would remain firmly committed to them, granting them due consideration in all his pronouncements and actions; his failing to do so would have meant that he was not fully compliant with his mandate.

The greatest challenge posed by this mandate was the need to reconcile everyday actions arising out of engagements and events—which are dictated by the demands of time and place—with a horizon that stretches out into the boundless future. As he engaged his reality, the Prophet (ﷺ) was aware that he was setting precedents for the future, since his primary task was messenger of the Lord of all creation. This was his objective and his duty, and every action that he undertook emanated from this mandate. Thus, that which would become the law and that which would be regarded as his normative practice (sunnah) arose out of reconciliation between the Prophet's (ﷺ) actions and their future implications. This is indeed a great burden that could be carried only by someone of great wisdom, who had insight into the far-reaching implications of his actions.

When we attempt to extract the principles of strategic praxis from the sīrah, we must remain conscious of the sphere of the divine mandate and its objectives, because of the continuous influence it exercises over the Prophet's (ﷺ) mind and spirit, and, consequently, on his actions and behaviour.

The first principle is a strong thread that runs through the story of Muḥammad's (ﷺ) life. It is the ethical-reformist nature of the prophetic strategic methodology, which strove to ensure the establishment of good character and the enjoining of all that was virtuous, and was developed through an interaction with inherited goodness, and an exposure of all contrived falsehoods. It was therefore a methodology that did not depart from the established moral legacy, but was instead its heir and was steadfastly consistent with it. This relates to the good that was brought by the prophets and messengers who preceded Muḥammad (ﷺ), and to what was brought by people of different religious affiliations at any other time. The sīrah attests to this in rich detail, and we will provide some examples of that detail in this book. The positive pronouncements made by the Prophet (ﷺ) about the Ḥilf al-Fuḍūl (Alliance of Virtue), which was consecrated in the home of ʻAbdallah ibn Jadʻān before the beginning of Islam, bears witness to this. The alliance was entered by idolaters, but it had a noble objective. The Prophet (ﷺ) regarded it as a virtuous initiative, and he later said that if he had been invited to endorse it after the beginning of Islam, he would have done so.

The second principle is that the prophetic methodology of strategic praxis was not exterminatory. It does not contain a thirst for victory-at-any-cost that can be observed in the biographies of numerous leaders who have been immortalised by history and who have redrawn the maps of the world.

The Prophet (ﷺ) did indeed change the world, but with an essential difference: he changed it in the pursuit of a divine mission and a higher calling, not in the pursuit of dominance and power. He was able to pursue transformation as part of a divine mission without being driven by vengeance, a desire for authority, or to gain monopoly over wealth. During his engagements with the Quraysh and other Arab tribes, he sought to make them partners in the divine mission, without conquering or subjugating them. His strategy was to elevate their status, protect their honour, and liberate them from the shackles of their misguided thoughts and beliefs. He did not desire their destruction or their extermination, as is confirmed by his recurrent supplication: "O Allah, guide my people, for they do not know." This principle of tolerance and patience is present in all Muḥammad's (ﷺ) strategies and plans, and it is illustrated in the following authentic ḥadīth.

> It has been narrated on the authority of 'Ā'ishah (May Allah be pleased with her), the wife of the Prophet (ﷺ), who asked the Prophet (ﷺ): "Messenger of Allah, have you experienced a day that was more terrible than the day of Uḥud?"
>
> He replied: "The harshest treatment that I received from your people was what I experienced on the day of al-'Aqabah. I had presented myself to Ibn 'Abd Yālayl ibn 'Abd Kulāl with the purpose of inviting him to Islam, but he did not respond to me in the way that I had expected. I therefore departed, with my distress visible on my face, and I did not recover until I reached Qarn al-Tha'ālib. There, I lifted my head and saw that I was covered by a cloud that cast its shade on me. I stared at it and saw the angel Jibrīl in it. He called out to me: 'Verily Allah, the Sublime and Honoured, has heard what your people have said to you, and how they responded to your call, and He has sent the angel in charge of the mountains to you to command him to do with them as you wish.' The angel in charge of the mountains called out to me, bid me peace, and said: 'O Muḥammad, verily Allah has heard what your people have said to you. I am the angel in charge of the mountains, and your Lord has sent me to you so that you may command me as you desire. If you desire that I should bring together the two mountains that stand opposite each other at the

two ends of Makkah to crush them in between, I will topple these two mountains on them.'"

But the Messenger of Allah (ﷺ) replied: "All I desire is that Allah produces among their descendants those who will worship only Allah, and will not associate partners to Him."[22]

In that very difficult moment, when the Prophet (ﷺ) tilted toward hope that the coming generation would be Muslims who believed in Allah alone, he also tilted toward the third important principle.

The third principle is the preference for long-term positive consequences and incremental progress over immediate and short-term solutions. Despite the bitter reality and the narrow horizons for success in Makkah, the Prophet (ﷺ) chose to continue along the longer, more treacherous path, and to reject the option of quick solutions. The Prophet (ﷺ) favoured a drawn-out engagement that required a long-term and intelligent strategy of transformation that would, ultimately, guarantee that Allah would produce from the children of idolaters a new generation that would worship Allah alone, and not associate any other with Him.

The fourth principle of the Prophet's (ﷺ) strategic vision, which guided his 23-year journey, was a deep-seated optimism and perpetual orientation toward a welcoming future, instead of drowning in the depths of the present moment and its complications. This fortified the Prophet (ﷺ) with perseverance and the endurance and long-term vision that such perseverance demands.

When the Prophet (ﷺ) prayed to Allah to provide the idolaters with progeny who would worship Allah alone, he was looking to the next generation, the generation of youth, the children of the arrogant Qurayshi leaders. Targeting the youth requires a perpetual orientation

---

22. This ḥadīth is muttafaq 'alayhi (agreed upon by the two eminent authorities of ḥadīth scholarship – al-Bukhārī and Muslim). See Muḥammad ibn Ismā'īl al-Bukhārī, *Saḥīḥ al-Bukhārī* (Damascus and Beirut: Dār Ibn Kathīr, 2002), "The Book on the Beginning of Creation, Chapter: If any one of you says *Āmīn*", vol. 1, Ḥadīth no. 3231, 797; and Muslim, "The Book on Jihād and Campaigns, Chapter: The harm that the Prophet (PBUH) encountered from the idolaters and hypocrites", vol. 3, 1420, Ḥadīth no. 1795. The wording of the ḥadīth as narrated here is that of Muslim.

toward the future, a focus on planning for its needs and challenges, constantly reflecting on it, and striving continuously to escape the psychological confines of the present moment. Islam, in the Prophet's (ﷺ) discourse, occupies the future, and it will be embraced by the coming generations. It has, therefore, to respond to the desire of the future generation to gain familiarity with everything that is novel and to break away from blindly following their elders. It is a methodology that addresses generations that have become fatigued by boredom and stagnation and are in search of an opportunity that will open new horizons, a generation characterised by a high degree of flexibility and one that embraces learning and adventure.

We will see how the Prophet (ﷺ) favoured this methodology at every strategic turn, in letter and spirit and without hesitation, even when it cost him dearly. He privileged the opinions of the youth during the battle of Uḥud, even though he personally preferred to remain in Madinah, and even though his senior companions agreed with him. This decision had direct security consequences when the leader of the hypocrites, 'Abdallah ibn Ubay, used it as an excuse to withdraw with a third of the army just before the battle began, saying that the Prophet (ﷺ) had "disobeyed me and followed boys and those who are inconsequential."

The fifth principle of the Prophet's (ﷺ) strategy was based on audaciously seizing the initiative. He refused to be restricted to the corner into which his opponents had attempted to push him, but would surprise everyone by moving forward, creating confusion, and forcing his enemies to react. There are many examples to illustrate this point. When the Prophet (ﷺ) became convinced that the Qurayshi leadership would stand arrogantly firm and was unrelentingly inclined to reject the call to Islam, he began thinking out of the Qurayshi box and set his sights on the second most prominent city in the Hijāz after Makkah. His visit to Ṭā'if was, thus, an exploration of new horizons. However, when the negotiation track with the leaders of the Banī Thaqīf tribe in Ṭā'if reached a dead end, he neither gave up nor was deterred. He again took the initiative and made an honourable return to Makkah under the protection of al-Maṭ'am ibn 'Adī, resumed his search for new allies, and reached out to tribal leaders during the ḥajj until the first and second 'Aqabah pledges were secured, and the Hijrāh (the migration to Madinah) had taken place.

As soon as he arrived in Madinah, he immediately took the initiative to integrate the Islamic ranks by forging fraternal links between the Makkan émigrés (al-Muhājirūn) and their Madinan allies (al-Anṣār). Thereafter, he integrated the Madinan ranks with the Charter of Madinah (Ṣaḥīfat al-Madinah). Settled in his new capital, he took the initiative to block Qurayshi caravans and created fear in the hearts of the idolaters at the possible collapse of the trade routes that linked them to the outside world. When the need arose to deal with problems on the Madinan front, he did not hesitate to expel the Banī al-Naḍīr and Banī Qaynuqā‘ tribes. When his army faced a setback during the Battle of Uḥud, he took the initiative to pursue the idolaters even before the blood of his wounds had dried. When the Quraysh attempted to wipe out the Muslims during the Battle of the Trench, by gathering the largest army as yet ever assembled, the Prophet (ﷺ) surprised them with the trench, upsetting their military plans. As for the Bedouin Arab tribes in the desert, the Prophet (ﷺ) was able to keep them destabilised with surprise attacks, not allowing them the opportunity to attack the Muslims. When the Quraysh exhausted all military options after their rapid collapse at the Battle of the Trench, the Prophet (ﷺ) undertook his greatest initiative at al-Ḥudaybīyyah; he changed the rules of the political game, surprising the Quraysh with what they least expected and forcing them into a truce that served as a foundation for the full recognition of the Muslim state. He then took the initiative to open channels of communication with foreign powers by sending his ambassadors to the kings of the ancient world and entering into military correspondence when required, as in the case of the Mu'tah campaign.

Muḥammad's (ﷺ) sixth principle was that he did not allow his internal front to divide; he was committed to maintaining the ranks, strengthening alliances, and building coalitions, not only among his Muslim companions but in Madinan society more generally, and with non-Muslim state partners as well. This principle can be captured in a single expression, which he pronounced when ‘Umar suggested killing the leader of the hypocrites. It was related in the story of Banī al-Muṣṭaliq by Ibn Isḥāq, who said that Muḥammad bin Yaḥyā ibn Ḥibbān, ‘Abdullah bin Abi Bakr and ‘Asim bin ‘Umar bin Qatadā narrated it to him.

While the Messenger of Allah (ﷺ) was in that area, Jahjāh bin Sa'īd al-Ghifārī, a hired hand for 'Umar, and Sinān bin Wabr fought over the water source. Sinān called out, "O Anṣār," while Al- Jahjāh called, "O Muhājirūn!" Zayd bin Arqam and several Anṣār men were sitting with 'Abdallah bin Ubay bin Sallūl at that time. When 'Abdullah heard what had happened, he said, "They are bothering us in our land. By Allah, the parable of us and these foolish Quraysh men is the parable: 'Feed your dog until it becomes strong, and it will eat you.' By Allah, when we go back to Al-Madinah, the Most Mighty will expel the weak from it." He then addressed his people who were sitting with him: "What have you done to yourselves? You let them settle in your land and shared your wealth with them. By Allah, if you abandon them, they will have to move to an area other than yours." Zayd bin Arqam, who was a young boy, heard these words and conveyed them to Allah's Messenger (ﷺ). 'Umar bin Al-Khattab was with the Messenger (ﷺ), and he said, "O Allah's Messenger! Order 'Abbād ibn Bishr to cut off his head at his neck." The Prophet (ﷺ) replied, "What if people started saying that Muḥammad kills his companions, 'Umar? No. Rather, order the people to start the journey [back to Al-Madinah]."[23]

Jābir ibn 'Abdallah reported another incident:

When the Messenger of Allah (ﷺ) was dividing the spoils of Hawāzin among the people at al-Ji'rānah, a man from Banī Tamīm said: "Be just O Muḥammad!" The Prophet (ﷺ) responded: "Woe unto you! Who will be just if I am not just? I will perpetrate a miscarriage and fail if I am not just." 'Umar ibn al-Khaṭṭāb then said: "O Messenger of Allah, should I not rise and kill this hypocrite?" The Prophet (ﷺ) responded: "I seek Allah's refuge should people come to hear that Muḥammad kills his companions."[24]

23. Abū Bakr al-Bayhaqī, *Dalā'il al-Nubūwwah* (Beirut and Cairo: Dār al-Kutub al-'Ilmīyyah & Dār al-Rayyān li al-Turāth, 1998), vol. 4, 52.

24. Narrated by Aḥmad ibn Hanbal, "Narrations on the ten people promised Paradise," Ḥadīth no. 14526. The original also appears in al-Bukhārī and Muslim.

The seventh principle was that the Messenger of Allah (ﷺ) was careful not to confront all his enemies at the same time. He worked actively to dismantle their alliances and to disunite them, even if this required making deals with some of them for a short period. This is what he did, for example, during the Battle of the Trench, when he negotiated with 'Uyanah ibn Ḥuṣn and al-Ḥārith ibn 'Awf, the leaders of the Ghaṭafān tribe. He offered them a third of Madinah's date harvest if they and their companions would withdraw from the battle. He justified this to Sa'd ibn 'Ubādah and Sa'd ibn Mu'adh, the leaders of al-Aws and al-Khazraj tribes in Madinah, by saying: "I see that the Arabs are shooting at you with one bow [in that they have developed a common front against you] and have you surrounded from all sides, so I wanted to break their unity for you."[25]

The Prophet (ﷺ) was careful not to fight two enemies in a single battle; only when he was done with one would he confront another. He confronted the Quraysh's caravans in the first year after the Hijrāh, but only after concluding an alliance with the Jews and ratifying it in the Charter of Madinah. He fought the Quraysh at Badr after reconciling with the coastal tribes such as Ḍimrah, Juhaynah, and Ghaffār. Furthermore, he did not deal with the Banī Qurayẓah until after the Battle of the Confederates and the consequent tempering of the Qurayshi threat. He also dispatched war parties against the Najd tribes to steer them away from Madinah and to ensure its safety while he travelled to al-Hudaybīyyah, and he conquered Khaybar only after he had neutralised the Quraysh with the al-Hudaybīyyah Peace Treaty. There are many other such examples.

The eighth principle is that Muḥammad's (ﷺ) strategy was flexible and multi-faceted. He utilised both soft and hard power in the appropriate context and at the appropriate time. It was in the interests of the Muslims to announce their security dominance in Madinah immediately after the migration. It was therefore a priority for them to demonstrate their hard power using raiding parties and military expeditions, thus allowing the Prophet (ﷺ) to keep the forces of the Quraysh unsettled by blocking their caravans, yet without any military confrontation, for a full year. Thereafter, alliances were concluded with the coastal tribes to increase

25. al-Bayhaqī, *Dalā'il al-Nubūwwah*, vol. 3, 430.

the economic burden on the Quraysh and to disrupt its trade, which passed through the desert. When the situation demanded direct military confrontation, the Prophet (ﷺ) led the Muslims at Badr and, thereafter, defended Madinah at Uḥud. When the Quraysh's options had run out after the Battle of the Trench, the Prophet's (ﷺ) strategy changed from defence to offence, combined with a good dose of soft power. The Treaty of al-Hudaybīyyah, then, was very different from what the Quraysh had been accustomed to, and it was different from the ideas around which they had built their strategy. It was an important transition that the Prophet (ﷺ) had crafted, and it bound the Quraysh in ways they were unable to escape without officially recognising the Islamic polity.

All this transpired over a six-year period, with Muḥammad's (ﷺ) diplomatic and military efforts accompanied by soft power. The Prophet's (ﷺ) poets, such as Hassān ibn Thābit and 'Abdallah ibn Rawāḥah, operated like official spokespersons of Madinah, reacting to events and transmitting ideas, positions, and directives to influence public opinion across the Arabian Peninsula. The Prophet (ﷺ), for his part, confronted the Qurayshi leadership and other influential parties in the tribe, while simultaneously addressing the downtrodden classes of Makkah. One example of this was when he lifted the embargo on the sale of wheat by Yamāmah to Makkah after being implored to do so by the Quraysh. The sanction had been imposed by the Yamāmah chief, Thumāmah ibn Athāl, after the Quraysh had treated him harshly for having embraced Islam. Also illustrative was the high moral standard displayed by the Muslims in their treatment of the captives from the Battle of Badr, and their forbidding the mutilation of the idolaters who had been killed, thus rejecting the principle of reciprocity.

We will see how the Prophet's (ﷺ) upstanding morals and wise actions became important factors in garnering the support of a marginalised community in Makkah, the Aḥābīsh, when the Muslims requested entrance to Makkah to perform the 'umrāh (lesser pilgrimage) in the same year as the signing of the Hudaybīyyah Treaty. We will also see how the masses of people in Makkah became increasingly impressed by the Prophet's (ﷺ) fairness and respect for the principle of equality in a tribal context where the status of the elite was elevated and the weak were forever challenged.

Makkah was conquered morally before it was conquered militarily, which is why its inhabitants did not put up a fight in the year of the conquest. In fact, they flung open the city doors for the Prophet (ﷺ) without fear, trepidation, or any expectation of retaliation.

The ninth principle was the Prophet's (ﷺ) methodical, objective, and strategic reading of events, which was fully concordant with prioritisation, and provided a careful assessment of the balance of forces while remaining ever-conscious of outcomes and consequences. He measured the extent of every action, placing each in the correct order of priority without agitation or haste. He showed leniency to the extent that one might think that he was not strict; but he was also decisive when that was required, to the extent that one might think that he knew no leniency. His actions arose out of a careful understanding of the context, taking into consideration its circumstances and strategic gravitas.

After he established that the Banī Qaynuqā' had acted treacherously, he decisively expelled them from Madinah; he did the same with the Banī al-Naḍīr. When he saw that the Banī Qurayẓah had indeed participated in the conspiracy to uproot Islam in Madinah, he decided to exterminate them. On the other hand, he was not decisive regarding the matter of 'Abdallah ibn Ubay ibn Sallūl and did not order his killing, incarceration, or expulsion. He dealt with ibn Sallūl with kindness and indulgence. All this was done with a deep awareness of the extent and nature of the harm that each of these parties was capable of inflicting upon the Muslims. The three Jewish tribes represented an existential threat and were planning to harm the Muslims militarily. Decisive action against them was therefore necessary. Ibn Sallūl, however, agitated people, spread rumours, and incited against the Muslims. He had allies and followers and an elevated status among the Khazraj, but his threat was not an existential one because he spoke much and acted little. He promised to assist the Banī Qaynuqā' and Banī al-Naḍīr, but then abandoned them and did nothing to help. He also had the opportunity to take control of Madinah during the Battle of Uḥud when the Muslim army was divided, but he did not do so. He was thus more of a noisemaker than a real threat, and the Prophet (ﷺ) decided to control the threat that he posed by winning over his followers rather than provoking them by targeting him.

The Prophet (ﷺ) engaged the tribes in a similar manner. The Khuzā'ah were the Prophet's (ﷺ) old allies. He reconciled with them and maintained contact, but when a clan of the tribe, the Banī al-Muṣṭaliq, tried to abandon the alliance, the Prophet (ﷺ) fought and subdued them. He later married a woman from the tribe and reconciled with them. On the other hand, the Prophet's (ﷺ) first military expedition was against the Ḍamrah tribe, which resided on the route followed by the Quraysh's caravans. They submitted without a fight, and he then reconciled with them. He did the same with the Juhaynah tribe: he won over their leaders and drew them into the security orbit of Madinah, which encouraged them to become helpful allies of the Muslims against the Quraysh and its caravans. In this way, the Prophet (ﷺ) was able to achieve a central strategic goal: to impede the Qurayshi caravans and place them under economic strain.

There was, however, a different calculation with regards to the Ghaṭafān tribe, since they were a conglomeration of Bedouin tribes located deep in the desert and extremely skilled in military raids and campaigns. The Prophet (ﷺ) therefore dealt with them with a combination of leniency and decisiveness, drawing them closer with promises of booty and dismissing them with the threat of the sword, each at the appropriate time and in accordance with a careful strategic assessment.

The Quraysh, who were the main opponents of the Muslims, were dealt with incrementally, beginning with a targeting of their economy, followed by military confrontation, and, finally, a ceasefire, each at the appropriate time and place.

CHAPTER ONE

Makkah's location and status

"Allah knows best where to place His Message" (Qur'ān 6:124).

Geography is the handiwork of Allah on earth, but history is the making of human beings in time and space.

Geographically, Makkah is of divine construction, since Allah chose that specific valley to be the cradle of the Ancient House, and guided Ibrāhīm (Abraham) to it so that he might establish a human presence and the first social formation around the House. Allah, the Glorious and Sublime, chose the location and afforded it its status. If it were not for this divine choice, human beings would not have settled, nor would life have flourished, in that valley. Even Ibrāhīm described the place as an "uncultivated valley" (Qur'ān 14:37), a barren valley deep in the heart of the desert, concealed among desolate mountains.

Today, when we study this choice from a strategic and historical perspective, we realise that it was truly the choice of the Most Honourable and Wise, as the final message could not have been born anywhere else except in Makkah, at that time and at that place, and "Allah knows best where to place His Message".

We begin our discussion on Makkah at the beginning of the fifth century, when it witnessed the birth of the political and social entity known to us as the Quraysh. Most historical accounts about Makkah before this period contain fanciful ideas, mythic tales and emotional ramblings that cannot be construed as reliable. However, even though historical sources differ in the way that they narrate the specific events of fifth-century Makkah, we are nonetheless able to grasp the most important and relevant events that led to the birth of the Quraysh as a socio-political entity shaped by the hands of the most prominent personality in its history, Quṣay ibn Kilāb.

Quṣay ibn Kilāb and Qurayshi exceptionalism

There is no significant disagreement between historians that the Makkah to which the Prophet (ﷺ) was sent was the political and social entity that had been built by his fourth-generation grandfather, Quṣay ibn Kilāb ibn Murrah ibn Fahar. While it is difficult to establish his birth and death dates with absolute certainty, it can confidently be asserted that he was born sometime around the beginning of the fifth century, and that he lived for about eighty years.

Ibn ʿAbbās described him as "the nobleman of the people of Makkah, with no challenger in this regard".[26] Quṣay's elevated status was a result of his many achievements, without which the Quraysh would not have had the reputation we associate with them.

It is indisputable that Quṣay was responsible for the Quraysh's ascendancy in Makkah, having wrested control of it from the Khuzāʿah tribe. While his father was Qurayshi, Quṣay's wife was the daughter of the Khuzāʿah chief, Ḥulayl al-Khuzāʿī. When Ḥulayl died, Quṣay felt that he and his people were more entitled to administer the Holy Sanctuary. He mobilised the tribal groups affiliated to Fahar ibn Mālik ibn al-Naḍr ibn Kinānah, which were collectively known as the Quraysh, and led them in an armed confrontation with the Khuzāʿah, leading to arbitration, in accordance with the prevailing Arab custom. The arbitration ruled in favour of the Quraysh being granted control over the Sanctuary and ordered the Khuzāʿah to pay blood money for the victims who had fallen during the clash.

This was the moment when the Qurayshis burst onto the stage of Arab history as the custodians of the Kaʿbah and the neighbours of the Holy Sanctuary. Thenceforth, the Quraysh occupied a high status among the Arabs, a position that may be attributed to the wisdom and cunning of Quṣay. By examining his actions after he took control of Makkah, we can see that he was a man with a vision. He understood that the Holy Sanctuary was at the very heart of Arab existence on the Peninsula, not only as the point of religious convergence, but also as a

26. Abū ʿAbdallah Muḥammad Ibn Saʿd, *al-Ṭabaqāt al-Kubra* (Beirut: al-Maktabah al-ʿIlmīyyah, 1990), vol. 1, 85.

centre of economic activity and political influence. Whoever managed to take control of the Sanctuary would reach a position and status that no one else could.

Historical records suggest that Quṣay was acutely aware of the distinguished and unique status of the Ka'bah, and that he wanted to project that same status onto the Quraysh; his ambition was to make them unique among the Arab tribes. Immediately after the arbitration between the Quraysh and Khuzā'ah, he took the first step in this effort by granting the Quraysh a standing that had not been attained by any tribe before it, including the Khuzā'ah, which had ruled Makkah for a period that was between two and three centuries. He gathered the Quraysh from the far ends of Makkah and from the neighbouring hinterland and surroundings and settled them on the Makkan plain, adjacent to the Sanctuary, thus making them neighbours of the Ka'bah. Historical reports suggest that this was not viewed favourably by the other tribes, since no one had lived in the Sanctuary before. It was regarded as sacred land; people entered it only for ritual circumambulation and daytime gatherings, and then returned to their dwellings in the hilltops and surrounding areas in the evening. Al-Ya'qūbī confirms this.

> In Makkah, there were no dwellings in the Sanctuary and people would enter during the day and leave at nightfall. When Quṣay - who was the most cunning of Arabs - gathered the Quraysh, he settled them in the Sanctuary, spent the night there with them, and woke with them [spread out] around the Ka'bah. He was approached by the noblemen of Banī Kinānah, who told him: "This is regarded as a great sacrilege by the Arabs. If we let you get away with it, the [other] Arabs will not." He responded: "By Allah, I will not leave this place." And he stood firm.[27]

It was clear that by building their homes in the Sanctuary - something no one before them had dared do - the Quraysh would be granted honour and a unique status over others, elevating them above the well-established tribal categories based on lineage, strength, and numbers. The Quraysh was not the largest tribe in numerical terms, nor was it the most powerful in terms of deterrent force; it was not even a well-

27. Abū al-'Abbās al-Ya'qūbī, *Tārīkh al-Ya'qūbī* (Najaf, Iraq: Manshūrāt al-Maktabah al-Ḥaydarīyyah, 1964), vol. 1, 209.

integrated tribal unit before Quṣay's intervention. It was through sheer shrewdness that he was able to give the Quraysh a status above the standards followed at the time, when comparisons between the tribes depended on ethnicity, lineage, numerical superiority and fighting strength. Although the Quraysh were unable to compete against other tribes in terms of these indicators, its new position as neighbours and custodians of the Sanctuary had effectively established a new criterion for status that none of the other tribes had been able to attain, and there was no way that the others could achieve this sublime honour.

Quṣay's purpose in settling on the Sanctuary plain was not only symbolic; it was also strategic par excellence. By gathering the Quraysh from the hinterland, the surrounding areas and hilltops, and settling them around the Ka'bah, he transformed them into a solid and tightly integrated unit, and entrenched their strength and tribal solidarity.

However, this bold move contravened the established traditions pertaining to the Holy Sanctuary. Since the Arabs regarded the Ka'bah as a religious symbol, it could not be the sole possession of a specific tribe. Quṣay's move, therefore, was not easily accepted. Al-Ya'qūbī indicates that the chiefs of Kinānah—the mother tribe to which the Quraysh were affiliated—condemned Quṣay's actions and informed him that even if they were to remain silent about the transgression, other Arabs would not. However, Quṣay had already prepared a plan to convince the Arabs that the relocation of the Quraysh to the environs of the Sanctuary was to their benefit. If they were to see this and benefit from it, he believed, then they would accept it and acquiesce. Again, al-Ya'qūbī's text is a useful reference.

> The time of the pilgrimage had arrived and Quṣay said: "The time of pilgrimage has arrived, and the Arabs have heard what you have done; they now hold you in high esteem, and I am not aware of a virtue held in higher regard by the Lord than food, so every one of you should set aside a portion of his wealth." They did so, and he accumulated a huge amount. When the first pilgrims arrived, he slaughtered a camel on every road leading to Makkah, as well as in Makkah. He constructed an enclosure and filled it with bread and meat, and he provided water and

> milk for drinking. He went to the Sanctuary and made a key and a covering for the Ka'bah and created a barrier between himself and the Khuzā'ah. The Sanctuary was now firmly in Quṣay's hands. He then built his house in Makkah, having thus built the first house in the city, and declared it to be the House of Assembly.[28]

Because Quṣay had realised that the legitimacy of the Quraysh could be affirmed if their control over the Sanctuary brought direct benefits to the pilgrims, he surprised them with lavish amenities that they had not been accustomed to in the time of the Khuzā'ah: food at the entrances to Makkah to welcome the visitors, water and milk for thirsty travellers who had traversed the desert for weeks on end, meticulous administration of the Sanctuary, and general order in Makkah, the like of which the Arabs had not previously known. Quṣay was thus able to show the advantages of having the Quraysh oversee the Sanctuary and tend to the needs of the pilgrims. He thus justified their resettlement in the Sanctuary and around the Ka'bah through providing essential services to the pilgrims. No one objected.

Quṣay's next initiative was to transform the Quraysh into an organised political entity. He established, for the first time in Makkah, a comprehensive administrative system that resembled an executive government with ministries that were aligned with the most prominent tasks of the Quraysh as the neighbours of the Sanctuary and the custodians of the Ancient House. He declared the feeding of pilgrims to be a permanent function and created salaried positions called al-Rifādah (Food Provisioner) and al-Siqāyah (Water Supplier, for supplying pilgrims with water and milk). The maintenance of the Ancient House became the third permanent function, al-Ḥijābah (Maintainer of the Ka'bah). He also built a large house, Dār al-Nadwah (the House of Assembly), close to the Ka'bah, and made it the centre of Qurayshi public life and a parliament for Qurayshi noblemen and elders. This became the seat of governance and leadership. The fifth permanent function that Quṣay established was that pertaining to matters of war; he called it al-Liwā'a (The Brigade). All these functions were under his direct leadership, making him the absolute leader of the Quraysh.

28. al-Ya'qūbī, *Tārīkh*, vol. 1, 209.

Though he never bestowed a royal title upon himself, the Quraysh, "in Quṣay's lifetime and after his death," according to al-Ya'qūbī, "saw his commands as religious obligations". The House of Assembly became the Qurayshi centre of existence for all aspects of life.

Ibn 'Abbās described the status of the House of Assembly:

> In his house, the door of which faced the Ancient House, all the Quraysh's affairs were conducted: matters of marriage or war or consultation among themselves. Even when [a Qurayshi] slave girl is given her freedom, she is emancipated there and only thereafter returned to her family. They do not raise the banner of war for themselves or for anyone else anywhere other than in the House of Assembly, and it is raised by Quṣay. Their slaves are only pardoned at the House of Assembly. A Qurayshi caravan always departs from it and, when they return, they stop there first, in honour of Quṣay, seeking his counsel and acknowledging his virtue. They follow his command as if it were a religious obligation; they followed no other, both during his lifetime and after his death. He held the positions of Maintainer of the Ka'bah, Water Supplier, Food Provisioner, Convener of the House of Assembly, and he ruled over all Makkah.[29]

Quṣay left his mark on Makkah by implementing the first town plan for the city. He divided it into districts and distributed these among the various clans of the Quraysh, so that each subdivision occupied a specific district. He was remembered as a person of bold initiatives. When the Quraysh settled on the plain around the Ancient House, they felt constricted and wanted to expand outwards and build new houses. Though custom dictated that plants and trees that grew in the Sanctuary could not be cut, Quṣay ordered that they be cut anyway so that the land could be made suitable for building. Because the Quraysh were afraid of the divine consequences of such an action, he took the initiative to cut down some of the vegetation himself. When other Qurayshis saw that no harm had come to him, they prepared the land and built the city.

29. al-Ya'qūbī, *Tārīkh*, vol.1, 211.

Quṣay died after having settled most of the Quraysh in the Sanctuary. They became known as the "Quraysh of the plains", due to the flat land that they occupied. Other clans settled on the hilltops and in the desert surrounding Makkah, and they were referred to as the "Quraysh of the hinterland". Only two branches from the lineage of Fahar were counted amongst the Quraysh of the hinterlands; the rest preferred a bedouin lifestyle and raiding. The future historic role of leading the Arabs thus fell to the Quraysh of the plains. They would be referred to as "the People of Allah" and gained a reputation as "the most cunning of Arabs, the most intelligent of people, and the most eloquent in speech".[30]

Quṣay's cunning and importance in Qurayshi history were manifested in his ability to build firm political and administrative structures. It was clear to him that custodianship of the Ancient House and tending to the needs of the pilgrims were the essential elements for establishing unparalleled legitimacy in terms of leadership and prestige. It was legitimacy that transcended the boundaries of tribal allegiance and complex associations, because it was specific to the Quraysh and not possessed by any other tribe. The Ka'bah was venerated by all Arabs, and even though some of the other tribes had sacred sanctuaries where religious rites were performed, the Ancient House in Makkah transcended the bounds of tribal and group association and was unanimously venerated by all inhabitants of the Arabian Peninsula.

Quṣay had four sons: 'Abd al-Dār, 'Abd Manāf, 'Abd al-'Uzza, and the last, 'Abd or 'Abd Quṣay. Before Quṣay died, he bequeathed five responsibilities to his first-born son, 'Abd al-Dār: maintenance of the Ka'bah, provisioning of food, supply of water, The Brigade, and the House of Assembly. 'Abd al-Dār was the weakest of the brothers, and the others were more prominent than he in the public sphere. His father wanted to raise his status by granting him all the positions of leadership. Even though these positions were collectively given to 'Abd al-Dār and to his children after him, 'Abd Manāf was the most prominent Qurayshi nobleman after his father, and he continued to entrench Makkah's position and expand its districts, organising the settlement of the subdivisions of the Quraysh. Ibn Sa'd narrates: "When Quṣay

30. Abū Manṣūr al-Tha'ālibī, *Thimār al-Qulūb fī al-Muḍāf wa al-Mansūb* (Beirut: al-Maktabah al-'Aṣrīyyah, 2003), 18.

ibn Kilāb perished, 'Abd Manāf ibn Quṣay took over, and the authority over the Quraysh was in his hands. He divided Makkah further, beyond the divisions that Quṣay had established for his people."[31]

Despite Quṣay's bequest in 'Abd al-Dār's favour, historical sources show that he was weak and unable to carry out the responsibility of leadership of the Quraysh, which led 'Abd Manāf to assume that role. This created a discrepancy: although the official leadership was bestowed on 'Abd al-Dār, effective leadership was in the hands of 'Abd Manāf. Even though 'Abd Manāf was able to live with this reality in deference to his elder brother and out of respect for his father's bequest, the future would witness conflict between the sons of 'Abd Manāf and 'Abd al-Dār over these leadership positions. This resulted in the most important factional development in Qurayshi politics: the establishment of the Alliance of the Scented (Ḥilf al-Muṭayyībīn) and the Alliance of the Allies (Ḥilf al-Aḥlāf).

After 'Abd Manāf, effective leadership of the Quraysh passed on to his son Hāshim, who had inherited the leadership of the Quraysh from his father, as well as discernment, administrative sophistication, and broad-mindedness from his grandfather. Hāshim's greatest achievement was the entrenchment of Makkah as a trading centre where desert transport routes crossed at the end of the fifth century. Historical sources paint a bleak picture of Makkah's economic status in the period before the trade pact established by Hāshim. The following quote is extremely striking and rich in significance:

> Hāshim ibn 'Abd Manāf was the first to establish the two journeys. His reason for doing so was to address the practice referred to as al-i'tifār [literally meaning "polluted by soil"]. According to this tradition, if a household was afflicted by poverty and it did not find food for its sustenance, the head of the family would take his family to a spot known for this purpose and set up a tent in which they would remain until they starved to death. It so happened that a household from the Banī Makhzūm tribe was afflicted by extreme deprivation and considered undertaking al-i'tifār. Hāshim heard of their plight

31. Ibn Sa'd, *al-Ṭabaqāt*, vol.1, 47.

> because one of their sons was an acquaintance of his son Asad. Hāshim addressed the Quraysh thus: "You have innovated a practice by which you are diminished while the [other] Arabs grow; you are shamed while the [other] Arabs are honoured. You are the people of the Holy Sanctuary and the people follow you, yet this i'tifār is almost overwhelming you." He then gathered the head of every household for two trade journeys. Whatever profit was generated by a person of wealth was divided between him and a poor person from his family, until the poor among them became just like the rich.[32]

Thus, if Quṣay is regarded as the creator of the Qurayshi entity, Hāshim—with his initiative, his sharp mind, and his good planning—was the instigator of the golden age in Makkah. He took Makkah out of extreme poverty and gave it a noble presence, opening the doors of regional trade to its caravans. Thereafter, Makkah was able to transcend its status as a small, isolated village visited by Bedouin pilgrims and became a frequently visited city, through which overloaded caravans passed as they crossed the desert. Makkah became a conveyor of cultures and a bearer of news and stories about the lands of Persia, Rome, Abyssinia, and Yemen. After a long slumber, Makkah was alive and active.

The trade pact and the beginning of the "Golden Age"

According to numerous chronicles, the flourishing of Makkah's economy began when, during a business trip to the Levant, Hāshim noticed that prices were more inflated there than in Yemen. He saw an excellent business opportunity that could put the Quraysh on the path to wealth and prosperity.

The phenomenon of high prices in the Levant and low prices in Yemen may be explained by examining the state of international trade at the end of the fifth century, when Hāshim visited the Levant. The international routes that joined the Chinese and Indian markets with the two global empires of the time—Persia and Rome—are relevant in

32. See also: Muḥammad ibn Aḥmad al-Anṣārī al-Qurṭubī, 1964, *al-Jāmi' li Aḥkām al-Qur'ān* (Cairo: Dār al-Kutub al-Miṣrīyyah, 1964), vol. 20, 205.

this regard. The Chinese and Indian markets were the most influential in the global economy of the ancient world. As a result, a network of land and sea routes developed, linking those markets to the Persian and Roman empires. The network of roads was called the "Silk Road"; it was not a single road but a network of pathways, the most important of which was the Northern Silk Road that had a tremendous impact on world history, and which China is currently trying to revive by way of a gigantic economic project.

For 2,000 years, the Northern and Southern Silk Roads—which cross overland from China to Central Asia, then over the Byzantine State to Europe—were, unquestionably, the most important international routes. They stretched over thousands of kilometres, passing through many lands, nations, and peoples, with caravans transporting a variety of merchandise, the most important of which was silk, from which the route derived its name. However, the merchandise was not restricted to silk; the caravans carried various other products, such as frankincense, perfumes, precious stones, and spices. The problem with the Northern and Southern Silk Roads was that they were under the control of several political authorities whose positions were influenced by each other and by the wars and conflicts that broke out between the various parties.

The Maritime Silk Route, on the other hand, was a sea route that took advantage of seasonal winds. Its south-to-north branch joined India to the Persian Gulf and terminated in Basra, from where the traveller could move over land to Iraq, which was under the control of the Sassanid Empire, and finally to Damascus. This route was subject to disruptions when conflict erupted between the Sassanid Persians and the Byzantine Romans. The east-to-west branch of the Maritime Silk Route stretched from India westwards to Aden. This route flourished especially when the land routes and the south-to-north maritime route were disrupted. Usually, when conflict broke out between the two international powers (the Persians and the Byzantines), the land route and the south-to-north maritime route would be suspended, while the west-to-east maritime route would remain active.

At the beginning of the fifth century, clashes between Turkish tribes in Central Asia were at their height, resulting in regular disruptions or even a shutting down of the Silk Road's land routes. In addition, the continual confrontations between the Persians and the Byzantine Romans brought activity on the south-to-north part of the Maritime Silk Route to a halt, causing the prices of imported goods such as silk, frankincense, perfumes, utensils, and fabrics to skyrocket. In these instances, only the east-to-west Maritime Silk Route remained active. Yemen was under Himyarite rule, and it had had sustained maritime contact with India for at least half a millennium. Considering the continual warring between the Persians and Romans, this maritime route was more stable than the other routes, since it lay beyond the contact points between the two great powers. Consequently, the cost of merchandise traversing this route was generally much lower.

From Aden, Byzantine ships (or Abyssinian ships, Abyssinia being an ally of Byzantium at the time) usually transported merchandise to Egypt's Red Sea ports. The goods were then carried to Alexandria over land, and from there to Europe. Alternately, other ships would transport merchandise from Aden to the Port of Elath, now known as Aqaba in Jordan, and from there over land to Damascus. Some merchandise found its way to Gaza and then to Europe by sea. The most transported product along this route was frankincense, which was used in church ceremonies. However, clashes between the two superpowers sometimes disrupted even the Red Sea Route, causing the merchandise to pile up in the Port of Aden and resulting in a drop in prices.

This is the background to the phenomenon that grabbed Hāshim's attention and changed the future of Makkah. The merchandise from India that reached Yemen by sea was relatively cheap compared to the merchandise sold in Damascus. Hāshim realised that if he were able to transport merchandise from Yemen to Damascus and Iraq via Makkah, he would be able to circumvent the conflict hotspots and tension points between the two empires. As a result, the Quraysh's trade would flourish, and Makkah would be enriched because of the huge price disparity between Yemen and Damascus.

A major problem for the caravans that were crossing the desert was their exposure to Bedouin raids, a common practice on the Arabian Peninsula. However, the status of the Quraysh among Arab tribes granted it a unique opportunity to use its symbolic position to protect its caravans from raids. The trade pact that we hear a great deal about, and that is mentioned in the Noble Qur'ān in Surah Quraysh (Surah 106) has two aspects to it. The first is an accord that allows for the passage of Qurayshi trade to the Levant, Yemen, Iraq, and Abyssinia. These states had borders with crossing points, and they levied taxation on trading caravans. Trade in these lands required formal permission, which resulted in the trade pact that would be realised by Hāshim and his brothers. The second aspect of the pact was an agreement with the Arab tribes residing along the trade routes that crossed the desert. The Qurayshi pact with these tribes secured the interests of both sides: the Quraysh gained protection for its caravans from raids, and, in return, the tribes benefitted directly from the protection fees that they received from the caravans, or from trade privileges that allowed them to conduct business with the caravans. This often entailed the bedouin tribes selling hides to the caravans and purchasing utensils, weapons, and clothing from them. In this way, the pact created a new economic and political map in the Hijaz and in the northern parts of the Arabian Peninsula, which placed Makkah at the very centre. This pact is essential if we are to understand the nature of the conflict that later broke out between the Prophet's (ﷺ) state in Madinah and the Quraysh. It also played a huge role in making sense of the network of alliances between the two groups, and the tribes inhabiting the areas along the trade routes, which will be explained later in greater detail.

Al-Tha'ālibī addresses the impact of the Qurayshi trade pact on Makkah and on the status of the Quraysh:

> The Quraysh traded only with people who came to Makkah during the pilgrimage seasons and would do so at the Dhī'l Majāz and 'Ukāẓ markets. They would not leave their homes during the sacred months, nor travel beyond the Sanctuary, due to a commitment to their religion and love for their Sanctuary and homes, and because they had undertaken to see to the needs of everyone who entered Makkah. They were in a barren valley, as Allah, the Sublime, related concerning Ibrāhīm: "Our Lord! I have settled some of my offspring in an uncultivated valley near Your Sacred House" (Qur'ān 14:37). In the Qur'ān, Allah

mentions Hāshim ibn 'Abd Manāf as the first Qurayshi to travel to the Levant, to call on kings, to undertake long journeys, to traverse the lands of enemies, and to enter a pact with them.

He used to undertake two journeys: a winter journey to the al-'Abāhilah. the kings of Yemen, and to Aksum in Abyssinia; and a summer journey to the Levant and the land of the Byzantine Romans. He would enter pacts with tribal leaders and clan heads for two purposes: the first was because Arab predators, vile bedouins, raiders and seekers of fortune did not leave the people of the Holy Sanctuary or anyone else in peace; the second was because some Arabs did not respect the sanctity of the Sanctuary or give importance to the sacred months. This group included the Banī Ṭay', Khath'am, and Qaḍā'ah. Other Arabs undertook the pilgrimage to the Ancient House and regarded its sanctity as a religious principle.

In terms of the pact, Hāshim set aside a share of his profits for the tribal leaders. He also transported some of their wares with his, and herded their camels with his. This alleviated some of their difficulties regarding travel, and it unburdened the Quraysh from the anxiety of enemy attacks. This arrangement benefitted both parties: the one that stayed at home profited, and the one that travelled was guaranteed safe passage. The Quraysh thus flourished and were able to access the best that the Levant, Yemen, and Abyssinia had to offer; their lot was improved, and their livelihood became pleasurable. When Hāshim died, al-Muṭṭalib took over; when he died, 'Abd Shams took over; and upon his death, Nawfal took over, and he was the youngest of them.[33]

Trade within the Arabian Peninsula spans millennia, and the land route that crosses from Yemen to the Levant was several centuries old. However, the organisation of this route within an established framework linked to trade agreements that traversed states and tribes was the work of Hāshim and his brothers from the Banī 'Abd Manāf. Based on extant historical accounts about Makkah, we may state that the first pact that

33. al-Tha'ālibī, *Thimār al-Qulūb*, 100-101.

Hāshim forged with Arab tribes signalled a turning point in the lives of the Qurayshis. Little Makkah, secluded in the heart of the desert, with its humble economy dependent on providing for the welfare of pilgrims, and its trade dependent on the seasons and the needs of its markets, soon became the centre of trade that crisscrossed the desert, linking the markets of the Levant, Iraq, and Yemen, and supplying them with their essential needs at the lower prices that generated higher profits. All this was a result of the disruption of the other international routes because of the continual clashes between the Persians and the Byzantine Romans.

Although the pact was initiated by Hāshim, it took its final shape only years after his death. Hāshim had probably first concluded a pact with the Byzantine authorities in the Levant, and had entered into agreements with tribal leaders along the trade route from Makkah to Damascus only on his return journey.

The pact was later expanded to include other territories beyond the Levant. The Banī ʻAbd Manāf forged a pact with the Negus (the king of Abyssinia), with the Iraqi authorities that represented the Sassanids, and with the Himyarite kings in Yemen. As a result, the caravans of the Quraysh were able to traverse the desert in peace and security, brimming with various merchandise. With the passing of time, and as the Qurayshi traders gained more experience in the various markets, five central trade routes developed. The first route ran from Makkah to Yathrib, then to Khaybar, on to Tabūk, and finally to Gaza, which was an important port from where merchandise was transported to Europe by sea. This was the trading route that Hāshim usually traversed. He died during one of his journeys to Gaza and was buried there (which is why it became known as "Hāshim's Gaza"). The second, coastal route headed out westward from Makkah to the Red Sea coastline, and then north toward the Levant. The third route was a maritime route from the Shuʻaybah[34] Port on the Red Sea to Abyssinia, the Kingdom of Aksum. A maritime offshoot from there headed northward towards Elath, now known as Aqaba. The fourth was the Najdi route, which went to Yathrib and then, via Najd, to Iraq. The fifth route ran south from Makkah,

34. A historical port on the Red Sea coast, south-west of Makkah. It was Makkah's central port for a time, until Jeddah became the main port during the reign of the third caliph, ʻUthmān ibn ʻAffān.

passed through Ṭā'if, then went from Najran to Yemen.

Makkah thus became a central node that joined four large markets: the Levant, Iraq, Yemen, and Abyssinia. Qurayshi trade was structured around, and took advantage of, the changing seasons and weather. The winter journey was to Yemen and Abyssinia, and the summer journey to the Levant, during which the traders travelled as far as the Ghassanid capital of Bosra (now in southern Syria). However, most of the Qurayshi trade was via Gaza, which was an important port for exporting goods to Europe.

These routes flourished as the Persian-Byzantine conflict intensified, since Makkah had become an alternative crossing point between the established trade routes. Makkah thus benefited from international destabilisation, especially when the conflict resulted in the suspension or disruption of the Red Sea maritime route. The Qurayshi caravans then became the only means by which to transport merchandise between Yemen and the Levant.

From trade to politics

In addition to his trading acumen, Hāshim is regarded as a central character in Qurayshi history, and much has been narrated about his extreme generosity, integrity, honour, judiciousness, and wisdom. Chroniclers also note his physical attributes. He was described as tall and light-skinned. While we may mention this image, we should be circumspect about accepting all these accounts as being authentic, since many of these biographical details were added retrospectively and much later, in an attempt to elevate Hāshim's status, since he was the Prophet's (ﷺ) great grandfather.

Considering Hāshim's leadership role in managing the trade pact, the political structure of the Quraysh had to be adjusted. The children of 'Abd al-Dār retained their symbolic leadership positions in Makkah on the grounds that they were the heirs of their grandfather's bequest. However, it was the children of 'Abd Manāf, including Hāshim, who executed administrative and other duties. This was particularly the case with the provisioning of food and water, which required much effort and a great deal of financial support. Hāshim was unhappy that the notional responsibility for the five essential duties remained that of his cousins, who were descended from ʻAbd al-Dār. He, along with the other sons of ʻAbd Manāf, believed it was unfair for their cousins to enjoy the symbolic honour of leadership while they undertook the actual daily work. They therefore tried to unite the formal authority of the five duties and the practical reality that the work required.

Consequently, a dispute broke out between the two parties. Some Makkan tribes supported the position of Hāshim and his brothers, while others stood with the sons of ʻAbd al-Dār, insisting on the inherited status of the authority. This incident marked the beginning of a huge rift that affected the entire Qurayshi political edifice and lay the foundation for the two most important alliances in Makkah's history: the Alliance of the Scented and the Alliance of the Allies. Standing with the Banī ʻAbd Manāf were the Banī Asad ibn ʻAbd al-ʻUzza ibn Quṣay, the Banī Zahrah ibn Kilāb, the Banī Taym ibn Murrah, and the Banī al-Ḥārith ibn Fahar. The Banī ʻAbd al-Dār were supported by the Banī Makhzūm, the Saham, the Jamaḥ, and the Banī ʻAdī ibn Kaʻb.

The Alliance of the Scented was the alliance of the Banī ʻAbd Manāf, so named because they had taken a container filled with perfume to the Kaʻbah, immersed their hands in it, rubbed the perfume onto the Kaʻbah, and there swore an oath allying themselves. The second alliance, that of the Banī ʻAbd al-Dār, was the Ḥilf Laʻqat al-Dam (Alliance of a Lick of Blood), alternately called the Alliance of the Allies. They were referred to by the first name because they had immersed their hands in the blood of a slaughtered camel and wiped it onto the Kaʻbah.

The two alliances gathered their forces and prepared for battle. Just before the conflict could erupt, they reconciled, after agreeing to share the leadership duties between the two sets of cousins. In terms of the agreement, the Banī ʻAbd Manāf were given the duties of supplying water and food, while the Banī ʻAbd al-Dār was responsible for Maintenance of the Kaʻbah, The Brigade, and the House of Assembly.

We should pause and reflect on this division of labour between the two parties. Water Supplier and Food Provisioner were both service duties, while Maintenance of the Ka'bah, The Brigade, and the House of Assembly were more ceremonial. The supply of food and water embodied the values of munificence, striving, and generosity, but also required the sons of 'Abd Manāf to provide direct assistance to the pilgrims and carry all its financial burdens. This does not mean that the Banī 'Abd Manāf spent exclusively from their wealth; other Makkan tribes also contributed financially to provide logistical support and water to pilgrims. Nevertheless, the greatest burden and responsibility fell on Hāshim, who was financially self-sufficient. He exerted the greatest effort of all the Quraysh in fulfilling these duties. Ibn Sa'd explains:

> They reached an agreement that Hāshim ibn 'Abd Manāf ibn Quṣay would be in charge of Water Supplies and the Food Provisioning. He was a man of wealth, and when the pilgrimage season approached, he addressed the Quraysh, saying, "O people of Quraysh. You are the neighbours of Allah and custodians of His house. Pilgrims are coming to you in this season to glorify the sanctity of His house. They are the guests of Allah, and the most deserving of esteem are the guests of Allah. Allah has selected you for this purpose and honoured you with this role. He protects your rights more than any other neighbour does. So respect His guests and pilgrims who come with dishevelled hair and covered in dust from every city on worn-out mounts. They have crawled, are covered in filth, have lice in their clothes, and have exhausted their provisions. Settle them and quench their thirst."
>
> The Quraysh would come to their assistance and every household would provide something, according to its means. Hāshim ibn 'Abd Manāf ibn Quṣay would set aside a huge portion of his wealth every year, the wealthy people of the Quraysh would also assist, and every person would contribute 100 Heraclian mithqals [of gold].
>
> Hāshim ordered the construction of cisterns (made of animal skins) near the well of Zamzam and filled them with water from the other wells of Makkah so that the pilgrims could drink therefrom. He

began feeding the pilgrims on the Day of Tarwiyah [the first day of the hajj pilgrimage] at Makkah and Mina, and on the Day of Jam'a at 'Arafah. He soaked the crumbs of bread in the soup of meat mingled with fat, parched barley, wheat, and dates. He provided them with drinking water in Mina when water in the cisterns ran low. When the pilgrims departed from Mina, the hospitality would end, and they then dispersed and returned to their homelands.[35]

We may conclude from this that when Hāshim undertook the responsibility of providing food and water, he was cognisant of the esteemed moral value of these duties. That is why he addressed his people using ethical language when enjoining them to fulfil the duty of hospitality in their capacity as "neighbours" of Allah and custodians of His house. Even though all members of the Quraysh contributed to these two duties, the greatest burden fell on Hāshim's shoulders, which is probably what contributed to the depletion of the wealth of the Banī Hāshim after him. Even though his descendants inherited virtue, ethical status, and a good reputation, they were never as wealthy as their cousins. This left its mark on the Alliance of the Scented; they upheld ethical values, entrenched generosity and justice, and embraced Muḥammad's (ﷺ) mission and provided him with social solidarity and tribal support. By contrast, the Alliance of the Allies retained possession of the duties of the House of Assembly, Maintenance of the Ka'bah, and The Brigade, which were linked to ceremony and status. This alliance thus became the ruling establishment, which was committed to its own vested interests and was prepared to transgress all that was sacred, if required, to preserve its hegemony and authority. They even used force against anyone who opposed them or challenged their political hegemony. The Alliance of the Allies combined wealth and politics and used these against Muḥammad's (ﷺ) mission. They were driven by arrogance and haughtiness into a violent confrontation with Islam that led to a prolonged struggle between the two camps and resulted, after twenty-three years, in victory for the alliance of virtue and magnanimity over the alliance of segregation and supremacy.

Hāshim ibn 'Abd Manāf likely died at the end of the fifth century. Chroniclers recorded that he married a woman in Yathrib named Salma

35. Ibn Sa'd, *al-Ṭabaqāt*, vol. 1, 63.

bint ʻAmr from the Banī al-Najjār tribe, which was affiliated to the Khazraj confederacy. Yathrib was located on the trade route between Makkah and the Levant. A son was born of his union with Salma, and she named him Shaybah. The boy remained with his maternal uncles of the Banī al-Najjār until he was an adolescent. Muṭṭalib ibn Quṣay, Hāshim's brother, took over the trade after his death, and gained a reputation for generosity. He travelled to Yathrib and returned to Makkah with Shaybah ibn Hāshim, carrying the boy behind him on his camel. When he approached Makkah, the Quraysh said al-Muṭṭalib had returned with a slave, to which he responded: "This is the son of my brother Hāshim." However, the story was not forgotten, and Shaybah ibn Hāshim became known as ʻAbd al-Muṭṭalib (the slave of al-Muṭṭalib).

We know that ʻAbd al-Muṭṭalib died when the Prophet (ﷺ) was eight years old, and that the Prophet (ﷺ) was born in 570, most likely on Monday, 15 Rabīʻ al-Awwal / 30 January 570. Thus, ʻAbd al-Muṭṭalib must have died in 578, and if we assume that ʻAbd al-Muṭṭalib lived to the age of eighty-two, as many reports suggest, then his birth was likely around the year 496. If, however, he lived to the age of ninety-two, as other reports suggest, then his birthdate was probably closer to 480, and we can conclude that this was the year in which Hāshim died. All the dates are speculative, of course, but we discuss them here to familiarise ourselves with the historical events that dominated the world around Makkah at that time, and, more especially, the political state of affairs in the Persian and Byzantine empires on the one hand, and in Abyssinia and Yemen on the other.

CHAPTER TWO

The world surrounding Makkah

"Do they not then see that We have made a Sanctuary secure, though all around them people are being snatched away. Then, how can they believe in that which is false and reject the blessings of Allah" (Qur'ān 29:67).

The first third of the seventh century witnessed the greatest geopolitical development in world history: the collapse of the Persian Empire, the decline of the Byzantine Empire and the dawn of Islamic civilization. However, the beginnings of the transformation in the structure of the international order had begun much earlier. To comprehend the international context within which the new religion was born, we must examine the international axis that dominated the world before Islam—the Persian-Roman axis—which was locked in a bitter battle lasting seven centuries. The international order that had prevailed until the arrival of Islam was a product of this battle, a comprehensive conflict, the impact of which transcended politics and strategy and encompassed economics, religion, and culture. Therefore, the breakdown of this axial order at the beginning of the seventh century was a massive collapse not only of the structure of the international order but of everything that it represented: the religious, cultural, social, and economic orders.

In this chapter, we will examine the roots of the transformation, beginning in the fifth century, since the fifth and sixth centuries had a profound impact on the structure of the international order. The most important event in these two centuries was the fall of Rome as the capital of the Roman Empire in 476, replaced by Constantinople as the throne of the Eastern Roman Empire, which came to be referred to as the Byzantine Empire, thus differentiating it from the Western Roman Empire. Another major event was the outbreak of a destructive world war between the Persians and the Byzantines in 602, which played out on several fronts. Both global poles were exhausted by the war that had irrevocably transformed the international order and ended only in 627, with the Byzantines vanquishing the Persians at the Battle of Nineveh.

This was the same year in which the Muslims decisively swung the balance of power in the Arabian Peninsula in their favour after the Treaty of Hudaybīyyah. Soon thereafter, they would prepare for the conquest of Makkah, followed by a series of conquests that would make them the heirs of the two wearied empires and the builders of a unique international civilisation.

The rise of Constantinople

The most noteworthy event of the fifth century was the collapse of the Western Roman Empire. Even though it was a gradual process that unfolded over three centuries, the official date for the collapse and dismantlement of the empire is fixed at 4 September 476, when its last emperor, Romulus Augustus, was deposed by the Germanic tribes that seized control of Italy. With the collapse of the Western Roman Empire, the Roman centre of gravity shifted to the Eastern Roman Empire, which was known to its inhabitants simply as "the Roman Empire". It later came to be referred to as the "Byzantine Empire", derived from Byzantium, the ancient Greek name for the empire's capital Constantinople, which is now called Istanbul.

The main reason for dividing the Roman Empire into western and eastern spheres was the sheer size and extent of its territories, the belief that it was not possible for one emperor to rule all these areas, and the need for a strong strategic centre in the east of the empire that would be capable of confronting the perennial threat posed by the Sassanid Persians. The Roman emperor Diocletian, who ascended the throne in 284, established an administrative capital for the Asian, Greek-speaking sphere of the empire in a village called Byzantium. Constantine I, who had become emperor in 306, made Byzantium the capital of his empire in 324, calling it "New Rome", and renaming it "Constantinople" in 330. Constantine I was the first Roman emperor to convert to Christianity and is famous for inviting Christian bishops to the most important and historic gathering in Christian history: the First Council of Nicaea, which was later referred to as the First Ecumenical Council. It brought together between 250 and 318 bishops to settle a major dispute between the Bishop of Alexandria, Alexander I, and the priest Arius, about the nature of the Messiah. The Bishop of Alexandria held the view that Christ was the son of God and was divine, while Arius advocated monotheism and denied the eternity of Christ. Arius argued that Christ was a created being (created by God), and that the Holy Spirit was also God's creation.

The council was convened on 20 May 325 in the town of Nicaea,[36] near the city of Bursa in contemporary Türkiye, and was opened by Constantine himself. After months of deliberation, the dispute was settled by a vote that saw Alexander's view prevail over that of Arius. The council thus adopted the Christian principle of faith that regards Christ as divine. Subsequently, particularly because of Arius's insistence on holding to his position, his view was regarded as a heretical innovation, his books were burned, his followers persecuted, and he was banished to Spain.

Even though Constantine had converted to Christianity, the official religion of the empire remained paganism until Emperor Theodosius I took the reins of power and changed it to Christianity. Theodosius (d. 395) was the last Roman emperor to rule over the whole of the Roman empire. Thereafter, it was divided into a Western Roman Empire with Rome as its capital, and an Eastern Roman Empire with Constantinople as its capital.

The Roman Empire's disintegration began with increasing attacks by the Germanic Vandal tribes, whose members likely held Arian beliefs, and with the dismantling of regions in Spain and Gaul that had been subservient to Rome. The Vandals invaded Rome in 455 and burned down much of the city. The last Roman emperor, Romulus Augustus, was finally overthrown on 4 September 476.

With Rome's collapse, Europe descended into chaos, conflict, and division, and superstition and belief in sorcery gained ascendancy in what became known as the Dark Ages. Constantinople, however, maintained strong centralised control over the eastern parts of the empire. There, the sciences and arts flourished, and it prospered as the

36. An ancient Greek town located on the Anatolian coast that was conquered by Orhan, the son of 'Uthmān the First, in the fourteenth century. It is currently named Iznik and is part of the Bursa province in Türkiye.

heir to Roman and Greek history.

As the strategic gravitas of Constantinople became dominant, its emperors saw themselves as the legitimate heirs of the entire Roman Empire, both Eastern and Western. Until the ascension of Justinian I (527–565), also known as Justinian the Great, the most prominent emperor in the history of the Eastern Roman Empire, they continued their attempt to regain the prestige of the empire and to reunite it. They also attempted to recolonise regions that had seceded.

Constantinople's Golden Age

Fortunately, Justinian's history has been preserved in great detail in the writings of the famous Greek historian Procopius, who was closely associated with the ruling elite. He accompanied several army generals on their military campaigns and was appointed to the Council of Elders by Justinian. An eyewitness with fine observation skills, he was well read, and he wrote several books which remain important references for Byzantine military, political, and architectural history.

There are several reasons why Justinian is regarded as the greatest emperor of Constantinople. He recaptured most of the territory that had been part of the historical Roman Empire, including North Africa, Italy, and Rome itself, which then remained under Byzantine control for two centuries. As an emperor, Justinian became known for his commitment to systems of law and administration. He rewrote the Roman constitution and established Roman civil law. It later became known as Justinian Law and is regarded as one of the most important sources of law globally. Many modern states still use certain of his constitutional provisions. The arts, literature, and architecture also flourished in his era. Justinian built Constantinople's famous Hagia Sophia Cathedral, which became the centre of Eastern Orthodox Christianity and remained so for several centuries.

His strategic achievements include the building of a powerful armada, which he used to dominate the Mediterranean Basin and its main ports, and also to patrol the Red Sea. Justinian forged alliances with kingdoms and political entities from Central Asia to the African Christian Kingdom of Aksum, which the Arabs referred to as Abyssinia. Roman ships carried merchandise from Abyssinian ports to the port of Elath (Aqaba), thereby circumventing the section of the Maritime Silk Route that joined India to the Arabian Gulf and was controlled by the Persians.

In 531, Justinian asked the Abyssinians, who ruled Yemen, to strengthen their maritime trade with India, hoping to rival the trade between the Sassanids and India. Byzantine historical records indicate that the Aksumian military general in Yemen, Abraha (Abraham), was not enthusiastic about carrying out the task he had been assigned and undertook several actions independently of Abyssinia. He appointed himself the independent king of Yemen, angering the king of Aksum and his ally Justinian. We will return to this event in our discussion on the strategic situation in Makkah.

Constantinople's flourishing Golden Age under Justinian's rule ended with the worst natural disaster that Europe had ever experienced, the plague that invaded Constantinople between 541 and 543, which became known as the Justinian Plague. It killed forty percent of the city's inhabitants before spreading to the rest of Europe, killing one quarter of its inhabitants. Economic production was suspended due to death, sickness, and poverty, and the condition of the empire deteriorated, as numerous provinces rose in rebellion against the central authority. This enfeebled the empire and weakened its resolve to confront the Sassanid Persians, who waited for an opportunity to attack Constantinople and start a new round of battles as part of a war that had been raging for seven centuries, making it the longest war in human history. These events paved the way for the final round of battles, which would be launched just before the commencement of the Prophet Muḥammad's (ﷺ) mission. Battlefronts were triggered in various corners of the ancient world. These battles ended with profound and fundamental changes in the international balance of forces and paved the way for the global ascendance of Islam, catching the two established powers by surprise and resulting in their collapse and annihilation.

Rome and religion

Religion formed an indivisible part of the official authority of the state in the Roman Empire, making it an extremely important political tool that was utilised by emperors and politicians to actively promote their interests. The Romans had adopted the worship of a plurality of gods from the Greeks. They gave their deities Roman names and built temples for them where sacrifices were offered, rituals performed, and religious celebrations held. These temples formed a defining part of Roman identity, and people visited them to consult the gods on all matters. The Romans believed that spirits possessed all things and that these spirits were capable of intervening in their lives. Thus, the belief in good and bad omens was commonplace. This belief created a need for an authority that would be capable of interpreting daily events and guiding one to appropriate action, a function that was carried out by temple priests, effectively making them intermediaries between the people and the gods. Of course, a visit to a temple also required that generous offerings be made to the gods.

The Roman religious heritage had twelve gods, six male and six female, each bearing the name of a planet. The highest-ranking and most important god was Jupiter, who was named after the largest planet in the solar system. He was effectively the king of the gods, as well as the protector and benefactor of Rome, the god of the sky and lightning, and the god of justice, in whose name all legislation was affirmed. Every god had a specific duty that was associated with a natural phenomenon or responsibility, such as harvesting, sowing, rain, love, and so on.

In the Roman religion, a deity was no different in form than a human, and yet they were characterised by perfection in body and in capabilities; a deity was thus a perfected and distinguished copy of a Roman person. However, the gods also conspired, forged alliances, and fought, just as humans did. For example, Jupiter attained his elevated status only after warring with his father Saturn and removing him from the throne with the help of his brothers Neptune, the god of the Sea, and Pluto, the god of the underworld. Jupiter thus became the king of the gods, as part of a holy trinity.

Roman religion was the backbone of national identity; the rejection of faith or any sacrilege was regarded as treason and was punishable by death. The ruling elite, of the noble class, were able to keep religion in check by ensuring that priests were elected. It was no surprise that the nobles and influential people won these elections and held a monopoly in representing the gods. Then, whatever laws or regulations the cunning Roman politicians were unable to pass through parliament, they would pass on the basis that these were divine injunctions. This pertained to all aspects of life—from the declaration of war, to the determination of election dates, to the passing of legislation.

Religious festivals were linked to major popular celebrations that were hosted in Rome. These gatherings were always important events for politicians and parliamentary candidates, allowing them to campaign. Ultimately, politics and religion were intertwined in Rome in such a manner that religion lost its independence from the state.

Interestingly, Julius Caesar was elected as High Priest of Rome and this position, in addition to his rank as head of the Republican Army and his assumed power to appoint magistrates, assisted him in imposing himself as dictator in perpetuity on, and in dominating, the senate, thereby threatening the democratic values of the republic. A rebellion in the senate resulted in senators stabbing him to death outside the senate chamber in 44 BCE. His assassination sparked a civil war that ended with Octavian, Caesar's adopted son, taking control of the state under the name Caesar Augustus. In 27 BCE, Augustus declared himself Emperor of Rome, putting an end to the republican era and inaugurating the age of the Roman Empire.

Augustus also exploited religion to claim a unique status for himself that none before him had held: he proclaimed himself divine. Augustus interpreted the appearance of a seven-day cometary outburst as the soul of Julius Caesar ascending to the heavens to join the other gods. He therefore requested the senate, which had become totally subservient to him, to officially recognise his adoptive father as a god, which it did. The senate also ordered the building of a huge temple in Rome for the new god. This allowed Augustus to add a significant new title to his many others; he was now also "the Son of God". He was thus able to appropriate all forms of authority to himself, becoming an absolute ruler with the final decision-making power on all matters—whether political, military, or religious. It is also worth noting that Jesus Christ was born during Augustus's rule, which ended in 14 CE. All Roman emperors thereafter inherited Augustus's status, until Constantine I, who was crowned emperor in 306 CE.

Constantine realised that Rome's institutions and its noble elite were both corrupt. He acknowledged that Rome's ethical spirit was likewise corrupt, and that a fundamental change was required to preserve the empire. To effect this change and revive the empire structurally and spiritually, he took two crucial steps. He first established a new capital at the eastern edge of the empire, in the village of Byzantium, which later became Constantinople. Thereafter, he converted to Christianity and encouraged its spread among his subjects.

It is unclear precisely why Constantine converted to Christianity. Some historians suggest that it was because his mother Helena was a Christian; others recount a myth that, during one of his battles, he had seen a cross in the sun just before it had set. Whatever the true reason for his conversion, the emperor, who was occupied with building his new capital, announced that he would pay money to every Christian who settled in Byzantium, and he began building churches, appointing Christians to senior positions, and declared Sunday an official public holiday.

As opposed to the old ways in Rome, Constantine wanted all that was new in Constantinople to be Christian. He therefore issued a decree in 314 that decriminalised Christian worship, granted legitimacy to Christianity, and paved the way for his successors officially to adopt Christianity as the religion of the Roman Empire. There is no doubt that Constantine's strategy was effective; changing the capital and elevating the status of Christianity breathed new spirit into the empire and ensured that it would survive another 800 years after the collapse of Rome in 476.

However, some clarification is necessary. From the time of Constantine's bold moves, the Roman Empire instrumentalised

Christianity, as if it were a new tool to be used to spread the empire's spiritual and moral influence over different nations of various cultures and religions. The ancient Roman religion was not suited to be a global religion. Moreover, it had lost its moral legitimacy when Rome's temples and priests had become pawns in the hands of the nobility and the ruling elite. The ancient religion had become an overused device that was devoid of any divine meaning, no more than a collection of superstitions and myths that granted legitimacy to the influential to hoard the wealth of the people.

Christianity provided an appropriate and suitable alternative, and it had the potential to become a global religion. In addition, it was seen as a pacifist religion that would not challenge the emperor's authority. Christ's statement "Render unto Caesar what is Caesar's and unto God what is God's" became widespread in the empire. The statement occurs in a longer passage in the Bible.

> They sent some of the Pharisees and supporters of Herod to trap him in his words. They came to him and said, "Teacher, we know that you're genuine and you don't worry about what people think. You don't show favouritism but teach God's way as it really is. Does the Law allow people to pay taxes to Caesar or not? Should we pay taxes or not?"
>
> Since Jesus recognized their deceit, he said to them, "Why are you testing me? Bring me a coin. Show it to me." And they brought one. He said to them, "Whose image and inscription is this?"
>
> "Caesar's," they replied.
>
> Jesus said to them, "Give to Caesar what belongs to Caesar and to God what belongs to God." His reply left them overcome with wonder.[37]

A close examination of this passage does not lead to the conclusion that Jesus placed the authority of Caesar on the same level as the authority of God. However, the emperor's interpretation and instrumentalization

37. *Common English Bible*, Mark 12, Verses 13-17.

of it effectively made Christianity a religion that was reconcilable with the state. From this perspective, Christianity was not to be feared, especially since it was linked to the state and enjoyed its blessing, support, and patronage. The potential for such a use of Christianity was, I believe, what encouraged Constantine to embrace Christianity and motivated him to encourage his subjects to convert as well.

Though Christianity was made the official religion of the state only after Constantine's death in 381, his influence on the religion was enormous. It was he who convened the First Ecumenical Council in Nicaea in 325 and delivered the opening address. The purpose of the council—in which as many as 318 bishops from all over the Christian world participated—was to settle a dispute over the nature of Christ between the priest Arius and Alexander, the Bishop of Alexandria. Arius believed that Christ was God's creation and not an eternal being, while Alexander held that the nature of Christ was the same as the nature of God. Alexander's view was upheld by the council after a vote, making it the official doctrine of the Church and the Roman Empire. Arius was subsequently denounced as an enemy of Christianity, and his followers were persecuted, with many fleeing to areas that were not under the authority of the Roman Empire, such as the Arabian Peninsula.

It is noteworthy that the body that settled the most critical doctrinal issue in Christianity—the official stance regarding the nature of Christ—was convened at the behest and under the patronage of the emperor. Even if one were to overlook whether Constantine and his inner circle influenced the Council's final decision, it set a precedent for the role of the empire. Thereafter, the empire's convening of ecumenical councils became an established tradition. In other words, the empire effectively became the administrator of Christian doctrine and the patron of Christian decision-making. Furthermore, the empire also implemented religious directives with the power of legislation. This development marked the beginning of the convergence of Christianity and the Byzantine state. It thus leads us to the conclusion that Constantine's conversion to Christianity was likely motivated not by a spiritual awakening and a desire for personal salvation, but by a conscious strategic decision to adopt a new religion with beliefs and organisational frameworks that were suited to a position as the official religion of the empire.

This hypothesis is strengthened by the steps that were later taken by the authorities in Constantinople, especially after the Council of Chalcedon in 451. The empire denounced the theology of the eastern Church of Antioch (whose contemporary inheritor is the Syriac Orthodox Church), and consciously reshaped the church so that it became more Roman. It did so by merging ancient Roman beliefs with the Christian religion. It also adopted the Greek language for liturgical purposes in place of Syriac and appointed Greek bishops to run the church's affairs. Gradually, the role of the state in church matters became more pronounced, and the Melkite Greek Orthodox Church emerged, deriving its name from the common semitic root M-L-K, meaning "royal," or loyal to the emperor. The church thus effectively became part of the state.

Taking control of the church was not easy, however. The Nicaea Council resolutions had major consequences. Doctrinal disputes overwhelmed churches, and conflicting claims emerged regarding the nature of Christ and the appropriate title for the Virgin Mary. Another prominent council that had later political consequences was the Third Ecumenical Council, or the First Council of Ephesus, convened in Ephesus in 431. It sought to interrogate the claims of Nestorius, the Bishop of Constantinople, that Christ had been created but that he was of two separate natures. When Jesus had been born, Nestorius argued, he was a natural person, but the divine word manifested in him after he was baptised by John the Baptist. Consequently, Mary was not the mother of God; she was not Theotokus ("Carrier of God"), but rather the mother of Jesus the man. This was a brazen departure from what had, by then, become official church doctrine. The official doctrine posited two hypostases for Jesus, the dwelling of the single Word in two natures, one divine and one human. The Council ruled the Nestorian doctrine false, and he was expelled from the church. The emperor went further, banishing Nestorius and persecuting his followers, prompting them to flee to Persian lands, where they were warmly welcomed by the Sassanid Persians, who hoped to weaken the Byzantine control over Christianity.

The most important schism in the Christian Church occurred after the Council of Chalcedon, or the Fourth Ecumenical Council, convened in

451 in Chalcedon (modern day Kadikoy, Istanbul, Türkiye) to address the dispute over whether Christ was of two natures in one person or of a single nature. The council adopted the position of the Roman and Constantinople churches, which held that Christ was of two distinct natures and two distinct volitions. As a result, the churches that believed that Christ was of a single nature in which the divine and human converge broke away. These were the Assyrian Church of the East and the Eastern Oriental Churches, comprised of the Coptic Orthodox Church of Alexandria, the Syriac Orthodox Church of Antioch, the Armenian Apostolic Church, the Malankara Orthodox Syrian Church, the Ethiopian Orthodox Tewahedo Church, and the Eritrean Orthodox Tewahedo Church.

The empire used its security apparatus to attack the dissenting churches and to punish the sects that did not uphold official Chalcedonian Christian doctrine. The Byzantine Empire realised that these divisions threatened the unity of the Church, which was an important weapon for its project of making official Christianity the collective religion of the citizens of the empire. Churches that professed doctrines contradicting the pronouncements of the officially recognised church councils departed from the official vision of the state. Some of these churches were culturally and ethnically distinct, such as the Syriac, Coptic, and Armenian churches. They were pressured to conform. Emperor Justinian I passed legislation affirming the resolutions of the four church councils; Christians who contradicted these resolutions were condemned as heretics and as contravening the law, and were threatened with severe punishment.

The only result of these aggressive policies of the emperors of Constantinople was to engender a general feeling among eastern Christians that they would not be able to practise their beliefs under Byzantine hegemony. This sentiment greatly influenced the positive reception later enjoyed by the Muslims, who many Eastern Christians saw as their saviours from Byzantine oppression. We will see later how the Prophet's (ﷺ) letter addressed Emperor Heraclius: "Submit to Islam and save yourself, and Allah will reward you twice over. But if you turn away, you bear the sin of the Arians." The Arians mentioned here are most likely the followers of the priest Arius. Many of the

Arians fled far from Byzantine influence, and many chose the Arabian Peninsula as a haven, making them a familiar presence among Arabs.

The Sassanid Persians

At this juncture, it is appropriate to introduce the second strategic player on the international stage: the Sassanid Persians.

The Sassanids were the third dynasty to inherit the throne of the Persian Empire. They took control of the empire in 224 after defeating their predecessors, the Parthians, who had taken the throne from the Achaemenids. The Sassanid Dynasty ruled for four centuries before falling to Muslim conquerors in 637. The founder of the Sassanid dynasty was Ardashir I, who was given the title of shahanshah, or king of kings, and was appointed the guardian of the holy fire, the symbol of Zoroastrianism, which was the official religion of the Sassanid Empire. Ardashir I moved his capital to the fortified city of Gur (modern day Firuzabad) and expanded his empire, joining to it Khurasan, Turkmenistan, Balkh, Khwarazm, al-Baḥrayn, and Nineveh. After the Romans tried to overthrow him in 230, he also attempted, unsuccessfully, to take over several regions that were vassals of the Roman Empire.

The conflict between the Persians and Romans persisted under the reign of the Sassanid emperor Shapur I, son of Ardashir I, and continued during the reigns of his successors. It was interrupted by peace treaties that lasted for brief periods. These agreements usually involved sharing disputed territories, the most important of which were Armenia and Upper Mesopotamia. The Romans were not the only enemy with whom the Sassanids clashed over the centuries; there were also the Hephthalite tribes, sometimes referred to as the White Huns, a collective of bedouins who had settled in Central Asia.

Historians differ over the origins of these tribes, with some claiming that they were of Turkic descent and others that they had originated in areas in current day Afghanistan, Pakistan, and Iran. They established a huge empire, the dominion of which stretched from

India to Central Asia. They fought numerous wars with the Persians and invaded Persian lands, but were repulsed by Sassanid emperors Bahram V and Yazdegerd II. However, the Hephthalites returned to Persian territory in the late fifth century and defeated Emperor Peroz I (457–484), causing havoc across the Persian Empire for two years. Peroz attempted an offensive against them, but he and his army were ambushed by the Hephthalites on the road to Herat. Peroz was killed and his army decimated, after which the Hephthalites occupied Herat. Wars between the two belligerents persisted until the Sassanid emperor Kavad I reached an agreement with the Hephthalites and joined forces with them in a war against Constantinople in 502. Kavad then took control of parts of Armenia, setting off a new round of wars between the Byzantines and the Persians.

For our purpose, the most pertinent element of these conflicts is that the wars between the Hephthalites and Persians created a state of chaos and contestation in the regions through which the most important trade route in the ancient world passed—the Northern Silk Road that linked China to Europe. Kavad's successor, Khosrow I, was one of the most important Sassanid kings. He had an expansionist policy that targeted lands in the east. He recaptured Persian lands from the Hephthalites around 565 and ultimately defeated the Hephthalite Empire.

Khosrow I ascended the Sassanid throne in 531 and ruled until 579. He was given the title of Anushirvān (the immortal soul). He was a contemporary of the Byzantine emperor Justinian and is regarded as the most famous Sassanid emperor. Known for his great achievements across the Empire, he passed, among other reforms, a tax law based on land ownership, and he exerted every effort to improve the empire's economy. He also limited the influence of feudal lords, affirmed the poor, organised the army on new foundations and divided it into specialist troops, and reformed the empire's administrative system.

Justinian I signed an accord with Khosrow I in 532. Known as "Perpetual Peace", the treaty required the return of all occupied territories by both sides and a once-off Byzantine payment to the Persian Empire of five-and-half metric tons of gold. Khosrow, however, reneged on the agreement in 540 when he believed that the Byzantine

Empire was fragile because of Constantinople's preoccupation with internecine wars, and because of the plague that had decimated a large part of the Byzantine population. Khosrow then invaded the Levant and the bloody conflict continued for more than two decades, until the Treaty of Dara (also known as the Fifty-year Peace Treaty) was agreed on in 562. By the terms of this treaty, the Byzantines were to pay an annual tribute of 30,000 gold coins to the Persians.

Justinian I died in 565 and was succeeded by Justin II (565–578), who was known for being impulsive. Justin suspended the payment of the annual grant that Constantinople had paid to the bedouin Arabs for the latter's ceasing their raids in the Byzantine territories in the Levant. Exploiting the Persian preoccupation with a revolution in Armenia, he also suspended the tribute to the Persians. The Byzantines allied with the Armenians and attacked Sassanid territories in 573. However, they were defeated, and the Persians again occupied the Levant, forcing Justin II to accept a new five-year truce and to pay a huge amount in compensation. Nevertheless, war quickly resumed, and the violent conflict between the two empires continued.

Persians and religion

The Persian Achaemenid, Parthian, and Sassanid dynasties all professed Zoroastrianism, one of the world's oldest religions, founded by Zoroaster, who likely lived in the seventh century BCE. In its first manifestation, Zoroastrianism professed monotheism and glorified Ahura Mazda (the Lord of Wisdom), who is One and Majestic, above in the heavens. It also professed the eternity of the soul, which is destined for either heaven or hell depending on its earthly actions. Zoroastrianism also regarded a person as being of free volition, but responsible for his or her actions. One's religious responsibility required one to maintain the balance that was created by God in the universe by doing good and speaking well, and by rejecting the chaos that results from deviating from the divine order.

Zoroastrianism rejects all forms of priesthood, and its adherents perform five daily prayers linked to the transition of night to day. Prayer involves meditation and the recitation of invocations from the Avesta, the Zoroastrian holy texts. Before beginning the prayer, a Zoroastrian performs ritual purification by washing the face and limbs three times. Zoroastrians regard water and fire as pure elements, and they pray in the presence of fire because it is the source of light. Water is regarded as the source of wisdom, and fire as the means by which wisdom is conveyed. Because Zoroastrians regard dead bodies as defiled, corpses should not mix with water and earth, which are pure, and thus should not be buried in soil. Further, since fire is also pure, corpses should not be cremated. The Zoroastrian tradition, therefore, is to construct towers, referred to as "dakhma", or towers of silence, and to place the bodies of the dead at the top of these towers, allowing birds of prey to strip the body and feed on the flesh, and the bones to be bleached by the sun. The dried bones, regarded as purified after the stripping and bleaching, are gathered and stored within the towers, ensuring that they do not mix with the earth's soil.

Arabs refer to Zoroastrianism as al-Majūsīyyah. As Jawwād 'Alī[38] explains, the term is derived from the Persian word magus, which means fire worshipper. The term also entered Greek vocabulary.

The Sassanids, who deposed the Parthians in 226, were the descendants of Zoroastrian priests, who were referred to as magi (singular magus); they used their well-established relationships as priests to legitimise their rule. As Christianity spread and the number of its converts increased, the Persian Empire feared that the spread of that religion would also aid the spread of Roman influence. The Sassanids therefore entrenched the status of Zoroastrianism as the official religion of the empire, and, to resist Christian expansion, their kings exhibited a public commitment to rituals and overt religiosity.

As with the Byzantines' instrumentalization of Christianity as the official religion, the Sassanids adapted Zoroastrianism to make it a comprehensive state religion that could be utilised to construct patriotic citizens and an all-encompassing identity for Persians and their vassals. They attempted to reconcile Zoroastrianism with ancient Persian religions that had venerated natural phenomena, creating a

38. Jawwād 'Alī, *al-Mufaṣṣal fī Tārikh al-'Arab qabl al-Islām* (Beirut: Dār al-Sāqī, 2001), vol. 12, 268.

new version of Zoroastrianism that was closer to fire worship, and advocating a duality that was expressed as a struggle between good and evil. Zoroastrianism became just a component of the structure of the empire; its priests were of a high social class and benefitted from imperial largesse. As the guardian of the holy fire, the king was located at the summit of the religious hierarchy, and Zoroastrianism became an imperial religion. Since its bond with the empire was ancient, the religion became a pliable tool in the hands of the Sassanid kings. The king, in turn, achieved the goal of all dictators across time; as the representative of the religion, he was bestowed with divine status, making him the king of kings, a status that was far above that of mere mortals.

Zoroastrianism spread because of the authority and influence of the empire beyond Persian territory. Historical sources mention its propagation to Azerbaijan and several other regions of the empire, but it remained essentially a Persian religion. The Sassanids appeared not to be concerned with proselytization in the manner that the Byzantines proselytized Christianity. Indeed, the opposite is true. Rather than trying to proselytize to non-Zoroastrians, the Persians welcomed the Nestorian Christians who had opposed the Melkite Church. By supporting the followers of the creed that opposed the official Byzantine doctrine, the Persian Empire attempted to spite the Byzantines and to widen the schism within Christianity.

The Persian Empire even allowed Nestorian Christians to propagate their religion to non-Persian citizens of the empire, because it wanted to retain Zoroastrianism as the national religion of Persians. Seemingly, it had realised that its non-Persian citizens would not embrace Zoroastrianism, so it rather encouraged them to convert to another religion that also enjoyed imperial patronage. Christianity did, in fact, spread among the Arabs who lived under the authority of the Sassanid Empire in al-Baḥrayn, Upper Mesopotamia and present-day Iraq. Some historians maintain, however, that Zoroastrianism had failed to spread beyond Persia's borders because other ethnic groups found some of the religion's rituals repugnant, especially its burial rites.

The Sassanid Empire forcefully suppressed all belief systems of its citizens that contradicted Zoroastrianism. At the beginning of the third century, the Sassanids violently opposed Manichaeism, a spiritual, gnostic religion that advocated dualism, believing that the world was dominated by the competing forces of good and evil, represented by light and darkness, respectively, and that forbade the pleasures of the flesh.

The Sassanids' problem with Mani—the eponymous founder of Manichaeism—was political, since he professed a faith that conflated Zoroastrianism with Christianity. He believed in Jesus and claimed that he was completing Christ's mission (and sometimes claimed to be the reincarnation of Jesus). Since the Sassanids regarded Christianity as the enemy's religion, it was to be expected that the empire would regard any rapprochement with Christianity as a threat to national security.

Another religion, Mazdakism, was persecuted in the era of Khosrow Anushirvān, who came to power in 531. Although it was founded during the reign of Emperor Kavad by Zaradust-e Khuragan, it derived its name from its most prominent advocate, Mazdak, who died in 528. He used the religion to fight against the influence of the feudal lords and their monopoly over wealth, advocating a socialist approach that regarded wealth and women as communal rights, on the basis that all men were equal. Initially, Kavad (Khosrow's father) tried to use Mazdakism to limit the influence of the feudal class when he feared its growing strength. However, when he died, his son Khosrow Anushirvān suppressed Mazdakism and labelled it an outlaw movement while simultaneously supporting Zoroastrianism and strengthening its influence.[39] The holy texts of Zoroastrianism, the Avesta, which contain sermons and hymns composed by religious figures and Zoroastrian priests, were written in this era.[40]

Since Mazdak's invitation to a kind of socialist ideology contradicted the policies of the empire, the temporary exploitation of Mazdakism in Kavad's era was clearly motivated by a specific goal, and thus it endured for only a short period. In general, however, the empire had adopted a feudal approach to administer the country and to collect taxes. The position of the empire regarding these matters was clear:

39. 'Alī, *al-Mufaṣṣal fī Tārikh*, 268.
40. "Zoroastrianism", *Encyclopædia Iranica*, online edition, 2015, http://www.iranicaonline.org/articles/zoroastrianism.

Zoroastrianism was a peaceful religion, part of the imperial structure and its official religion, and any Persian who sought another religion was a threat who had to be destroyed.

There are reports of some Arabs having converted to Zoroastrianism, such as Zarārah ibn 'Adas and his son Ḥājib ibn Zarārah, al-Aqra' ibn Ḥābis, and Abū al-Aswad, the grandfather of Wakī' ibn Ḥassān.[41] These individuals were leaders of the Tamīm tribe, and, if reports of their conversions are true, it is possible that they converted for some vested interest. These leaders of Tamīm were in conflict with Bakr ibn Wā'il, and they may have believed that converting to Zoroastrianism would strengthen their bonds with the Persians, from whom they had hoped to gain some influence and financial benefit. In any event, these were isolated cases, and Zoroastrianism did not spread among Arabs. In fact, many Arabs from al-Ḥīrah and Upper Mesopotamia, which were under Sassanid control, converted to Christianity, and when Yemen was under Persian influence, it was Judaism that spread among its people. The Persian Empire's policies regarding Christianity were clear: it was welcome if it was different from the Orthodox Christianity that was aligned to Constantinople. If it was associated with Melkite Orthodox Christianity, it was a threat that had to be stopped. The Sassanid Empire therefore welcomed the conversion of the Manādhirah Arabs to Eastern Orthodox Christianity. The Sassanids also provided protection to the Nestorians and allowed them to build churches in Naṣībīn and al-Raha. In Yemen, the Sassanid Jewish ally Dhū Nuwās massacred Christians in Najrān and Dhamar at the beginning of the sixth century under the pretence that they had been Byzantine and Abyssinian agents.

International struggle over Yemen

Yemen's importance in international trade can be traced back centuries before the advent of Christianity. Greek historian and geographer Agatharchides, who lived in the second century BCE, wrote:

> [N]o nation seems to be wealthier than the Sabaeans and Gerrhaeans, who are the agents for everything that falls under

41. 'Alī, *al-Mufaṣṣal fī Tārikh*, 268.

> the name of transport from Asia to Europe. It is they who made Ptolemaic Syria rich in gold, and who provided profitable trade and thousands of other things to Phoenician enterprise.[42]

Sabaeans and Gerrhaeans were ferocious warriors and skilful sailors who navigated large ships to their colonies and returned with products that were available only there.

For us to grasp the strategic significance of Yemen in the fifth and sixth centuries, we must examine the oldest and most important kingdom in the history of the Arabian Peninsula and Horn of Africa, the Kingdom of Sheba, whose control extended across Yemen and Abyssinia. The Kingdom of Sheba dominated the southern Arabian Peninsula for more than a millennium, with its authority stretching over parts of Abyssinia, particularly the region in which the Kingdom of Aksum was later established, after the collapse of Sheba. The Kingdom of Sheba is mentioned in archaeological relics, engravings, and writings that date to the eleventh century BCE. It persisted until the first century CE, when the Himyarites seized control of the Yemeni portion, and the Aksumites the African side.

Accounts of the wealth and prosperity of the Kingdom of Sheba occupied the popular imagination in ancient times, and its impact on Arab and African heritage is still felt. The migration of Yemeni tribes after the collapse of the Ma'rib Dam (which was built between 1750 and 1700 BCE, and was breached around 575 CE) created a population displacement in the Arabian Peninsula that reached as far as Iraq and the Levant, creating well-known tribal migrations which remain familiar to this day. After the fall of Sheba, which had been an extremely bountiful and resilient kingdom and people, ancient Yemeni civilisation began to decline, losing its sovereign and independent political identity. It then became part of the strategic axis of the two great powers of the time: the Persian and Roman empires.

We saw how repeated clashes between the Persians and the Byzantines—the superpowers of the day—disrupted the Northern Silk Road and South-to-North Maritime Silk Route, resulting in the growing

42. Quoted in George Fadlo Hourani, *Arab Seafaring in the Indian Ocean in Ancient and Early Medieval Times* (Princeton: Princeton University Press, 1951), 21.

importance of the East-to-West Maritime Route from India to Aden. Thus, the main objective of the two empires' feverish competition to subjugate Yemen was to control its strategic location in international trade.

The Byzantines were desperate for trade with the east, but their trade with India and China had to pass through volatile regions—either Central Asian lands occupied by rebellious tribes in perpetual revolt and entrenched Sassanid influence, or the Persian Empire itself. The Byzantines had realised much earlier that they needed a route that was not controlled by the Persians and that was able to supply them with merchandise with relative ease. They, therefore, actively attempted to secure a maritime trade route between Aden and Elath (Aqaba) across the Red Sea. To protect this route, they also wanted to establish political influence on the opposite shores of the Red Sea. To this end, the longstanding Roman alliance with Abyssinia was useful, in that it had secured the western shores of the Red Sea for Rome. However, the people on the eastern shores remained determined not to submit to Byzantine domination.

Rome had been trying to establish its influence on the eastern shores of the Red Sea from the time of Emperor Augustus (27–14 BCE). During his reign, Roman forces were dispatched from Egypt, and they crossed the Red Sea to the Arabian Peninsula. After travelling to Yathrib from the coast, they headed south to Najrān (currently in southwestern Saudi Arabia, close to the border with Yemen), but failed to establish a continuous presence in the southern part of the Peninsula. The Byzantines persisted in their attempts to establish a permanent presence on the Arabian Peninsula until the opportunity to subdue Yemen arose during the reign of Justinian. Under the pretence of seeking revenge for the genocide of Christians in Najrān by the Jewish Himyarite king Dhū Nuwās, a Persian ally, the Byzantine-Abyssinian alliance occupied Yemen in 525 and terminated Dhū Nuwās's rule. The Abyssinians' military presence in Yemen did not last long, though Yemen remained in Abyssinian control for around half a century. Meanwhile, the Persians sought any opportunity to regain their influence in the southern part of the Arabian Peninsula.

Such an opportunity presented itself in 570, when the Himyarite

Sayf ibn Dhī Yazan called on the Sassanid emperor Khosrow and requested his support to defeat the Abyssinians and expel them from Yemen. The Persians took advantage of this opportunity to strike a blow at Byzantine influence in the southern Arabian Peninsula. They realised that, by supporting Sayf ibn Dhī Yazan, they would weaken the Byzantine-Abyssinian influence in Yemen as well as across the Red Sea. Further, if they succeeded in capturing the strategic strait of Bab al-Mandab, which connects Yemen to Djibouti and Eritrea on the African side, the movement of Byzantine ships through the Red Sea would be at the mercy of Persian forces.

The second Persian goal was to dominate and monopolise the international trade routes of the ancient world. They were already in control of the main Silk Road that traversed Central Asia, as well as the South-to-North Maritime Silk Route that reached Iraq via the Gulf, but if they also controlled Yemen, the endpoint of the East-to-West Maritime Silk Route, they would become the world's preeminent trading power.

Khosrow dispatched a small army of 5,000 soldiers (some reports give the number as 800) across the Arabian Sea to take up a position close to Aden. Although initially defeated in battle, the Persian army went on to defeat the Abyssinian occupiers, and Sayf ibn Dhī Yazan was crowned king in 575. However, he was unable to maintain stability. A civil war and various rebellions broke out, and Sayf was assassinated by his Ethiopian servants. The Persians intervened again, installing Sayf's son Ma'd Yakrab on the throne. However, such flagrant Persian interference in Yemeni affairs led to a revolution that resulted in the expulsion of the Persians. The Sassanid Empire dispatched another army, which occupied Yemen in 598 and annexed it. Yemen remained under Persian rule until its Sassanid governor, Bādhān ibn Sāsān, embraced Islam shortly after the death of Khosrow II in 628. This will be explained later.

World war

The ancient conflict between the Persian Empire on the one hand and, on the other, the Roman Empire and its successor Byzantine

Empire, continued for seven centuries, making it the longest conflict in human history. However, the wars were punctuated by treaties and reconciliation efforts that quickly broke down when one side saw an opportunity to subjugate the other. By the end of the sixth century, political life in Ctesiphon, the Sassanid capital, had undergone a profound transition as a result of an internal power struggle, and this resulted in the toppling of the new king, Khosrow II (also known as Khosrow Parviz).

We should pause here to point out that Islamic historiography is rich in its recollection of two important Persian kings, both of whom bore the name "Khosrow", which is a proper name and not a monarchical title, as the writings of many Muslim historians suggest. In Sassanid history, there are two kings that bear the name Khosrow. The first was Khosrow I, also known as Anushirvān, who we mentioned earlier and who ruled from 531 to 579. Prophet Muḥammad (ﷺ) was born during his reign. The second was Khosrow II, the grandson of Khosrow I, who lived during the period of the Prophetic mission and ruled from 590 to 627. He was also known as Parviz (the Victorious).

After the death of Khosrow I, his son Hormizd IV ascended the Sassanid throne, but he was killed eleven years later, in 590, in a coup orchestrated by the heads of a few prominent Persian families. They replaced him with his two-year-old son Khosrow II. However, the powerful general, Bahrām Chōbīn, refused to pledge allegiance to the new king and appointed himself king in 591, forcing Khosrow II to flee into exile in the Levant and to seek Byzantine protection.

The fugitive king was welcomed and supported by the Byzantines, who led a military campaign that toppled Bahram and returned Khosrow II to the Persian throne in the same year. The Byzantine service to Khosrow was not free, however. The Byzantine emperor, Maurice, got Khosrow to agree to cede territory to the Byzantines, including northeast Iraq and some areas in Armenia and the Caucasus. He also exempted the Byzantine Empire from the annual tribute that it had been paying to the Persians. Khosrow's relationship with the Byzantines was undoubtedly a stain on his legacy; no Persian king could take pride in the fact that the most important enemy of his kingdom was responsible for returning him to the throne. In addition, Khosrow's concessions to the Byzantines were not acceptable to his military leaders and subjects. Khosrow therefore patiently waited for the appropriate moment to reclaim his prestige and the lost territories of his kingdom. Such an opportunity arose in 602, when Maurice was killed in a military coup led by Phocas, the general of the Byzantine forces in the Balkans. This was followed by clashes and an insurrection across the Byzantine Empire. Khosrow II exploited the chaos and fragility, as his grandfather Khosrow I had done. He launched an attack against the Byzantines, attempting to recapture the territory that he had conceded, and conflict between the two sides broke out on several fronts.

The Byzantine Empire was in a difficult position. Phocas's usurpation of the throne in Constantinople and his incompetence and brutality left the empire paralysed and in disarray. Many of his subjects believed that he was not qualified to rule. With the increasing number of Byzantine defeats at the hands of the Persians, Phocas's popularity waned. Byzantine's Exarch of Africa, Heraclius the Elder, rebelled against him, and his son, also named Heraclius, led his father's army to save what he could of the disintegrating empire. He took control of Egypt, then led the army against Constantinople, entering the city and killing Phocas. In 610, the year in which the Prophet's (ﷺ) mission began, Heraclius pronounced himself emperor.

The war between the two empires continued, with the Persians gaining the upper hand. In the decade that followed, Heraclius was not able to successfully confront the Persians or to halt their advance. In 611, Khosrow II invaded Upper Mesopotamia and Armenia, occupied Syria, and took control of Antioch (modern day Antakya, Türkiye).

Byzantine defeat

In 613, the Byzantine army was defeated in a decisive battle outside Antioch, and the Persians occupied more Byzantine territory, including Jerusalem in 614. Because of Jerusalem's religious significance, this was the most traumatic defeat for the Byzantines. The Persians took the Sacred Cross (also known as the True Cross) and the Sacred Spear to their capital Ctesiphon. These were the most important religious symbols of the Byzantine Empire, as Christians believed that Jesus was crucified on the Sacred Cross, and the spear was the one that a Roman soldier had used to stab the crucified Christ in his side.

In the same year—the fourth year of the Prophetic mission—the surah of the Qur'ān entitled "Al-Rum" (The Romans) was revealed to the Prophet (ﷺ), drawing his attention to the international strategic reality that would be created by the defeat of the Byzantines (or Eastern Romans, as they were also known at the time) in the Levant. The Qur'ān also advised him that the Byzantine defeat would be temporary. Between this defeat and the future victory, there would be years filled with bloody clashes and great conflict between the Byzantines and the Persians, and the outcome would be the weakening of both superpowers. Cracks would thus emerge in the established international order, which would allow a youthful new power to fill the vacuum and become the de facto heir to the two competing empires.

Persian military victories occurred on several fronts and, after taking control of Jerusalem and the Levant, Persian troops moved on to Egypt—the breadbasket of the Byzantine Empire. They occupied Alexandria in 619 and the rest of Egypt in 621.

While the fall of Jerusalem was a painful blow to the legitimacy of the Byzantine Empire, which saw itself as the protector of the Christian faith, the fall of Egypt was a fatal economic blow, since it was the richest Byzantine province and its capture resulted in the suspension of wheat exports to Constantinople. Egypt had, for centuries, been the most important wheat source for both the Western and Eastern Roman Empires, and the suspension of Egyptian exports caused crippling inflation in Constantinople. The Byzantine Empire seemed to be on the road to certain collapse, especially when the Persians took advantage of the state of confusion and fear that was spreading through the Byzantine provinces and laid siege to Constantinople itself. By the time the Persian armada reached the waters of the Bosphorus, the Byzantine capital was already on the verge of collapse.

In these extremely trying times, a miraculous event occurred that saved the Byzantine Empire. After sneaking away and uniting what remained of his army, as well as entering an alliance with Khazar and Turkish tribes, Heraclius rallied in Central Asia and unexpectedly attacked the Sassanids. This 622 attack was rare and shrewd; it penetrated Persian territory from the north and set off a series of military victories that lifted the morale of the Byzantine army and disillusioned the Persians. The Persian army was already spread thin and required long supply lines, thus making centralised control extremely difficult. This gave Heraclius a unique opportunity to achieve a few strategically important military victories. In December 628, Heraclius surprised the Persians with a decisive mid-winter attack on Nineveh (just outside modern-day Mosul), dealing the Persians a humiliating defeat before continuing his advance southwards alongside the Tigris River and plundering one of Khosrow's palaces along the way. However, the Persians destroyed the bridge that crossed over the Nahrawan Canal leading to Khosrow's capital, Ctesiphon, thus preventing its fall to Heraclius. The Byzantine emperor withdrew to Diyala in northern Iraq, and he continued his conquests on his return home, staging a victorious return to Constantinople.

Khosrow's resounding defeat in Nineveh was received as a great insult to the prestige of the king. Consequently, Khosrow II was callously murdered in 628 by his son Shīrūya, better known by his later dynastic name Kavad II. According to many reports, Shīrūya imprisoned his father in a cupola, had him bound with chains and left him to die without food or water. Thus ended Khosrow II's thirty-eight-year reign. His name appears often in the works of Arab historiographers and in the works of sīrah. In fact, Khosrow Parviz was of such importance to Arabs that they came to refer to all Persian kings as "khosrow", making it a generic word for Persian kings, when it was actually a proper name. Khosrow I had been in power when the Prophet (ﷺ) was born, and biographers of the Prophet (ﷺ) date his birth as having occurred in the fortieth year of Khosrow I's reign. Khosrow II, also known as Parviz, was the last of the great Sassanid kings. He was the Persian king to whom the Prophet (ﷺ) sent a letter with 'Abdallah ibn Ḥudhāfah al-Sahamī in 628, after the treaty of Hudaybīyyah and soon after Khosrow's defeat in Nineveh.

Al-Bukhārī[43] narrates the story in the Book of Jihād in his Saḥīḥ.

> On the authority of 'Abdallah ibn 'Abbās: Allah's Messenger (ﷺ) sent his letter to Khosrow and ordered his messenger to hand it over to the governor of al-Baḥrayn, who was to hand it over to Khosrow. When Khosrow read the letter, he tore it up. Sa'id bin al-Musayyab said, "The Prophet (ﷺ) then invoked Allah to tear them to shreds, [to destroy Khosrow and his followers]."[44]

The letter of Allah's Messenger (ﷺ) most likely reached Khosrow after the Nineveh defeat, when he was not in the best of moods. Biographers of the Prophet (ﷺ) record that the Persian king became extremely angry when, upon reading the letter, he noticed that the Prophet (ﷺ) had written his own name before Khosrow's. Ibn Hishām narrates that the text of the letter began with the words: "From Muḥammad the Messenger of Allah to Khosrow the Great of Persia." This formulation did not please Khosrow, who was filled with pride even after his great defeat at Nineveh, which likely provoked his already-inflated sensitivities even further. As he tore up the letter, Khosrow retorted: "He writes to me thus and he is my slave?"

He then wrote to his Yemen proxy Bādhān and commanded him to send the man who had appeared in the Hijaz to the imperial court. "Send two of your strong men," he instructed Bādhān, "and order them to bring him to me." Bādhān did, in fact, appoint two men to carry a letter to Allah's Messenger (ﷺ), commanding him to accompany them to Khosrow without delay. However, Allah's Messenger (ﷺ) replied in a letter to Bādhān: "Verily Allah has promised me that Khosrow will be killed on such a day in such a month." When Bādhān received the letter, he paused, reflected, and then said: "If he is a prophet, then it will be as he says." Ibn Hishām wrote, "Allah then killed Khosrow on the day reported by the Messenger of Allah (ﷺ), and when Bādhān was informed of this, he sent the news of his [acceptance of] Islam and the [acceptance of] Islam of those Persians who were with him to Allah's

43. al-Bukhārī, *Saḥīḥ*.
44. al-Bukhārī, *Saḥīḥ*, "Book of Jihād and Expeditions, Chapter: Inviting the Jews and Christians, and on what they fought over, and what the Prophet (ﷺ) wrote to Khosrow and Caesar and the Call before fighting", (1/723), Ḥadīth no. 2939.

Messenger (ﷺ)."[45]

Shīrūya killed his father and assumed power after him, calling himself Kavad II. Once again, the Byzantines influenced a change on the Persian throne. To save the Persian Empire, Kavad ended the war with Heraclius and signed an accord that guaranteed the withdrawal of Persian troops from the territories occupied by his father's army. As a result of this accord, Heraclius retrieved the Sacred Cross in 629 and returned it to the Church of the Holy Sepulchre in Jerusalem in 630. He tried to use this action as a way of entrenching his political and religious status. According to Christian sources, Heraclius walked barefoot, in simple clothing, and imitated Christ by carrying the cross on his shoulders down the Via Dolorosa (the "Path of Pain").

Plagued by internecine wars and disputes, the Sassanid Empire under Kavad was unable to stage a revival. Kavad was killed barely months after he took the throne, and that office was then occupied by five emperors over a period of four years, with true power vested in the hands of competing military leaders. When the Islamic conquering armies reached Iraq, the Sassanid Empire was in its death throes. The Muslims delivered the final blow when they entered the Persian capital and conquered its vast lands.

Regional powers

In the period leading up to Prophet Muhammad's (ﷺ) mission, the Sassanid Persians and Byzantine Romans dominated the international stage, and the struggle between them charted the map of the global balance of forces. However, the struggle between the two major powers did not prevent the existence of regional powers in the Arabian Peninsula and surrounding areas. They played important roles in shaping the political reality in the region and, specifically, in Makkah. Even though these regional powers were either subservient or allied with the two major powers, they were still actively engaged politically and economically with their neighbours. It is, therefore, a worthwhile exercise to examine them and study their impact on Makkah.

---

45. Ibn Hishām, *al-Sīrah al-Nabawīyyah* (Cairo: Muṣṭafa al-Bābī al-Ḥalabī, 1955), vol. 1, 69.

Kingdom of al-Ḥīrah

Al-Ḥīrah was an ancient Arab city, the ruins of which are to be found near Kūfah in Iraq. Reports of the city's establishment date back to the first century, but it gained fame when it became the capital of the Lakhminid Manādhirah Arabs between 268 and 633. Al-Ḥīrah exercised great influence on Arab life in general, as it was the greatest, the most beautiful, and wealthiest Arab city for a long period after its establishment. It was also the capital of poets, musicians, and artists, and the cradle for the development of Arabic writing, which, according to recent studies, came to Makkah from al-Ḥīrah. These studies contradict earlier theories that traced the language's origins to Yemen.[46]

Al-Ḥīrah's stature and influence is linked to the Manādhirah dynasty, which is affiliated to the Lakhm tribe of Yemeni origin. The Manādhirah remained in power in al-Ḥīrah for more than three centuries, with eighteen consecutive kings, the first of whom was 'Amr ibn 'Adī, and the last—effectively—being al-Nu'mān ibn al-Mandhar, who was killed by Khosrow II, probably in 609, at about the same time as the beginning of the Prophetic mission.

Reports about al-Ḥīrah and its kings dominated the ancient Arab popular imagination. Numerous anecdotes and narrations about them occur in the works of many chroniclers, including stories of poets such as al-Nābighah al-Dhubyānī, Imru' al-Qays, and 'Antarah al-'Absī; accounts of al-Ḥīrah's palaces, such as al-Kharānaq and al-Sudayr; and tales of al-Nu'mān's good and bad omens. While Al-Ḥīrah occupied this elevated status, the Manādhirah exercised political authority in Iraq, Upper Mesopotamia, al-Baḥrayn, and as far as Oman. The king of al-Ḥīrah called himself the king of the Arabs, and the city had links to other contemporary Arab kingdoms in al-Ḥaḍar, Tadmur (Palmyra) and to the land of the Nabataeans. Moreover, its trade caravans traversed the peninsula and participated in its seasonal festivals and markets under the protection of a special guard. The most famous and important market in the area was al-Ḥīrah's own annual market that was held at Dumat al-Jandal. The Quraysh's caravans also patronised al-Ḥīrah's markets, and Qurayshi leaders met and engaged with the city's kings,

46. See 'Alī, *al-Mufaṣṣal fī Tārikh.*

returning to Makkah with merchandise, news, and wonderful tales.

Nestorian Christianity spread among the Manādhirah. Based on the teachings of Bishop Nestorius, it differed from official Byzantine Christianity on the question of the nature of Christ; the latter followed the position of the Chalcedon Council held in 451. Nestorians therefore fled to areas outside Byzantine influence and settled under the protection of the Persian Empire. Al-Ḥīrah housed several churches and monasteries, and it was home to many Christians who were affiliated to the Eastern Roman Church and who actively spread Christianity among the Arabs.

Politically, the Manādhirah were somewhat independent, to the extent allowed by the Sassanid Empire. The most accurate assessment of the political situation can be gleaned from the way in which Byzantine historians referred to the Manādhirah and Ghassanid kings. They called the Manādhirah "Persian Arabs" and the Ghassanids "Roman Arabs".[47] This is the clearest strategic assessment of the regional influence of the Manādhirah: they were subservient to the Persians and deferred to their interests, as demonstrated in the Manādhirah's role in maintaining order on the borders of the Persian Empire with the Arab desert. Bedouin raids often created chaos and upheaval on the outskirts of the empire, and the Manādhirah's influence needed to be strengthened so they could protect the empire's periphery. They were more capable than the Persians in maintaining control over the bedouins, and placated them with gifts, grants, and trade, while simultaneously threatening them with punitive military action.

The second strategic dimension of Manādhirah dependency on the Persians is manifest in the perennial conflict between the Manādhirah and the Ghassanids. These wars were integral to the international conflict between the Persians and the Byzantines. Often, Arabs participated in the battles between these two powers on both sides; the Manādhirah fought alongside the Persians against the Byzantines, and the Ghassanids fought as part of the Byzantine army.

Historical accounts about the killing of al-Nu'mān ibn al-Mandhar may not be accurate in terms of specific details, but they are important

47. 'Alī, *al-Mufaṣṣal fī Tārikh*, vol. 5, 165.

in understanding the nature of the relationship between the Manādhirah and the Persians. These accounts report that al-Nu'mān refused to give his daughter in marriage to the Persian king, and, on another occasion, refused to gift the king one of his horses. As appealing as they may be in their popular renditions as displays of bravery, we cannot rely on these narratives to understand the real reason that al-Nu'mān was killed by Khosrow II. However, the context within which these events are narrated do help us to understand, in small measure, Khosrow's anger.

As explained earlier, Khosrow II ascended the Sassanid Throne in 590, but was soon overthrown and fled to the Byzantine Empire. The Byzantine emperor, Maurice, helped Khosrow II regain his throne in return for a long-term truce between the two empires, which resulted in fighting between the two powers being suspended until 602, when Maurice was assassinated by one of his generals. Khosrow II used that as an opportunity to resume the war against the Byzantines. Several reports indicate that al-Nu'mān ibn al-Mandhar had not supported Khosrow II when he had been toppled, and had not migrated with him to Byzantine territory when he had fled there seeking protection. Nor did al-Nu'mān support Khosrow in his most recent war in the Levant.

The Sassanid Empire began its war against the Byzantines in 602 by recapturing Upper Mesopotamia from the Byzantines, after which the confrontation spread to the Levant. It was expected that, as was usually the case, the Manādhirah would play a decisive role in supporting the Persians in both territories. However, since they were Arabs, as were the inhabitants of Mesopotamia and the Levant, al-Nu'mān's inclination toward independence made him hesitant to unconditionally involve himself in the war. This convinced Khosrow to remove Nu'mān and replace him with an obedient and submissive king. With this in mind, Khosrow lured al-Nu'mān to the Persian capital Ctesiphon.

According to various reports, when Khosrow's messenger arrived to summon al-Nu'mān to Ctesiphon, he realised Khosrow's intentions and considered fleeing. He consulted the Arab tribes, but none was prepared to support him, fearing Persian retaliation. Hāni ibn Mas'ūd al-Shaybānī advised the embattled king to go to Khosrow. Hāni told him:

To die with honour is better than to taste humiliation or to revert to being a commoner after being a king. And that is if you survive. Go to your patron bearing gifts and money and submit yourself to him. He will either pardon you and you will return an honoured king, or you will be punished. Death is better than becoming a plaything for the wretched Arabs, becoming their inferior, and having your wealth eaten, and to live in poverty or be overpowered and killed.[48]

Nu'mān asked, "What about my wives?" Hāni replied: "They are under my protection; no one will reach them without reaching my daughters first." Nu'mān then said: "By my father! This is the correct opinion; I will not ignore it." Al-Nu'mān accepted the offer and did leave his family, wealth, and armour in Hāni's care while he set off to meet his fate.

There are many historical accounts about how al-Nu'mān was killed, including one that Khosrow had imprisoned him and he had succumbed to the plague. The manner of his death is, however, unimportant. The result of his meeting with Khosrow was that al-Nu'mān was murdered, and Khosrow replaced him with a new king. The primary role of Khosrow's replacement, Īyās ibn Qabīṣah al-Ṭa'i, was to assist the Persians in their war against the Byzantines and their Arab allies. Īyās did as expected; he went to the battlefront and fought against the Byzantines at Sātīdmā River near Arzĕn in what is now southeastern Türkiye.[49]

The events unleashed by al-Nu'mān's murder proved that Khosrow had taken a hasty, unwise decision. It opened a door that had previously been firmly shut: the enmity of the Arab tribes and their retributive attacks. Īyās, the al-Ḥīrah king appointed by the Persians, attempted to appropriate al-Nu'mān's armour and wealth, but Hāni ibn Mas'ūd remained true to his word; he refused to hand anything over. Īyās then sought the assistance of the Persians and led an army that included Persian soldiers and several Arab tribes loyal to him. Hāni sought the assistance of other Arab tribes, and was joined by the tribes of Bakr ibn Wā'il when he marched to Dhī Qār. The tribes of Ṭa'i, al-'Abbād,

48. 'Abd al-Qādir Al-Baghdādi, *Khizānat al-Adab* (Cairo: Al-Khānjī Library, 1997), vol. 1, 385.
49. Yāqut al-Ḥamawī, *Mu'jam al-Buldān* (Beirut: Dār Ṣadar, 1993), vol. 3, 169.

Īyād, and all the Arabs loyal to the Persians secretly communicated with Hāni even though they were part of Īyās ibn Qabīṣah's army, and they reached an agreement with the Banī Bakr that they would switch sides during the battle.[50]

The coalition of Arab tribes fought bravely against the Persian army, defeated it on the second day, and pursued its remnants into the fertile territories of Iraq. A direct consequence of this battle was that Īyās ibn Qabīṣah was removed from his post by Khosrow and replaced by a Persian governor, Azadveh-i Banegan Mahan-i Mihr-Bondad, who became the first Persian governor of Al-Ḥīrah. He, however, failed to re-establish the level of stability that had characterised the old relationship between the Manādhirah and the Persian Empire.

The precise date of the Battle of Dhī Qār is not known. Some historians argue that it was in the year in which the Prophet's (ﷺ) mission began, in 611; others hold that it was in the second year of his mission, in 613; yet others state that it took place after the Prophet's (ﷺ) migration (Hijrah) from Makkah to Madinah, or after the Battle of Badr in 624.[51] The *Encyclopedia Iranica* states that modern studies place the Battle of Dhī Qār in the period between 604 to 611, which is most likely.[52] Arab historians also disagree on the date of the battle, but it remains a famous and highly significant event that Arabs celebrated in poetry and prose, because it gave them a sense of unity and a newfound sense of confidence.

The Persians were surprised by their defeat, since the Arab tribes had not been expected to demonstrate organised military capacity in the face of the experienced Persian military. Moreover, the battle was small compared to the massive clashes between the Persians and Byzantines. Due to its relatively limited scale, Persian historical sources do not even mention the battle. Arab historians put the number of Persian fighters at 2,000, in addition to 3,000 allied Arab fighters. However, the symbolism of the defeat and its repercussions had a negative impact on

50. For the entire episode, see Abū Ja'far Muḥammad ibn Jarīr ibn Yazīd al-Ṭabarī, *Tārīkh al-Ṭabarī*, The Dhakā'ir al-'Arab Series (Cairo: Dār al-Ma'ārif, 1968), vol. 2, 193-212.
51. See Muḥammad Bayūmī Mahrān, *Dirāsāt fī Tārīkh al-'Arab al-Qadīm* (Alexandria: Dār al-Ma'rifah al-Jāmi'īyyah, 1968), vol. 1, 533.
52. Ella Landau-Tasseron, *"Ḏū Qār", Encyclopædia Iranica,* https://www.iranicaonline.org/articles/du-qar.

the exhausted empire, which was trapped in a protracted war with the Byzantines. Arab lands were extremely close to the heart of the Persian empire, and any instability in these areas would echo in the Persian capital. Furthermore, the traditional function of the Manādhirah, which was to keep the bedouin Arabs in check, could no longer be exercised. The direct strategic impact of the security instability in the desert was acutely felt after Dhī Qār, since the Persians needed to be in communication with their agents in Yemen, which was, at the time, occupied by Persia. Caravans and delegations travelling to Yemen had to pass through Arab territories, which posed a great threat. Chroniclers recorded several tribal attacks on these caravans.

The most important outcome of the Battle of Dhī Qār was psychological. The Arabs were liberated from their overwhelming fear of the Persians, whose dominating image had been shaken in the Arab imagination, after they had dared to stand up to them. The Battle of Dhī Qār marked the beginning of an audacious streak of defiance in the face of the aging empire. That defiance was set to grow stronger over the next years, finally bearing fruit with the coming of Islam. The Arab tribes welcomed the Muslim conquering armies two decades later and pressed forward with the new message, dealing the deathblow to the Persian Empire and uprooting it completely.

The Ghassanids

The Ghassanids, like the Manādhirah, had their origins in the Yemeni tribes. They migrated at intermittent periods due to the uncertain security situation in Yemen, the accompanying deterioration in living conditions, and the collapse of the Ma'rib Dam. The Ghassanids, who are from the al-Azad tribe, settled on the northern periphery of the Arabian Peninsula, neighbouring the Byzantine territories of Balqā' and Ḥawrān. Their home base was Jābiyah, near the Golan Heights. The Byzantine authorities regarded the Ghassanids as an important tool to protect their territories from bedouin raids, and granted them official recognition, allowing them to extend their influence over the rural Levant. The Byzantines also charged them with security responsibilities that ranged from maintaining the peace in the northern part of the peninsula to fighting the Persians and their Manādhirah allies. The Ghassanids and the Manādhirah thus became vassals of the two warring global powers.

With the blessing and support of the Byzantines, whose influence was linked to Christianity, the Ghassanids had converted to Christianity and were active in spreading the religion among the Arab tribes. However, Byzantine sources indicate that in the sixth century, a few Ghassanid emirs joined the Jacobite sect. The Jacobites believed that Christ was of a single nature, as opposed to the official Byzantine position that he was of a dual nature. This created tension between the Byzantines and the Ghassanids, but the Byzantines were keen to overlook the discrepancy for the sake of their security interests. They reconciled with the Ghassanids so that the latter could continue their role as protectors of Byzantine interests.

Pre-Islamic poetry is rich in praise of the Ghassanid kings, elevating them to a status higher than they deserved. This praise was sung by poets such as al-Nābighah al-Dhubyānī and Ḥassān ibn Thābit. Before Islam, Ḥassān profusely praised the Ghassanids, visited them often, and was showered with gifts by them.

Without doubt, the title "king", in reference to the Ghassanids, was exaggerated, since they were merely Byzantine vassals, despite their grand titles. Byzantine sources confirm that Justinian conferred the title "Phylarch" on al-Ḥārith ibn Shammar al-Ghassānī in 528, after his victory over the Manādhirah king, al-Mandhar ibn Mā' al-Samā'. The title meant "Governor" and was used for the Byzantine governor of any region. This honour was granted in recognition of the security role the Ghassanids had played, which, in this case, was to fight their Manādhirah cousins, the vassals of the Sassanid Empire.

Clearly, the Byzantines did not care about the Ghassanids and did not see them as more than a security force to be used to protect their interests. This was also how the Sassanid Persians regarded the Manādhirah. So, when we talk about the kingdoms of the northern peninsula, we are really talking about functional entities that had been stripped of sovereignty, or that exercised it only regarding their battles with each other or with the bedouin Arab tribes from the desert.

The Ghassanid influence ended when Palestine and the Levant fell under Persian occupation in 613. When the Byzantine emperor Heraclius regained control of these territories in 628, he tried to rekindle the role of the Ghassanids, again placing them at the forefront of events in the peninsula, but with less effect and for a shorter period. The Islamic conquest put an end to Ghassanid influence. Sīrah works from this period refer to Jablah ibn al-Ayham al-Ghassānī as the last Ghassanid emir. He fought with the Byzantines against the Muslims during the Battle of Yarmūk. Later, in the era of ʻUmar ibn al-Khaṭṭāb, he embraced Islam, but then reverted to Christianity and relocated to Constantinople.

Kingdom of Aksum

Narrations in the Torah, the Christian Bible, and the Qur'ān about the Kingdom of Sheba and the historic meeting between its queen and the Prophet Sulaymān shed some light on the characteristics of this kingdom, its vast wealth and strength, and its centrality in the tenth century BCE. Its impact continues to inspire the imaginations of writers, poets, and artists and serves as the basis of many tales, myths, and popular narratives. The kingdom was located on extremely important trade routes in the ancient world. It was therefore a node for trade between the Chinese and Indian markets, Egyptian and Greek markets, and Roman and Persian markets. It developed a system of writing using the Musnad (ancient South Arabian) script and transmitted this system to regions that it controlled in the northern Arabian Peninsula and Abyssinia. It also developed a second system of writing that used the Zabūr script. Its citizens used the Musnad script to record historical events and the Zabūr script (also known as South Arabian minuscules) for daily communications. The origin of the Arabic, Amharic, and Tigrinya alphabets was the Musnad script, which was written from right to left.

In Africa, the Ethiopians immortalised the culture of the Kingdom of Sheba. They believe that the Ethiopian kings descended from King

Menelik (Menelik means "son of the Wise"), who was the son of King Solomon and the Queen of Sheba. She is referred to as "Makeda" in Ethiopian writings, especially in *The Glory of Kings*, a reference work on the legitimacy of Ethiopian kings who claim to be from Solomon's lineage. According to Ethiopian legend, the Queen of Sheba gave birth to Menelik on her return from visiting Solomon. Menelik visited his father when he was twenty-five-years old. Solomon, extremely pleased with his son, gifted to him the Holy Ark, which contained the staff of Moses. Menelik returned to Abyssinia with the Ark and made Judaism the official religion of Sheba. His descendants continued to rule Ethiopia until the tenth century, when the Kingdom of Aksum declined.[53]

Most historians regard this story as an unfounded fabrication. The commonly accepted understanding is that, during Solomon's rule, the Kingdom of Sheba had not yet spread far enough to encompass Abyssinia. Furthermore, there is no verification for the story of a son born out of the relationship between Solomon and the Queen of Sheba. It is more likely that later Ethiopian kings wanted to create an identity that was specific to them and that conferred religious legitimacy on them by tracing their lineage to Solomon. *The Glory of Kings* was written in the twelfth century and has become a cornerstone of Ethiopian identity and a justification for its ruling dynasty. Even in the modern era, the Ethiopian constitutions of 1931 and 1955 both contained clauses that granted emperors who are descendants of Menelik a divine right to rule. Hence Haile Selassie, the last Ethiopian emperor (who ruled from 1928 to 1974) regarded himself as a descendant of Solomon and claimed that he was the 225th king descended from Menelik. One of his official titles was, therefore, "Lion of Judah". The name "Haile Selassie", in fact, means "power of the trinity". The references to Solomon and Menelik were removed, however, in the last two Ethiopian constitutions, 1987 and 1995.

The Kingdom of Aksum was created at the beginning of the first century and prevailed until the tenth. In its golden age, its authority stretched over a large territory that included Eritrea, east Sudan, Ethiopia, Djibouti, and reached as far as the city of Barbar in northern Somalia.

53. *Kebra Nagast (The Glory of Kings): The True Ark of the Covenant*, trans. Miguel F. Brooks (Asmara, Eritrea: The Red Sea Press, 1996).

King Ezana was the first Aksumite king to embrace Christianity. Minted coins of the period suggest that he converted to Christianity in 330, around the same time that Roman emperor Constantine also converted.

Of the many factors that impacted Makkah politically, socially, and economically in the fifth and sixth centuries, the Kingdom of Aksum, or Abyssinia as the Arabs called it, is regarded as one of the most important influences. There are several reasons for this assertion.

First, Aksum was regarded as a natural geographical extension of the Arabian Peninsula. The argument that the Red Sea is a natural barrier that separates the Hijaz from East Africa and sets them apart, and that the people of Makkah were simply bedouins who were not familiar with maritime navigation, is inaccurate. In fact, the Arabs easily crossed the Red Sea, as evidenced by the many ports dotting both its shorelines. Ships regularly crossed between them according to fixed schedules. According to the sīrah, the Muslims who migrated to Abyssinia boarded two ships that were about to depart from al-Shu'aybah Port, rendering the Quraysh unable to catch up with them, and that the fare for a single passenger was half a dinar, or one Byzantine gold coin. When winds were favourable, it took around two days to cross the Red Sea, which is short compared to the weeks it took to traverse the desert to reach the Levant or Iraq, or even to reach the south of Yemen. The Red Sea was, then, an easy crossing route and not a barrier that separated the peninsula from Abyssinia.

Second, economic links between the two sides of the Red Sea were well established, and Abyssinia was a regular trade destination for the Makkans, where they exchanged merchandise such as animal hides, rare timber, precious stones, and perfumes. Abyssinia was not just a trade destination; it was also a node in a trade route that led to markets deeper in Africa, up to Nuba and Merowe, an ancient Sudanese city on the banks of the Nile about 300 kilometres from Khartoum. Some reports show that Qurayshi traders often sailed with their merchandise to Abyssinian ports, and from there by sea, southwards to the Yemeni port of Aden. This was a faster route than the land route that crosses the southern Peninsula, especially in periods of political upheaval and civil war in Yemen.

It is clear that the Abyssinians viewed the Makkans as respected and valued partners. They were, in the Abyssinians' opinion, "People of Allah", which is a moniker that many Arab tribes also used to describe them. Some Makkan traders, such as 'Amr ibn al-'Ās, forged a strong relationship with al-Najāshī. The case of 'Amr will be examined in the discussion of Muslim migration to Abyssinia.

Third, language ties between the two sides were very strong. The ancient al-Ja'zīyyah language, which is regarded as the origin language for Amharic and Tigrinya, the two key languages in contemporary Ethiopia, was a Semitic language that was strongly associated with ancient Arabic dialects such as al-Sab'īyyah, al-Ma'īnīyyah, and al-Ḥimyarīyyah. These dialects gave more recent Arabic its strong links with al-Ja'zīyyah. Arabic and the two main Ethiopian languages share some vocabulary and syntax. Communication between the Arabs and the Abyssinians was likely possible without the need for translation, as is clear from the conversation between Ja'far ibn Abī Ṭālib and al-Najāshī, which will be recounted later.

The results of this language exchange were still present in the Islamic era. Much of the vocabulary that appears in the Noble Qur'ān, and in religious texts in general, is of al-Ja'zī-al-Sab'ī origin. One example is the word "Quraysh", which means "traders" in the Ja'zīyyah language. Other words include minbar, miḥrāb, suḥt, jibt, ṭāghūt, qaswarah, mansa'ah, and mishkāt. There is also a prophetic tradition (ḥadīth) stating that the word "muṣḥaf", which was used for the first time after the Qur'ān was compiled as a book, was taken from Ge'ez, an Abyssinian language that is also referred to as Classical Ethiopic. Some scholars, however, claim that the word had a common Semitic origin with the Abyssinian language, and was not directly adopted from that language.[54]

Fourth, many inhabitants of Makkah were of Abyssinian origin. Some, such as Bilāl ibn Rabāḥ, were slaves; others were traders or manufacturers. This indicates that the Makkans engaged regularly with the Abyssinian language and its culture in terms of food, drink, and dress. At this point, we should recall that Barakah Umm Ayman,

54. 'Abd al-Ṣabūr Shāhīn, *Tārīkh al-Qur'ān* (Cairo: Dār al-Nahḍah, 2007), 143.

the Prophet's (ﷺ) nurse, was also Abyssinian. She looked after him after his mother's death and stayed by his side throughout his life. He said of her: "Umm Ayman is my mother, after my mother." It is also narrated that, when he saw her, he was filled with joy. He said, "She is the remaining part of my household."[55] Thus, Abyssinian culture, language, and habits were closely associated with the Prophet's (ﷺ) household. The ḥadīth that the Prophet (ﷺ) stood with 'Ā'isha on the day of 'Īd to watch Abyssinians as they performed with their spears also suggests that the Abyssinian presence in Madinah was an ordinary and familiar part of everyday life.

55. Ibn Ḥajar al-'Asqalānī, *al-Iṣābah fī Tamyīz al-Ṣaḥābah* (Beirut: Dār al-Kutub al-'Ilmīyyah, 1994), vol. 13, 198.

CHAPTER THREE

Makkah – From periphery to centre

"For the pacts [of security enjoyed] by the Quraysh, secure in their winter and summer journeys" (Qur'ān 106:1-2).

After the previous chapters, which discussed the political map and regional and international centres of power in the fifth and sixth centuries, we can conclude that, in the era of Quṣay and 'Abd Manāf, Makkah was a small settlement, and that its existence and economy depended primarily on the pilgrimage season. Furthermore, local trade was dependent on merchandise brought by pilgrims to Makkah's markets. The economic boom and resultant prosperity began after Hāshim ibn 'Abd Manāf secured agreements with Byzantine Syria and when Arab tribes settled along the land route between the Levant and Makkah, and Makkah and Yemen. These agreements increased in number after Hāshim's death, and came to include Iraq and Abyssinia. This complex of agreements entrenched the practice of safe trade in an era when the war between the Persians and Byzantines was at its height and negatively affected international trade, since the war was being fought in areas around the maritime and land routes that linked the markets of the ancient world. Makkah was the fulcrum of this safe-trade arrangement, which the Qur'ān refers to as Īlāf Quraysh (the Quraysh Pact).

To preserve its safe-trade function, Makkah had to maintain a posture of political non-alignment toward the ongoing regional and international contestation; maintaining relations with both major warring parties required that Makkah not be seen as favouring one side over the other. It was not in Makkah's interest to be hostile toward the Persians, who controlled the Iraqi and Yemeni markets, nor was it expedient to be hostile toward the Byzantines, since they controlled Egypt and the Levant. Makkah needed cordial relations with both sides to guarantee its pacts and ensure that permission was granted for its merchandise-laden caravans to cross their borders. To maintain cordial relations with the two powers, warm relations were also required with their allies. These allies included the Christian Kingdom of Aksum, Makkah's closest neighbour, which had thrown in its lot with Constantinople; the kings of al-Ḥīrah in Iraq, who were allied to the Persians; and the Levantine Ghassanids, who were vassals of Constantinople. It was essential that cordial relations with all these parties be maintained in order, first, to guarantee communication through them to the Byzantine and Persian empires, and, second, because their territories and peoples represented both the markets for Qurayshi caravans, as well as the sources of their merchandise.

Makkan non-alignment and the lesson of Najrān

This commitment to non-alignment led Makkah to reject all attempts to drag it into the vicious competition between the two great powers. The Makkans remembered how Najrān had suffered bitterly because of its involvement in the Byzantine-Persian contestation, and of how that war had created major upheaval in Yemen. These experiences had resulted in the deep-rooted conflict that they constantly heard about, and which had not left them untouched.

Najrān was an important trading centre located between Yemen and the Byzantine and Persian markets. It was also an important crossroad for trade caravans on the frankincense route. The road from Yemen split into two at Najrān: one proceeded northwards through the Hijaz to Egypt and the Levant, and the other followed a northeasterly route toward Hajar and the lands of the Persian Empire. From Najrān, then, caravans linked Yemen with both the Byzantines and the Persians, making it inevitable that it would become a conflict hotspot between the two empires from an early stage in their war.

Rome's attempts to take control of Najrān began in 25 BCE when the Roman prefect of Egypt, Aelius Gallus—acting on orders from Emperor Augustus—dispatched an army to capture the trade routes in the Arabian Peninsula in an attempt to appropriate the wealth generated by trade in dates and frankincense, and also to exercise control over the sea by suppressing the pirates who sought refuge along the Yemeni and Hijazi coastlines. Gallus also ordered the appointment of guards to protect ships that crossed the Red Sea from pirates. However, his army failed miserably, primarily because of the harsh environment and the prevalence of disease.

A close friend of Gallus, the Greek geographer and historian Strabo (36 BCE–24 CE), narrated a provocative account of this military campaign. He wrote that the Roman army had arrived in Yathrib and had established friendly relations with its people before heading south to Najrān, which Strabo described as a vassal of the Kingdom of Sheba. The Romans occupied Najrān and converted it into a base for launching attacks on Ma'rib, the capital of Sheba. However, the Roman army was forced to retreat after an unknown disease broke out within its ranks, causing the deaths of many soldiers.[56]

The Himyarites captured Najrān when they revolted against Sheba in 280. Ancient Himyarite records, however, tell of a popular rebellion that was supported by Abyssinia, but which the Himyarites managed to extinguish. These records also mention another party that was close to the Persians and that attempted to capture Najrān in 328: the king of the Manādhirah, Imru' al-Qays ibn 'Amr. This attempt was encouraged and supported by the Persians, who regarded the Manādhirah as allies and preferred proxies for intervening in the Arabian Peninsula.

The Abyssinians also repeatedly attempted to control Najrān by forging ties with its people, who began converting to Christianity and found in their Abyssinian brethren an important ally against the Himyarites. The latter oppressed and cruelly suppressed the followers of the new religion. The Himyarites, who were loyal to the Persians, regarded the special relationship between Najrān Christians and Abyssinians as treason, since the Kingdom of Aksum was a strong ally of Rome. This was the context for Dhū Nuwās's savage campaign against the Christians in 523, in an attempt to exterminate them and remove all Abyssinian-Byzantine influence.

The Makkans still remembered Dhū Nuwās's Najrān genocide ninety years later, when the Prophet (ﷺ) began his mission. The persistent

56. 'Alī, *al-Mufaṣṣal fī Tārīkh*, vol. 3, 43.

memory of that event in the Makkan mind is reflected in the Qur'ān's drawing attention to it in the first phase of the prophetic mission. The story, as narrated in Arab and Byzantine sources, recalls that the Jewish Himyarite king Dhū Nuwās—or "Dounaas" in Byzantine sources—was a Persian ally who realised that the spread of Christianity in Yemen would lead to the entrenchment of Byzantine authority. In 523, with encouragement from his Persian allies, he led an extensive campaign against Christians in Mocha, Dhafar, and Najrān.

Ancient sources relate that Himyarite soldiers poured oil onto the heads of the women in Najrān and burnt them alive. Byzantine and Syriac sources say that Dhū Nuwās attacked Christians and Abyssinian expatriates in Dhafar, before heading to Najrān where he burnt down the churches and compelled Christians to choose between being burnt alive or renouncing their faith. Ancient Sabaean texts discovered in Yemen claim that Dhū Nuwās killed more than 22,000 Christians during this campaign. An extremely important Sabaean text in the Musnad (Ancient South Arabian) script, carved onto a rock in Bi'r Hima, 193 kilometres northeast of Najrān, describes the atmosphere in which these campaigns were undertaken.

> 1. May God, to whom belongs heaven and earth, bless King Yusuf As'ar Yat'ar, king of all communities, and may He bless the Qayls [tribe],
>
> 2. Laḥay'at Yarham and Simyafa' Aswa' and Sarah'il Aswa' and Sarahbi'il As'ad, sons of Sarahbi'il Yakmul, Yazanids, Gadanids,
>
> 3. henchmen of their Lord King Yusuf As'ar Yat'ar. Now he destroyed the church and massacred the Habashites in Zafar, and waged war in al-As'ar and Rakban, and
>
> 4. Farasan and Mocha, and went to war against and besieged Najrān, and the fortification of the chain of al-Mandab. So he mustered [troops] under his own command, and dispatched [the Qayls] with an independent detachment. And what the king successfully

5. took in spoils in this campaign was 12,500 slain, 11,000 captives, and

6. 290,000 camels, oxen, and sheep. This inscription was written by the qayl Sarah'il the Yazanid, when he was taking precautionary measures against Najrān

7. with the Hamdanid tribesmen, both townsfolk and bedouin, and a striking force of Yazanites and bedouin of Kinda, Murad and Madhij. Meanwhile, his brother Qayls were with the king for defence

8. on the sea from the Habashites, and were fortifying the chain of al-Mandab. All that they have recorded in this inscription in the way of killings, booty, and precautionary measures were on a campaign, the termination of which,

9. when they turned homeward, was thirteen months [after its commencement]. May God bless their sons Sarahbi'il Yakmul and Ha'an As'ar, sons of Lahay'at.[57]

Byzantine sources also discuss the Najrān incident and mention that a certain Dūs Dhū Tha'labān, the sole survivor of the genocide, fled to Constantinople, from where he provided a report to the Byzantines. Emperor Justin I, who regarded himself as the protector of the Christian faith, was so enraged that he encouraged the Abyssinian king to occupy Yemen and rescue the Christians. Byzantine sources also indicate that Justin I provided the Abyssinian king with ships to transport his soldiers to Yemen. The Abyssinians killed Dhū Nuwās and ended Himyarite rule in Yemen in 527.

The story of Dhū Nuwās is also related in a letter sent by Bishop Simon from Yemen to Justin I in 524. It contains alarming details of what occurred in Najrān, narrating the individual tribulations of several people and detailing their suffering at the hands of Dhū Nuwās.[58]

---

57. A. F. L. Beeston, "Two Bi'r Ḥimā Inscriptions Re-Examined", *Bulletin of the School of Oriental and African Studies – BSOAS* (vol. 48, no. 1, 1985), 45.
58. Joel Thomas Walker, *The Legend of Mar Qardagh: Narrative and Christian Heroism in Late Antique Iraq* (Oakland: University of California Press, 2006).

Aksumite sources relate that a man named Umayyah arrived at the Abyssinian court and narrated a detailed account of what had happened, prompting the king to prepare an army of 7,000 soldiers, led by a man named Abraha. It was this army, according to Abyssinian sources, that ended Himyarite rule and reasserted Abyssinian control over Yemen.

The Najrān genocide is an important event in Christian history. Even though the Christians of Najrān belonged to the Eastern Orthodox Church, the Catholic Church nonetheless bestowed sainthood on the leader of Najrān's Christian community, al-Ḥārith ibn Ka'b, and canonised him Saint Arethas. It is clear from the context of Dhū Nuwās's war against the Christians and Abyssinians in Yemen that he wanted to quell the Byzantine presence there. The Greek historian Procopius of Caesarea, who lived in the sixth century, wrote in *History of the Wars* that Dhū Nuwās had been deeply committed to fighting Constantinople.[59] This determination prompted him to attack every Byzantine merchant vessel that sailed through the Red Sea; he justified this by claiming that Constantinople was persecuting Jews everywhere in the Mediterranean Basin. Dhū Nuwās's actions disrupted Red Sea trade, which in those days centred around markets controlled by Byzantine in Egypt and the Northern Red Sea ports in Palestine.

The negative economic impact also affected Abyssinian markets, and its king wrote to Dhū Nuwās in protest of his policies towards Constantinople, outlining the damage it was causing to Abyssinian trade in the Red Sea, and threatening not to stand idly by if Dhū Nuwās continued with policies that harmed Abyssinian interests. When the Yemeni king continued with his anti-Byzantine policies and his targeting of Christians in Yemen or those who sailed into Yemeni and Abyssinian ports in the southern Red Sea, al-Najāshī, the Abyssinian king, declared war on Dhū Nuwās. He announced that the war was in support of oppressed Christians in Yemen.[60]

59. Procopius Caesariensis, *History of the Wars,* translated by H.B. Dewing (Massachusetts: Harvard University Press, 1914).
60. Ja'far Mīrghanī, *Awrāq al-Mu'tamar al-Duwalī li al-Islām fī Ifrīqīyya* (Khartoum: International Africa University, 2006), 9.

Makkah inherits Najrān

The lessons from the international battle over Najrān were undoubtedly an important factor in alerting the Quraysh to the risks of falling into the trap of global polarisation. The Najrān episode occurred around the same time that Hāshim had concluded his pacts with various parties. It is clear from this context that Makkah was about to inherit Najrān's position as the trade crossroads of the desert. The Makkans, then, had to have learnt critical lessons from the outcome of the battle over Najrān that would help them protect themselves from a similar fate and affirm the Quraysh's strategy of non-alignment.

The consequences of Najrān impacted negatively on Makkah. It created a justification for the external Abyssinian-Byzantine intervention that did away with the Himyarite Dhū Nuwās and replaced Persian with Byzantine influence in a manner that led, within a few years, to Abraha's army marching on Makkah to uproot the foundation of Makkan exceptionalism embodied in the Ka'bah.

After the Abyssinians had seized control of Yemen in 525—with Byzantine logistical support—the Negus, Kaleb, appointed a Christian Himyarite, Sumuafa' Ashawa', as governor of Yemen. He immediately began reconstructing the churches that Dhū Nuwās had destroyed. However, Sumuafa' did not remain in power for much longer. Byzantine sources indicate that he was unable to fulfil his mandate, and that:

> Emperor Justinian sent his envoy, Julianus, to the Negus and to Sumuafa' Ashawa' to ingratiate himself to them and to request, in the name of the common faith that bound them, to form a common front with Constantinople to fight the Sassanids and to rise with the Arab tribes that would join them in the attack. The envoy carried a second request to Sumuafa', seeking his permission to appoint an Arab leader, Qays, as the governor [phylarch] over an Arab tribe called "Ma'dīnī", i.e., the Ma'ad tribe, to join him and a large number of fighters from his tribe in an attack on the Sassanids. The envoy returned, pleased, and gave [Justinian] glad tidings of the success of his mission, based on the promises he had extracted from the two leaders,

who, nevertheless, did nothing and did not implement any of the promises they had made.[61]

Justinian was disappointed by Sumuafa‘'s inability to fulfil his mandate. He dismissed Julianus and replaced him with someone more loyal and more capable of implementing Constantinople's strategic goals. This is when the name Abraha (Abraham or, in Latin, Abrahamos) came to prominence. There is some dispute about Abraha's specific role, if any, before ascending to power in Yemen. Some sources suggest that he had been an Abyssinian army general who had ended Himyarite rule, while Procopius referred to him as a Christian zealot and as a slave of a Byzantine trader working at the Adulis Port on the Ethiopian coast on the Red Sea. Whatever the truth might be, Abraha killed Sumuafa‘ and took control of Yemen. He bestowed on himself the Himyarite royal title of "King of Saba, Dhū Raydān, Hadramaut and Yamanat and of their Arabs on the plateau and the lowland".

Most sources agree that the Abyssinians were unhappy with the role that Justinian had envisaged for Yemen. The Byzantines had realised that the Abyssinians would not fully support Constantinople against the Persians because their past experience had taught them that the Persians were capable of brutal vengeance. The sources mention a campaign by a Persian armada against the Kingdom of Aksum in which the Persians had captured Dahlak Island on the Aksumite coastline in the Red Sea. The Negus therefore decided to maintain a back channel with the Persians in case they returned and reoccupied Yemen. His political calculation was accurate: the Persians would indeed return to Yemen soon thereafter.

Significantly, the Byzantines supported Abraha, who took advantage of Aksum's preoccupation with its war with Nubia and fulfilled his ambition of becoming the king of Yemen, the richest country at that time, which Byzantine chronicles appropriately refer to as "the land of happiness". The Negus was infuriated by Abraha's coup against Sumuafa‘ and dispatched an army under Aryat to destroy him, but Abraha emerged victorious. Abraha sent an envoy to the Negus with a placatory message pledging allegiance to the Aksumite king. This resulted in a truce between Aksum and Abraha, and the Negus gave

61. ‘Alī, *Al-Mufaṣṣal fī Tārīkh*, vol. 7, 171.

Abraha his blessing to rule as king of Yemen.

Let us pause here to reflect on Qays, who the Byzantine envoy had recommended, and for whose appointment as chief of the Ma'ad tribe he had sought the support of the rulers of Abyssinia and Yemen. This Qays is none other than Imru'l Qays ibn Ḥajar, the poet who composed the famous hanging ode, and who had striven to become king of the Arabs. Arabic sources mention his journey to Constantinople to meet the emperor. However, due to some illness, he died in Ankara on his return journey. Historians attribute a poem to him that he supposedly recited before his death. In it, he discusses his journey to the land of the Byzantines and his ambition to become king. With his death, the Byzantines tasked Abraha with taking control of the tribes of Ma'ad ibn 'Adnān.

Some of Abraha's activities and accounts of his campaigns were fortuitously recorded in six inscriptions in the Musnad script, four of which are signed in his name. They were found in the 1950s in a region called the Well of al-Murayghān, near Najrān. One inscription records Abraha's battles against Yazīd ibn Kabshah, the leader of the Kindah tribe, and mentions Abraha's meetings with Persian and Byzantine envoys; another records his clashes with the Ma'ad tribes, one with 'Āmir ibn Ṣa'ṣa'ah near Ṭā'if, and another in Ḥalbān, in the northeast region of the peninsula. The inscriptions state:

> With the power of the All-Merciful and His messiah, King Abraha Zībmān, King of Saba'a, Dhū Raydān, Hadramaut and Yamanat, and of their Arabs on the highlands and on the coast, wrote this inscription when he had raided the Ma'ad [during] the Battle of al-Rabiya in the month of Dhū al-Thābah [April], [and] when all the Banī 'Āmir had revolted. Now the king appointed Abū Jabar with Kindah and 'Alī [tribes] and [appointed] Bishr ibn Ḥusn with Sa'd and Murād, and they presented themselves in front of the main army. Against Banī 'Āmir were Kindah and 'Alī in the valley of Dhū Markh, and Murād and Sa'd in a valley on the Tarbin road. They slaughtered and captured the enemy and took booty in great quantity. The king, on the other hand, did battle at Ḥalibān and pursued Ma'ad like their shadow

> and forced them to give hostages. After all this, 'Amr ibn al-Mundhir negotiated [with Abraha] and agreed to give hostages to Abraha from al-Mundhir, for al-Mundhir had invested him ['Amr] with the governorship over Ma'ad. So Abraha returned from Ḥalibān by the power of the Merciful One in the month of Dhū 'Ilān [September] in the year 662 [of the Sabean era, corresponding to around 550 CE].[62]

According to this inscription, these campaigns ended with the subjugation of those regions. It is worth noting that the inscription does not mention Makkah. It is likely that this was not the well-known campaign that entered Makkah with the objective of destroying the Ka'bah. The army that hoped to destroy the Ka'bah had reached Ṭā'if, which is close to Makkah. This is confirmed by the reports of Arab chroniclers who mention Abraha's visit to Ṭā'if, where the Thaqīf tribe pledged subservience to him, before he proceeded.

> When he passed al-Ṭā'if, Mas'ud ibn Mu'attib ibn Mālik ibn Ka'b ibn 'Amr ibn Sa'd ibn 'Awf ibn Thaqīf came out to meet him with a delegation of the men of [the tribe of] Thaqīf and said to him, "O King, we are but your slaves and we listen and obey and we have no quarrel with you. Our house is not the house that you want [meaning the house of the idol al-Llāt]. What you want is the house in Makkah. We will send with you one who will guide you to it." And so he passed by them.[63]

This account is strengthened by another of Abraha's inscriptions that talks about a cathedral that he had built in Ma'rib,[64] probably a reference to al-Qullays, which is mentioned in Arab history books.[65] The word "qullays" is derived from "qalsan" in Himyaritic and means church. The failure of the six inscriptions to mention Makkah is not only understandable but also justifiable. These texts are not impartial narrations or objective journalistic reports; kings only recorded their victories and conquests so that they could be immortalised. Abraha

62. 'Alī, *Al-Mufaṣṣal fī Tārīkh*, vol. 6, 185.

63. Ibn Kathīr, *al-Bidāyah wa al-Nihāyah* (Damascus: Dār al-Fikr, 1986), vol. 2, 171.

64. One of the present-day provinces of Yemen, located about 173 km northeast of the capital Sanaa.

65. See Ḥusayn Mu'nis, *Tārīkh Quraysh: Dirāsah fī Tārīkh Aṣghar Qabīlah 'Arabīyyah Ja'alahā al-Islām A'ẓam Qabīlah fī Tārīkh al-Bashar* (Jeddah: al-Dār al-Sa'udīyyah, 1988), 155.

was defeated in Makkah, and such a defeat would not be included in accounts of his glory and victories. It was, therefore, not in his interest to record or even mention this episode.

Nonetheless, the general context of Abraha's six inscriptions leads to the conclusion that his campaign across the Hijaz had a central objective: to capture the caravan trading routes by subjugating the Hijazi tribes. He knew that if he were able to achieve that, he would have accomplished a great goal, since control of these routes would grant him strategic gravitas with Constantinople, which had appointed him for this very purpose.

Abraha decided to destroy the Ka'bah mainly because it was through its presence that Makkah—which was on the trade route—had successfully entrenched its status above that of other trade cities. No other city on the trade route, neither Najrān, Ṭā'if, Yathrib, nor Khaybar, possessed such an important icon and gathering place. Furthermore, if Abraha was a Christian zealot, as Byzantine sources claim, he would have been driven by a "treacherous plan"—in Qur'ānic parlance—to destroy the Ka'bah to fulfil two objectives. First, he hoped to weaken Makkah and destroy its symbolic status, bringing it within his sphere of influence; second, he intended to proselytise Christianity to the Arabs. Muslim historians refer to this with the expression "he wanted to turn the Arabs to his church", meaning that he sought to convert them to Christianity. Even though the Arabs did not follow one particular religion, they all venerated the Ka'bah, thus making it a symbol of Arab unity. Destroying the Ka'bah would, therefore, open the door to the propagation of a new religion, especially if this religion was supported by an important tri-partite alliance: the Byzantine Empire, Abraha's kingdom in Yemen, and the Kingdom of Aksum. Certainly, Abraha's propagation of Christianity was not solely for religious reasons; he knew that Arab conversion to Christianity would result in political allegiance to his kingship and to Constantinople.

Abraha was unable to impose his control over the Hijaz and the northern part of the Arabian Peninsula. He died sometime between 560 and 565, and was succeeded by his son Yaksum, who ruled for a brief period before being succeeded, in turn, by his brother Masrūq.[66] That was when the Persians violently retaliated. First, by supporting the Himyarite leader Sayf ibn Dhī Yazan against Masrūq, then by the direct occupation of Yemen in an attempt to limit Byzantine-Abyssinian influence. The Persian occupation persisted until 628, when the Persian governor of Yemen, Bādhān ibn Sāsān, embraced Islam, as will be explained later.

It is pertinent at this juncture to point to an important matter concerning the account of the Prophet's (ﷺ) birth in the "Year of the Elephant". It is clear that Abraha died at least seven years before the Prophet's (ﷺ) birth. Therefore, if Abraha had led a campaign against Makkah, it must have occurred before the Prophet (ﷺ) was born, which, in all probability, was in 570.[67] This issue requires detailed inquiry. It is worth noting that there are varying accounts in the sīrah texts regarding the Prophet's (ﷺ) birth date, including one suggesting that he was born ten years after the Year of the Elephant, and al-Zuhrī's view that it was thirty years thereafter.[68] Another view that may resolve this problem holds that the Abraha who tried to destroy the Ka'bah was not Abraha I, who became the king of Yemen after Aryat's murder. In his important book on the Prophet's (ﷺ) life, the Turkish scholar Mehmet Apaydin differentiates between three individuals with the name Abraha.[69] The first was Abraha al-Ashram, who died long before the prophetic era. He had seized power in Yemen, and his family remained in control of the country for thirty years. The second was Abraha, the son of al-Ṣabāḥ, the grandson of Abraha al-Ashram from his daughter Rayḥānah, and whose father was a Himyarite, thus making this Abraha a Himyarite. He, Apaydin argues, was the one who attempted the attack on the Ka'bah as related in the incident of the elephant. He was also about the same age as 'Abd al-Muṭṭalib. The third Abraha was the son of Sharḥabīl, the son of Abraha, the son of al-Ṣabāḥ, the grandson of Abraha the Himyarite who attacked the Ka'bah and then embraced Islam and visited the Prophet (ﷺ).

66. Mu'nis, *Tārīkh Quraysh*, 155.

67. Mehmet Apaydin, *Siyer Kronolojisi* (Istanbul: Kuramar, 2018). We will rely on the dating of all the events in the sīrah as related in this book. These dates are not only accurate due to Apaydin's rigorous research methodology, but also because they match many of the dates that we have affirmed by our reading of events from various angles and from Arabic and non-Arabic sources.

68. Ibn Kathīr, *al-Bidāyah wa al-Nihāyah*.

69. Apaydin, *Siyer Kronolojisi*.

Abraha's failure to subjugate the Hijaz and the northern part of the Arabian Peninsula had important later consequences for the international balance of forces, and it was an indicator of declining Byzantine influence on the Yemeni and Arabian fronts in the second half of the sixth century. The Persian king, Khosrow Anushiruwān (531–579), famous for his erudition and political strategy, monitored the attempts of his opponent Justinian to capture international trade. In particular, he monitored Justinian's expulsion of Persians from Yemeni ports and his consolidation of maritime routes via the Red Sea, as well as his attempt to take full control of the land routes traversing the Arabian Peninsula. An additional concern for Khosrow was Constantinople's support of Abraha, and its alliance with him in Yemen. This led to the Persians supporting Sayf ibn Dhī Yazan with an army that defeated the Abyssinians in spectacular fashion and crowned Sayf as the king of Yemen.

Understandably, news of the Abyssinian defeat and Sayf ibn Dhī Yazan's victory was received positively in Makkah, creating a celebratory mood in the city. There are several reasons for this. First, it was viewed as retribution for the failed Abyssinian attempt to destroy the Ka'bah. Second, the Persian return to Yemen would disrupt the Red Sea trade route and boost the desert route, resulting in increased profits for Makkan businesses. Constantinople had preferred the Red Sea trade route due to its low cost and because the Red Sea was within the Byzantine sphere of influence.

A delegation of Makkan elders, led by 'Abd al-Muṭṭalib ibn Hāshim and including Umayyah ibn 'Abd Shams, 'Abdallah ibn Jad'ān, Khuwaylid ibn Asad and Wahb ibn 'Abd Manāf, travelled to Yemen to congratulate Sayf ibn Dhī Yazan on his victory. 'Abd al-Muṭṭalib addressed him as "the king of the Arabs, the spring that brings fertility to their land, and the head of the Arabs to whom obedience is shown". In one account of this visit, there is an indication of the economic decline in Makkah because of Byzantine control over Yemen and the Red Sea. It is narrated that 'Abd al-Muṭṭalib told Sayf ibn Dhī Yazan:

> We are, O King, the people of Allah's sanctuary, its servants, and the custodians of His House. The One who brought us before you has also guided you to lift the calamity that has belittled us.

> We are a delegation that brings salutations and not one that has incurred loss.[70]

'Abd al-Muṭṭalib's delegation established a strong relationship with Ibn Dhī Yazan and historians note that he gave them generous gifts, with 'Abd al-Muṭṭalib receiving tenfold what any other individual received.

Clearly, the Qurayshi delegation did not undertake that journey simply to convey salutations and to celebrate the expulsion of the Abyssinians. The Quraysh had realised that a new era had begun in Yemen, and that it was incumbent upon them to affirm their pact with the new king and to resume with Yemen the trade that had been halted during Abyssinian rule. Furthermore, they knew from past experience that strong Persian influence in Yemen presented a great opportunity for the Quraysh to revive its trade, since Persian control of Yemen would disrupt the maritime trade route along the Red Sea, leading to price increases in the Levant, thus making it possible for Qurayshi caravans to double their profits, since they would be the sole transporters of Yemeni merchandise originating in India.

After Sayf ibn Dhī Yazan ascended the Yemeni throne, the Persians tried to encourage him to implement their policies and serve their interests, which had been their rationale for supporting him. However, the new king felt disinclined to serve the Persians; his inflated sense of importance and elevated stature among his people seemingly prevented him from becoming subservient to his erstwhile supporters. The Persians responded by sending a second army to remove him and to take full control of Yemen. They annexed it to the Persian Empire and appointed a Persian governor to implement Khosrow's policies.

Desert ship replaces sea ships

After Constantinople lost Yemen and the movement of its ships in the Red Sea was impeded, it began plotting to take control of the desert land route that passed through Makkah and to appoint a Christian king in Makkah to guarantee its trade interests.

---

70. Ibn Kathīr, *al-Bidāyah wa al-Nihāyah*, vol. 3, 554.

Historians mention a certain ‘Uthmān ibn al-Ḥūwayrith who had travelled to Byzantium and asked Caesar (the sources do not mention which “Caesar” this was) to grant him authority over Makkah. He argued, “It will be an addition to your realm, like Khosrow’s Sana’a.” Caesar was convinced and wrote a letter bearing his seal, appointing ‘Uthmān ibn al-Ḥūwayrith as Makkah’s ruler. He also adorned him with lavish clothing and provided a mule with a gold bridle. ‘Uthmān told the people of Makkah:

> O People, as you are aware, Caesar has granted you protection in his country and [you are also aware that you benefit from] the trade that he commands. He has appointed me your king. I am your cousin and one of you, and all I ask of you is a bagful of acacia leaves, a pouch of fat and some hides.[71] Gather these and send them to me. I fear that if you refuse, the Levant will no longer be accessible to you. So do not take the risk and lose the benefits you obtain there.[72]

The report continues that, when he addressed them, it evoked in them fear of Caesar, their hearts were seized by the threat of their potential loss of trade, and, even before they dispersed, they agreed to place a crown on ‘Uthmān’s head the next day.

‘Uthmān addressed the Quraysh using language that appealed to their interests. He reminded them of the security they enjoyed in Caesar’s lands (a reference to the Qurayshi Pact), and stoked their fear of losing their Levantine trade if they refused to obey Constantinople’s orders. His words had an impact on their psyche, and they decided to obey Caesar’s letter.

However, the idea of having a king in Makkah appointed by Constantinople undermined the Qurayshi strategy of non-alignment. If they accepted a king chosen by Constantinople, they would antagonise the Persians and would have to sacrifice their relationship with Yemen, which was under Persian influence. Therefore, they had no choice but to reject ‘Uthmān’s appointment, and so they did. The historian Ibn

71. The essence of his message was that the taxes they would have to pay were minimal and not burdensome. Acacia leaves were used to tan animal hides in Arabia at that time.
72. Ibn Manẓūr, *Mukhtaṣar Tārīkh Dimashq* (Dimashq: Dār al-Fikr, 1984), vol. 16, 82.

Manẓūr narrated that ʻUthmān's cousin Abān:

> shouted at the top of his voice when the majority of the Quraysh were gathered round the Kaʻbah: "O for the servants of Allah, a king in Tihama [the Red Sea coastal plain of the Arabian Peninsula]?!" They flocked toward him like a herd of zebras, and responded: "You have spoken the truth, by al-Llāt and al-ʻUzzah; there has never been a king in Tihama." And the Quraysh went back on what they had initially said, and [ʻUthmān ibn al-Ḥūwayrith] went to Caesar and informed him thereof.

Sound strategic logic was victorious, and Makkah remained "immune and unpossessable".[73]

The Quraysh's understanding of the struggle between the Persian and Byzantine empires was clear: whenever tensions escalated between the two great powers, the trade routes were disrupted and reliance on intermediaries increased, making it a source of profit and wealth for Makkah's caravans. The Northern Silk Road joining India to Central Asia and heading toward Europe was disrupted for extended periods as a result of the Persian-Byzantine conflict over Central Asia and because of attacks by Turkish tribes. The South-to-North Maritime Silk Route from India to Oman and other Gulf ports was disrupted whenever conflict broke out over Upper Mesopotamia, which was hotly contested by the two powers. The only route that remained constantly operational was the East-to-West Maritime Route between India and Yemen.

Persian-Byzantine rivalry did not disrupt the maritime route that reached Aden, but it affected the way in which the merchandise was transported from Aden to the Persian and Levantine markets. The Quraysh clearly anticipated the consequences of such a scenario: if Yemen was under Byzantine influence, Byzantine ships would transport merchandise from Yemen via the Red Sea northward to Egyptian ports and to the port of Elath (Aqabah) at a much lower cost than if they used overland caravans. This would threaten the land route that traversed the desert, and it would weaken Makkah economically. However, if Yemen

73. Ibn Manẓūr, *Mukhtaṣar Tārīkh Dimashq*, vol. 16, 82.

was under Persian influence, Byzantine ships would not ply the waters of the Red Sea with ease, and trade across the desert would then be revitalised, allowing Makkah to flourish. This was why the Quraysh had been pleased with Sayf ibn Dhī Yazan's victory over the Abyssinians. After Abyssinian rule collapsed in Yemen, Yemeni ports no longer welcomed Byzantine ships, because the Persians were determined to prevent Byzantine ships from transporting their merchandise. As a result, the number of Byzantine merchant ships in the Red Sea declined, and Constantinople's trade with Abyssinia was restricted.

As per Qurayshi calculations, desert trade flourished whenever shipping in the Red Sea was disrupted, and camels replaced Byzantine ships in linking Yemeni ports with the Levant for both the summer and winter journeys. As the sixth century came to a close, the golden age of Makkah began. Many chroniclers point out that the Qurayshis were no longer prepared to work for profits that were less than 100 percent, being fully aware of the monopoly that they enjoyed over most merchandise.

Makkah's growth

With the strengthening of Makkah's strategic position and the increased wealth of its traders, various aspects of the Makkan lifestyle began to change; the economic boom influenced political and social thinking, as well as buying patterns. Makkah began to see itself and the world around it anew. Cities that were located on trade routes that crossed borders were usually characterised by certain essential features that left their mark on the lives of their citizens and on their social and political habits. Trading caravans did not exclusively transport merchandise; they also carried news, ideas, religious teachings, and different lifestyle patterns. Makkah thus became deeply influenced by its changing status. On the political level, the city's strategy of non-alignment called for diplomatic skills, caution, sound praxis, balance, and courage.

The grim portrait of Makkah from the end of the fifth century—when the only hope of its poor was to wait for death—was transformed by the end of the sixth century into a picture of abundance, wealth, and ostentation. The wealth of Qurayshi traders grew to such phenomenal levels that popular legends circulated concerning some of them, such as 'Abdallah ibn Jad'ān, who was rumoured to have found a secret cave in the mountains filled with gold. Makkan traders used their wealth to entrench their stature, social standing, and dominance. They competed against each other in hosting banquets and distributing food, and they developed a taste for gold and silver utensils, adopting the Roman practice of using knives and spoons. Some Qurayshi leaders began paying special attention to their personal appearance and would dress in ostentatious clothing; some extended the length of their expensive robes so that they dragged on the ground as an expression of pride and arrogance. They also had young servants and slaves follow them around in procession, in imitation of the customs of rich Romans.

Makkah had entered a time of security and abundance while the rest of the world was steeped in poverty, sickness, and fear. The international political economy was in turmoil by the sixth century because of the brutal war between the Persians and the Byzantines. The spread of plagues added another level of tragedy. The Justinian Plague, for example, had resulted in the deaths of forty percent of Constantinople's population, and had spread across Europe and to Persian lands. It left hunger and poverty in its wake, followed by unrest, conflict, and rebellion. The Quraysh, however, lived a life completely unaffected by the misery that surrounded them. Allah, the Most High, alludes to this in the Qur'ān: "Can they not see that We have made [them] a secure sanctuary though all around them people are snatched away? Then how can they believe in what is false and deny God's blessing?" (29:67).

Makkah's economic boom left a deep impression on its social, political, and ethical structure. It contributed to reshaping its social and political structure and facilitated the city's shift from being a simple polity to becoming a complex political reality. The era of distinctions and alliances had begun, and two of the most important alliances in Makkah's history became prominent in this era: the Alliance of the Scented (Ḥilf al-Muṭayyībīn) and the Alliance of the Allies (Ḥilf al-Aḥlāf). The first was a coalition that was committed to an image of the Quraysh as the People of Allah and the neighbours of the Holy Sanctuary, while the second represented the camp of influential authority and savage capital.

CHAPTER FOUR

Qurayshi exceptionalism

"So let them worship the Lord of this House, Who provides them with food against hunger, and with security against fear" (Qur'ān 106:3-4).

The Quraysh were never the largest or the strongest of the Arab tribes, nor were they known for their ferocity. In fact, compared to other Arab tribes, such as the powerful and strong Hawāzin, Tamīm and Ghaṭafān, the Quraysh was small. These other tribes relied largely on raiding, pillaging, and the enslavement of their enemies for their livelihood. Consequently, the land routes of the Arabian Peninsula were targeted by tribal bandits, forcing caravans to stick to established routes that were protected by tribal leaders who were able to repel bedouin attacks. In return, the caravans paid tributes and provided certain services to their benefactors.

However, the Qurayshis were special, not because of their numbers or wealth, but because of their custodianship of the Ka'bah and their responsibility to tend to the pilgrims. Aware of this, the Quraysh began to entrench its unique status among the Arab tribes. Acknowledged as "the People of Allah and the neighbours of the Holy Sanctuary", they exploited this position to the fullest. First, they entrenched the concept and significance of dual sanctity—sacred months and sacred land—thus winning for Makkah a unique protected status in a tumultuous environment. This was even more exceptional because normal customs and laws did not apply to the city in the same manner as it applied to other regions.

The Quraysh exploited the concept of "sacred months" for their benefit. Arab tribes upheld the sacred months (Muḥarram, Rajab, Dhī'l Qa'dah and Dhī'l Ḥijjah), which was a practice derived from the law of Ibrāhīm (Abraham), since they needed a regular truce during which they would be able to protect themselves and allow pilgrims to safely visit the Holy Sanctuary. The remaining eight months were unrestricted, and the tribes were free to attack and raid each other and engage in war. If it were not for the sacred months, the pilgrimage would not have been possible, and Makkah's markets would not have thriven. The city would, in all probability, have perished, both economically and religiously.

In the year 580, a conflict broke out in the sacred months between the Quraysh and Kinānah tribes on the one side, and the Qays 'Ilān tribes (Hawāzin, Ghaṭafān, Salīm and Thaqīf) on the other. It ended only in 590. To express the outrage over the transgression of the sacred months and to affirm that conflict in this period violated custom and established practice, these clashes were named the "Immoral Wars" (Ḥurūb al-Fijār).

The Quraysh also entrenched a spatial understanding of sanctity by designating neutral territory wherein tribal aggression was prohibited. The demarcated sanctuary covered a wide area around Makkah, and it provided security and protection throughout the year, not only during the sacred months. None dared commit any act of aggression in this sanctuary.

The concept of dual security founded on the sanctification of time and space was not specific to Makkah, but would, in time, extend to Qurayshi individuals as well, wherever they may be. Over time, Qurayshis came to be referred to as "sanctified" (ḥaramīyūn), resulting in their being more protected than others during their travels outside Makkah. In his commentary on the chapter of the Qur'ān entitled "The Quraysh" (Surah 106), the famous exegete al-Ṭabarī[74] quotes opinions that illustrate this special status, such as the view of Qatādah. In his commentary on the verse: "For the pacts [of security and safeguard enjoyed by] the Quraysh" (Qur'ān 106:1-2), al-Ṭabarī asserts:

> The People of Makkah were traders whose trading [patterns] alternated between winter and summer, and they were protected among the Arabs. While the Arabs undertook raids against each other, they could not [undertake similar raids against the Quraysh] out of fear. As for the Quraysh, if one of their people

74. Abū Ja'far Muḥammad ibn Jarīr ibn Yazīd al-Ṭabarī, *Jāmi' al-Bayān 'an Ta'wīl al-Qur'ān* (Gezah: Dār Hajar, 2001).

> was attacked in any Arab quarter, and it was said that he was a ḥaramī' (sanctified), he was left alone and his wealth was left untouched in veneration of the protection that Allah had granted them.[75]

Regarding the verse: "Who provides them… with security against fear" (Qur'ān 106:4), Qatādah explains: "[In the period before Islam,] they would say: 'We are from Allah's Sanctuary,' and no one would touch them. They were thus protected, while Arabs from other tribes would be attacked when they travelled." Ibn Zayd comments on this verse: "The Arabs would raid one another and enslave one another but [the Quraysh] were protected from that due to the status of the Holy Sanctuary." He then quoted the following verse: "Have We not established for them a secure Sanctuary, to which fruits of all kinds are brought as tribute, as a provision from Us? But most of them do not understand" (Qur'ān 28:57).[76]

The second way in which the Quraysh utilised their special status as neighbours of the Sanctuary was by inventing a new system of exceptionalism for themselves that they referred to as al-Ḥums (the Sanctified People). Ibn Isḥāq described the notion of the Sanctified People and its mechanisms.

> The Quraysh invented, adopted, and managed the concept of the Sanctified People. They said: "We are the progeny of Ibrāhīm and we are a sanctified people. We are also the administrators of the Holy House and the original settlers and inhabitants of Makkah. Therefore, no Arab enjoys the rights that we do, nor does any Arab have the status that we do; nor do the Arabs show the same regard for others as they do for us. So do not venerate anything unsanctified in the same manner as you venerate the Sanctuary, because if you did, the Arabs would make little of your sanctity, and they would say that you have venerated the unsanctified just as you venerate the Sanctuary." Thus did [the Quraysh] abandon the practice of maintaining the vigil at 'Arafah and the dispersal therefrom, knowing full well and affirming that it was part of the rituals of the pilgrimage

75. al-Ṭabarī, *Jāmi' al-Bayān*, vol. 24, 654.
76. al-Ṭabarī, *Jāmi' al-*Bayān, vol. 24, 655.

> and part of the religion of Ibrāhīm. They held that all other Arabs were obliged to maintain the vigil at ʻArafah and to disperse therefrom, and they said [in justifying their actions]: "We are the People of the Sanctuary and therefore cannot leave the state of sanctity and venerate any other place as we venerate the Sanctuary. We are al-Ḥums, and al-Ḥums are the Sanctified People." They then granted any Arab who was born in the Sanctuary—whether [their parents] were inhabitants of the Sanctuary or from beyond—the same status as their own, making lawful for them what was lawful for the Quraysh and prohibiting for them what was prohibited to the Quraysh.[77]

It is necessary to reflect on this text. The justifications forwarded by the Quraysh emphasised their exceptional character and unique status. They were "the progeny of Ibrāhīm, a sanctified people, and the administrators of the Holy House." This gave them a position and status that no other Arab enjoyed. While this is obviously correct, exploiting this position was rather devious and contradicted the idea of their being closely associated with Ibrāhīm, especially because they exempted themselves from performing one of the major pilgrimage rituals, the vigil at ʻArafah, which was advocated by the religion of Ibrāhīm. They claimed that it was inappropriate for them to leave the confines of the Sanctuary, and since ʻArafah lay outside the Sanctuary, they performed the vigil in Muzdalifah and dispersed from there, while all other Arabs followed the tradition of holding the vigil at ʻArafah.

"Al-Ḥums" thus became an expression of superiority and an exploitative utilisation of the status of the Quraysh. This should be assessed within the context of the ascension of the wealthy, power-hungry section of the tribe; the use of the notion of a sanctified people had a purely materialistic motivation in the quest for direct economic benefits. Abusing this idea, they introduced the rule that outsiders were not to undertake the circumambulation ritual of the Holy House in clothing that was not sourced from the Sanctified People. Pilgrims were thus forced to buy clothing in Makkah or be given clothes by the Sanctified People; whoever was unable to do so was obliged to do the

77. Quoted in ʻAbd al-Malik Ibn Hishām, *al-Sīrah al-Nabawīyyah* (Cairo: Muṣṭafa al-Bābī al-Ḥalabī, 1955), vol.1, 199.

ritual while naked. Any person who violated the rule and walked around the Holy House in clothing not sourced from the Sanctified People had to discard the clothes thereafter and never use them again. Furthermore, pilgrims from outside Makkah were not allowed to eat food that they brought with them from outside the sanctuary.

It is clear that these two rules—that Makkan traders forced pilgrims to buy clothing and food inside the sanctuary—resulted in enormous profits and benefit for the Makkans. Alternatively, whoever could not afford to purchase from the Makkans had to depend on the generosity of the Sanctified People to provide them with clothing so that they could perform the circumambulation ritual, and had to suffice with food freely provided to the pilgrims by the Quraysh.

Cultural centrality

From earlier discussions we may conclude that the Holy House, the Sanctuary, the pilgrimage, and all their related rituals and practices were the pillars upon which Qurayshi exceptionalism was built. The Quraysh were able to convert these elements into tools that strengthened their presence among the Arabs and elevated their status, making them unique and their status unattainable by any other tribe. While the basis of this exceptionalism was religious, the Quraysh were skilful enough to transform it into a revenue stream through trade and by exploiting the notion of a Sanctified People. They benefited from the pilgrimage season by establishing three important annual markets that were linked to the pilgrimage: 'Ukāẓ, Dhū al-Majāz and Majnah.

Historical narratives describe people visiting the markets while in their pilgrim garb. The link is also clear from the times of the year when these markets were held. The 'Ukāẓ market was held over 20 days, from 1 Dhī'l Qa'dah; the Majnah market was in session in the last ten days of Dhī'l Qa'dah; and, immediately thereafter, the Dhū al-Majāz market would commence, doing business in the first eight days of Dhī'l Ḥijjah. Thereafter, people would disperse to complete the pilgrimage.

'Ukāẓ was the most important market. It was set up at a venue that was a three-day march from Makkah and a one-day march from Ṭā'if. It brought together Arab merchants and their merchandise from the various tribes, as well as trade delegations and their wares from al-Ḥīrah, Yemen and Abyssinia. However, the basis of the 'Ukāẓ market's reputation and popularity was not merchandise but its literary and political symbolism. The poetry and oratory performances of 'Ukāẓ, especially the poetry competitions and the heated exchanges between orators, were major attractions for the Arabs. A judging panel was comprised of senior poets of great literary calibre. It convened annually to listen to and consider new poems. The fate of new poets would be decided at 'Ukāẓ; if their poems were praised and endorsed, they would attain a special status among Arabs, but if they were not endorsed, the aspiring poets would effectively be forced to abandon poetry. With the passage of time, 'Ukāẓ became the high cultural academy of the Arabian Peninsula.

The poems that received commendation and were spread across the peninsula by visiting Arab delegations conveyed a mixture of ethical values. Poetry was a means of individual and societal expression, as well as a social and political expression of incidents and positions, and the poet was an important spokesperson for the tribe. In other words, poetry functioned similarly to media and propaganda tools in contemporary times, which is why the tribes honoured their poets and instrumentalised their poetry to glorify and enhance their status and power.

The poetry and oratory competitions at the 'Ukāẓ market saw the audiences supporting one or other side, and competition was so intense that it would often end in argument, and sometimes even physical fights, especially when the topic concerned the virtues of one tribe over another. In fact, the Immoral Wars were sparked at 'Ukāẓ.

These markets enhanced the reputation of the Quraysh and entrenched their symbolic power in several ways. They served as huge trade exhibitions where merchants made deals, exploited business opportunities, and familiarised themselves with recent trading practices, prices, and the needs of various regions and tribes. The markets also served as political gatherings, where leadership elites from all over the peninsula congregated. Tribal leaders met and created opportunities for the resolution of conflicts and the settlement of longstanding inter-tribal disputes regarding retribution and clashes. They also provided opportunities to forge new alliances and make new political deals. Culturally, the markets represented an annual festival that contributed to strengthening the Qurayshi Arabic dialect and spreading it among the tribes; the poetry was recited in this dialect and transmitted across the peninsula by the dispersing pilgrims. This is how it became the official dialect of high literature and authorised poetry. The Quraysh also benefited from the symbolic status of the Ka‘bah, since some great poets were honoured by having their poems hung inside the Ka‘bah. These then became known as the Hanging Odes (al-Mu‘allaqāt) and are regarded as the finest of Arabic poetry, conveying important insights into the social, political, and tribal conditions of the time.

Makkah's political structure

The political map of Makkah was entirely structured around tribal hierarchies. The political status of individual tribes, clans, and sub-clans was based on their lineage, just as their economic standing was based on their wealth. Unlike Yemen and the territories ruled by the Manādhirah and Ghassanids, Makkah had neither a king, nor a strong central authority, nor a system of governance that was enforced by the power and might of a powerful state. Instead, the moral authority of tribal leaders was respected, and there was consideration for their views when decisions were made. The tribe was the political and societal actor; the individual had no worth without tribal protection. To its members, the tribe extended its protection and cover against aggression, and it intervened to aid the individual who might encounter problems or fall into debt. Everyone in a tribe contributed toward blood money if one of its members killed someone from outside the tribe, just as they contributed to ransoms to free their prisoners. The tribe also entered alliances and covenants with its own clans and sub-clans and with other tribes to strengthen itself, entrench its authority, and widen the circle of protection for its members. Such arrangements created a safe sphere for tribe members within which they could move freely and conduct trade. If an individual found himself without tribal affiliation due to their being cut off from their family or because of migration to a new territory, they would need to seek protection from another tribe by becoming its client (mawla). In this way, they benefited from the same protected status as tribe members themselves.

The tribe was a participatory, consultative entity in which sovereign authority was vested in the person who was most capable of bearing the burdens of leadership; authority was not necessarily inherited through lineage. The needs of the tribe were always pressing and could not be delayed. Thus, whoever offered better service and was more skilled in serving the tribe was pushed forward and was appointed to a leadership position. If the person failed or was not up to the task, he was removed from leadership, which was bestowed on another. A tribe might also have several leaders, but its internal matters were always resolved through consultation amongst senior members and leaders, and the majority acceded to the consensus of the elders.

Similarly, the general affairs of the Quraysh, its alliances and its interests, were all debated in the House of Assembly (Dār al-Nadwah), which took consensual decisions after in-depth discussions. Located close to the Ka'bah, the House of Assembly was established by Quṣay and remained the Qurayshi political, social, and economic centre. Its members were leaders over forty years of age of all the clans of the Quraysh. There were, however, exceptions. Certain youth were allowed to participate if they distinguished themselves from their peers in public affairs. Their presence was useful, their opinions valued, and they participated in the assembly's deliberations.

The Quraysh were extremely careful to ensure that other tribes perceived it as a united front, so as to entrench its prestige and religious and commercial credentials. However, cracks began to show in Qurayshi society after Quṣay's death. These fissures created internal political momentum and an appropriate space for the protection of the Islamic message in its early years, and they remained an important element in the development of the relationship between the Quraysh and the Prophet (ﷺ) and his companions after their migration to Madinah. The Messenger (ﷺ) shrewdly exploited these cracks and saw in them opportunities to divide his enemies. This will be explained later. Furthermore, the effects of these differences and splits continued to influence the formation of the political map of the Islamic empire for a long time into the future.

Leadership split

The most significant split in the Quraysh was in its political leadership, within what could be regarded as the ruling family of the Quraysh, from a group of clans that were related to Quṣay himself. We examined earlier how Quṣay enjoyed the status of being the founder of the Quraysh, how his people received his orders as religious commandments, and how he attained a status that no one else was able to attain. He developed a good reputation and was remembered fondly by later generations. His reputation resulted in his descendants and their clans inheriting a special status, and they came to be regarded as a "ruling family," in terms of political custom and practice. These clans were affiliated to Quṣay's four sons: 'Abd Shams, 'Abd Manāf, 'Abd al-Dār, and 'Abd Quṣay. Since 'Abd Quṣay did not have any sons, the other clans represented what might be considered the ruling family of the Quraysh, both in terms of de facto authority and in terms of honour, status, and dominance. Having Quṣay's name in a man's lineage was enough to win him respect in Makkah and among all the Arab tribes.

To his oldest son, 'Abd al-Dār, Quṣay bequeathed the five central duties of the Quraysh: al-Rifādah (Food Provisioner), al-Siqāyah (Water Supplier), al-Ḥijābah (Maintenance of the Ka'bah), Dār al-Nadwah (the House of Assembly) and al-Liwā'a (The Brigade). However, the de facto leader who carried the burden of leadership was not 'Abd al-Dār but his brother 'Abd Manāf. We also saw how 'Abd Manāf's son Hāshim was unhappy that his cousins from 'Abd al-Dār monopolised the leadership of the central duties, and how he regarded it as unfair that he had to carry the burden of leadership while the privileges and recognition of leadership fell on someone else. He therefore decided to officially take over the leadership of all five duties. That decision led to the first political dispute in Makkah between these two branches of the family and their supporters. One faction favoured the sons of 'Abd Manāf and the other supported the sons of 'Abd al-Dār. 'Abd Manāf's sons were supported by the Banī Asad ibn 'Abd al-'Uzza, Banī Zahrah, Banī Taym ibn Murrah, and Banī al-Ḥārith ibn Fahar. 'Abd al-Dār's sons had the backing of the Banī Makhzūm, Banī Saham, Banī Jumaḥ, and Banī 'Adī ibn Ka'b.

The camp aligned to the Banī 'Abd Manāf was known as the Alliance of the Scented (Ḥilf al-Muṭayyībīn) because they immersed their hands in perfume to symbolise the sealing of their alliance. The other camp was the Alliance of the Allies (Ḥilf al-Aḥlāf), alternately referred to as the Alliance of a Lick of Blood (Ḥilf La'qat al-Dam). They formed their alliance by immersing their hands in camel's blood, after which one of them licked his hand. The rest of those forming the alliance followed his lead, resulting in the moniker they were given.

Reports suggest that the two sides were on the verge of war, but the Qurayshi custom of avoiding conflict asserted itself, and they sought arbitration to resolve their differences. The result was that the duties of Food Provisioner and Water Supplier were given to 'Abd Manāf's sons, and the duties of Maintenance of the Ka'bah, The Brigade, and the House of Assembly to 'Abd al-Dār's sons. Though fighting was avoided and reconciliation achieved, this incident laid the foundation for new political practice within the Quraysh and spawned what resembled two large political parties. This political classification persisted and was strengthened on many occasions, as will be mentioned later.

By carefully examining the formation of these two alliances, we can assert that this development saw the Quraysh transition from simple politics to a new era of complex politics. The political momentum that resulted from the emergence of different alliances was generally positive, because it enriched Qurayshi political life and led to the creation of organised mechanisms for conflict resolution. These political developments laid the basis for the first formalised social contract to protect the weak and vulnerable non-Makkans, the Alliance of Virtue (Ḥilf al-Fuḍūl).

The Alliance of the Virtuous was formed to protect a Yemeni merchant who was cheated in Makkah when the Prophet (ﷺ) was around twenty years of age. Al-'Āṣ ibn Wā'il, a wealthy and influential Makkan, had purchased the Yemeni's merchandise but had refused to pay for it. The Yemeni appealed to the Alliance of the Allies, which comprised of the tribes of ʻAbd al-Dār, Makhzūm, Jumah, Saham and ʻAdī, but they refused to support him against al-ʻĀṣ ibn Wā'il and rebuked him. He then climbed the Abī Qubays Mountain at sunrise—while the Qurayshi elite were gathered in groups around the Kaʻbah—and shouted out verses of poetry, demanding justice. Consequently, the Banī Hāshim, under ʻAbd al-Muṭṭalib's leadership, met with other representatives of the Alliance of the Scented—the Banī al-Muṭṭalib ibn ʻAbd Manāf, Banī Taym and the Banī Zahrah—at the house of ʻAbdallah ibn Jadʻān in the month of Dhī'l Qaʻdah, 590.

> They pledged and swore by Allah to be as one hand with the oppressed against the oppressor until he hands over to the oppressed what is rightfully his, as long as the ocean wets wool [meaning: it will always be as it is now] and [the two mountains in Makkah called] Ḥirā' and Thubayr remain pegged in place, until mutual assistance is extended to the oppressed.[78]

The Quraysh called this pledge the Alliance of the Virtuous. They said, "These people have entered into a virtuous matter." Members of the Alliance of the Virtuous walked to al-ʻĀṣ ibn Wā'il, confiscated the Yemeni's merchandise, and returned it to him. The Prophet commended this pledge, which he witnessed when he was 20 years old. He said about it: "I bore witness, along with my uncles, to a pledge [the Alliance of the Virtuous] in the house of ʻAbdallah ibn Jadʻān that was more beloved to me than a herd of red camels.[79] If I were invited to it in the time of Islam I would have accepted." In another narration, the Prophet (ﷺ) is reported to have said: "As a young man, I bore witness, with my uncles, to the Alliance of the Scented, and I would not transgress it even in exchange for a herd of red camels."[80]

---

78. Jawad ʻAlī, *al-Mufaṣṣal fī Tārīkh al-ʻArab Qabl al-Islām* (Beirut: Dār al-Sāqī, 2001), vol. 14, 135.
79. This Arabic phrase, current at the time, referred to anything that was extremely valuable or priceless.
80. Al-Imām Aḥmad, *al-Musnad,* al-ʻAsharah al-Mubashshirīn bi'l Jannah (Beirut: Resalah Publishers, 2001), (3/210), Ḥadīth no. 1676. Verified as sound by al-Albānī. This ḥadīth has been narrated in several versions.

Alliance of values and justice

An initiative of the Alliance of the Scented, Alliance of the Virtuous included a mechanism for implementing civil law by delivering justice to the oppressed and holding the oppressor accountable. It also embodied a social contract by which people provided mutual assistance to each other in terms of everyday needs; they stood in solidarity and helped each other so that ordinary people could make a decent living. It is noteworthy that the alliance began by applying the law to a leader of the Alliance of the Allies, al-'Āṣ ibn Wā'il, the leader of the Banī Saham, forcing him to return the Yemeni's merchandise. The Alliance of the Virtuous came to play an important role in entrenching the principles of justice in Makkah, and it was consulted by the disenfranchised, especially foreigners and the weak, who were exploited by notables and tribal leaders.

If we examine the parties that entered the Alliance of the Virtuous, we find differences between it and the Alliance of the Scented. The latter encompassed all the Banī 'Abd Manāf, while the former, which was formed at least two decades later, was restricted to the Banī Hāshim and the Banī al-Muṭṭalib ibn 'Abd Manāf. The Banī 'Abd Shams and Banī Nawfil ibn 'Abd Manāf did not enter the Alliance of the Virtuous because of a leadership dispute between Hāshim and Umayyah ibn 'Abd Shams.

The dispute led to a form of litigation or arbitration that was known as al-Munāfarah. Typically, a mutually acceptable soothsayer would be presented with the dispute; the soothsayer's judgement would be final and its implementation obligatory. The arbitrator in the case of Hāshim and his cousin Umayyah was a soothsayer from the Khuzā'ah tribe. He ruled that Hāshim was of more noble lineage than Umayyah and more deserving of leadership. Umayyah therefore had to pay a fine of fifty camels and was banished from Makkah for ten years. Historical accounts suggest that he spent his exile in the Levant, and, through him, a special relationship developed between the Banī Umayyah and that region. Umayyah benefited from the urban Levantine lifestyle and from its political activity and mercantile experience. He passed this heritage on to his grandchildren, which led to Mu'āwīyyah ibn 'Abī

Sufyān establishing the Banī Umayyah kingdom there after his victory over the Hāshimites.

Nawfil ibn 'Abd Manāf, the half-brother of the remaining sons of 'Abd Manāf, seized lands and farms belonging to 'Abd al-Muṭṭalib ibn Hāshim, prompting 'Abd al-Muṭṭalib to seek the aid of his uncles from the Banī al-Najjār tribe in Yathrib. They came to his aid by sending a force of eighty warriors, forcing Nawfil to return what he had illegally appropriated. This was the reason the sons of Nawfil did not join the Alliance of the Virtuous.

As indicated earlier, the four sons of 'Abd Manāf together enjoyed the status of the Quraysh's ruling family. Each of them enjoyed influence among their people. Hāshim had the highest status, since he had forged the pact with Constantinople. His brothers had broadened the pact to encompass the three remaining regions: 'Abd Shams with Abyssinia, al-Muṭṭalib with Yemen, and Nawfil with Persia. Ibn Kathīr[81] asserts that 'Abd Manāf's sons "came to possess the leadership and they were referred to as the protectors (al-mujīrūn) because they secured for their people the protection of regional kings who allowed trade into their countries".

The split between the Banī Hāshim and the Banī Umayyah affected the leadership structure in Makkah and left its mark on Qurayshi politics for a long time. This was apparent even after the commencement of the prophetic mission; the Banī Hāshim and Banī al-Muṭṭalib sided with the people of Abū Ṭālib in granting protection to the Prophet, with only Abū Lahab dissenting. The Banī Umayyah and Banī Nawfil, on the other hand, sided with the rest of the Quraysh in opposing the Prophet and his people. This struggle in Qurayshi politics continued until Abū Sufyān ibn Ḥarb ibn Umayyah took over the Qurayshi leadership and led the war against the Hāshimite Prophet (ﷺ) after the Hijrah, or the Prophet's (ﷺ) migration to Yathrib. The split remained active until it erupted in a violent confrontation between the Hāshimite camp, led by 'Alī ibn Abī Ṭālib, and the Umayyad camp, led by Mu'āwīyyah ibn Abī Sufyān.

A careful examination of the constituent parts of the Alliance of the

81. Ibn Kathīr, *Al-Bidāyah wa al-Nihāyah*, vol. 2, 253.

Virtuous reveals that it was built on strong relationships, which enabled it to persist for a long period. In addition to the sons of Hāshim and al-Muṭṭalib ibn 'Abd Manāf, another prominent participant was the Taym ibn Murrah tribe. Even though it was not one of the larger Qurayshi tribes, it was well known because of the prominence of its leader, 'Abdallah ibn Jad'ān, in Qurayshi affairs. He was mentioned earlier as a member of the Qurayshi delegation that had been sent to congratulate Sayf ibn Dhī Yazan. He also hosted, in his home, the meeting that resulted in the establishment of the Alliance of the Virtuous.

'Abdallah ibn Jad'ān was the nephew of 'Abū Quḥāffah, the father of Abū Bakr al-Ṣiddīq. He was a rich merchant who had been given the nickname "Ḥāsī al-Dhahab" (Gold Touch) because he ate with utensils made of gold. Historians have narrated numerous accounts, many of them exaggerated, of his magnanimity and generosity. When he became old, members of his tribe tried to curb his excessive generosity. Chroniclers describe huge cauldrons in which he would prepare food, so large that a rider would be able to eat from them while sitting on his camel. One story is about a boy who drowned after falling into one of the cauldrons.

The Prophet of Allah (ﷺ) referred to one of Ibn Jad'ān's feasts when explaining to his companions how to identify the body of Abū Jahl after the latter had been killed. "Seek him among the dead. You will know him by a fracture on his knee. He and I were squeezed together at Ibn Jad'ān's banquet and I [accidentally] pushed him. He fell on his knee, smashing it, and leaving a mark on it."[82] 'Abdallah ibn Jad'ān died a short time before the beginning of the Prophetic mission.

Other prominent personalities from Taym that supported Islam included the companion Ṭalḥa ibn 'Ubaydallah and Abū Bakr al-Ṣiddīq, along with his entire household. The Banī Zahrah were also members of the Alliance of Virtue. Their leader was Wahb ibn 'Abd Manāf ibn Zahrah ibn Kilāb, the father of Lady 'Āminah, the Prophet's (ﷺ) mother. The Banī Zahrah and the Banī 'Abd Manāf were closely linked, such that 'Abd Manāf ibn Quṣay and 'Abd Manāf ibn Zahrah were referred to as "the two Manāfs". The two tribes lived next to each

82. Ibn Kathīr, *Al-Bidāyah wa al-Nihāyah*, vol. 3, 287.

other, and the two men were also linked through marriage; ʻAbdallah ibn ʻAbd al-Muṭṭalib had married ʼĀminah bint Wahb. The men of Banī Zahrah were, therefore, the Prophet's (ﷺ) uncles. Their fondness for him prompted them to withdraw from the Battle of Badr because they refused to fight their beloved nephew, after they had been reminded of their relationship with the Prophet (ﷺ) by al-Akhnas ibn al-Sharīq. He told them:

> Verily Muḥammad is one of you, the son of your daughter. If he is indeed a prophet, you should be most pleased with him. If he turns out to be a liar, it is better if someone else kills him than for you to kill your nephew. So turn back and let the cowardice of this fall on me. There is no need for you to pursue what is of no benefit.[83]

Other prominent individuals from the Banī Zahrah who believed in the Prophet (ﷺ) and followed him included ʻAbd al-Raḥmān ibn ʻAwf, Saʻd ibn Abī Waqqāṣ, and al-Musawwar ibn Makhramah.

The Alliance of the Virtuous, then, represented the firm core that had emerged from the Alliance of the Scented. It was an alliance of those who were committed to commendable values, protecting the oppressed, feeding the pilgrims, providing pilgrims with drink, and striving to meet the needs of the impoverished. In other words, they represented the trend of high moral values within the Quraysh.

The Alliance of Virtue occupied a special place in Muslim hearts because of the Prophet's (ﷺ) participation in it. There is a significant incident, narrated by Ibn Hishām and dating to the early Umayyad era, in which al-Ḥusayn ibn ʻAlī drew attention to the Alliance of Virtue in a dispute with al-Walīd ibn ʻUtbah ibn Abī Sufyān. Ibn Hishām says that the dispute, at Dhī'l Marwah, was over some amount of money. Al-Walīd ibn ʻUtbah ibn Abī Sufyān was the governor of Madinah, appointed by his uncle Muʻāwīyyah ibn Abī Sufyān.

> Al-Walīd had treated al-Ḥusayn unjustly regarding what was rightly due to him under his authority, so al-Ḥusayn told him: "I swear by Allah that you will treat me justly regarding what is

83. Muḥammad ibn ʻUmar al-Wāqidī, *Kitāb al-Maghāzī* (Beirut: Dār al-ʼAʻlamī, 1989), vol. 1, 44.

> rightfully mine, or I will take my sword, stand up in the mosque of the Messenger of Allah (ﷺ) and invite to a Pledge of Virtue." 'Abdallah ibn al-Zubayr, who was with al-Walīd at the time, responded: "And I swear by Allah that if he invites to such a pledge, I will take my sword and will stand with him until he justly receives what is rightfully his, or we will all die together." Al-Musawwar ibn Makhramah ibn Nawfil al-Zuhrī heard about this and responded in the same way [as 'Abdallah]; 'Abd al-Raḥmān ibn 'Uthmān ibn 'Ubaydallah al-Taymī heard about this and also responded in the same way. When al-Walīd ibn 'Utbah heard about this he gave al-Ḥusayn what was rightfully his until he was satisfied.[84]

It is significant that, in this incident, the person who threatened to invite others to a pledge of virtue, al-Ḥusayn ibn 'Alī, was the grandson of Abū Ṭālib of the Banī Hāshim, one of the founding members of the Alliance of Virtue, and that the call would have been against al-Walīd ibn 'Utbah from the Banī Umayyah, who had not been party to the original pledge. Furthermore, the individuals who announced their support for al-Ḥusayn were the grandchildren of the original founders of the pledge. Al-Zubayr ibn al-'Awwām was from the Banī Asad ibn 'Abd al-'Uzza; al-Musawwar ibn Makhramah was from the Banī Zahrah; and 'Abd al-Raḥmān ibn 'Uthmān was from the Taym tribe.

Alliance of power and wealth

Another face of the Quraysh was that of an alliance of power and wealth. It was a coalition of the wealthy and powerful, characterised by opportunism and a determination to protect the status quo, even if that meant exploiting the poor, leveraging one's social standing, and showing partisanship and stubborn opposition to transformation, truth, and justice. The most important constituents of the Alliance of the Allies were the sons of 'Abd al-Dār ibn Quṣay, the Banī Makhzūm, Banī Saham, Banī Jumaḥ, and Banī 'Adī.

A glance at the list of names of the Qurayshis who led the campaign

84. Ibn Hishām, *al-Sīrah*, vol. 1, 135.

against the Prophet (ﷺ), were vulgar towards him, and treated him with extreme cruelty will show that the majority were from the Alliance of Allies. They included al-Nuḍar ibn al-Ḥārith, the leader of the Banī 'Abd al-Dār. Ibn Hishām described him as "one of the devils of the Quraysh". He tormented the Prophet and incited enmity toward him, as illustrated in these verses of the Qur'ān: "Woe to every sinful liar who hears God's Signs being recited to him, yet persists in his arrogance as if he had not heard them. So give them news of a painful punishment." (45:7-8).

About al-Walīd ibn Mughīrah from the Banī Makhzūm, Allah says: "Indeed he contemplated and he plotted. So may he be destroyed. How he plotted. Then may he be destroyed; how [ferociously] he plotted." (Qur'ān 74:18-20).

Another individual from the Banī Makhzūm to whom Allah refers in the Qur'ān is 'Amr ibn Hishām, better known as Abū Jahl. "Do not revile those whom they call upon besides Allah in case they, in their enmity and ignorance, revile Allah." (Qur'ān 6:108).

The following verses were revealed about Umayyah ibn Khalaf from the Banī Jumaḥ: "Woe to every slanderer [and] backbiter who amasses wealth and counts it [repeatedly]." (Qur'ān 104:1-2).

An entire (though short) chapter ("al-Kawthar" or "The Abundance", Surah 108) was revealed about al-'Āṣ ibn Wā'il of the Banī Saham after he described the Prophet (ﷺ) as cut off from any good (al-abtar) because he did not have any sons.

From the constituents of the Alliance of the Allies, the Banī 'Adī was an exception in terms of how its members related to the Prophet (ﷺ). They took a more neutral, rather than a hostile, stance toward him, because one of its prominent members, 'Umar ibn al-Khaṭṭāb, embraced Islam. Hence, for example, none of them participated in the Battle of Badr.

The third bloc

There was also a third bloc that was distinct from the Alliance of the Allies and the Alliance of Virtue. This comprised the sons of 'Abd Shams ibn 'Abd Manāf, who were originally part of the Alliance of the Scented, but who broke their alliance with the Banī Hāshim due to a dispute. They also did not join the Alliance of Virtue. The genesis of the dispute was a quarrel between Hāshim ibn 'Abd Manāf and his nephew Umayyah ibn 'Abd Shams. Even though the precise reasons for their conflict are not clear, they essentially relate to the issue of leadership and administration of the duties of supplying food and water. The Banī 'Abd Shams came to prominence after the Immoral Wars that were fought between 580 and 590, when the tribes of Qays 'Ilān united to fight against the Quraysh. These tribes were aggrieved over what they saw as the Quraysh's monopoly over wealth and its rising status, and they resolved to try to break this dominance. The Banī 'Abd Shams led the Quraysh's response in an outstanding manner. This enhanced the prominence of the Banī Abī 'Aḥīḥah al-'Āṣ ibn Umayyah (known as al-'A'yāṣ) and the sons of Ḥarb ibn Umayyah (known as al-'Anābis), the most important of whom was Abū Sufyān ibn Ḥarb. This episode resulted in the Banī 'Abd Shams and its leadership gaining respect in Makkah. Since they were also prominent merchants, they were able to leverage their status and authority with their prosperity and wealth to achieve the Quraysh's political objectives.

The enmity between the Banī Umayyah and the Banī Hāshim continued and even deepened after the beginning of the Prophetic mission; the Banī Umayyah was at the forefront of the groups that opposed the Prophet. 'Utbah ibn Rabī'ah and his younger brother Shaybah were the leaders of the Banī 'Abd Shams when the Prophet (ﷺ) declared his mission. The second leadership tier was made up of Abū Sufyān ibn Ḥarb and 'Uqbah ibn Abī Mu'īṭ. All of them strongly opposed the new message.

It is worth noting that the enmity of the Banī 'Abd Shams toward the Prophet (ﷺ) was driven by very different motives from that of its allies, such as the Banī Makhzūm. This is because the Banī 'Abd Shams was cognisant that the Prophet (ﷺ) was, according to tribal custom, their cousin, even if he was from the Banī Hāshim clan. They also knew that the primary motive for the Banī Makhzūm's enmity towards the Prophet (ﷺ) related to its competition with the Banī 'Abd Manāf and that their hostility was not limited to the Banī Hāshim but also encompassed the Banī 'Abd Manāf and the Banī Quṣay, thus including the Banī 'Abd Shams. This enmity was well known; Abū Jahl had been vocal about it on many occasions.

Ibn al-Qayyim al-Jawzīyyah narrates the following example.

> al-Musawwar ibn Makhramah asked his uncle Abū Jahl the truth about Muḥammad (ﷺ): "O Uncle, did you accuse Muḥammad of lying even before he said what he said?"
>
> Abū Jahl responded: "O my nephew, Muḥammad was one of us and as a young man he was called al-Amīn (the Trustworthy). We never encountered any lie from him, ever."
>
> "O Uncle, why do you not then follow him?" Musawwar asked.
>
> "O my nephew," Abū Jahl replied, "we competed with the Banī Hāshim over who was the most honourable. They used to feed [the poor] and we used to feed [the poor]; they used to provide water and we used to provide water; they would provide protection and we would provide protection; until we sat down [to settle our scores] and we were like competing steeds. Then they said: 'We have a Prophet.' When will we be able to say the same?"[85]

Ibn Kathīr narrated another incident.

> The Prophet came across Abū Jahl and shook hands with him. Someone asked Abū Jahl: "Did I just see you shaking hands with one who has left the religion of his fathers?" Abū Jahl responded: "By Allah, I know that he is a prophet, but since when have we been subservient to the Banī 'Abd Manāf?"[86]

Al-Wāqidī tells a similar story.

> Al-Akhnas ibn Sharīq told Abū Jahl on the day of Badr: "O Abū

85. Ibn al-Qayyim al-Jawzīyyah, *Hidāyat al-Ḥayāra fī Ajwibah al-Yahūd wa al-Naṣārah* (Makkah: Dār 'Ālim al-Fawā'id, 2008), 41.
86. Ibn Kathīr, *Tafsīr al-Qur'ān al-'Aẓīm* (Beirut: Dār al-Kutub al-'Ilmīyyah, 1998), vol. 3, 224.

al-Hikam, tell me about Muḥammad. Is he truthful or is he a liar? There is no one here from the Quraysh who is listening to us except you and I." Abū Jahl replied: "Woe unto you! By Allah, Muḥammad is truthful and has never lied, but if Banī Quṣay take the duties of The Brigade, Maintenance of the Ka'bah, Water Supply and have prophethood as well, what will remain for the rest of the Quraysh?"[87]

Perhaps this conversation is what prompted al-Akhnas ibn Sharīq to advise the Banī Zahrah to leave the battlefield and to return to Makkah before the Battle of Badr. If the issue was one of tribal solidarity, then the Banī Zahrah were the Prophet's uncles. How then could they accept Abū Jahl's logic and fight their nephew? An interesting point of difference in these three narrations is that one mentions the Banī Hāshim, the second mentions the Banī 'Abd Manāf, and the third attributes the origins of the dispute to Quṣay.

The competition between the Banī 'Abd Shams and the Banī Makhzūm is illustrated in an account about two parties from these clans meeting in al-Ḥijr. They reminisced over honour and might, but soon began to argue. The Banī Makhzūm claimed that they were the more honourable and more powerful, while the Banī 'Abd Shams insisted that they were. An argument broke out between Usayd ibn Abī al-'Ayṣ, the leader of the Banī 'Abd Shams, and al-Walīd ibn Mughīrah, the leader of the Banī Makhzūm. Al-Walīd insisted: "I am better than you in matrilineal and patrilineal descent, and I have a stronger lineage." Usayd responded: "I have a higher position than you and a stronger lineage in the Quraysh than you." Deciding to seek arbitration, they asked Suṭayh—a soothsayer to whom the Arabs often referred their disputes—to judge. Both men agreed that fifty camels would be awarded to the person who would win the arbitration. Suṭayh judged in al-Walīd's favour.[88]

The motive of tribal solidarity behind Usayd's words was clear to the Banī Makhzūm and their allies. The dispute was not about support for a specific deity, nor denial of prophethood, but about competition

87. Ibn al-Qayyim al-Jawzīyyah, *Hidāyat al-Ḥayāra*, 41.
88. Muḥammad ibn Ḥabīb al-Baghdādī, *Kitāb al-Munammaq fī Akhbār Quraysh* (Beirut: 'Ālim al-Kutub, 1985), vol. 1, 105.

over leadership and its resultant benefits and interests. Their motives for rejecting the Prophet (ﷺ) and their hostility toward him were also related to tribal solidarity—between two of the houses of Quṣay, the Banī Umayyah ibn ʿAbd Shams, and the Banī Hāshim ibn ʿAbd Manāf. It was, in effect, an internal dispute within the same house. Despite this, many men and women of the Banī ʿAbd Shams were among the first to become Muslims. It is noteworthy that most of them were youth and were children of the leaders of the Banī ʿAbd Shams. This included the son of Abū Hudhayfah ibn ʿUtbah ibn Rabīʿah; ʿAbdallah ibn Saʿīd ibn al-ʿĀṣ, who would later be one of the migrants to Abyssinia; and ʿUthmān ibn ʿAffān, who the Prophet (ﷺ) honoured by giving him two of his daughters in marriage. ʿUthmān was subsequently called Dhā al-Nūrayn (the Possessor of the Two Lights).

The Banī ʿAbd Shams women who embraced Islam included Abū Sufyān's daughter, Umm Ḥabībah, who was one of the first Muslims. She later migrated, with her husband ʿUbaydallah ibn Jaḥash al-Asadī, to Abyssinia. The Prophet (ﷺ) married her after her husband had reverted to idolatry. Another prominent woman to join the ranks of the early Muslims was Umm Kulthūm bint ʿUqbah ibn Abī Muʿīṭ, even though her father was extremely antagonistic and vulgar toward the Prophet (ﷺ). The following Qur'ānic verse refers to him: "The day on which the wrongdoer will bite his hands, and will say, 'I only wish I had taken the [same] path as the Messenger!'" (25:27).

Despite the penetration of Islam into the homes of the Banī ʿAbd Shams, their official position was represented by two of their leaders: ʿUtbah ibn Rabīʿah and his successor Abū Sufyān ibn Ḥarb, who took over the leadership after ʿUtbah had died in the Battle of Badr. They both supported and articulated the Quraysh's enmity toward the Prophet (ﷺ). Nevertheless, the splits between the two idolatrous sides—the Banī Makhzūm and the Banī ʿAbd Shams—were clear because their different motives produced different positions. The splits became obvious when the Banī ʿAbd Shams tried to avoid fighting the Muslims at Badr.

After Abū Sufyān's caravan had escaped the Muslim ambush, ʿUtbah ibn Rabīʿah, then leader of the Banī ʿAbd Shams, advised the

Quraysh to return to Makkah. However, Abū Jahl, the leader of the Banī Makhzūm and of the Alliance of the Allies, insisted on advancing to Badr. A heated argument broke out between the two sides. Abū Jahl provoked 'Utbah by accusing him of cowardice, and he attributed it to the fact that 'Utbah's son Abū Hudhayfah was in Muḥammad's (ﷺ) army. "We will not return [to Makkah] until we reach the wells of Badr and the slave girls sing and the drums are beaten and the Arabs hear about us,"[89] Abū Jahl asserted. The angry 'Utbah responded: "No one else is able to divide the people like [Abū Jahl] Ibn al-Hanẓalīyyah."

Abū Sufyān also sent a message to the Quraysh asking them to withdraw, but Abū Jahl insisted on marching on, because he wanted to strengthen his position in relation to that of 'Utbah, so that he might be seen as a strong leader who decisively issues orders and is obeyed. It was clear that the leadership of the Quraysh was hotly contested between the Banī 'Abd Shams and the Alliance of the Allies. Even though 'Utbah ibn Rabī'ah was the oldest of the Qurayshi leaders and one of its elders, Abū Jahl insisted on undermining and disregarding him. This competition continued even after the most senior of the Qurayshi leadership were killed at Badr. Abū Sufyān was then given the leadership of the Banī 'Abd Shams, but he too adopted an approach different from that of Abū Jahal. This created conflict between him and the second-generation leaders of the Alliance of the Allies, led by Ṣafwān ibn Umayyah and 'Ikrimāh ibn Abī Jahl. This internal conflict persisted for five years after Badr, until Abū Sufyān surrendered Makkah to the Prophet (ﷺ) to avoid spilling Qurayshi blood.

Despite this intricate Qurayshi political posturing—including power struggles, alliances, and splits—the broader perspective reveals that the symbolic authority over the Quraysh nevertheless remained in the hands of Quṣay's sons, though within two opposing camps. One was the camp of wealth and power, which was part of the Alliance of the Allies. The Banī 'Abd Shams, motivated by tribal prejudice, was aligned to this camp in their view of the Prophet (ﷺ). The other camp was led by the Banī Hāshim and their allies from the Alliance of the Scented. The first camp represented tribal prejudice, reflected in its historical and current prioritising of material interests. In contrast, the second camp

89. Ibn Hishām, *al-Sīrah*, vol. 1, 618.

was committed to the values entrenched by Quṣay, which were derived from traditions such as the provisioning of drink for pilgrims, tending to pilgrims' needs, and uniting under the Pledge of Virtue to settle disputes and hold oppressors to account. The second was, thus, a far more open-minded and altruistic alliance. Significantly, the percentage of youth in the second camp was greater than that in the first camp; and youth, by nature, were psychologically more inclined to discard blind tribal solidarity and inherited customs.

Alliance of the marginalised

The two alliances, the Alliance of the Scented and the Alliance of the Allies, belonged to the core of Qurayshi ancestry, the clans and sub-clans whose lineages could be traced back to Fahar ibn Mālik ibn al-Nuḍar ibn Kinānah who, genealogists believe, was also called "Quraysh". Of course, not all of Makkah's inhabitants descended from these tribal roots. As the city's trade wealth increased and it opened to the world, the number of non-Qurayshi citizens in the city also increased. Many citizens were clients (mawālī) who chose to live in Makkah and entered client alliances that provided them the protection of one or another Makkan tribe. The city's inhabitants also included craftsmen, slaves, and others who were not Qurayshi. A closer examination of the social make-up of Makkah will provide important context. As the city's trade gained momentum at the end of the sixth century, and caravan traffic to and from the city increased, the number of newcomers to the city, both in groups and individually, also increased. This included bedouin groups from deep within the desert who sought stability, liberated slaves seeking a new life, the children of slave women and Qurayshi free men, and migrants from distant lands seeking new opportunities in a stable and thriving environment. In a tribal society that privileges lineage, Qurayshi custom automatically regarded these social groups as less important.

An artisanal class also developed in the city. It included carpenters, blacksmiths, weapon makers, tanners, and so forth. The Makkans generally looked down on artisans, some of whom were not Arabs. Historical reports about the construction of the Ka'bah mention that the Quraysh sought the assistance of either a Byzantine artisan or a Coptic carpenter named Bāqūm who resided in Makkah, to build its roof. Another report states that this person was on a ship loaded with marble, wood, and iron equipped by the Byzantine emperor for building a church. The ship anchored at the al-Shu'aybah port. The Quraysh purchased the leftover wood and sought the assistance of the Byzantine artisan Bāqūm to build the Ka'bah's roof.

There are also reports of other non-Arabs in the city, including one of a young man named Bal'ām who the Prophet (ﷺ) used to visit and who, perhaps, gave lessons to the Prophet (ﷺ). Other accounts suggest that the man the Prophet learnt from was a Christian called Abū al-Yusr. The following Qur'ānic verse is believed to have been revealed in this regard: "We surely know that they say: 'It is a man who teaches him,' but the language of the person they refer to is foreign, while this is in clear Arabic." (16:103).

Historians mention other Christian inhabitants of Makkah, including Naṭās, a client of Ṣafwān ibn Umayyah; Nusṭūr the Roman; Yuḥannā, the client of Ṣuhayb the Roman; and Ṣuhayb himself, who was originally from the Levant but settled in Makkah. Ṣuhayb entered a partnership with 'Abdallah ibn Jad'ān but later went off on his own and became one of the wealthiest inhabitants of Makkah. He later embraced Islam and became a close companion of the Prophet (ﷺ). There is also mention of a Greek client who married Sumayyah, the mother of Bilāl ibn Rabāḥ, and of 'Addās, who the Prophet (ﷺ) met at a farm in Ṭā'if that belonged to 'Utbah ibn Rabī'ah. 'Addās was from Nineveh. He believed in Muḥammad's (ﷺ) prophethood and, it is said, embraced Islam.[90]

This diverse social matrix was an expected result of Makkah's transformation into an urban settlement and a trading centre that was open to the world. The mixture of inhabitants was significant; some researchers estimate that, just before the beginning of the Prophetic mission, half the Makkan population was comprised of people from outside the city. These people and groups, however, had little if any political impact. The Quraysh (and Makkah) was controlled by its elite,

90. 'Alī, *Al-Mufaṣṣal fī Tārīkh*, vol. 7, 121.

not by its commoners.

One reason for opposition to the Islamic message was that the Qurayshi elite was afraid of the novel ideas, including the notion of equality, that the new religion was spreading among commoners. Many of the Prophet's (ﷺ) earliest followers were from marginalised groups and the Quraysh feared the loss of their privileges. They therefore launched a tireless war against the weak and marginalised converts, even killing some of them. The parents of 'Ammār ibn Yāsir, for example, were murdered by Abū Jahl. He also tortured other converts, such as his blinding of Zunayrah, a slave woman who belonged to the Banī Makhzūm. Umayyah ibn Khalaf committed similar atrocities; he tortured Bilāl ibn Rabāḥ and many other Muslims.

The marginalised classes had certain common concerns and interests. In the tribal Makkan society, these classes began to coalesce into something resembling a tribal structure, but without a common lineage and a common ancestor. Historians mention a non-Quraysh coalition called the Alliance of the Aḥābīsh. It included various tribes, such as Banī al-Muṣṭalaq, al-Ḥayā from the Khuzā'ah, and the Banī al-Hawn ibn Khuzaymah. There are different theories as to why the alliance was named "Aḥābīsh". Some believe the term was derived from a word that means "to come together"; others argue that the alliance was named after the place where the groups had gathered, close to the al-Aḥbash Valley or the al-Aḥbash Mountain in Makkah. There are various stories about the Alliance of the Aḥābīsh, with some regarding it as the first alliance in Makkah, forged after the Quraysh had expelled the Khuzā'ah tribe from the city. Others suggest that the alliance was forged between the Quraysh, the Banī al-Muṣṭalaq, and al-Ḥayā against the Banī Bakr, that the Aḥābīsh tribes had fought against the Banī Bakr during the Dhāt Nakīf battle, in which they emerged victorious, and that the Aḥābīsh participated in the Immorality Wars.

Considering all the narrations that mention the Aḥābīsh, it is clear that the term was used in several ways. History books often use the term together with the name of one or another of the important clans of the Quraysh, with expressions such as "Banī 'Abd Manāf and their Aḥābīsh" or "Banī 'Abd Shams and their Aḥābīsh". There are also mentions of the Quraysh "gathering their Aḥābīsh to fight the Prophet on the day of the Conquest of Makkah". This last usage prompted some researchers to suggest that the Alliance of the Aḥābīsh was a military force made up of African slaves and mercenary Arabs tasked with defending Makkah.

Yet others suggest that the expression Aḥābīsh was used in reference to inhabitants of Makkah of Abyssinian origin, since it was well known that contact between Abyssinia and Tihama, the coastal area of the Arabian Peninsula, was ongoing. This contact resulted in two-way migratory exchanges, making it possible that Abyssinians mixed with and married people from the Kinānah tribe much earlier, or that the subjugation of Kinānah to Abyssinian rule at certain times resulted in their being referred to as Aḥābīsh, and that it then came into common usage to refer to Kinānah and its allies. Thus, not all the Aḥābīsh were necessarily of Abyssinian descent; they were likely a combination of Arabs, slaves, and mercenaries who had become naturalised in Makkah.[91]

However, in the context of our discussion on the Aḥābīsh, we find that they were an organised group with a respected leader. Ibn Hishām narrated that the leader of the Aḥābīsh, Ibn al-Daghannah of the Banī al-Qārah of al-Hawn ibn Khuzaymah, had granted Abū Bakr al-Ṣiddīq protection in Makkah, and had stopped him from migrating to Abyssinia. He also mentions another Aḥābīsh leader, al-Ḥulays ibn Zabbān, who had:

> passed Abū Sufyān ibn Ḥarb while he was striking the jaw of Ḥamzah ibn 'Abd al-Muṭṭalib with a spearhead, after he had been killed in the Battle of Uhud. [Abū Sufyān] said: "Taste this for your disobedience." Al-Ḥulays said: "O Banī Kinānah, is this a leader of the Quraysh abusing his dead cousin?" Abū Sufyān responded: "Woe unto you. Conceal my actions for they were a lapse.[92]

Al-Ḥulays is also mentioned positively on another occasion. When he visited the Muslim encampment at al-Hudaybīyyah, the Prophet (ﷺ) described him as being from a devout people, a people who worshipped

91. 'Alī, *al-Mufaṣṣal fī Tārīkh.*
92. Ibn Hishām, *al-Sīrah*, vol. 2, 93.

and venerated Allah. At al-Hudaybīyyah, al-Ḥulays was extremely moved by the sight of the Muslims in their pilgrims' dress, and of their sacrificial animals, emaciated due to the prolonged delay. He returned to the Quraysh and pleaded for the Muslims to be allowed to enter Makkah. They responded: "Sit down! You are but a bedouin who knows nothing." Enraged, al-Ḥulays said:

> O people of Quraysh. By Allah, we did not pledge allegiance to you for this, nor did we agree to this. Do you prevent entry to the House of Allah to those who come to show veneration to it? By the One who holds the life of al-Ḥulays in His Hands, you will allow Muḥammad to do what he came for, or I will mobilise the Aḥābīsh to the very last man.

They then called on him: "Show restraint, al-Ḥulays, so that we may make [a decision] with which we are satisfied."[93]

From these accounts, we may identify some characteristics of the Aḥābīsh. They were a people whom the Quraysh regarded with disdain, which was demonstrated by how some of them mocked the Aḥābīsh leader at al-Hudaybīyyah, calling him an ignorant bedouin. They would not have said such a thing about the leader of one of the well-known tribes.

In addition, it is apparent that the Aḥābīsh was an organised force. This is indicated by the warning of al-Ḥulays after the Quraysh had angered him, when he threatened to mobilise the Aḥābīsh against them, and pointed out that he was able to do so to the last man. Clearly, the Qurayshi leaders took his threat seriously and attempted to placate him by asking to be allowed to discuss the matter further among themselves. If the Aḥābīsh were insignificant and divided, the Quraysh would not have taken al-Ḥulays's oath and threat seriously.

These three incidents involving two leaders of the Aḥābīsh also suggest that they were wise and judicious men and that the Aḥābīsh were not clannish. They upheld the sanctity of the Holy Sanctuary, as can be inferred from the Prophet's (ﷺ) reference to them as devout people. This is further proof that they did not display the same tribal

93. Ibn Hishām, *al-Sīrah*, vol. 2, 312.

partisanship as the Arabs before Islam. Further, they also adopted a rational approach to dealing with problems. It is possible that some of them may have been Christians, and not followers of the Qurayshi religion.

Within this context, we might suggest that the Aḥābīsh included several groups and categories of people. These would be subdivisions of small tribes, groups of people who settled in Makkah, bedouins who also settled there, as well as the artisans and migrants who came to work in Makkah. The Aḥābīsh, therefore, did not constitute a fixed tribal collective, as did the Alliance of the Scented or the Alliance of the Allies. This is why they inclined toward consensus based on values common to the various groups that made up their collective, and why they were more just and not obsessed with partisanship. On this basis, we can affirm that they were from among the common folk of Makkah, who were the majority in the city. Furthermore, they were marginalised and weak, resulting in Makkah, which was associated with the central Qurayshi ancestry arising from the sons of Fahar Ibn Mālik, not regarding the Aḥābīsh as anything more than scattered remnants who were subservient to the city.

That is, until the emergence of Islam, which enriched them with a new vision of equality and brotherhood. We will see in the following chapters how the Prophet (ﷺ) pursued a deliberate strategy to win over this marginalised class by strengthening their sense of a common humanity, and by turning them into a political force that compelled the Quraysh to take notice of their presence, as the incident with al-Ḥulays at al-Hudaybīyyah illustrates.

CHAPTER FIVE

Makkah contends with the future

"Their leaders depart, (saying), "Walk away and remain constantly [devoted] to your gods! For this is indeed just a scheme (against you)!" (Qur'ān 38:6)

The Quraysh constituted the tribal senate of Makkah, with the representatives in the House of Assembly being drawn from the leaders of Qurayshi households. Representation was not limited to a single member of each clan or sub-clan; influential persons and intellectuals also participated in the meetings. By carefully examining the reports of various meetings and events that took place in the House of Assembly, and the many decisions taken there, we can compile a list of the permanent representatives of the Qurayshi tribal senate at the beginning of the Prophetic mission.

Representing the Banī 'Abd Shams ibn 'Abd Manāf: 'Utbah and Shaybah, sons of Rabī'ah ibn 'Abd Shams; Abū Sufyān ibn Ḥarb; 'Uqbah ibn Abī Mu'īṭ; and Sa'īd ibn 'Abī al-'Āṣ ibn Umayyah.

Representing the Banī Hāshim ibn 'Abd Manāf: Abū Ṭālib ibn 'Abd al-Muṭṭalib.

Representing the Banī 'Abd al-Dār ibn 'Abd Manāf: al-Nuḍar ibn al-Ḥārith.

Representing the Banī Nawfal ibn 'Abd Manāf: al-Muṭ'am ibn 'Adī and his brother Ṭa'īmah.

Representing the Banī Asad ibn 'Abd al-'Uzza: Abū al-Bukhtarī; al-'Āṣ ibn Hishām ibn al-Ḥārith; al-Aswad ibn al-Muṭṭalib; Nawfal ibn Khuwaylid; and Ḥizām ibn Khuwaylid.

Representing the Banī Makhzūm: al-Walīd ibn al-Mughīrah; al-'Āṣ ibn Hishām ibn al-Mughīrah; Abū Jahal 'Amr ibn Hishām ibn al-Mughīrah ibn ʻAbdallah; ʻAbdallah ibn Abī Umayyah ibn Mahsham ibn al-Mughīrah and his mother ʻĀtikah.

Representing the Banī Saham*:* Nabīh and Munabbih, sons of al-Ḥajjāj; and al-ʻĀṣ ibn Wā'il al-Sahamī.

Representing the Banī Jumaḥ: Umayyah ibn Khalaf ibn Wahab ibn Ḥudhāfah and his brother Ubay ibn Khalaf.

Representing the Banī Zahrah*:* al-Aswad ibn ʻAbd Yaghuth.

Representing the Banī ʻĀmir ibn Lu'ay: Suhayl ibn ʻAmr.

Representing the Banī Taym: ʻAbdallah ibn Jadʻān.

Revelation first descended on the Prophet (ﷺ) on Monday, 17 Ramaḍān / 8 March 611, a year in which there was much to debate in the House of Assembly. A key issue that the House discussed was the war between the Persians and Byzantines, which had reached a climax. This included discussion of Khosrow's attack on Upper Mesopotamia and Anatolia and his haranguing of Byzantines in the Levant. The year before, the Byzantine general Heraclius the Elder had captured Constantinople and deposed Emperor Phocas, who had alienated large sections of the population.

Despite the geopolitical turmoil all around them, the Makkan leadership was unconcerned about the city's commerce. On the contrary, an escalation of hostilities between the Persians and Byzantines usually meant that international trade routes would be disrupted and the Makkans would be in even greater demand as alternative commercial intermediaries; the trading caravans from their safe sanctuary in Makkah would also increase in size. This was an era in which a single caravan could comprise 2,000 camels, and most in Makkah were involved and taking home profits as high as 100 percent.

The more their wealth increased, the greater the ostentation and competition within the Qurayshi elite. Some from among the elite brought chefs from Persia and Yemen to prepare unheard-of dishes so that they might gain renown and boast about their superiority. Such individuals' reputations could be boosted by a few mentions in poetic verses. Of course, these wealthy patrons filled the poets' stomachs with food and their pockets with money. Other Arabs had previously scoffed at the Quraysh for eating al-sakhīnah, a simple dish made from flour and dates that they "ate in hard times, when struck by inflation and when money was scarce".[94] Now, however, Makkah was introduced to al-fālūdhaj, a Persian dessert made from flour and honey, by 'Abdallah ibn Jad'ān, or the "Gold Touch". Ibn Jad'ān invited a talented young Persian chef who specialised in this dessert to prepare it for him, and he presented it to his guests in Makkah. He laid out tables in front of the Ka'bah and a caller invited anyone who wanted al-fālūdhaj to his tables.

Among the elite were rich traders with vast wealth, such as al-Walīd ibn al-Mughīrah, who constructed one corner of the Ka'bah at his own expense, while the Quraysh paid for the remainder of the construction. He was called "Makkah's One and Only" (Wahīd Makkah) because the Qurayshi clans together paid for the Ka'bah covering for one year, and he alone covered the cost of it the following year.

Others showed ostentation in dress and through conspicuous consumption. They ate from gold and silver utensils; drank from crystal goblets; wore turbans of Chinese silk imported through Yemen, velvet clothing produced in Iraq, or brightly coloured Yemeni gowns and jewellery made from precious stones from India. They walked with Abyssinian slaves holding umbrellas over their heads and cooling them with hand-held fans. Their commercial interests were managed by white Byzantine or Persian slaves bought in the slave markets of the Levant and Iraq.

The Qurayshi elite owned estates and gardens in Ṭā'if, where they spent the summer months because of its moderate weather, abundant water supply, and superior fruit. Some even owned estates in the Levant. Abū Sufyān, for example, maintained an estate in Balqa (currently in Jordan, northwest of Amman). Qurayshi leaders regularly met in the House of Assembly. It was their political centre and social gathering point, where marriages were contracted, children circumcised, contracts

94. 'Alī, *Al-Mufaṣṣal fī Tārīkh.*

signed, war banners unfurled, alliances debated, and disputes settled. Much of the negotiation that took place there was through consultation, but with consideration for status and age. 'Utbah ibn Rabī'ah, Abū Ṭālib ibn 'Abd al-Muṭṭalib, al-Walīd ibn al-Mughīrah, and 'Abdallah ibn Jad'ān, all of similar age, were Qurayshi elders who enjoyed high status and great respect. Even though Abū Ṭālib was not as wealthy as the others, nor as well-established in trade, his leadership of the Banī Hāshim, who were responsible for al-Siqāyah (Water Supply) and al-Rifādah (Food Provisioning), and his famous generosity and sound intellect made him the equal of others who were respected for their immense wealth.

The younger generation of the Makkan elite—including Abū Jahl, Abū Sufyān, Umayyah ibn Khalaf, Suhayl ibn 'Amr and Ḥakīm ibn Ḥizām—represented the second leadership tier. They recognised the status of the elders and never acted without their approval.

These individuals represented their tribes or clans. Tribal members would present their needs to these leaders, who would find solutions and settle disputes. General matters affecting the Quraysh as a whole were settled through consultation and decisions made by consensus. If a dispute arose between two or more leaders, they would seek the arbitration of an Arab soothsayer whose judgement was binding and had to be upheld by all parties. Such arbitration was referred to as al-Munāfarah.

In Makkah, wealth was not the preserve only of men; there were many wealthy women, too. Some of these women, such as Khadījah bint Khuwaylid, were traders. Makkan women enjoyed an elevated status: they married by choice, expressed their opinions freely, and influenced their husbands' decisions.

In the first decade of the seventh century, Makkah was resplendent with wealth and bustling with activity, and the 'Ukaẓ and Majannah markets overflowed with merchandise. The Makkans had also just completed rebuilding the Ka'bah after its destruction by a flood. They draped the Ka'bah with silk cloth, and it was quickly acknowledged as the most perfect construction for the building, elevating it and the

Quraysh's status in the eyes of pilgrims from the various Arab tribes. The Qurayshi commitment to religious matters was predicated on the benefit and status they derived from the Arab veneration of the Holy Sanctuary. These benefits included the entrenchment of the system of al-Ḥums (the Sanctified), and the maintenance of the Ka'bah, provisioning of food, and supply of water. The most senior of their gods was the idol Hubal, which was erected inside and in the centre of the Ka'bah. The drawing of lots[95] for the purpose of divination took place in front of Hubal. The idols Isāf and Nā'ilah stood in front of the Ka'bah. More than 300 other idols, representing objects venerated by various Arab tribes, were placed around the Ka'bah. The Quraysh hoped to convert the Ka'bah into a pantheon of gods, and therefore allowed anyone to place their idol in the Ka'bah, ensuring that all Arab tribes felt that their religions were represented, thus guaranteeing that everyone would undertake the pilgrimage to it.

The spiritual life of the Quraysh was generally shallow. A few exceptions were the exhortations of people such as Waraqah ibn Nawfal, who taught remnants of the teachings of the monotheism of the prophet Ibrāhim, the aphorisms of Qis ibn Sā'idah, or the stories of Jews and Christians. Some of their visitors listened with a passing interest before re-immersing themselves in their material pursuits and conceited boasting about their lineages.

In contrast, the common folk—such as the artisans, shepherds, labourers, and servants—suffered under the burdens of exploitation and deprivation. If any of them needed money, they were forced to borrow from the rich at exorbitant rates of usury, which condemned them to exploitative debt traps that ended, for many, in enslavement to their creditors. Slaves were generally obedient to their masters, some of whom forced their female slaves into prostitution, and sold the resultant offspring for a profit.

95. The drawing of lots (*al-azlām*) was a pre-Islamic custom. A *zalam* (singular for *azlām*) was a featherless arrow on which a specific act was written. If a person wanted to decide a matter by divination, he would bring someone who specialised in this practice and give him some money. The Diviner would pull out his arrows from their quiver and cast them on the ground, and the way they fell would determine whether the questioner should proceed with his intended action. If the arrows fell in another way, it meant he should not proceed with his intended course of action. Such customs were later forbidden by Islam.

This was the state of Makkah at the beginning of the seventh century. It was a society immersed in materialism; distracted from its heritage; and attached to the drapes of the Ka'bah only for profit, trade, and status, while making a show of faith, guidance, and religious commitment.

While at the apex of their trivial and materialist preoccupations, travels, and commercial dealings, the Makkan elite began to sense a new spirit impinging on their dreams and entering their homes. It was taking shape far from the bustle of Makkah's markets and festive gatherings. It began as a whisper, which they dismissed as a passing exhortation, like those of Waraqah ibn Nawfal. When it became louder, they were forced to take notice, because it entered the very foundations of their existence, penetrated their dreams and their homes, and threatened to undermine their interests, social balance, and trade. The words being uttered by Muḥammad ibn 'Abdallah (ﷺ) had special resonance, embodied a revolutionary spirit with an uplifting message, and carried the promise of a new future.

Read in the Name of your Lord who created

A journey that lasted twenty-three years and changed the future of the world began in a small inconspicuous cave called Ḥirā', situated on a mountaintop overlooking Makkah. The story began with a sublime command to "Read", and the Prophet's (ﷺ) response: "I cannot read." The reply to his plea was emphatic.

> Read! In the Name of your Lord Who created. He created the human from a clinging substance. Read! And your Lord is Most Bountiful. He taught (by means of) the pen. He taught humanity what it did not know (Qur'ān 96:1-5).

These few words embodied a unique discourse and called for a break from the form of the usual rhetoric taking place in the valley at the foot of the mountain. The command to read was not what the Prophet (ﷺ) had initially understood it to mean. It was not an order to read a written text or speech, but to engage in a vast universal reading that connected the name of the Creator at the very apex, to all His creation. This was a new kind of reading, conveying a novel and unique understanding of the universe, of humankind, and of existence, and emphasising that everything emanated from a single Divine Will. Furthermore, this vast universal reading was articulated in the name of a Lord Who is Most Bountiful, and whose bounty is ever-giving. This reading, in this world of created beings, was therefore rich and boundless.

These verses of the Qur'ān, the first to be revealed to the Prophet (ﷺ), remind us of the proof that Allah gave Ibrāhīm when he needed to respond to questions from his people. Allah showed him the treasures of the heavens and earth, and he began to read to his people from Allah's book of nature, drawing their attention to the fact that the planets, the moon, and the sun were not self-sustaining, but were part of a single dominion whose Sublime Lord alone was worthy of worship (Qur'ān 6:74-79).

Biographers of the Prophet note that when these verses were revealed, the Prophet (ﷺ) was alarmed and scared, which was a natural response, since a meeting of a human being with the Divine Spirit is a connection between the earthly and heavenly spheres and no means a casual event. Such an experience would require a profound psychological predisposition and tremendous courage. By its very nature, this was an extremely weighty encounter, and one that brought many questions to mind. Did this really happen or was it a dream? Was this really a transcendent, sublime encounter, or was it whisperings emanating from the world of the jinn?

The Prophet (ﷺ) sought solace in the comforting presence of his calm and rational wife. Khadījah allayed his fears and whispered in his ear: "Rejoice! For I swear by Allah that He will never bring shame upon you. You maintain family ties, are truthful in your pronouncements, carry your own burdens, provide for those in need, show hospitality to the guest, and stand for the truth." With great wisdom and a calm confidence, she began searching, questioning, and inquiring, engaging with the event in a composed and collected manner. She approached Waraqah ibn Nawfal to seek his council. He reassured her and the Prophet (ﷺ) by explaining the concept of revelation: "This is the same one [the Angel Jibrīl] who came to Mūsa. I wish I were young and could live until the time when your people will banish you." The Messenger of Allah asked, "Will they banish me?" Waraqah responded, "Yes. Anyone who comes with that which you bring is treated with hostility. If I should remain alive until that day, I will support you fully."[96] This is when the vision began to be clarified. The Prophet's composure returned, and he began to prepare himself for the greatest task that a person could be burdened with.

Only a few scattered accounts deal with the first three years of the Prophetic mission. Historians describe this period as the years of secret propagation. The Prophet (ﷺ) began his mission by approaching people closest to him: his wife Khadījah, his ten-year-old cousin 'Alī ibn Abī Ṭālib, and his adopted son Zayd ibn Ḥārithah, who was called "Zayd ibn Muḥammad". They all affirmed the truth of his message and professed their belief in him. He then approached his close companion Abū Bakr ibn Abī Quḥāfah al-Taymī, who did not hesitate but immediately declared his belief. He then approached 'Uthmān ibn 'Affān al-Umawī and 'Abd al-Raḥmān ibn 'Awf of the Banī Zahrah, the tribe of his uncles, and Sa'd ibn Abī Waqqāṣ. This small group of intimate confidantes constituted a strong psychological support base, which the Prophet surely needed at the beginning of his mission. The mission was a weighty burden that required strong will and spiritual fortitude, and having his household and closest companions supporting, following, and helping him was invaluable.

All great projects require two essential elements: a clear and coherent vision, and a team that believes in the vision and is fully committed to and actively engaged in its realisation. The first three years were, therefore, a formative training exercise of the highest order for the Prophet (ﷺ) and his small team.

The great rapprochement with existence

The first chapters of the Qur'ān to be revealed to the Prophet (ﷺ) include the first five verses of Chapter 96 (The Clinging Clot), the first seven verses of Chapter 74 (The One Wrapped Up), followed by

96. Narrated by 'Ā'ishah, an authentic prophetic tradition (*Ḥadīth Ṣaḥīḥ*), al-Bukhārī (1/1263), Ḥadīth no. 4953; Muslim (1/139), Ḥadīth no. 252.

Chapters 106 (Quraysh), 93 (The Glorious Morning Light), 94 (The Expansion of the Breast), 103 (Time Through the Ages), 91 (The Sun), 107 (The Small Kindnesses), 86 (The Night Star), 95 (The Fig), 99 (The Earthquake), 101 (The Great Calamity), 100 (Those Who Run) and 92 (The Night).[97]

An analysis of the major themes in these chapters reveals a new discourse that lifts the human intellect to an unprecedented level of reflection concerning the universe, the self, and the objectives of existence. Revelation in this period covered concepts that laid the foundation for a new way of understanding, prompting the Prophet (ﷺ) and the small group of Muslims to intimately engage with life and the universe, and opening wide horizons that traversed the heavens and the earth. This discourse linked the wide and expansive universe with the very essence of the human self, providing new directions for human existence, and linking what was previously separated by the limited capacity of the human intellect.

In that era, the human intellect examined existence only partially. It pondered the sun and concluded that it was an independent self-sustaining and miraculous entity with a life and a will and should be worshipped out of either hope or fear. That intellect considered the moon and saw an entity that existed autonomously and was worthy of humans prostrating to it. If it could not understand the links between and functions of the various entities in the universe, it attributed divinity to a stone, animal, or tree, creating deities to represent every aspect of life. Thus, fertility and rain would each be said to have a god; as would the wind, the sea, and other natural phenomena. Even human actions, such as war, revolution, and love were each said to have a god. The universe had become crowded with gods.

Since the human intellect always strives to personify the abstract, it imagined these "gods" in its image, with human form and characteristics. These gods fought, reconciled, and entered alliances. Humans, in comparison, were portrayed as weak and subservient, with no recourse in this strange and violent existence except to seek protection through total submission to the various gods. Since these gods did not communicate

97. Mu'nis, *Tārīkh Quraysh*.

with their worshippers, sorcerers, soothsayers, and voyeurs were needed to interpret the will of the gods. These intermediaries read the stars and cast lots and, for this service, collected gifts and sacrifices from weak human subjects who firmly held onto the hope that no evil would come to them, or that they would not have to face the gods' destructive wrath. However, the humans did not know what incurred the wrath of the gods, nor how to appease them—except through the intervention of the soothsayers, sorcerers, and voyeurs.

These were the limits of the perplexed intellect, with its partial view of existence. That was why the first verses of revelation sought to reconcile all of creation and existence, to end confusion, and to return order, rationality, and balance to the universe. Everything that exists—the sun, the moon, night, and day, and even the human being—all belong to a system that was created with precision by a single Creator Who gave them purpose and order, of which they are a part. On its own, no creation possesses the ability to provide benefit or cause harm.

> And the night is also a sign for them: We strip the daylight from it, and behold, they are in darkness. And the sun runs its course for a period determined for it. That is the decree of the Almighty, the All-Knowing. And We have determined phases for the moon until it returns to looking like an old date stalk. The sun is not permitted to overtake the moon, nor can the night outrun the day: each floats in (its own) orbit (Qur'ān 36:37-40).

The first Qur'ānic verses to be revealed drew the attention of the Prophet (ﷺ) and his companions to the fact that that the order that exists in creation and the purpose of existence do not exclude the human being, except that the Creator had granted all human beings the will to choose.

> By the sun and its (morning) splendour; by the moon as it follows it; by the day as it reveals (the sun's) glory; by the night as it conceals it; by the heaven and (He) Who constructed it; by the earth and (He) Who spread it; by the soul and (He) Who proportioned it, and inspired it (to know) its own wickedness and its own righteousness. Indeed, the one who purifies (his

> soul) succeeds; and, indeed, the one who corrupts (his soul) fails. (Qur'ān 91:1-10).

The Qur'ān presents existence as a unified whole and describes a symmetric structure that encompasses all the phenomena of the universe and is composed of pairs, such as night and day. This structure is linked to humanity that is also paired as male and female. All of this is intertwined to achieve a higher purpose.

> By the night as it conceals; by the day as it appears in all its brightness; and by (He) Who created male and female. Verily, your strivings differ greatly. As for the one who gives and is ever-conscious (of Allah), and who testifies to the best, We will smooth his path towards ease. But as for the one who is miserly and thinks of himself as self-sufficient, and who denies goodness, We will smooth his path towards misery, and his wealth will not help him when he falls (Qur'ān 92:1-11).

The initial verses of the Wise Book, revealed in the first years of the Prophet's (ﷺ) mission, built, fashioned, and trained the psyche of the strong core of individuals who had gathered around him. These verses transformed their mindset to something very different from the objectives and agendas that had been commonplace in Qurayshi society. This core of people placed no value on the Qurayshi competition to accumulate wealth, to privilege their lineage, or to sacrifice to idols. The training methodology of this core of first believers was more sublime and encompassed concepts far above the decayed disputations of the Quraysh, their idle concerns, and their pedestrian, inherited understandings. These believers were, instead, exposed to an unfamiliar discourse that was absent from Makkah's hanging odes or famous sermons.

The group that laid the foundation

A careful examination of the first group of believers shows that it was distinguished by two characteristics. The first of these characteristics was that these individuals had a strong bond with the Noble Prophet (ﷺ)

and were the closest people to him: his nuclear household that included Khadījah, ‘Alī, and Zayd; his closest companion Abū Bakr; his future son-in-law ‘Uthmān; and ‘Abd al-Raḥmān ibn ‘Awf, Sa‘d ibn Abī Waqqāṣ, and Talḥah ibn ‘Ubaydallah, all of whom were relatives of the Prophet (ﷺ) or his wife, or were his companions.

Beyond that core, the circle expanded to a wider range of people, but still included only confidantes who were close to those within the first circle: Abū ‘Ubaydah ‘Āmir ibn al-Jarrāḥ, Abū Salmah al-Makhzūmī, al-Arqam ibn Abī al-Arqam, ‘Uthmān ibn Maẓ‘ūn, ‘Ubaydah ibn al-Ḥārith ibn al-Muṭṭalib, Sa‘īd ibn Zayd and his wife Fāṭimah bint al-Khaṭṭāb, Abū Bakr’s daughters Asmā’ and ‘Ā’isha, and Khabbāb ibn al-Arat.

Biographers of the Prophet (ﷺ) estimate that, by the end of the first three years of his mission, the community of Muslims comprised around sixty persons. This group was made up of individuals from across the Makkan social spectrum. It included people from the major Qurayshi clans and sub-clans, clients and slaves, and men and women, with most of them being youth. In this first phase, no prominent Qurayshi or leader of any of its clans had yet embraced Islam.

That first group of Muslims also included individuals with various talents and from various occupations. These were individuals connected to the commercial sector, such as ‘Uthmān ibn ‘Affān and ‘Abd al-Raḥmān ibn ‘Awf; those linked to the various clans that were part of the Alliance of Allies (Ḥilf al-Aḥlāf), such as al-Arqam ibn Abī al-Arqam al-Makhzūmī and ‘Uthmān ibn Maẓ‘ūn al-Jamaḥī; and people with ties to the client community (al-mawālī), such as Khabbāb ibn al-Arat, an ally of the Banī Zahrah, Ṣuhayb al-Rūmī, ‘Ammār ibn Yāsir and his parents; and slaves, such as Bilāl ibn Rabāḥ. Abū Bakr was valuable for his other talent; he was the most knowledgeable Qurayshi on tribal genealogy, a useful expertise for one who wanted to communicate with Makkan society. To understand lineage was to understand family and social ties, both through blood and marriage, and it encompassed important information on demographics, resources, and alliances. That expertise was more comprehensive than the general statistical information that we are familiar with in the contemporary context. Abū

Bakr thus became the Prophet's (ﷺ) best assistant when he wanted to reach out to the tribes and their clans; he provided essential information about them, their ancestry, and their potential predisposition toward protecting the new religion.

The core group was also unique because it stood outside the social system and the established Makkan hierarchy. It was virtually unheard of for such a diverse group to coalesce in a single formation where all members were equal. It was, therefore, a rare social phenomenon, a rare group and a rare message, and the Quraysh were confused about how it might be dealt with using established norms.

From an early stage, the Quraysh were aware of the Prophet's (ﷺ) group and his mission, but its leaders did not pay attention to it in the first three years. They regarded his message as similar to the pronouncements of other monotheists and ascetics, such as Waraqah ibn Nawfal and his companions. Since the Quraysh generally inclined toward temperate action and the maintenance of peaceful tribal and social relations, it did not wish, at that stage, to convert the matter of a handful of Makkans into a public spectacle that might be viewed as a threat. As far as they were concerned, the Qur'ānic verses that were being circulated were largely meaningless. They were unconcerned that Muḥammad focused his followers' minds on the sun and moon, and night and day.

The Quraysh's heedlessness of the new religion gave the Prophet a wonderful opportunity to prepare the first group of Muslims, granting them his full attention, without external distractions. The group chose the house of al-Arqam ibn Abī al-Arqam (whose real name was 'Abd Manāf ibn Asad) of the Banī Makhzūm as a venue for their gatherings. Only al-Arqam and his elderly blind father lived in the huge house that was situated on the road between the hills of al-Ṣafā and al-Marwah. The Prophet (ﷺ) and his companions probably headquartered their group in al-Arqam's house in the second year of his mission; they continued to meet there for three years thereafter, until the fifth year of the mission.

Perhaps the only cause for discomfort for the Qurayshi leadership was that the new group operated outside the established class structure, forged relationships contrary to the tribal hierarchy, and encouraged free mixing with slaves and clients, thus violating entrenched norms. While this was disconcerting for the senior leaders, it was not, however, a reason for much anxiety.

The beginning of confrontation

Numerous accounts discuss the commencement of the Prophet's (ﷺ) propagation to the Quraysh and the moment when the call shifted from addressing specifically the Banī Hāshim and Banī al-Muṭṭalib to addressing the Quraysh generally. Some historians suggest that this occurred after the revelation of "And admonish your nearest kinsmen" (Qur'ān 26:214). Others hold that it occurred after the revelation of "Therefore expound openly what you are commanded, and turn away from the idolaters" (Qur'ān 15:94).

Ibn Kathīr and Aḥmad narrated the event, from Ibn 'Abbās.

> When Allah, the Most Sublime, revealed "And admonish your nearest kinsmen", the Prophet ascended the hill of al-Ṣafā, then called out: "O People." The people gathered, either in person or by sending representatives, and Allah's Messenger (ﷺ) said: " O Banī al-Muṭṭalib, O Banī Fahr, O Banī Lu'ay. What would you say if I informed you that horsemen stood at the bottom of this mountain and intended to attack you? Would you believe me?" They responded, "Yes." He then said: "I am, to you, a warner of the coming of a terrible punishment." Abū Lahab retorted: "May you perish! Have you gathered us just for this?" In response, Allah, the Most Sublime, revealed about Abū Lahab]: "Perish the hands of the father of flame! Perish he!" (Qur'ān 111:1).[98]

Ṣaḥīḥ Muslim recorded it slightly differently.

> When the verse "And admonish your nearest kinsmen" was revealed, Allah's Messenger called together the Quraysh and

98. See Ibn Kathīr, *al-Bidāyah wa al-Nihāyah*, vol. 4, 97.

addressed specific groups and individuals and the community in general. He said: "O People of Quraysh, save yourselves from the fire; O People of Banī Ka'b, save yourselves from the fire; O People of Banī Hāshim, save yourselves from the fire; O People of Banī 'Abd al-Muṭṭalib, save yourselves from the fire; O Fāṭimah, daughter of Muḥammad, save yourself from the fire. [I swear] by Allah that I cannot provide [any protection] for you from Allah [by virtue of our kinship], except that [we] have family ties that I will strive to uphold.[99]

Ṣaḥīḥ Muslim also recorded that 'Ā'isha said:

> When the following verse was revealed, "And admonish your nearest kinsmen", Allah's Messenger (ﷺ) invited his close relatives to a banquet. After they dined, he stood up and said: "O Fāṭimah, daughter of Muḥammad; O Ṣaffīyah, daughter of 'Abd al-Muṭṭalib; O Banī 'Abd al-Muṭṭalib; I cannot provide [any protection] for you from Allah [by virtue of our kinship]. Ask for as much of my wealth as you wish."[100]

These narratives may be reconciled by speculating that the time between the banquet that the Prophet (ﷺ) hosted for Banī Hāshim and Banī 'Abd al-Muṭṭalib, and his public address to all the clans of the Quraysh was short. We may therefore conclude that the permission to call his family members to Islam and the command to fulfil his mission in general occurred at the same time or, at least, very close together.

Ibn Isḥāq, however, provides a different perspective. He suggests that the dispute with the Quraysh occurred after the Prophet began to confront the Quraysh's corrupt system—through his attack on their gods, rather than immediately after the general call.

> When Allah's Messenger (ﷺ) began introducing Islam to his people and publicly declared what he was commanded by Allah, his people neither withdrew from him nor did they refute him—

99. This is an authentic narration in accordance with the stipulations of the two Shaykhs. *Ṣaḥīḥ Muslim*, "Kitāb al-Īmān", Chapter: "On Allah the Sublime's pronouncement": "*And admonish your nearest Kinsmen*", (1/192), Ḥadīth no. 204. It is also narrated by al-Tirmidhī, al-Nisā'ī and Aḥmad in his Musnad.

100. *Ṣaḥīḥ Muslim*, (1/192), Ḥadīth no. 205.

> according to what has been conveyed to me—until he mentioned their gods and found fault with them. When he did that, they rejected him, gathered in opposition, and displayed their enmity toward him, except for those who Allah, the Sublime, had protected by guiding them to Islam. These, however, were few, and hid their faith. The uncle of Allah's Messenger (ﷺ), Abū Ṭālib, showed sympathy to him and protected him, and Allah's Messenger (ﷺ) continued fulfilling Allah's command openly and was not deterred by anything.[101]

The Prophet's (ﷺ) criticism of the Quraysh's gods was carefully calculated. From the Quraysh's perspective, it was safer to ignore Muḥammad's (ﷺ) call, thereby minimising its import. However, he decided to shift the discourse away from the Qurayshi comfort zone and to follow a new strategy, the contours of which he was able to shape. This strategy aimed to provoke the Quraysh into reacting, which is exactly what the Prophet (ﷺ) achieved. Showing initiative and refusing to be confined to the corner his opponents had chosen for him were prominent strategic principles throughout the prophetic era. The Prophet (ﷺ) never allowed his enemy to restrict him to a fixed course of action, and he often surprised them with one initiative after another, forcing them into a state of perpetual reaction. Thus, it was the Prophet (ﷺ) who chose the moment to launch his call, and it was he who chose to push the Quraysh into a reactive mode by criticising and finding fault with their gods.

The Quraysh were not known for a strong sense of spirituality, nor was their religion a system of sublime beliefs and piety. It was, rather, a system of practical religiosity for a tribe that was driven by interests, benefits, and the balance of forces. They viewed religion through the prism of benefits and attainable privileges. Thus, a belittling of their beliefs was not, in itself, a provocation. The monotheists among them followed the religion of Ibrāhīm; they criticised the Quraysh for worshipping idols that brought neither benefit nor harm. In their hearts, the Quraysh knew that Allah was the only one to be worshipped, but they used their idols as a pretext to construct a unique identity. In the words of Ibrāhīm: "You have taken (for worship) idols instead of Allah,

101. Ibn Hishām, *al-Sīrah*, vol. 1, 264.

out of mutual love between yourselves in this life" (Qur'ān 29:25).

The Quraysh instrumentalised the idols for their material benefit. Further, they worshipped well-known idols such as Hubal, Isāf, and Nā'ilah, but allowed the other Arab tribes to bring their own idols and place them around the Ka'bah. In allowing this, the Quraysh used the presence of the other tribes' idols to entrench Makkah as a religious centre for all Arabs, a status that garnered huge trade and political benefits. Why else would they place more than 360 idols around the Ka'bah? The idols, the pilgrimage season, and the system of al-Hums were all tools that the Quraysh utilised to shore up their power and increase their material benefit. The Prophet's criticism of these gods and rituals, therefore, was direct criticism of the entire system: tribal superiority, financial exploitation, and the abuse of religion. It attacked the heart of the Qurayshi political, economic, and social structure and was, therefore, not something they could afford to overlook or ignore.

The Qurayshi strategy

Makkah was a tribal mercantilist society; business always prefers stability and hates surprises. The Quraysh worked hard to maintain the status quo. In cases where it found itself forced into a reactive and defensive stance, it followed a scripted strategy: its response would be incremental, beginning with negotiations, switching to measured threats if diplomacy yielded no satisfactory results, and taking escalatory measures only if the other options failed.

The Quraysh's strategic decisions were taken through consensus in the House of Assembly, where the leaders of all its clans and sub-clans were present. However, in a case where the antagonist was a Qurayshi and was supported by two important clans, the Banī Hāshim and the Banī al-Muṭṭalib in this case, the decision-making would take place outside the Dār al-Nadwah, with the various parties consulting their closest allies. Since the Prophet (ﷺ) was from a house that was affiliated to the Alliance of the Virtuous, it was expected that the other camp—the Alliance of the Allies—would consult and discuss appropriate responses within its ranks. Furthermore, since the Banī

'Abd Shams was not a part of the Alliance of the Virtuous due to an ancient dispute between Hāshim and Umayyah ibn 'Abd Shams, they were co-opted into these consultations.

The leadership structure of the Quraysh had two levels. The first was made up of senior leaders; they were tribal elders who were advanced in age and status. The most prominent of these were al-Walīd ibn al-Mughīrah, the head of the Banī Makhzūm; Abū Uḥayḥah ibn al-'Āṣ ibn Umayyah ibn 'Abd Shams; and 'Utbah and Shaybah, the sons of Rabī'ah. These elders possessed vision, an inclination to resolve conflicts through negotiation, and a desire to maintain the integrity and unity of the Quraysh.

The second level was the younger generation, most of whom were the Prophet's (ﷺ) peers. It included Abū al-Ḥakam 'Amr ibn Hishām, a nephew of al-Walīd ibn al-Mughīrah who the Muslims came to refer to as Abū Jahl; Abū Sufyān Ḥarb ibn Ṣakhar, 'Utbah's nephew and son-in-law; al-Nuḍar ibn al-Ḥārith; 'Uqbah ibn Abī Mu'īṭ; al-Aswad ibn 'Abd Yagūth; and al-Ḥārith ibn Qays ibn 'Adī. This group was more impetuous and impulsive. The role of the senior leaders had become mostly ceremonial, but it could also be decisive when the need arose. Everyday executive leadership was, however, delegated to the second level.

The escalation of the confrontation between the Muslims and the Quraysh was sparked by a few isolated incidents. The first, which was also the first case in which blood was spilt in Islamic history, occurred when Sa'd ibn Abī Waqqāṣ and a few Muslims journeyed to a mountain pass outside Makkah to pray. When a group of idolaters confronted them and criticised their prayer, Sa'd struck one of them with a camel bone, cutting him open. Ibn Ḥajar mentions that the first Muslim killed was the stepson of Allah's Messenger (ﷺ), al-Ḥārith ibn Abī Hālah. Ibn al-Kalbī and Ibn Ḥazm said that al-Ḥārith "was the first person killed in the path of Allah, at the Yemeni corner [of the Ka'bah]." Al-'Askarī states in *al-Awā'il*: "When Allah commanded his Prophet (ﷺ) to openly proclaim what he was commanded, he stood up in the Holy Sanctuary and said: 'Say there is no god but Allah and attain success.' But they attacked him, and the screams were heard by his family. Al-

Ḥārith ibn Abī Hālah came to his aid and struck some of them but they struck back, and he was killed. He was the first martyr."[102]

The most significant escalation occurred when Abū Jahl and a few impulsive Qurayshi leaders confronted the Prophet (ﷺ) and the Muslims, not long after the Prophet (ﷺ) had declared his mission. This incident suggested that tensions had reached dangerous levels and warned of the possibility of open conflict within the Quraysh. The confrontation concerned the senior leaders, who were afraid that further escalation could see tribal alliances being mobilised and the conflict spiralling out of control. Two of these elders, al-Walīd ibn al-Mughīrah and 'Utbah ibn Rabī'ah, were, at the time, holidaying in Ṭā'if. This was usual for the rich Qurayshi leaders; they escaped Makkah's sweltering summer heat by taking refuge in their Ṭā'if farms and homes. When the elders heard about the incident with Abū Jahl, al-Walīd and 'Utbah ended their vacation and returned to Makkah to contain the tensions.

The Qurayshi elders decided to personally intervene and find a solution to the Muḥammad (ﷺ) problem. They implemented a series of steps, beginning with a conversation with and direct advice to the Prophet (ﷺ).

Ibn Isḥāq reports on these meetings, which were initiated by 'Utbah ibn Rabī'ah.

> 'Utbah sat by Allah's Messenger (ﷺ) and said: "O my nephew. You are aware of your status in the family and your standing in terms of lineage. But you have come to your people with a serious matter that has divided them and ridiculed their customs. You have criticised their gods and their religion, and you have denounced their forefathers. Listen to me and allow me to present some proposals for your consideration. Perhaps you will accept some of them.
>
> Allah's Messenger (ﷺ) said: "I am listening, O Abū al-Walīd."
>
> He said: "O Nephew, if you want wealth, we will gather for you from our wealth so that you will be the richest among us; if

102. Ibn Ḥajar, *al-Iṣābah*, vol. 1, 696.

you want prestige, we will make you our leader so that we will not take any decision without you; and if you want to become a king, we will coronate you as our king. And if this that comes to you is such that you cannot be rid of it, we will seek a cure, and spare no expense until you have been cured, for a man is sometimes overcome until he is treated."

When 'Utbah stopped, the Prophet (ﷺ) asked him: "Are you done, O Abū al-Walīd?"

He said: "Yes."

The Prophet then said: "Now listen to me."

He said: "I will."

Allah's Messenger (ﷺ) then recited [these verses of the Qur'ān]: "In the name of Allah, The Most Gracious, the Most Merciful. Ḥa Mīm. A revelation from the Most Gracious, the Most Merciful. A book whose verses are explained in detail; a Qur'ān in Arabic, for people who understand" (Qur'ān 41:1-3). Allah's Messenger (ﷺ) continued to recite verses from this chapter of the Qur'ān. When 'Utbah heard them, he listened intently, and put his hands behind his back, leaning on them, as he listened to the Prophet.

Allah's Messenger (ﷺ) continued the recitation until he reached the verse commanding prostration [Qur'ān 41:37], and he prostrated. He then said: "Have you heard, O Abū al-Walīd?"

He said: "I have heard."

The Prophet then said: "It is up to you to do as you please."

'Utbah then returned to his companions and some of them said to each other: "We swear by Allah, Abū al-Walīd has come back to you with a very different look on his face, not like that when he had left." When they gathered around him, they asked: "What's the matter, O Abū al-Walīd?" He said: "What it is, I swear by Allah, is that I have just heard something the like of which I have never heard before. I swear by Allah that it is not poetry, nor is it the whisperings of a soothsayer. O people of Quraysh, take my advice and do as I am doing. Do not come between this man and what he is engaged in; leave him be. For I swear by Allah that the words I heard from him carry a prediction. If the Arabs kill him, then others will have rid you of him. And if he is victorious over the Arabs, then his sovereignty is your sovereignty and his honour is your honour, and you will be most pleased with him."

They said, "He has bewitched you with his tongue , O Abū al-Walīd."

He said, "I offer you my opinion, so do what you feel is correct."[103]

Another narration claims that it was al-Walīd ibn al-Mughīrah who addressed the Prophet (ﷺ). It is likely that al-Walīd made a second attempt, but that the outcome was similar to that of 'Utbah's, and that al-Walīd did not take a final stand after having listened to the Prophet (ﷺ). Ibn Isḥāq relates that it was Abū Jahl who convinced al-Walīd to take a firmer stand against the Prophet.

[Abū Jahl] went to [al-Walīd ibn al-Mughīrah] and said: "O Uncle, your people want to collect money for you." He asked, "Why?" [Abū Jahl] replied: "As a gift to you, since you have gone to Muḥammad, and so that you oppose that which he has accepted." [Al-Walīd] said: "The Quraysh know that I am one of the richest among them." Abū Jahl said: "Then say something about him that will convince your people that you reject him."

Al-Walīd did go back to his people and suggested to them that they say that Muḥammad was a sorcerer, since he had caused dissension between relatives.[104]

The context of this narrative suggests that the senior leadership was initially hesitant to adopt a unified harsh position against the Prophet (ﷺ), because that would hasten a confrontation. They knew

103. Ibn Hishām, *al-Sīrah*, vol.1, 293-294.
104. Ibn Kathīr. *al-Bidāyah wa al-Nihāyah*, vol.4, 152.

that the outcome of such a decision would be strife within the Quraysh, and they wanted to avoid such a situation. In another similar incident, we observe the hesitation of another leader of equal stature to al-Walīd and 'Utbah in terms of seniority. Abū Uḥayḥah ibn al-'Āṣ spoke to his people by addressing their interests.

> Abū Uḥayḥah ibn al-'Āṣ said: "Leave Muḥammad alone and do not confront him. If what he says is true, he is one of us and not someone outside the Quraysh. If he is a liar, the Quraysh will confront him without you having to."
>
> The Prophet (ﷺ) would walk past Abū Uḥayḥah, and he would say: "Verily he speaks from the heavens." Al-Nuḍar ibn al-Ḥārith then went to him and said: "I have heard that you say positive things about Muḥammad. How is that possible, when he curses the gods, claims that our forebears are in the fire, and promises those who do not follow him a grievous punishment?" Thereafter, Abū Uḥayḥah became hostile toward Allah's Messenger (ﷺ), condemned him, and criticised his message. He said: "We have not heard anything like that which he has brought, neither in Judaism nor in Christianity."[105]

In both these cases, younger leaders intervened to pressure al-Walīd and Abū Uḥayḥah to change their stances: Abū Jahl in the case of al-Walīd and al-Nuḍar ibn al-Ḥārith in the case of Abū Uḥayḥah.

Despite these efforts, the Qurayshi leaders failed to dissuade the Prophet (ﷺ) from spreading his message. This was expected, since the Qurayshi approach, consistent with its outlook, was to view all matters in terms of interests that could be resolved by promises of material gain or leadership and authority. In contrast, the Prophet (ﷺ) addressed issues on a principled basis, which was an approach on a higher ethical plane. The Quraysh were, therefore, unable either to refute him or to ignore him. They were aware that their unique legitimacy derived from the Ancient House and the Sanctuary, which was undeniably tied to the legacy of Ibrāhīm (Abraham). The Prophet (ﷺ) threatened that legitimacy with his claim that he followed the creed of Abraham the monotheist, who never worshipped anyone or anything except Allah,

105. Aḥmad ibn Yaḥyā al-Balādhurī, *Ansāb al-Ashrāf* (Beirut: Dār al-Fikr, 1996), vol. 1, p. 141.

the One and Only, and that his call was for them to return to the purity of the Abrahamic faith. It was that faith that had laid the foundation for their symbols of exceptionalism: the Ka'bah, the Holy Sanctuary, the sacred months, and the pilgrimage. The Prophet (ﷺ) also invited them to embrace fairness, justice, and equality; to abandon greed and commercial crookedness; and to uphold family ties. On what basis, then, could they malign his message?

Direct negotiations with the Prophet (ﷺ) produced no results for the Quraysh and only made them angrier; they knew in their hearts that his message was both serious and dangerous, that it transcended all existing discourses about the gods, and that it went as far as to subvert the entire Qurayshi system of values. Moreover, Muḥammad (ﷺ), who they had known as al-Amīn (the Trustworthy one), did not seek temporal authority or worldly gain. This made both message and messenger inherently immune to any obvious shortcomings in capacity and legitimacy. For the Quraysh, it therefore became imperative to raise the bar of negotiations and to approach the leader of the Banī Hāshim, the Prophet's (ﷺ) uncle and protector.

Abū Ṭālib was a respected Qurayshi elder, leader of the Banī Hāshim, and responsible for the duties of Food Provisioning and Water Supply. He was known as a champion of the values that defined the Hāshimites, such as assistance to the needy, resistance to oppression, and defence of the truth. Abū Ṭālib was, however, not wealthy like other Qurayshi leaders who were his equals. The first delegation that visited Abū Ṭālib to discuss this issue comprised ten individuals: Al-Walīd ibn al-Mughīrah and Abū Jahl from the Banī Makhzūm; 'Utbah and Shaybah, the sons of Rabī'ah, and Abū Sufyān ibn Ḥarb, all from the Banī 'Abd Shams; Abū al-Bukhtarī al-'Āṣ ibn Hishām and al-Aswad ibn 'Abd al-Muṭṭalib from the Banī Asad ibn 'Abd al-'Uzza; and Nabih and Munabbih, the sons of al-Hajjāj, and al-'Āṣ ibn Wā'il, all from the Banī Saham.

The first round of negotiations with Abū Ṭālib was calm, and the delegation addressed him respectfully, asking him to force Muḥammad (ﷺ) to end his campaign against them. They recounted their problems with the Prophet (ﷺ): he criticised their gods, regarded their customs as nonsensical, and confronted them in the markets and their places of gathering. Abū Ṭālib responded with kindness and words of reassurance, and he promised to do his best to convince Muḥammad (ﷺ).

It is noteworthy that most of the members of the delegation were not signatories to the Alliance of the Virtuous. The exception was the Banī Asad ibn ʻAbd al-ʻUzza, which was represented by Abū al-Bukhtarī and al-Aswad. The delegation did not include anyone from the Banī Zahrah, the Banī Taym, the Banī Hāshim, or the Banī al-Muṭṭalib.

Abū Ṭālib discussed the delegation's visit with the Prophet (ﷺ) and conveyed their request that he stop ridiculing their gods and confronting them in the markets and places of gathering. Their obvious intention was to coerce him into altogether abandoning conveying his message to the people. However, the Prophet (ﷺ) made it clear that he would continue his mission. Abū Ṭālib did not act to prevent him from doing so; he simply remained silent when the Prophet (ﷺ) responded.

The second round of negotiations was marked by a dangerous escalation. Members of the delegation did not mince words; they threatened Abū Ṭālib, asked him to lift the protection he had extended to his nephew, and instructed him not to stand between them and Muḥammad (ﷺ). He was warned that if he refused their requests, the situation would escalate into violence and a resort to arms.

> [They told him:] "O Abū Ṭālib, you are a man of a venerable age and honour, and you enjoy a high status among us. We asked you to keep your nephew away from us and you have not done so. By God, we will not restrain ourselves when our ancestors are insulted, when our customs are ridiculed as nonsensical, or when our gods are insulted. Unless you stop him, we will fight both him and you until one of us is destroyed."
>
> Abū Ṭālib then summoned the Prophet (ﷺ) and told him: "O nephew, your people have come to me [with their protests and threats]. Consider both my and your [predicament], and do not burden me with more than I can bear." Allah's Messenger (ﷺ) thought that his uncle was about to despair and would submit to the Quraysh's demands, and that his resolve to protect and stand

with him was weakening. Allah's Messenger (ﷺ) replied: "O Uncle, I swear by Allah, even if they were to put the sun in my right hand and the moon in my left to convince me to abandon my mission, I will not do so until Allah makes it manifest or I die trying." His eyes welled up with tears, and when he turned to leave, Abū Ṭālib called to him: "Come closer nephew." Allah's Messenger (ﷺ) approached. He then said: "Go forth, my nephew, and say whatever you please. I swear by Allah that I will never give you up, no matter what."

In the third round of negotiations, the Quraysh presented a desperate offer, suggesting that they had run out of options. They asked Abū Ṭālib to hand Muḥammad (ﷺ) over to them so that they could kill him. They offered to give Abū Ṭālib one of the handsomest young men in the Quraysh, 'Ammārah ibn al-Walīd, as a substitute son in Muḥammad's (ﷺ) place. Abū Ṭālib responded sarcastically to the ludicrous offer: "What a terrible offer! I must give you my son so that you may kill him, and you will give me your son so that I may feed him on your behalf! I swear, by Allah, that this will never happen."[106]

Infiltration of the homes of the elite

With negotiations having collapsed, it was clear that the Quraysh's attempts to stop the Prophet (ﷺ) had failed, and that the situation was completely out of their control. The accusation that he was a "sorcerer", which some of the Quraysh had concocted, did not produce the hoped-for result of inhibiting those who had already embraced the new religion, nor did it prevent others from converting. In addition, the negotiations with Abū Ṭālib and the Banī Hāshim had reached a dead end.

The Quraysh were keen to deal quickly with the issue of the Prophet (ﷺ), before news of his mission could negatively affect their status among the Arab tribes. Gatherings in the 'Ukāẓ, Majannah, and Dhi'l Majāz markets, as well as the pilgrimage season, helped spread news to all corners of the Arabian Peninsula that something was awry in Makkah. The Quraysh subsisted on status and reputation,

106. For the full account see Ibn Hishām, *al-Sīrah*, vol. 1, 266.

and reputation and stability were the foremost assets of Makkah as a commercial centre. The Quraysh's concern was that the dissemination of news about the Prophet (ﷺ) would leave a negative impression of its internal affairs and undermine its image of coherence and unity that had earned it respect and praise. Many tribes hoped for divisions to emerge in Makkah. The Khuzā'ah, for example, would not forget its expulsion from Makkah by the Quraysh; the Qays 'Īlān tribes had fought against the Quraysh for three decades during the Immoral Wars and would be pleased to see the Quraysh weakened.

The second pressing problem facing the Quraysh, which required them to act quickly, was that the number of followers of the new religion was continuously increasing. Moreover, its converts came not only from among the weak, the client class or the slaves; most were from Qurayshi clans and many of the youth belonged to the homes of the leadership elite.

It was surprising that the Prophet's (ﷺ) message was able to infiltrate the homes of the Qurayshi elite and spread in the hostile Qurayshi heartland in the early Islamic period. Many sons and daughters of Qurayshi leaders embraced Islam, and not a single Qurayshi noble house was left untouched by Islam in its first five years. For a society that prides itself on its lineage, sanctifies the heritage of its ancestors, and is committed to following their guidance, it is no easy task to convince its children to abandon the religion of their fathers and to embrace a new faith. Even more remarkable was the fact that the converts were sons and daughters of leaders from all the Qurayshi clans. They were not only from Banī Hāshim or Banī 'Abd Manāf or from the Alliance of the Scented; some of the new recruits were from Banī Makhzūm, Banī Saham, Banī Jumaḥ, Banī 'Āmir, Banī 'Adī, Banī Taym, Banī Zahrah, and Banī 'Abd Shams.[107]

It is instructive to consider the case of the most malicious Qurayshi clan in the violent campaign against the Prophet (ﷺ): the Banī Makhzūm. From this clan, Al-Walīd ibn al-Mughīrah led the war of words and politics against the Muslims, while 'Amr ibn Hishām led the campaign of terror and violence, which earned him the moniker of Abū Jahl (Father

107. Ibn Hishām, *al-Sīrah*, vol. 1, 266.

of Ignorance). Some commentators suggest that 'Amr's uncle al-Walīd was the first to call him by the name Abū Jahl, after he witnessed his arbitrary, dismissive, and harsh treatment of the Muslims. However, it was more likely Muslims who gave him this nickname. Both these homes were infiltrated by the very message that they were campaigning against. This is probably what angered Abū Jahl almost to the point of insanity; there could be little that could infuriate a man more than the loss of his family's support and his children siding with his enemy, unflinchingly abandoning his religion, and dismissing his opinion as nonsense. Even if one could tolerate sons defying their fathers, in a patriarchal society, daughters defying their fathers was unthinkable.

It was quite amazing, then, that among the first Muslims, including those who emigrated to Abyssinia, were many young men and women of the Banī Makhzūm. Salamah ibn Hishām ibn al-Mughīrah, Abū Jahl's full brother and a nephew of al-Walīd ibn al-Mughīrah, was one of the first to embrace Islam and was among the Muslims who emigrated to Abyssinia in the fifth year of the Prophetic mission. Others included Hishām ibn Abī Hudhayfah ibn al-Mughīrah, Abū Jahal's nephew, and his half-brother 'Ayyāsh ibn Abī Rabī'ah; and Umm Salamah bint Abī Umayyah Hudhayfah ibn al-Mughīrah, the full sister of 'Abdallah ibn Abī Umayyah and of Abū Jahl's cousin, who migrated to Abyssinia with her husband.

Other Qurayshi houses were also infiltrated. Converts from the Banī 'Adī included Zayd ibn al-Khaṭṭāb and his sister Fāṭimah. Islam and the Muslim community were then strengthened by the conversion of 'Umar ibn al-Khaṭṭāb, the son of Abū Jahl's sister Ḥantamah bint Hāshim ibn al-Mughīrah. Another of Abū Jahl's nephews to embrace Islam was Hishām ibn al-Āṣ ibn Wā'il, a chief of the Banī Saham, whose mother was Ḥarmalah bint Hishām. Al-Ḥajjāj, the son of the leader of the Banī Saham, Munabbih ibn al-Ḥajjāj, also embraced Islam.

'Uthmān ibn Maẓ'ūn, a nephew of Umayyah ibn Khalaf, the chief of the Banī Jumaḥ, was another convert. Other converts included 'Abdallah and Abū Jandal, the sons of Suhayl ibn 'Amr, the chief of the Banī 'Āmir ibn Lu'ay, as well as his brother Sulayṭ ibn 'Āmir, and his daughter Sahlah bint Sahl. Furthermore, Sahlah migrated to Abyssinia with her husband Abū Hudhayfah, who was the son of the chief of the Banī ʻAbd Shams, ʻUtbah ibn Rabīʻah, one of Makkah's most cunning leaders and, later, the Quraysh leader at the Battle of Badr.

Converts from the Banī ʻAbd Shams included ʻAmr and his brother Khālid, who were the sons of Saʻīd ibn al-ʻĀṣ, a chief of the Banī ʻAbd Shams. One of the most well-known early converts was ʻUthmān ibn ʻAffān, Abū Sufyān's nephew. Abū Sufyān's daughter Umm Ḥabībah also embraced Islam and was one of the émigrés to Abyssinia. The conversion of the Prophet's wife Khadījah bint Khuwaylid, from the Banī Asad ibn ʻAbd al-ʻUzza, led to the conversion of many people from the Banī Asad, including her nephews al-Zubayr ibn al-ʻAwwām ibn Khuwaylid and Khālid ibn Ḥizām. Khālid was the son of the Banī Asad leader (and Khadījah's brother), Ḥiẓām ibn Khuwaylid, and the brother of another chief, Ḥakīm ibn Ḥizām. Firās, son of the malevolent al-Nuḍar ibn al-Ḥārith, the leader of the Banī ʻAbd al-Dār, also embraced Islam and emigrated to Abyssinia, with two others from the Banī ʻAbd al-Dār: Muṣʻab ibn ʻUmayr and his brother Abū al-Rūm.

Beyond these individual conversions, Qurayshi leaders were even more unsettled by their failure to convince the Banī Hāshim and the Banī ʻAbd al-Muṭṭalib to withdraw their protection from the Prophet (ﷺ). In fact, Abū Jahl's callousness convinced Ḥamzah ibn ʻAbd al-Muṭṭalib—an uncle of the Prophet who was renowned for his courage—to openly declare his Islam. When Ḥamzah heard that Abū Jahl had physically accosted the Prophet (ﷺ) and insulted him, he sought him out and struck him with his bow, cutting open his head. Ḥamzah then told Abū Jahl: "Do you dare to curse him while I follow his religion and proclaim what he proclaims? Direct your curses to me if you can."

Islam's entry into the homes of the Qurayshi leaders caused them immense distress. When their gentle persuasion failed to convince their children to reconsider their new religion, they resorted to compulsion, incarceration, and torture. The elite tribal status of these Muslims did not afford them any protection; indeed, it became the cause of their oppression by their fathers. The preferred punishment was incarceration. Abū Jahl imprisoned his nephew Hishām after the latter's return from Abyssinia, and Hishām was able to migrate to Madinah only after the

Battle of the Trench, about four years after the other Muslims had migrated. Abū Jahl also imprisoned his older brother Salamah ibn Hishām and pursued his half-brother 'Ayyāsh ibn Abī Rabī'ah all the way to Madinah, returning him to Makkah in chains, and keeping him prisoner until after the Battle of the Trench.

Muṣ'ab ibn 'Umayr was tortured and incarcerated by his mother. Hishām ibn al-Āṣ ibn Wā'il was incarcerated by his family, and 'Abdallah and Abū Jandal by their father Suhayl ibn 'Amr. 'Abdallah escaped before the Battle of Badr and joined the Muslims in Madinah, while Abū Jandal remained imprisoned until after the Treaty of Ḥudaybīyyah, four years after his brother's escape. The Quraysh resorted to incarceration as the most common form of sanction because they were, in general, unwilling to use extreme forms of punishment against the sons and daughters of the elite. Some Muslims were beaten, as in the case of numerous attacks on 'Uthmān ibn 'Affān and Abū Bakr. However, tribal pride and the network of tribal alliances, in addition to the common practice of granting amnesty to those who sought it, all helped constrain the Quraysh from going to extremes in inflicting harm on the Muslims from the elite.

From a small band to a community

By the fifth year of the Prophet's (ﷺ) mission, the Muslim community was fully formed, with an identifiable social structure. It had grown in number, with close to 300 adherents from every social class in Makkan society. In this period, the Muslims were from a range of tribal groups and social backgrounds, coalescing in a unique manner. In addition to those from the elite who had embraced Islam, the community also included clients, slaves, and other marginalised people.

This group included Zayd ibn Ḥārithah, a client of Allah's Messenger (ﷺ); the family of Yāsir, which was allied to the Banī Makhzūm; Bilāl ibn Rabāḥ, a slave owned by Umayyah ibn Khalaf; Ṣuhayb al-Rūmī, a client of 'Abdallah ibn Jad'ān; and Khabbāb ibn al-Arat, who belonged to a woman slave-owner called Umm Anmār. It also included 'Abdallah ibn Umm Maktūm, because of whom Allah reprimanded His Messenger (ﷺ).[108] The reprimand happened after the Prophet (ﷺ) had ignored Ibn Umm Maktūm's question, because he was trying to convince some Qurayshi leaders to accept Islam. Whenever the Prophet (ﷺ) met him after that incident, the Messenger of Allah (ﷺ) smiled and said: "Welcome to the one because of whom my Lord reprimanded me."

Other converts from marginalised sections of Makkan society included 'Abdallah ibn Mas'ūd, a goat herder who worked for 'Uqbah ibn Abī Mu'īṭ; and Sālim, a client of Abū Hudhayfah. The community also included former slaves who had been liberated by Abū Bakr. Bilāl ibn Rabāḥ was the most well-known of them, but the group also included others, such as 'Āmir ibn Fuhayrah, Fakīh al-Azdi, Umm Shumays, Zunnayrah, al-Hindīyyah and her daughter, the slave girl from the Banī Mu'mil who had been held by the Banī 'Adī, and Umm 'Umays, who had been held by the Banī Taym.

The Quraysh severely punished converts from these marginalised groups. They were dealt with more harshly than the children of the elite. Some were tortured to death, such as Sumayyah bint al-Khayyāṭ, the first female martyr in Islam, and her husband Yāsir ibn 'Āmir. Both were murdered by Abū Jahl. Their son 'Ammār ibn Yāsir managed to escape only after he dissimulated and agreed to curse the Prophet (ﷺ), though he remained a Muslim. Some from the marginalised classes were branded with fire, such as Khabbāb ibn al-Arat; others, such as Bilāl ibn Rabāḥ, were tortured with rocks, which were placed on their bodies while they lay supine in the sweltering desert heat. Ṣuhayb al-Rūmī, a client, repeatedly lost consciousness due to the severity of his torture. He was allowed to migrate to Madinah only after he handed over all his wealth to his persecutors.[109]

By this stage, in the fifth year of the Prophet's mission, the Quraysh were divided, and its leaders had lost control over the course of history. This might explain their abuse and brutality. For these Qurayshi leaders, the most painful fact was that the majority of the Prophet's (ﷺ) followers were themselves Qurayshi. His strategy to entrench the idea of a "New Quraysh" that confronted the "Old Quraysh" had succeeded.

108. Ibn Kathīr, *Tafsīr al-Qur'ān*, vol. 8, 320.
109. Ibn Hishām, *al-Sīrah*, vol. 1, 477.

The New Quraysh was Muslim, predominantly young, and looked forward to the future. The basis of its worldview was monotheism and all that this entailed, including liberation, equality, and justice. The Old Quraysh, however, was idolatrous, elderly, clung to ancient values and customs, remained committed to venerating their ancestors' heritage, lived in the past, and was trapped in a hierarchy of lineage and status.

The first deployment

The Prophet's (ﷺ) choice of Abyssinia (the Kingdom of Aksum) as the destination for the migration of his companions in the sixth year of his mission was a strategic, carefully considered, and insightful choice. The Abyssinians were Christians, or People of the Book, and understood the concept of divine revelation. Since they had long engaged the Quraysh and other Arab tribes, they knew the Arabs as idol worshippers. Therefore, if some Arab was to appear and proclaim beliefs similar to the Christian doctrine, that person would be more easily understood and more deserving of respect than someone who worshipped idols.

From another perspective, a Muslim presence in Abyssinia would give them a strategic advantage over the Quraysh because of the country's importance to Qurayshi trade. The Quraysh did not have many options in how to respond. They also had to be careful not to anger the king of a country with which they traded. It is apparent that the Prophet (ﷺ) was familiar with the political climate of Abyssinia, which explains the manner in which he described its king to his companions when he suggested Abyssinia as a destination for their migration. "If you were to go to the land of Abyssinia," he told them, "you would find a king who does not oppress anyone. It is also a land of truth, [where you may remain] until Allah grants you respite from the state in which you find yourselves."[110]

The first group of the Prophet's (ﷺ) companions departed for Abyssinia in the fifth year of his mission and included twelve persons, led by 'Uthmān ibn 'Affān. He was accompanied by his wife Ruqayyah, the daughter of Allah's Messenger (ﷺ).

110. Ibn Hishām, *al-Sīrah,* vol. 1, 321.

Most historical texts suggest that the migration to Abyssinia was for asylum from the persecution of the Quraysh. This is a correct but not a complete interpretation. The meaning and significance of the migration suggests much more than simply oppressed people seeking asylum. A careful examination of the names of the early migrants to Abyssinia reveals that they belonged to respected families and held notable positions within the Quraysh; it is unlikely, therefore, that they had been forced to flee Qurayshi tyranny. In addition to the Umayyad 'Uthmān ibn 'Affān and his Hāshimite wife Ruqayyah, the group included other sons and daughters of the Makkan elite, such as Abū Hudhayfah ibn 'Utbah ibn Rabī'ah and his wife Sahlah bint Suhayl ibn 'Amr; al-Zubayr ibn al-'Awwām ibn Khuwaylid ibn Asad; 'Abd al-Raḥmān ibn 'Awf from the Banī Zahrah; 'Abdallah ibn Jaḥsh from the Banī Asad and his wife Umm Ḥabībah bint Abī Sufyān. Almost the entire delegation was comprised of individuals from well-known clans of Makkah rather than from the marginalised classes. The only exception was 'Abdallah ibn Mas'ūd, an ally of the Banī Zahrah, who had worked as a goat herder for 'Uqbah ibn Abī Mu'īṭ.

The Quraysh severely targeted the Muslims in this period, but those who suffered the most were believers from the marginalised classes: the clients, slaves, and liberated slaves. Men such as 'Uthmān ibn 'Affān, 'Abd al-Raḥmān ibn 'Awf, and Abū Hudhayfah ibn 'Utbah were not from these classes, and tribal custom granted them sufficient protection that they would not have to flee.

The migration was, therefore, more likely a fact-finding and diplomatic mission that sought to establish relations with the Abyssinian king. This explains why the delegation returned after a short period and began preparations for a second migration to Abyssinia for more than eighty persons. This second group did include people from Makkah's marginalised classes. The first migration was, thus, a diplomatic deployment for the purpose of establishing relations and to prepare the ground for the reception of other migrants; the second migration comprised a larger group, most of whom sought asylum.

Reports on the migration to Abyssinia show that the relationship between the Muslims and the political administration of the Kingdom of Aksum strengthened as a result. The Muslims now had an established embassy in Abyssinia, headed by the Prophet's (ﷺ) cousin Ja'far ibn Abī Ṭālib. The Negus was personally touched by the Islamic message and later embraced the new faith. He also provided full support and protection to the migrants, rendering unsuccessful the efforts of 'Amr ibn al-'Āṣ, the Quraysh's envoy, to convince the Negus to hand over the Muslims.

This argument is strengthened by the fact that some of the migrants stayed there for a long time and the last group—under the leadership of Ja'far ibn Abī Ṭālib—returned only after the signing of the Treaty of Ḥudaybīyyah. If the main objective of the Muslim presence in Abyssinia was to escape to a place where they could freely practise their religion, they would have returned and joined the Prophet (ﷺ) in Madinah after his migration to that city. However, their long stay in Abyssinia suggests that they had other priorities, such as spreading the message and maintaining and strengthening relations with a friendly political power. These were necessary tasks and part of the project to firmly establish the foundations of the Islamic state in Madinah; a hostile Abyssinia could have posed an additional threat to the fledgling Muslim polity, adding to the many other dangers that surrounded them in the Arabian Peninsula. Ja'far's deployment to Abyssinia began before the Muslim migration to Madinah, and it lasted until the Khaybar campaign. It is not clear whether there was Muslim representation in Abyssinia after Khaybar, but it is likely that some Abyssinians had embraced Islam and continued to spread the message after Ja'far and his companions had returned.

It must be stressed that the conversion of the Negus to Islam did not mean that the Abyssinian political administration had been Islamised. The king had secretly converted, and the kingdom remained Christian. Christianity was the backbone of political legitimacy in Abyssinia, and the king would have lost his throne had he announced his conversion to another religion. He kept his Islam concealed and allowed the Muslims to practise their religion and to invite others to it.

Ibn Isḥāq relates that a group of Christians who had become familiar with the Prophet's (ﷺ) message in Abyssinia visited him in Makkah and embraced Islam.

> Then about twenty Christians came to Allah's Messenger (ﷺ) while he was in Makkah, after news about him had reached them in Abyssinia. They found him in the mosque and sat with him, conversed with him, and questioned him, while men of the Quraysh sat in their regular gatherings around the Ka'bah. When they had finished questioning Allah's Messenger (ﷺ), he invited them to Allah, the Most Sublime, and recited the Qur'ān to them. When they heard the Qur'ān, their eyes welled up with tears and they accepted Allah's call, believed in the Prophet (ﷺ), and confirmed the truth [of his message]. They recognised in him what their scriptures had described about him. When they left the Prophet (ﷺ), Abū Jahl ibn Hishām and a few other Qurayshis confronted them. He told them: "By Allah, what a disappointing delegation! Your co-religionists sent you to gather news about this man on their behalf, but your meeting with him was so unsettling that you renounced your religion and believed him and his claims. We are not aware of a delegation more foolish than yours." Or words to that effect. They responded: "Peace be upon you. We do not disregard what you say, but it is for us to decide what we follow, and for you that which you follow. We only want what is best for ourselves."[111]

The context of this exchange makes it clear that Abū Jahl and the Qurayshi leaders with him were aware of the purpose of the Christian delegation, that it was a fact-finding mission sent by their people to establish the truth about the new prophet. According to some accounts, the delegation had come from Najran, but they were more likely from Abyssinia, sent by the Negus to establish the truth about the new religion. When the delegation returned to the Negus having become Muslims, he was further motivated to embrace Islam himself.

Locating the Negus

In order to view the full picture, we should corroborate the places and names related to the migration to Abyssinia; this will help clarify the political map and identify the strategic relationships at the time. There

111. Ibn Hishām, *al-Sīrah*, vol.1, 391-392.

is an ongoing debate, which raged in the 1980s and 1990s and continues today, on two critical issues: the precise destination of the migration, and the identity of the king to whose lands the Muslims had migrated. I witnessed these debates in the early 1990s when I was a student of African Studies at the International African University in Khartoum. The College of African Studies was consumed by discussions and research on both these questions.

There are divergent views regarding the destination of the migration, with all views being backed up by evidence. Some suggest that the migration was to Aksum, in current-day Ethiopia, while others hold that it was to Massawa, in current-day Eritrea, on the Red Sea coastline. Several Sudanese scholars—led by the late ‘Abdallah al-Ṭayyib—believe that the migration was to Suakin, a city in northeast Sudan and previously the country's main port. Suakin is located on the opposite bank of the Red Sea, across from the port of al-Shu‘aybah, from where the Makkans had sailed to Abyssinia. This debate arose, in part, from legitimate queries about the journey's route, but it was also motivated by the national pride of three countries—Ethiopia, Eritrea, and Sudan—that were competing for the honour of being the first country to which the Muslims migrated.

Such debates are not easily resolved. It is therefore useful to pursue more in-depth research on this matter. It is also important that the research goes beyond Islamic source material and encompasses the histories of other nations and the disciplines of archaeology, philology, genetics, and other modern sciences to shed light on this and other issues in the Prophet's (ﷺ) life. His biography has not yet been subjected to a serious inquiry that brings together modern sciences with historical sources. This is a task for scholars from a range of specialisations, and one that will enable us to serve the Prophet's (ﷺ) life with the best available tools of our time.

Regarding the objective of this book, which focuses on the strategic dimensions of the Prophet's (ﷺ) life, it is sufficient that the expression al-Ḥabashah (Abyssinia) was used by Arabs to indicate the regions located on the opposite bank of the Red Sea. In the seventh century, the Kingdom of Aksum did not encompass the territories that cover the current state of Ethiopia; the consolidation of different kingdoms and regional authorities into a centralised structure that approximates the current Ethiopia, with a state machinery for the territory, started under Tewodros II in 1855. The Abyssinia of Aksum was located in the northwest of contemporary Ethiopia, in territory that is currently part of contemporary Eritrea, parts of Somalia, the Adwa Valley (in the central Tigray region of Ethiopia), and the Bijat Mountains on the Red Sea. Lake Tana, Addis Ababa, and the Ethiopian Highlands were not connected in any way to the migration of the Prophet's (ﷺ) companions.[112]

Regarding the king who granted asylum and protection to the Muslims, Islamic sources mention a few variations of his name, including, inter alia, Aṣḥamah ibn Abjar, Aṣḥamah ibn Abḥar, and Saham ibn Abḥar. However, there is no mention of a king with any such name in the records of the Kingdom of Aksum. It is quite possible that the Negus to whom the Muslims had migrated was not the king of Aksum, but rather the king of a coastal region that was autonomous but was a vassal of the Kingdom of Aksum. Aksum comprised several regions, each having its own king, or "Negus" in Ge'ez, the ancient Ethiopian Semitic language. The Arabs pronounced it "al-Najāshī". The king who reigned from his capital Aksum was known as "Najūsā Najāst", meaning the "king of kings".

From written accounts about the migration, we may conclude that the Muslims' journey across the sea from al-Shu'aybah port lasted two nights. Thus, their final destination could not have been the port of Adulis, the main port of Aksum, which is much farther away. They probably cast anchor at the Bāḍi' port in current-day Massawa on the Eritrean coast. The port was part of a region controlled by the Negus of the Sea (Baḥri Najāshī), whose capital was in Debarwa (currently in Eritrea), about twenty-five kilometres from Eritrea's capital Asmara. He was likely the Negus Aṣḥamah, who is mentioned in biographies of the Prophet (ﷺ). Umm Ṣalamah narrated a lengthy story about a duel that was fought between the Negus and a man who tried to depose him. She narrated that al-Zubayr ibn al-'Awwām was:

> observing the event for the Muslims. They inflated a hide for

112. 'Abdallah al-Ṭayyib, *Majallat Dirāsāt Ifrīqīyyah*, (International African University, 1998).

> him, which he placed under his chest and then swam across the river to the other side to join the people who had gathered… We prayed to Allah to grant the Negus victory over his enemy and control over his country.[113]

The river that she mentioned was probably the Mareb River that forms the border between Eritrea and Ethiopia today. Historically, it separated the coastal region north of the river and Tigray to its south.

The city of Debarwa has both Muslim and Christian inhabitants; the latter are affiliated to the Eritrean Orthodox Tewahedo Church. "Tewahedo" is a Ge'ez word that means "united as one". It was derived from the Arabic word tawḥīd, meaning monotheism.

The siege

At the beginning of the seventh year of the Prophetic mission in 618, the Quraysh had lost all faith in their ability to contain the problem. This, after they had observed that the Muslims had become receptive to the idea of going to Abyssinia. The Quraysh then escalated the situation by besieging the Banī Hāshim and the Banī al-Muṭṭalib and subjecting them to a social and economic boycott.

The decision was taken after deliberations among senior Qurayshi leaders. Some of them had proposed murdering Muḥammad (ﷺ), but this view was not unanimous, since his murder would certainly spark a civil war, which the Quraysh wanted to avoid. Hence the decision to enforce a siege and boycott of the Banī Hāshim and the Banī al-Muṭṭalib. No one was to buy from or sell to them, nor would marriages to them be allowed. Truces with them were proscribed, and no one was to show them any leniency until they surrendered Allah's Messenger (ﷺ) and allowed him to be killed. Confirming the determination and desperation of the Quraysh, this agreement was written and hung in the Ka'bah.

The Banī al-Muṭṭalib and the Banī Hāshim moved to Abū Ṭālib's shi'b,[114] or valley. Many of their members already lived close to each

113. Ibn Hishām, *al-Sīrah*, vol. 1, 338.
114. A sh'ib is a valley or an opening between two mountains. Certain clans of the Quraysh settled

other, but those who were further away moved to the same area. It is likely that the decision for them all to resettle in the same area was forced on them by the Quraysh. This view is corroborated by an account related by Ibn Sayyid al-Nās in his *'Uyūn al-Athar*, where he indicates that the idolaters agreed to cast out the Banī Hāshim and the Banī al-Muṭṭalib and to expel them from Makkah to the valley. In any case, the Quraysh hoped that by besieging them, they could control the communications of these clans with the outside world, and to effect the implementation of the resolutions in their declaration. However, the siege was not an absolute confinement of the people to the valley. Reports indicate that the Prophet (ﷺ) regularly visited the gatherings of the Quraysh, debated with them, and invited them to Islam. Others from the Banī Hāshim and the Banī al-Muṭṭalib also moved around freely in Makkah and attended its gatherings.[115]

It is likely that the confinement was only in terms of residence. Even though the Quraysh's intentions were evil, the siege did result in some good. Forcing the Banī Hāshim and the Banī al-Muṭṭalib into a confined space gave them a sense of security. In addition, living together strengthened their unity and social solidarity at a difficult time. Various reports make it clear that the Banī Hāshim and the Banī al-Muṭṭalib reached a consensus not to surrender the Prophet (ﷺ) and to unite under Abū Ṭālib's leadership. The only dissenting voice in this agreement was Abū Lahab. We will see later how tribal solidarity between the Banī al-Muṭṭalib and the Banī Hāshim became one of the most significant factors contributing to the failure of the siege, which, nevertheless, persisted for three years. The convergence of besieged Muslims and non-Muslims around a unified position subverted the Qurayshi plan to subjugate and dismantle the Prophet's (ﷺ) base of support. This unity had other consequences too, especially for people from the Qurayshi clans that were connected to the Banī Hāshim and the Banī al-Muṭṭalib by lineage or through marriage.

It is important to note that the siege itself was a desperate, ill-considered move. For the Quraysh to demand that the Prophet (ﷺ) be surrendered to be murdered ignored the fact that such an act did not

and lived in these valleys.

115. Ibn Sayyid al-Nās, *'Uyūn al-Athar fī Funūn al-Maghāzī wa al-Shamā'il wa al-Siyar* (Beirut: Dār al-Qalam, 1993), vol. 1, 147.

accord with the prevalent tribal customs. Surrendering the Prophet (ﷺ) would have been a major insult and a disgrace that would have haunted the Banī Hāshim and the Banī al-Muṭṭalib for the foreseeable future. They would, therefore, never give in to such a disgrace, especially since they were the most esteemed of the Qurayshi houses due to their pristine genealogy that linked them directly to Quṣay, who had entrenched the Quraysh's control over Makkah.

The siege was an unprecedented violation of the notion of co-existence previously adhered to in Makkah, and the destruction of the most important pillar of Qurayshi society: decision-making by consensus and the containment of internal crises. The Quraysh was a social entity before it became a political entity, and its constituent parts were deeply bound together. Because of the practice of the Qurayshi clans marrying outside of their families, the besieged people had relatives in and family links to other Qurayshi clans through lineage, marriage, and ancient alliances.

The siege did hurt the Banī Hāshim in its first few months, especially since most of their income was derived from trade. Furthermore, Abū Jahl and some other Qurayshi leaders strictly enforced the declaration, sometimes resorting to violence against those who sent food to the valley. This was the case, for example, of Ḥakīm ibn Ḥizām, who tried to take food to his aunt Khadījah, since the besieged were suffering after they had run out of supplies and were overcome by starvation.

With this background, and the fact that relations of the Banī Hāshim and the Banī al-Muṭṭalib with the other Qurayshi clans were strong, the social identity of the Quraysh was prioritised over its political one. Marriage ties linked them to the Banī Zahrah, who were the maternal uncles of the Prophet (ﷺ), Khadījah was from the Banī Asad ibn 'Abd al-'Uzza, and Ḥamzah ibn 'Abd al-Muṭṭalib's maternal uncles were from the Banī Wahb. Similarly, all the besieged people had links to other Qurayshi clans. These relationships were ever-present in people's minds and persuaded some Qurayshis—especially the youth—to secretly violate the declaration.

Historical reports show that Hishām ibn 'Amr ibn Rabī'ah, from the

Banī 'Āmir ibn Lu'ay, and his mother, from the Banī Hāshim, ignored the Quraysh and dispatched consignments of food to the valley. The texts of these reports provide important insights into the distressing psychological atmosphere that was created by the siege in a society that was founded on tribal custom and pride of lineage.

> We were informed by Muḥammad ibn 'Umar, who said: "Abū Bakr ibn 'Abdallah ibn Abī Sabrah informed me, on the authority of Isḥāq ibn 'Abdallah ibn Abī Salamah al-Ḥaḍramī, who said: 'Hishām ibn 'Amr al-'Āmirī was a Qurayshi who was regularly in contact with the Banī Hāshim when they were besieged in the valley. One night, he sent them three consignments of food, about which the Quraysh found out. They confronted him about this in the morning. He said: "I will not return to anything that you oppose." They then left him. However, he resumed sending food to the valley. One night, when he had sent a consignment or two, the Quraysh responded harshly and considered [harsher measures]. Abū Sufyān ibn Ḥarb then said: "Leave him be; he is a man who is [upholding the duty] of maintaining family ties. I swear by Allah that if we were to do what he has done, it would be best for us, or at the very least we should allow them to buy [what they require] with their own wealth. I did not like what the Quraysh have done to them, and showing hostility could have been much more graceful than this." The people remained silent, then dispersed.'"[116]

Another account, transmitted by Ibn Isḥāq, is just as important. It narrates the attempts by Ḥakīm ibn Ḥizām to bring wheat to Khadījah, his aunt.

> It is mentioned that Abū Jahl ibn Hishām came across Ḥakīm ibn Ḥizām ibn Khuwaylid ibn Asad, who was accompanied by a boy carrying wheat that Ḥakīm wanted to deliver to his aunt, Khadījah bint Khuwaylid, who was with Allah's Messenger (ﷺ) in the valley. Abū Jahl ibn Hishām grabbed him and demanded: "Are you going with food to the Banī Hāshim? I swear by Allah, you will not take a step with your

116. Abū 'Abdallah Muḥammad Ibn Sa'd, *al-Ṭabaqāt al-Kubra: Mutamam al-Sahaba* (Taif: Siddq Library, 1993), vol. 2, 453.

food before I expose you to all of Makkah." At that moment, Abū al-Bukhtarī ibn Hāshim ibn al-Ḥārith ibn Asad approached them and asked: "What is [the problem] between you and him?" Abū Jahl responded: "He is taking food to the Banī Hāshim." Abū al-Bukhtarī then told him: "[It is] food that belonged to his aunt that was left with him, and that she [has now] sent for. Will you prevent him from taking her own food to her? Make way for the man!" Abū Jahl refused and the two men exchanged blows. Abū al-Bukhtarī picked up a camel jawbone and struck Abū Jahl with it, cutting him open and knocking him down hard. Ḥamzah ibn 'Abd al-Muṭṭalib watched from close by. They did not want Allah's Messenger (ﷺ) and his companions to hear about what happened, as they would be disappointed by their actions. Allah's Messenger (ﷺ) was inviting his people [to Islam] day and night, openly and in secret, undertaking what Allah had commanded without fear for any person.[117]

The stance of Abū Sufyān and Abū al-Bukhtarī deserves some reflection. They were both Abū Jahl's peers and men of repute among their people. Their stance was not unexpected, if we consider the nature of tribal pride and solidarity. Abū Sufyān was from the Banī 'Abd Shams ibn 'Abd Manāf and was close to the Banī Hāshim and the Banī 'Abd al-Muṭṭalib through family relations; Abū al-Bukhtarī was from the Banī Asad ibn 'Abd al-'Uzza, relatives of Khadījah, who was his cousin, and Ḥakīm ibn Ḥizām was his nephew. This is why he could not tolerate Abū Jahl insulting Ḥakīm. Lineage and marriage ties thus played a significant role in undermining the Qurayshi consensus and in impeding the implementation of the boycott, ultimately collapsing it.

The kindness and fairness of people such as Abū al-Bukhtarī was later repaid. During the Battle of Badr, for example, the Prophet (ﷺ) ordered that Zama'ah ibn al-Aswad and Abū al-Bukhtarī not be killed, even though they were part of the enemy army. Ibn Isḥāq explains the Prophet's (ﷺ) decision.

Allah's Messenger (ﷺ) prohibited the killing of Abū al-Bukhtarī because he never disparaged Allah's Messenger (ﷺ) while he

117. Ibn Hishām, *al-Sīrah*, vol. 1, 354.

was in Makkah. He never harmed the Prophet, nor did he say anything to the Prophet that he found offensive. He was also one of the persons who defied the declaration [of the siege] issued by the Quraysh regarding the Banī Hāshim and the Banī al-Muṭṭalib.[118]

As time passed, more honourable Qurayshis began to agitate to end the suffering of the besieged people. Gradually, more Makkans openly called for the complete lifting of the siege. The most active individuals supporting this call were, among others, Hishām ibn ʻAmr, al-Muṭʻam ibn ʻAdī, Abū al-Bukhtarī al-ʻĀṣ ibn Hishām, Ḥakīm ibn Ḥizām, Zuhayr ibn Abī Umayyah al-Makhzūmī, and Zamaʻah ibn al-Aswad ibn al-Muṭṭalib. They mobilised sympathetic individuals from the Quraysh and addressed them in their gatherings, arguing that there were many negative aspects to the siege, including that it was shameful for the Quraysh and that, after three years, it had not achieved any of its goals. The siege should end, they said, to prevent the embarrassment of being viewed by other Arabs as people who cut family ties.

Biographies of the Prophet (ﷺ) generally credit Hishām ibn ʻAmr ibn Rabīʻah, whose mother was from the Banī Hāshim, with the honour of transforming this groundswell of displeasure into a defiance movement. He contacted many Qurayshis who were displeased with the siege and were related to the Banī Hāshim. His first contact was with Zuhayr ibn Abī Umayyah ibn al-Mughīrah al-Makhzūmī, son of ʻĀtikah bint ʻAbd al-Muṭṭalib. He was followed by al-Muṭʻam ibn ʻAdī ibn Nawfal ibn ʻAbd Manāf; Abū al-Bukhtarī ibn Hishām ibn al-Ḥārith ibn Asad ibn ʻAbd al-ʻUzza, whose father was the cousin of Khadījah; and Zamaʻah ibn al-Aswad ibn al-Muṭṭalib ibn Asad ibn ʻAbd al-ʻUzza, whose father also was Khadījah's cousin. Clearly, this group, which organised the public campaign to oppose the declaration, represented others who did not dare make their views known. The campaign then transformed into a rebellion. Ibn Isḥāq narrates the events of the day on which the declaration collapsed, and the group's planning that preceded the collapse.

They gathered at night at Khaṭm al-Ḥajjūn above Makkah, agreed by consensus, and pledged to oppose the declaration until it was annulled. Zuhayr said: "I am the first among you

118. Ibn Hishām, *al-Sīrah*, vol. 1, 354.

so I will be the first to speak." In the morning, they gathered. Zuhayr ibn Abī Umayyah approached them wearing a robe and circumambulated the Ka'bah seven times. He then approached the people and said: "O People of Makkah, will we eat food and wear clothing while the Banī Hāshim perishes, not [being allowed to] buy or sell? By Allah, I will not sit until this divisive and oppressive declaration is shredded." Abū Jahl, who was on the other side of the mosque, responded: "By Allah, you lie; it will not be shredded." Zama'ah ibn al-Aswad said: "You, by Allah, are more untruthful. We were not happy with the declaration when it was written." Abū al-Bukhtarī added: "Zama'ah has spoken the truth. We are not happy with what has been recorded in it, and we do not affirm it." Al-Muṭ'am ibn 'Adī said: "Both of you have spoken the truth. Whoever says otherwise has lied. We seek Allah's exoneration from it and from what was written therein." Hishām ibn 'Amr said something similar. Abū Jahl then responded: "This is a matter that was resolved in a night and was consulted over at a place other than this one." Abū Ṭālib was sitting at the other end of the mosque. When Al-Muṭ'am rose and approached the Ka'bah to tear up the declaration, he found that termites had eaten it, leaving [only the words]: "In Your Name, O Allah.[119]

The declaration was thus nullified and the Qurayshi boycott collapsed. The Muslims emerged victorious, and it became clear that the Quraysh were unable to defeat the unity and resolve displayed by the Banī Hāshim and the Banī al-Muṭṭalib to protect the Prophet (ﷺ). They were forced to find another strategy to contain Muḥammad's (ﷺ) message. They attempted to reach some compromise with the Prophet (ﷺ). One suggestion was for the Quraysh to worship "Muḥammad's God" on one day, and for him to worship their gods on the next. They also tried to reach an agreement with Abū Ṭālib. They had abandoned the idea of his handing Muḥammad (ﷺ) over to be killed – as they knew that this was impossible – but they sought a compromise through which the Muslims would make some concessions.

119. Ibn Hishām, *al-Sīrah*, vol. 1, 356.

Visit to Ṭā'if

According to most accounts, the Prophet (ﷺ) visited Ṭā'if in the tenth year of his mission, after the death of his uncle Abū Ṭālib and after the loss of the tribal protection that Abū Ṭālib had extended to him. The Prophet (ﷺ) wanted to open new vistas for his message and test new audiences that would potentially be more receptive to Islam. Ṭā'if was the city closest to Makkah, so it was to be expected that the Prophet (ﷺ) would consider it for his message. He took Zayd ibn Ḥārithah with him and spent ten days in the city, meeting and discussing with its elders. They, however, were not only unresponsive, but also hostile, and incited the city's mobs to attack the Prophet (ﷺ).

Ṭā'if, with its moderate climate, had a strong trade and tourism relationship with the Quraysh; the Makkan leaders owned farms and homes there, where they often spent their summers. The Prophet's (ﷺ) visit coincided with the presence of some of these leaders. The leaders of the Banī Thaqīf in Ṭā'if wanted to maintain good relations with the Quraysh and wanted its leaders to know that they categorically rejected anything that harmed the welfare of the Quraysh. This is probably what motivated them to treat the Prophet (ﷺ) with such contempt. At least two Qurayshi leaders, 'Utbah and Shaybah, the sons of Rabī'ah, were spending the summer at their farm in Ṭā'if and witnessed the manner in which the Prophet (ﷺ) was treated.

Returning to Makkah protected by a historical bond

When the Prophet returned to Makkah, he did not immediately enter the city, because he knew that the Quraysh—who had already received news from Ṭā'if—would be even more hostile and violent toward him. He needed to make appropriate security arrangements and thus stayed in Nakhlah, which is close to Makkah, while he prepared. When he reached Ḥirā', he sent someone from the Khuzā'ah tribe to al-Muṭ'am ibn 'Adī, requesting their protection. Al-Muṭ'am granted him tribal protection, allowing him to enter Makkah safely.

We should reflect on the Prophet's (ﷺ) choice of a man from

Khuzā'ah to be his emissary. The Khuzā'ah were allies of 'Abd al-Muṭṭalib due to a famous incident that bore direct relevance to al-Muṭ'am's protection of the Prophet (ﷺ) and to the alliance that was to develop between the Prophet (ﷺ) and the Khuzā'ah, which lasted until the conquest of Makkah.

Many years earlier, before 'Abd al-Muṭṭalib had any children, Nawfal ibn 'Abd Manāf had cheated his nephew 'Abd al-Muṭṭalib by confiscating the inheritance he was to receive from his father Hāshim ibn 'Abd Manāf. The dispute was over a tract of land called al-Arkāḥa, which had been earmarked for irrigation. When Nawfal illegally appropriated the land, 'Abd al-Muṭṭalib sought the help of his immediate kin, but no one assisted him. Having witnessed how his own people let him down, he sought the assistance of his maternal uncles from the Banī al-Najjār tribe in Yathrib. They came to his assistance with a force of seventy or eighty men and forced Nawfal to reinstate 'Abd al-Muṭṭalib's inheritance.

The Khuzā'ah tribe was monitoring the developments in Makkah, as they were old enemies of the Quraysh. When they saw that 'Abd al-Muṭṭalib had been strengthened by his uncles' support, they decided to enter an alliance with him. The alliance was facilitated on behalf of the Khuzā'ah by Warqā'a ibn 'Abd al-'Uzza, the father of Budayl ibn Warqā'a, who later emerged as an important role-player during negotiations for the Treaty of Ḥudaybīyyah. The alliance was sealed in the House of Assembly and was captured in writing. It confirmed the alliance between the Khuzā'ah and the Banī Hāshim, and committed them both to "assist one another and to console one another in a comprehensive alliance that does not differentiate elder from elder, junior from senior, or the present from the absent… [It is] a permanent alliance for all time".[120]

This alliance persisted with the sons and grandsons of 'Abd al-Muṭṭalib, down to the Prophet (ﷺ), and became extremely important in his life story. All the Khuzā'ah remained faithful to the alliance, including those who embraced Islam as well as those who did not. It was, thus, understandable that the Prophet (ﷺ) delegated a man from the Khuzā'ah to request protection for him. But why was it al-Muṭ'am

120. Al-Baghdādī, *al-Munammaq* (Beirut: 'Ālam al-Kutub, 1985), 87.

ibn ʻAdī from whom he sought protection?

Al-Muṭʻam ibn ʻAdī was the grandson of Nawfal ibn ʻAbd Manāf. He remembered that, when his grandfather had violated the rights of Muḥammad's (ﷺ) grandfather, the results had been catastrophic. ʻAbd al-Muṭṭalib had to seek help from beyond his closest relatives, and found allies in Yathrib. Thereafter, he developed an alliance with the Khuzāʻah. These developments proved to be disastrous for the Banī Nawfal, and they suffered their consequences for many generations. Suddenly, ʻAbd al-Muṭṭalib's grandson placed Nawfal's grandson in a unique situation, seeking his protection with a request carried by a man from the Khuzāʻah. If al-Muṭʻam were to refuse, Muḥammad (ﷺ) would find an alternative from among his grandfather's protectors, or from other allies. Al-Muṭʻam, a man of sharp intellect, understood this and realised that an important opportunity had been presented to him. He was unwilling to repeat his grandfather's mistake and acceded to the Prophet's (ﷺ) request for protection. Al-Muṭʻam's sons armed themselves and announced before the Quraysh that he had granted protection to Muḥammad (ﷺ). The Prophet (ﷺ) thus returned to Makkah and continued with his mission of inviting people to Allah.

This incident and its antecedents are proof of the Prophet's (ﷺ) deep understanding of tribal dynamics and politics within Qurayshi society. He instrumentalised this understanding for his mission on this occasion and others in later years.

It must be noted, however, that al-Muṭʻam ibn ʻAdī was one of the most tolerant and balanced of the Qurayshi leaders and was always extremely fair toward the Muslims. He also strove to end the siege of his kin in the valley and would later adopt many more positions that were helpful for the Muslims when they began their migration. He was also the father of Jubayr ibn Muṭʻam, a companion of the Prophet (ﷺ). Al-Muṭʻam died before the Battle of Badr, aged ninety. The Muslims were saddened by his death, and the Prophet's (ﷺ) poet, Ḥassān Ibn Thābit, elegised him in a famous poem.

CHAPTER SIX

Migration towards the future

"And say, 'My Lord, grant me an honourable entry, and grant me an honourable exit; and give me a supporting authority from Yourself'" (Qur'ān 17:80).

A major element of the prophetic strategy was to be proactive and seize the initiative. This meant that the Muslims were constantly the ones determining the contours of the Muslim-Quraysh struggle, deciding on the fields and schedules for battles. In addition to courage and wisdom, initiative also requires deep insight into the internal and external balance of forces, and the ability to determine the opponent's possible reactions. The element of surprise and the ability to unsettle one's opponent and to force a reaction on one's own terms are critical elements in this battle to gain the initiative.

Repeatedly seizing the initiative ensured that the Prophet (ﷺ) did not put himself in a position where he would be forced to react. Such pressure could place additional stress on his project, preoccupy him with battles designed by his opponent, and rob him of the ability to maintain focus on his primary strategic objectives.

After the formation of his core team, which took shape over three years, the Prophet (ﷺ) announced his mission with confidence, strength, and determination. That assertiveness left the Quraysh bewildered, disputing with each other, and in a state of confusion. When most of the Qurayshi clans colluded in their hostility to the Muslims, the Prophet (ﷺ) again took the initiative and deployed a delegation to open a channel of communication with the neighbouring Abyssinian leadership, confusing the Quraysh and forcing it to react. The Quraysh sent 'Amr ibn al-'Āṣ to bring the Muslims back from Abyssinia as captives, but he failed. Later, the arrogant Qurayhsi leadership formulated a desperate and unwise tactic to besiege the Banī Hāshim. This foolish response undermined tribal consensus, which was an important principle of Qurayshi politics, and the siege failed.

Thereafter, the Prophet (ﷺ) took the initiative of communicating with the various Arab tribes and visiting Ṭā'if. Even though that visit was unsuccessful, the exercise of dealing with its consequences was an important lesson in conflict management. The Prophet (ﷺ) was able to contain the crisis by utilising his deep knowledge of the nature of Qurayshi alliances and its internal balance of forces. He returned to Makkah and sought a new initiative that would again force the Quraysh to respond to a strategic escalation that would change the rules of the political game and remove the Prophet (ﷺ) and the Muslims from the trap that the Quraysh was trying to set for them.

It was during this period, in 621, that al-Isrā', or the Prophet's (ﷺ) ascension to Jerusalem, occurred. This event was preparation and guidance for the Prophet's (ﷺ) upcoming migration. The "Ascension" chapter in the Qur'ān (Surah 17) was revealed fourteen months before the migration to Madinah (Hijrah). The ascension was preparation and an opening of new horizons. It provided insights into the experiences of a past nation that had built a state but, due to its deviation from the laws of Allah, saw that state collapse and be destroyed. The establishment of a state does not mean an end to defeat and the attainment of victory. A state is simply a tool; if it is abused, it becomes a source of evil.

Al-Isrā' (the ascension) was training for the Prophet (ﷺ) regarding the norms of state building and the capacity required to maintain a virtuous state. It was also his preparation to understand the political structure and psychological nature of the Banī Isrā'īl (the "Children of Israel", the term that the Qur'ān uses in references to Jews), who he would soon encounter in Yathrib.

After these norms were outlined in the chapter on the ascension (Qur'ān Surah 17), which deals with the nature of the state, its mission, and the balance of forces required to ensure its perpetuation, Allah directed his Prophet (ﷺ) to ponder another norm related to the Hijrah. Allah gave him glad tidings that his departure from Makkah would mark the beginning of the Quraysh's defeat and the victory of the Islamic call. "They planned to scare you off the land, but they would not have lasted for more than a little while. Such was Our way with the messengers We sent before you, and you will find no change in Our ways." (Qur'ān 17:76-77). Therefore, his exit from Makkah and his migration to Madinah should not be construed as a defeat for him or his mission. It was, rather, the beginning of the defeat of the Quraysh and their religious and ideological approach.

The Qur'ān then directed the Prophet (ﷺ) to call on Allah, the Most Sublime, to make the Hijrah easy for him and to grant him the authority that would aid him to establish the truth and to defeat and eliminate falsehood. "And say, 'My Lord, grant me an honourable entry, and grant me an honourable exit; and give me a supporting authority from Yourself.' And say: 'Truth has arrived and falsehood has perished. Indeed, falsehood is bound to perish.'" (Qur'ān 17:80-81).

The broad outline of the future became clearer to the Prophet (ﷺ). The trajectory of his mission had reached the moment that demanded a break with the Quraysh and Makkan society, both of which were unresponsive to change. From this point onward, all efforts had to be directed at a new base that would give the Muslims authority and assistance. Makkah could never serve that purpose, and it had become obligatory to act on that realisation. Within this context, the ascension was a signal, a preparation, and a shift toward the second phase of the Prophetic mission: the Hijrah.

The road to Yathrib

The Prophet's (ﷺ) choice of a new base was Yathrib. It was a calculated and strategic decision; it happened neither by chance, nor simply because some people of Yathrib came to Makkah, met with him, and invited him to migrate to their city. The Hijrah to Yathrib, and the way in which it was executed, indicated deep reflection and careful planning by the Prophet (ﷺ) and his companions.

The Qur'ānic directive in Surah 17 clearly advocated the search for an "honourable exit", an "honourable entry", and a "supportive authority". Let us then examine the available options that would fulfil these three criteria.

Ṭā'if?

We saw how the Banī Thaqīf deliberately and maliciously rebuffed the Prophet (ﷺ), intending, thereby, to send a message to the Qurayshi leadership that Ṭā'if would not be the seat of an opposition against them. The Banī Thaqīf were fully cognisant that the Qurayshi economy was essential to Ṭā'if's sustenance, especially after the Makkan elite had invested in Ṭā'if with their purchases of farms and villas, and had made the city their preferred summer holiday destination. It was obvious that the people of Ṭā'if would not sacrifice these benefits to grant shelter to a man without influence or wealth comparable to that of the Qurayshi leaders. Thus, Ṭā'if did not qualify as an "honourable entry", "honourable exit", or a "supportive authority".

And Abyssinia?

Abyssinia was a land of truth. If the migration was to be a search for a refuge where the Prophet (ﷺ) could find shelter from the tyranny of the Quraysh, or for a temporary self-imposed exile where he could spend some time before returning to Makkah, Abyssinia would have been a suitable choice. It was within the Prophet's (ﷺ) means to migrate to Abyssinia, especially since the Negus had secretly converted to Islam, had welcomed Muslims who had migrated to his lands, and had given them hospitality and refuge from the Quraysh's tyranny.

Despite all this, would the Muslims find a supportive authority in Abyssinia?

Abyssinia was suitable for general Muslim migrants, especially the disenfranchised who sought security and refuge, but it was not appropriate as a refuge for the Prophet (ﷺ) in his capacity as a leader, or for the core group accompanying him. He was a man with a mission, and he needed to be able to continue propagating his call and spreading his message. He knew that this religion would spread and grow, to the far east and the far west. He was, therefore, not looking for a refuge or a place of exile; he needed a capital from which he would be able to manage the course of his mission and the strategy to spread it and to elevate the word of Allah. Abyssinia was not fit for this purpose; it already had a stable system of governance, with its own interests, alliances, and a national and religious identity. While its ruler had embraced Islam in his personal capacity, its system of governance and its official state religion was Orthodox Christianity. Thus, even if Abyssinia had accepted Muḥammad (ﷺ) the individual refugee, it would never accept Muḥammad (ﷺ) the prophet and leader.

Khaybar, a commercial centre inhabited by Jews, was also not a viable option for the Prophet's (ﷺ) migration. It did not meet the requirements for his migration and was, additionally, very far from Makkah.

Migration to Sana'a was also not viable, since it was under Persian authority. Nor was al-Ḥīrah, the capital of the Manādhirah, a viable option, because the Persians and Byzantines were fighting over the Levant, and neither of those warring parties would tolerate an independent religious movement that they would be unable to instrumentalise for the advancement of their own interests.

There was, then, only one option that met all the requirements for a successful migration: Yathrib.

An honourable entry

Yathrib was a unique settlement with a long history. It was surrounded by fertile lands, populated by a diverse group of inhabitants, had a moderate climate, and was strategically located. However, it had just emerged from a major tribal conflagration that challenged its peace and security and therefore needed a leader who would be able to reset its moral compass and rebuild its society.

There are important differences between Yathrib and Makkah that made the former an obvious destination for the migration of a messenger and his message, a community and a calling, rather than a migration of individuals seeking shelter and refuge.

The most significant difference between the two cities was that

Yathribi society was much more egalitarian than Makkan society. Qurayshi society was mercantile, very hierarchical, and had been founded on rank and pride over wealth and progeny. Classist hierarchy therefore occupied an important place in the minds and imagination of the Quraysh. The Makkan trading elite possessed great wealth and large caravans and made a point of flaunting their power. In contrast, Yathribi society was more balanced; the disparity between rich and poor was not as extreme as in Makkan society, since agriculture was the backbone of the Yathribi economy. Trade and some manufacturing were carried out, but this did not create a large wealth gap between citizens. Furthermore, such an agrarian society was more relaxed and more tolerant, allowing it to engage more comfortably with the Prophet's (ﷺ) message of brotherhood and equality. In Makkah, this message posed a direct threat to the authority of the small rich elite that subjugated the marginalised masses.

A second difference was that Yathribi society was more religiously tolerant than its Makkan counterpart. For the Quraysh, religion was about tribal solidarity linked to Qurayshi exceptionalism. The Holy Sanctuary represented a centre of distinction that the Quraysh exploited and used to assert their leadership over all Arabs. Religion, for the Quraysh, was about status, authority, and economics. When the Prophet (ﷺ) found fault with and cursed their gods, he was simultaneously criticising their belief system and threatening the foundations of their authority and superiority. That is why they strongly opposed him, even if they did see some truth in his message; they were defending their interests and privilege.

In Yathrib, religion was not a matter of consensus, the backbone of tribal solidarity, or a means of attaining wealth or success in trade. Yathrib's population included Jews, who were "People of the Book", as well as illiterate Arabs who worshipped various gods. If someone professed a new religion, the unlettered people of Yathrib were more likely to engage with it in a balanced and fair manner, unlike the unlettered people of Makkah.

A third difference relates to the structure of the political systems in the two cities. The Qurayshi political consensus—represented by the House of Assembly and its main duties of Maintenance of the Ka'bah, Food

Provisioning, Water Supply, and The Brigade—was a system of collective governance that was able to impose its decisions on its clans. They also had a mechanism for conflict and dispute resolution. The responsibility for maintaining public order was, thus, that of the Qurayshi elite. The authority of the elite was, in turn, related to inherited relationships between and within Qurayshi clans, as well as trade interests that were determined by consensus in the House of Assembly. The House of Assembly authority was able to create a stable society in Makkah, but it also trapped Qurayshi society in a fixed mindset that rejected change and treated inherited traditions as if they were religious obligations. The Qurayshi leadership thus regarded the coming of Islam as an existential threat to its consensus, and it therefore rejected and fought against the new religion.

This form of communal authority was not replicated in Yathrib, primarily because the city had a very different demography. Its inhabitants were divided between five main clans and a few smaller ones. The Aws and the Khazraj were clans whose lineages were derived from maternal cousins of Yemeni descent. The Banī Qurayẓah, Banī al-Naḍīr, and the Banī Qaynuqā‘ were three Jewish clans that had settled in Yathrib centuries earlier. Each clan in Yathrib had its own leadership; some were allied to each other, but there was no collective governing institution for all the tribes and clans of Yathrib. Without a centralised administration, tribal conflict in Yathrib was commonplace and frequent, especially between the Aws and the Khazraj. Historians have recorded a series of battles and wars between these two clans and their respective Jewish allies. The absence of internal political consensus also made Yathrib society more open to new ideas; change was therefore easier to effect than in Makkah.

A fourth difference between the two cities was their strategic priorities. Makkah's strategic enemy was always an outside threat, and the Immorality Wars loomed large in the Qurayshi consciousness. The fear of an external onslaught pushed them to embrace internal consensus and solidarity. The spectre of an enemy from abroad was ideal for the purpose of forging unity, but it was also a pretence for opposing Muḥammad's (ﷺ) message, by accusing it of causing division.

In contrast, Yathrib's strategic challenge was always internal, represented by the continuous conflict between the Aws, Khazraj, and their allies. The most recent chapter in the conflict, before the Prophet (ﷺ) got involved, was the Bu'āth War, which had a destructive effect on life in Yathrib.

Having erupted five years before the Hijrah, that war had engulfed most of the tribes in Yathrib. It pitted the Aws—with its Banī Qurayẓah, Banī al-Naḍīr, and Banī Muzaynah allies—against the Khazraj and Banī Qaynuqā', and their Banī Ashja' and the Banī Juhaynah allies. The Khazraj was defeated, its members' homes and date orchards were torched, and its leader, 'Amr ibn al-Nu'mān, was killed, as was Aws leader Khuḍayr al-Katā'ib. Khuḍayr was succeeded by his son Usayd.[121]

The war destabilised Yathrib internally; but an important outcome was a change in leadership structures in the city, with younger leaders taking over. Many elders from both sides were killed, allowing the accession of the youth leadership tier that included Usayd ibn Khuḍayr and Sa'd ibn Muā'dh from the Aws, and Sa'd ibn 'Ubādah from the Khazraj. All three individuals accepted Islam before the Prophet's (ﷺ) migration to Yathrib, and their conversions helped prepare the ground for an appropriate welcome for him and his companions. Perhaps the leadership elite and Yathribi society in general were motivated by the deep wound that affected them and by the collective will to find an escape from the cycle of endless conflict. This convinced them to welcome wise leadership from the outside, one that was not party to the conflict and the cycles of revenge in Yathrib, and which provided an opportunity to establish a consensus that might open a new horizon for the exhausted city. The Prophet's (ﷺ) Hijrah was thus an appropriate opportunity for the astute citizens who sought new horizons.

A supportive authority

The Aws and Khazraj leaders and their representatives who met the Prophet (ﷺ) at the Second Pledge of 'Aqabah were fully aware of the security implications of his Hijrah to Yathrib. For his part, the Prophet (ﷺ) clearly explained to the Yathrib delegation his expectations of a

121. Ibn Hishām, *al-Sīrah,* vol. 1, 556.

"supportive authority". Two texts are illustrative in this regard, by al-Ṭabarī and Ibn Isḥāq. Al-Ṭabarī writes:

> When the people gathered to pledge allegiance to Allah's Messenger, al-'Abbās ibn Naḍlah al-Anṣārī said, "O People of al-Khazraj, are you aware of what it means to pledge allegiance to this man?" They replied, "Yes." He said: "You pledge allegiance to him to wage war on people, black and white, and if you feel that it is a calamity when your wealth has been depleted and your leaders have been killed [and you therefore decide] to surrender him [to the enemy], know now that, by Allah, it is a disgrace in this world and the hereafter if you were to do so." They said: "If we were to take this pledge in spite of the loss of our wealth and the killing of our leaders, what will we gain therefrom, O Messenger of Allah, if we are faithful?" He said: "Paradise." They said: "Extend your hand." He extended it, and they pledged their allegiance to him.[122]

Ibn Isḥāq narrated, on the authority of Ka'b ibn Mālik:

> We gathered in the valley, waiting for Allah's Messenger (ﷺ), until he came [to us] accompanied by his uncle, al-'Abbās ibn 'Abd al-Muṭṭalib, who at that time still followed the religion of his people, but wanted to be present for this matter pertaining to his nephew, and to support him and bear witness on his behalf. When the Prophet sat, the first to speak was al-'Abbās ibn 'Abd al-Muṭṭalib. He said: "O people of al-Khazraj [referring to the people of the particular district, which included the Khazraj and the Aws]. Verily Muḥammad is one of us, as you know. We have protected him from our own people, who share our opinion on him. He is honoured among his people and protected in his home. Nevertheless, he has chosen to incline towards you and to join you. If you feel that you are faithful to what you have promised him, and are able to protect him from his opponents, then you bear that responsibility. But if you feel that you will betray him and abandon him after taking him with you, then leave him right now, as he is honoured and protected among

122. Al-Ṭabarī, *Tārīkh*, vol. 2, 363.

his people and in his abode." We replied, "We have heard what you have said. Now speak, O Messenger of Allah, and choose for yourself and for your Lord whatever you please." Allah's Messenger (ﷺ) then spoke. He recited the Qur'ān and invited to Allah and inclined [us] towards Islam. Then he said, "I invite your pledge that you will protect me as you protect your women and children." Al-Barā'a ibn Ma'rūr took his hand and said: "Yes, by the One who has sent you with the truth [as a prophet], we will protect you as we protect our women. Accept our pledge, O Messenger of Allah. By Allah, we are the sons of war and a people of resilience; this is our legacy through many generations." Al-Barā'a was interrupted by Abū al-Haytham ibn al-Tayyihān, who said: "O Messenger of Allah, we have ties with certain other people [the Jews in Madinah]. We will sever these ties [for your sake]. After we do this, what will you do if Allah then grants you victory? Will you return to your people and abandon us?" Allah's Messenger (ﷺ) smiled and replied: "Blood is blood and destruction is destruction. I am of you and you are of me. I fight against those against whom you fight, and I keep peace with those with whom you keep peace."[123]

There is another text that Ibn Isḥāq relates that is also relevant to this discussion. On the day of the Battle of Badr, when the Prophet (ﷺ) learnt that the Quraysh had mobilised to meet him at Badr, he wanted to establish whether the Anṣār, "the helpers" who had welcomed him to Yathrib, would fight alongside him. After asking his companions their opinion on fighting, three of them, all Muhājirūn who had migrated with him from Makkah responded. However, he was not satisfied and continued to inquire so that he might hear the opinion of the Anṣār.

Allah's Messenger (ﷺ) said, "Advise me, O people." He wanted to hear from the Anṣār since they were in the majority, and because, when they had pledged allegiance to him at al-'Aqabah, they had promised: "O Messenger of Allah, we are absolved of protecting you until you reach our city. When you do, you will be under our protection, and we will secure you as we secure our children and wives." Allah's Messenger (ﷺ) was

123. Ibn Hishām, *al-Sīrah*, vol.1, 441.

> now concerned about whether the Anṣār felt compelled to come to his assistance only against those of his enemies who attacked him in the city of Madinah, and they might not feel obligated to leave their city and march out with him against his enemies.[124]

The terms of the pact of allegiance with the Yathribis had included the protection of the Prophet (ﷺ) only after he had reached Madinah and was within the city itself. It was unclear whether the protection and assistance extended to any fighting outside Madinah. The Prophet (ﷺ) therefore wanted to ascertain whether the Anṣār would fight with him at Badr, since it was not located within Madinah.

We quote these texts to emphasise an important issue: the understanding of the two parties, the Anṣār and Muhājirūn, of the strategic dimensions of the pledge, and their willingness to interrogate these dimensions and reaffirm them. In particular, this applied to those provisions concerning protection, support, and their political and security consequences. This is why the second pledge with the Yathribis was referred to as a "war pledge", to distinguish it from the first pledge, which did not include the obligation of military support. It was as a result of the second pledge that the Muslims of Madinah were called al-Anṣār (the Helpers).

On the occasion of the pledging, Al-'Abbas was careful to clarify the security dimensions of the oath in a way that had left no room for doubt. Importantly, his presence, even though he still was not a Muslim, drew attention to the strategic nature of the pledge. He attended in his capacity as the leader of the Banī Hāshim, the Prophet's (ﷺ) tribal protectors in Makkah. Al-'Abbas was explicit that the Prophet's (ﷺ) migration was not for the purpose of seeking shelter and a place to live. He was neither a fugitive seeking refuge, nor an ally seeking patronage; he was already protected by his own people, who were fully capable of continuing in that role.

He was, rather, a prophet and a leader, a person with a mission that no longer had a future in Makkah in the face of Qurayshi stubbornness. This was the reason for his migration, which the people of Yathrib needed to understand. They also needed to grasp the implications of their support for him.

124. Ibn Hishām, *al-Sīrah*, vol.1, 615.

Their welcoming him had to be with the recognition that he was a messenger of Allah and a man with a mission, and that he would continue with his mission from Yathrib, which would serve as his capital. By agreeing to protect and support him, the people of Yathrib were committing to participate in his struggle, and to pay the price for this involvement in wealth and blood. This was precisely what the Prophet (ﷺ) had meant by his brief speech. If Abū al-Haytham al-Tayhān's question had been reasonable in terms of the drafting of such a pledge, then the Prophet's (ﷺ) response was also clear and transparent: he undertook to make Yathrib his home, not a temporary refuge or a place of transit on his way to a new destination. He would join Yathrib in its quest and was committing to become one with them as they commited to be one with him. They would both fight whoever fought against them, and grant peace to whoever granted them peace.

The historical texts are clear that the people of Yathrib who had participated in the Second Pledge of ʻAqabah, comprising seventy-three men and two women from the various houses of Yathrib—including ʻUsayd ibn Khuḍayr, an Aws leader, and Saʻd ibn ʻUbādah, a Khazraj leader—were fully cognisant of the consequences of the Prophet's (ﷺ) migration. There were strategic and political calculations that had to be made; hosting the Prophet (ﷺ) and his companions was, after all, an automatic declaration of hostility toward the Quraysh. Since the Quraysh had great influence among the Arabs, allying with its enemies would create many problems.

Yathrib's economy would certainly be affected by the Hijrah. The city was bound to the Quraysh by trade ties. Qurayshis crossed Yathrib during their journeys to the north while Yathrib's merchants and farmers sold their products and harvests at many markets controlled by the Quraysh. Like many other Arabs, the people of Yathrib were also linked to Makkah through their pilgrimages to the consecrated House of Allah.

The delegation from Yathrib also needed to consider the balance of forces within Yathrib. The Prophet (ﷺ) would not migrate alone; he would take a group of Muslims from the Quraysh who would form a new social group and an influential political bloc within the city. Its members would be the closest people to the prophet and leader and would thus be able to influence the balance of forces and affect the fortunes of those in Yathrib who aspired to power, such as ʿAbdallah ibn Ubay ibn Sallūl al-Khazrajī, a prominent Yathribi elder. Because ʿAbdallah ibn Ubay had not participated in the Buʿāth War that had ripped Yathrib apart, he had become its most important beneficiary. He had offered himself as a consensus candidate to the warring parties and was almost crowned king of Yathrib; the Prophet's (ﷺ) Hijrah suspended his aspirations.

Another internal political issue that required consideration was the possible reactions of Yathrib's Jewish tribes. They would suddenly be confronted with a unique situation: a man proclaiming a single deity, as they did, and who had a scripture that affirmed his claims as well as the claims of the Torah of Moses, but a man who was neither from their people nor affiliated to their religion. He would also forge a rare consensus between the Aws and the Khazraj and lay the foundations for a political reality that was unique for Yathrib, with potentially serious consequences for its Jewish inhabitants.

The day of the crowd

We return to Makkah, where the Quraysh had realised that Muḥammad (ﷺ) was on the verge of migrating. Many of his companions had already secretly slipped away to Yathrib, and he was poised to do the same. The Quraysh were confused, and they were afraid of the consequences of the migration. They had contained his mission for thirteen years, but he was about to break free from their clutches and their sphere of influence, moving far beyond their reach and robbing them of the ability to monitor his plans. They feared the consequences of his independence in a territory that protected and supported him, especially since it was on their caravan route, the lifeline of the Qurayshi economy. They found the implications of his migration to be horrific and decided to stop him at any cost, even if it meant his physical elimination.

Ibn Isḥāq explains:

> When the Quraysh saw that Allah's Messenger (ﷺ) now had

> supporters and companions from people other than from their ranks, and in another land, and they saw his companions—the Muhājirūn—migrating to these new supporters, they knew that the Muslims would settle in [a new] abode and that they had received their hosts' protection. They warned of the implications of the departure of Allah's Messenger (ﷺ), understanding from his decision that he had decided to fight them. They gathered in the House of Assembly—which was the House of Quṣay ibn Kilāb in which the Quraysh always made their decisions—to deliberate over their course of action regarding Allah's Messenger (ﷺ). They now feared him.[125]

Biographies of the Prophet (ﷺ) refer to the day that this meeting took place as "the day of the crowd" because the House of Assembly was packed with Qurayshi elders. Their fear that the migration to Yathrib was for the purpose of mobilising to fight against them drove them to override the entrenched Qurayshi custom of not killing one of their own. The leaders agreed that Muḥammad's (ﷺ) assassination should be a collective effort so that the responsibility for it could be shared among the clans, thus preventing the Banī Hāshim from targeting any individual for revenge. However, Allah, the Most Sublime, protected the Prophet (ﷺ) from the plot; he exited his home and safely left the city with his companion Abū Bakr. Their journey had been carefully planned, and all necessary security measures had been taken to ensure that they would not be overtaken by any Qurayshi group in pursuit.

Forward planning and careful preparation were prominent features of Prophetic praxis. The Prophet (ﷺ) knew that he was protected by Allah, and he was confident of Allah's assistance, but he still worked in earnest and strove to block every gap and to plan for every scenario. His faith and confidence in Allah did not prevent him from deliberate planning, careful preparation, and considering all options.

Calculations and balances

The Prophet's (ﷺ) decision to migrate to Yathrib was a critical

125. Ibn Hishām, *al-Sīrah*, vol.1, 480.

turning point in the course of his mission. It required his intense fore-planning, which continued incrementally and in secret over a period of three years and three months. He began by making contact with various people from Yathrib who had visited Makkah for pilgrimage or trade. However, these exchanges did not bear fruit until after the Prophet (ﷺ) met with six individuals from the Khazraj during the pilgrimage season. The meeting did not occur by chance; it was preceded by the gathering of information and by a great deal of communication. The Khazraj were the uncles of the Prophet's (ﷺ) grandfather 'Abd al-Muṭṭalib, and there was already an existing relationship with them; the Prophet (ﷺ) undoubtedly benefitted from his lineage in his effort to strengthen the relationship with the six delegates. The fact that they were from the Khazraj meant that they had been on the losing side in the Bu'āth War and that they desperately needed a change in the balance of forces in Yathrib in order to restore some semblance of civil peace. A message of brotherhood, equality, and peace from outside the city could, they hoped, become the foundation of a post-war Yathrib.

The six Khazrajis embraced Islam and accepted the responsibility given them by the Prophet (ﷺ) to widen the circle of Islam in Yathrib, both in terms of numbers and diversity. They succeeded in this task and, a year later, the Prophet (ﷺ) met a larger delegation of twelve men. This group, however, included representatives from the two most important factions in Yathrib, the Aws and the Khazraj. The meeting came to be known as the First Pledge of 'Aqabah. After the Prophet (ﷺ) ascertained the ability of the group to prepare to receive him and his companions in Yathrib, he instructed Muṣ'ab ibn 'Umayr to join as his ambassador and special envoy to prepare for the momentous event of migration and to evaluate the situation inside the city. The Prophet (ﷺ) also tasked him with spreading the message as widely as possible and ensuring that Islam reached most of the houses in Yathrib, especially those of the Aws and Khazraj leaders. When Muṣ'ab returned a year later with good news, the larger meeting was arranged, with seventy-three men and two women from Yathrib. The Messenger (ﷺ) was accompanied by his uncle al-'Abbās ibn 'Abd al-Muṭṭalib. This was the Second Pledge of 'Aqabah. The two sides held discussions and concluded an agreement. All its provisions and their implications were clarified for all attendees. The Messenger (ﷺ) then commenced with the practical arrangements for his Hijrah, and his companions began migrating in secret. The Prophet (ﷺ) coordinated the migration plan, as well as its route and logistics with Abū Bakr. Three months after the Second Pledge of ʻAqabah, the Prophet (ﷺ) and Abū Bakr began their own migration, following a carefully designed plan.

For the people of Yathrib, the decision to host the Prophet (ﷺ) was profoundly strategic, and also required interrogation and debate. The first Muslims from among the Anṣār—those who welcomed the Prophet (ﷺ) to Yathrib—undoubtedly deliberated over the Hijrah, its potential and implications. It is evident from discussions that transpired on the eve of the Second Pledge of ʻAqabah that these deliberations were profound and frank, and the resolution was decisive. The decision to fulfil the pledge was made by consensus, with full consideration of its implications.

While the primary motivation for welcoming the Prophet (ﷺ) to Yathrib was the new religion that many Anṣār had freely embraced, their decision about the Hijrah was also expedient and beneficial from another perspective: it served the desire of both the Aws and the Khazraj for a new beginning for their city. The process of reaching the decision was assisted by a combination of the circumstances of Yathrib's unfolding transition, the political and social vacuum that had been created after the Buʻāth War, and the new young leadership. This was bolstered by the Yathribi community's willingness to consider all options that might help move the city from division and conflict to security and stability.

In conclusion, the Hijrah benefitted both parties: a prophet and his community seeking a land that would be receptive to his message, and a land seeking a leader to give it a new start.

The world around the Arabs: Collapse of the old, emergence of the new

As well as can be ascertained, the Prophet (ﷺ) left Makkah for his Hijra to Yathrib on Monday, 26 July 622. Let us pause here briefly to consider the global situation at the time, so that we may locate the Hijrah in its international strategic context. This will assist in an understanding of the implications of the Hijrah and its importance, in light of the prevailing regional and global balance of forces.

A critical turning point was reached in the global balance of forces in 622. The raging war between the Persians and the Byzantines was about to take a new turn. In 622, the Persians still held the military advantage. They controlled the most important Byzantine provinces—Syria, Egypt, Armenia, and large portions of Anatolia—and their ships had lain siege to Constantinople, the Byzantine capital.

The Byzantine-Persian War was being fought on several fronts, and the Byzantines were being defeated on all of them. In addition to fighting the Persians, the Byzantine army was also battling an enemy in the Balkans: Slavic tribes that were looking for an opportunity to attack Constantinople, either unilaterally or with the Persians.

The Byzantines needed a miracle to prevent a total collapse of the empire, and Emperor Heraclius delivered that miracle. He assumed power in Constantinople in 610—just before the beginning of the Prophetic mission in 611. The Byzantine-Persian war was in its eighth year, with the Byzantines being pushed back on all fronts. The Persians soon won a resounding victory, occupying Jerusalem—the Byzantine symbol of religious legitimacy, and Egypt, the breadbasket of the Byzantine empire. When Heraclius realised that his army was incapable of defeating the Persians, he sued for peace. The armistice agreement required him to pay huge amounts in compensation, but the truce also allowed him to rebuild his army and reorganise the affairs of his kingdom. He infused a new fighting spirit into Byzantine society, driven by the exhortation to a holy war to liberate Jerusalem from Persian occupation. His standard, a portrait of Jesus, was hoisted by Byzantine soldiers on all fronts, and the church joined in the military mobilisation both financially and theologically.

By the beginning of 622, Heraclius felt ready for war. With a small but well-trained army, he attacked Persian forces in Asia Minor and Armenia and achieved important, morale-boosting victories that revived Byzantine self-confidence. He returned to Constantinople and resumed his offensive in the spring of 623, attacking Azerbaijan and entering Tabriz, the Sassanid capital. The Byzantines razed Tabriz's Great Zoroastrian Temple in retaliation for the Persians having gutted the Church of the Holy Sepulchre in Jerusalem. This battle marked the end of Byzantine subservience and the beginning of Persian collapse. Heraclius then returned to Asia Minor and began preparations for a decisive encounter, which was launched on 25 March 624—around the time that the Battle of Badr took place in the Arabian Peninsula. The Byzantine campaign began in the Caucasus, and it included the forging of alliances with certain of the Turkic tribes that were extremely hostile towards the Persians.

The year of the Prophet's (ﷺ) migration was, thus, a significant year in terms of global geopolitics; the balance of global power was tipped in a different direction and the map of the ancient world was being redrawn. Constantinople's vigorous attack against the Persians and the attempt to destroy their aging empire resulted in the Byzantines exhausting their armies by fighting simultaneously on several fronts. Nevertheless, they achieved a huge victory in the Battle of Nineveh at the end of 627 and captured Ctesiphon, the Sassanid capital. The war ended with the murder of Khosrow II by his son Kavad, who hastily made peace with Constantinople. All Byzantine territory that had been occupied by the Persians, most importantly Syria and Egypt, was restored to Constantinople. The Byzantines also retrieved the True Cross from Ctesiphon and mounted it in the Church of the Holy Sepulchre in a solemn ceremony led by Heraclius. Despite these gains, Constantinople had suffered tremendous losses, both economically and in terms of human lives. Before they would have enough time to rebuild their fatigued empire, a new energetic enemy, which the Byzantines had not previously considered, would emerge from the desert. This enemy would descend on the remnants of the Persian empire and uproot it before surprising Constantinople and conquering its most prized and richest provinces: the Levant and Egypt. This territory would forever be lost to the Byzantine empire.

With the Prophet's (ﷺ) arrival in Yathrib, the final chapter of the historical clash between the two great empires was closing. It would be accompanied by a violent disruption in the balance of forces, with the world entering a state of tension and uncertainty. Such an environment is usually associated with periods of global strategic transformation and represents the best opportunity for weaker entities that are located far from the chaos of conflict and its catastrophic consequences to relocate from the periphery to the centre. This is what the Muslims were able to do. As the Byzantine-Persian war was ending in 628, the Islamic state in Madinah had extracted Qurayshi recognition after the Treaty of al-Hudaybīyyah. Not long thereafter, the new Muslim state disposed of the old Qurayshi entity. Furthermore, three other entities in the Arabian Peninsula—Yemen, the Manādhirah and the Ghassanids—also began to shrivel due to their links to the two conflicting global powers: Byzantine and Persia. This allowed Madinah to quickly become the most important power in the Arab region. It was then only a matter of a few years before the Muslims were catapulted from regional leadership to global power.

After the Byzantine-Persian war, the Muslims saw an opportunity. They exploited the strategic vacuum that the war had created and began knocking on the crumbling wall of the decrepit bipolar edifice, collapsing a world order that had dominated the ancient world for seven centuries. They pushed forward, using the force of their message of monotheism, armed with a global ethical vision, and offering a new order that was able to replace the deadly conflict of the past.

From Yathrib to Madinah

The Prophet's (ﷺ) strategic objective for migrating to Yathrib was clear and is succinctly conveyed in Surah al-Isrā' (Night Journey) in the Qur'ān. "And say, 'My Lord, grant me an honourable entry, and grant me an honourable exit; and give me a supporting authority from Yourself.'. And say: 'Truth has arrived and falsehood has perished. Indeed, falsehood is bound to perish'" (Qur'ān 17:80-81).

The purpose of the migration to Yathrib, a land of truth and honour, was to find an authority that could provide aid. "Authority" in this context encompasses all the elements of power. The supporting authority would also be a social and political compact that would allow a new power to develop and become entrenched, since a leader is always in need of allies. Muḥammad (ﷺ) was aware that he was the bearer of a universal message that would persist until the end of time; it did not stop at the borders of Makkah and could not be restricted to Yathrib or to Arab territory; it would penetrate the veils of both time and space. Therefore, if Makkah refused to be the supporting authority for the fulfilment of his mission, it was necessary for him to migrate elsewhere.

Placed within this context, the migration can be understood not as a human exodus or a means for persecuted people to secure themselves, but as part of the project to create an authority that would be capable of fulfilling the global and perpetual dimensions of the mission. In other words, it would provide the Prophet (ﷺ) and the Muslims a base and a fulcrum for manifesting the truth and eliminating falsehood. This project would require a firm foundation, an integrated society, and a leadership that is obeyed. The leadership also had to be able to plan, meet its obligations, implement, and evaluate. The leader was made manifest, the message had been prepared, and the foundational team that had cohered around the Prophet (ﷺ) in the early years of his mission was ready for action. The team members possessed diverse capacities, were from diverse backgrounds, had forged their skills in the Makkan crucible, and had been infused with an intense motivation for action and innovation by the Hijrah. This is the condition of all new beginnings: souls overflowing with desire and charged with energy.

With the leadership, the message, and the team being in place, all that remained was for its awareness and positivity to penetrate the state of affairs in the new land so that it could become the mission's cradle and launchpad. Yathrib was still a tribal city with inherited conflicts that compromised its social structure, and with several centres of political power that harboured conflicting ambitions. For the city to become the launchpad for a new universalism, it had to be restructured in a way that enabled it to undertake this responsibility.

From the day that the Prophet (ﷺ) arrived in Yathrib, its inhabitants were clear that they stood before a new kind of leader, not one seeking sovereignty, fame, authority, or wealth. This was a leader of a special type, and his characteristics included virtue, insight, extraordinary resolve, and deep ethical values. He was welcoming and hospitable to all who called on him; he brought glad tidings rather than fear, and he did not discriminate between master and slave.

Their attention was drawn to the fact that he accepted gifts with humility, but did not accept charity due to his modesty. Deviating from the tradition of leaders before him, he dissociated from tribal partisanship. He did not favour his uncles from the Banī al-Najjār nor anyone of means and influence from the tribes of Yathrib, despite the determination of each of the noble houses of Yathrib to host him. When he entered Yathrib for the first time, he refused to accept any invitation from the different neighbourhoods of Yathrib for him to settle among them, because he did not want to be seen to be choosing any particular tribe, clan, or family over another. Instead, he released his camel and declared that it was "under [Divine] command". When the animal sat on a plot of land, he announced that this would be where the mosque and his family home would be built. He insisted on paying for the plot from his own wealth, because it would be the heart of the new political establishment and, thus, neutral ground that would be accessible to all without exception. It was, therefore, inappropriate for any one person or family to claim a right or ownership over it.

When the Muslims began constructing the mosque, he worked with them, carrying mud and stones and building with his own hands, teaching by his example that he was different from other leaders. His actions impressed on the minds of all the people of Yathrib—Muslims, idolaters, and Jews—that they were in the company of a unique leader. They should not expect him to issue familiar directives or undertake stale initiatives, like those that had been adopted by their leaders who had been driven by tribal bias, and who had sought status and pride in lineage.

The Prophet (ﷺ) was about to begin rebuilding Yathrib from its very foundations; he would reconstruct it politically and socially in a manner that was unfamiliar to the Arabs. To entrench the uniqueness of the new project, the city was renamed. The familiar "Yathrib" was replaced by "Madinah". The Prophet (ﷺ) prohibited the use of the old name and announced a new beginning; names express personality and carry meanings and memories. The time had arrived for Yathrib—with its tribal heritage and painful memories—to be erased and for Madinah—with its wide-open horizons and promising future—to be born. The new name offered everyone an opportunity to transition from an inherited consciousness to a new awareness that was liberated from history's shackles, complexes, and disturbing standards and structures, and to welcome initiative, renewal, and innovation.

From House of Assembly to House of Allah

The first institution that the Prophet (ﷺ) established in Madinah was the mosque, which would become the city's heart and the centre of its spiritual, political, and social life. Yathrib had not had a governing institution like the House of Assembly in Makkah, but had different centres of power affiliated to the various tribes. The Madinah Mosque would assume this unified function for the first time in the city's history and would become the gathering point and daily meeting place for its people, as well as the centre of public policy and decision-making. It thus fulfilled the role of Makkah's House of Assembly, but was fundamentally different in terms of its principles and precepts, and was much more open and representative. The House of Assembly was the meeting place of Qurayshi leaders and elders; members of the public were not partners in decision-making, and clients and slaves had no representatives or delegates in the House. Furthermore, the main purpose of the House of Assembly was to preserve the customs and interests of the Quraysh and their leadership over other Arabs. It effectively protected the interests of the rich and powerful and was the centre of their influence and authority.

The Madinah Mosque, in contrast, realised the public interest through gatherings and consultations that were not restricted to the leadership elite or tribal elders. It was open to all citizens and entrenched a principle that was absent in Makkah: equal citizenship for all who lived in the city.

The second difference relates to the relationship between religion and worldly affairs. We saw how the Quraysh used religion to fulfil their worldly and class interests and how, by inventing the notion of al-Ḥums (the Sanctified) and by exploiting their status as custodians of the Holy Sanctuary, they distinguished themselves from other Arabs. They had instrumentalised the Holy Sanctuary, the sacred months, and the pilgrimage season for their mercantile interests and accumulation of wealth. Their religiosity was not characterised by a deep spiritual connection or a sublime belief, but by tribal partisanship and adherence to their ancestors' customs and heritage. The Quraysh subjugated religion and modified it for their material benefit.

In contrast, the new paradigm in Madinah sprung from a single source: belief in Allah, the One and Only. The mosque provided a space for the harmonious manifestation of this monotheism in its worldly and religious dimensions and allowed for the fulfilment of public functions, political and social consultations, the signing of contracts, and the sealing of alliances. In addition, it was the religious centre of the community, used for obligatory prayer, supplication, supplementary prayer, or other devotional practices. This combination of functions in one institution was unprecedented, since the Arabs placed their worldly affairs at the top of their priorities, and religion was secondary.

While the mosque represented a central physical-spatial gathering point, it also exemplified a vision that combined the objectives of religion with worldly interests in an integrated model that had no separation or duality. From a devotional perspective, the mosque is the house of Allah; from a worldly perspective, it is the house of the people. Therefore, any worldly matter conducted in a mosque where prayer is offered and supplications are made cannot be devoid of religious objectives and consequences. Islam reset society's compass so that striving over good deeds and competing to attain the pleasure of Allah, the Most Sublime, could happen simultaneously; it encouraged its adherents to draw closer to Allah through sound worldly governance, while worshipping Him through sound religious practice.

The third difference between the Qurayshi House of Assembly and the Prophet's (ﷺ) Mosque relates to the mosque's educational and intellectual function. It was a veritable university, in which the Islamic mindset was cast in its new dye. Madinah was on the verge of adopting a new existential vision emanating from firm doctrines of faith that manifested in ethical teachings that permeated trade, social transactions, legislation, and political and strategic visions. The construction of the "Muslim self" is a continuous educational process in both its theoretical and practical dimensions, and the mosque offered the space for the fulfilment of this function. In this way, the functions of the most important central institution in the city were realised. It began playing this role a few months after the Prophet's (ﷺ) arrival in the city.

From patronage to forging brotherly bonds

The Prophet (ﷺ) introduced a unique approach to address a twin economic-tribal challenge in Madinah. He united pairs of individuals so that they would regard each other as brothers. The migrants who arrived in droves had abandoned most of their belongings and wealth and had reached a new land as strangers with no experience of earning a living in an economy that was very different from Makkah's. Agriculture was the primary economic activity in Yathrib, followed by trade and artisanship. The new immigrants were skilled traders, but they lacked capital and knowledge of the new market.

The second problem was that tribal partisanship in Madinah—even if not as pronounced as in Makkah—was pervasive. The Anṣār were recently converted to Islam, a number of groups in Madinah were still idol worshippers, and the Jewish tribes were joined together by religion and tribal affiliation. In contrast, the Muhājīrun (the Muslim immigrants from Makkah), were, as a migrant bloc, entering a society that was tribally settled. Somehow, they had to be integrated into it.

Tribal custom prescribed a system of client patronage in which a migrant would join a particular tribe and become its "client", enjoying the same rights as its other members and having the same responsibilities. This practice entrenched the custom of tribal partisanship. Islam, however, strove to create a new type of society founded on bonds of faith rather than partisanship, in which all believers were brothers and sisters, and the most honoured among them in the sight of Allah were the ones who were most conscious of Allah. The bonds created by the Prophet's (ﷺ) innovative plan became so strong that, initially, a man would even inherit from his "brother". This practice continued until its annulment by the revelation of Qur'ānic verses pertaining to inheritance.

The benefits of forging brotherly bonds went beyond the economic and social integration of the Muhājīrun into Madinan society; the bonds of faith became as important as the bonds of blood, and a new contract of citizenship emerged in which religion, rather than tribal affiliation, represented the essence of identity and belonging.

Political constitution and social contract

The Prophet's (ﷺ) most important initiative in Madinah was the Charter (al-Ṣaḥīfah), an extremely important declaration that effectively announced the death of the old Yathrib and the establishment of a new city on constitutional foundations.

The Charter is regarded as the *grundnorm* of Madinah; it engaged foundational concepts, the regulation of authority, and the principles of governance. It was also a social contract that reflected a profound understanding of the tribal and demographic reality of Madinah. Unfortunately, not much is known about the process of its drafting and the manner in which it was promulgated. However, an examination of its articles suggests that it was a collective effort in which the people of Madinah participated, especially those with a deep knowledge of its tribes and alliances. It is also apparent that the document was approved by the various social groups in the city, thereby granting it legitimacy and the status of a constitution that had to be implemented and adhered to.

Ibn Isḥāq presents the Charter as a document that encompassed the political contours of the new entity, providing a prophetic frame of reference, defining citizenship, regulating alliances, outlining social and political obligations, explicating principles of governance, and resolving on unity of purpose in its position toward the Quraysh. In its prologue, the Charter clearly expresses the source of its legitimacy, the Prophet (ﷺ), then states its main purpose: the declaration of the establishment of a single nation (ummah), distinct among people, comprising of believers, Muslims and those allied to them.

> In the name of Allah, the Beneficent, the Merciful. This is a written [declaration] from Muḥammad, the Prophet (ﷺ), between the believers and Muslims of the Quraysh and Yathrib and those who follow them, join them, and fight alongside them. They are one community (ummah), distinct from all other people. The Muḥājīrūn from the Quraysh keep to their tribal organisation and leadership, cooperate with each other regarding blood money, and ransom their captives according to what is amicable and just among the believers.[126]

The expression "the believers and Muslims of the Quraysh and Yathrib" deserves some reflection; the insertion of "Quraysh" here is particularly significant. The Charter highlights the Qurayshi affiliation of the Muḥājīrūn, thus emphasising that the name "Quraysh" and its status among the Arabs would not remain the strict preserve of the Makkan idolaters. The name of Quraysh had tremendous gravitas, and the Prophet (ﷺ) and the Muḥājīrūn were more entitled to it than the Makkan idolaters. The Arabs felt obligated to hold the Quraysh in high regard, since they were the "People of Allah and the custodians of the Holy Sanctuary". In Madinah, the Muslim section of the Quraysh, under the leadership of a prophet from the most senior branch of the Quraysh, the Banī Hāshim, declared a new, organised social entity that was unfamiliar to the idolatrous Quraysh. It was an unprecedented declaration for the Quraysh, but the correct model of what the Quraysh should adhere to. These Madinan Quraysh affiliated themselves to the monotheistic Abrahamic legacy that the Quraysh had corrupted and that laid the foundations for a message that was open to wide horizons, leaving behind the idolatrous Quraysh who were trapped in an inherited past.

Indeed, the worst fears of the idolatrous Quraysh was soon to

126. Ibn Hishām, *al-Sīrah,* vol. 1, 602. [Translator's Note: I have relied on Dr Ovamir Anjum's excellent translation in rendering the Charter into English, but have made changes where I deemed necessary. For Dr Anjum's translation and commentary, see: "The "Constitution" of Medina: Translation, Commentary, and Meaning Today": (https://yaqeeninstitute.org/read/paper/the-constitution-of-medina-translation-commentary-and-meaning-today).]

be realised; Muḥammad (ﷺ) did not migrate to Yathrib to seek refuge from the harm they had caused him, but to challenge them as representatives of the tribe, and to present himself and his allies as the true representatives of Qurayshi legitimacy. He gave glad tidings of an elevated ethical consciousness that rose above a parochial exploitative utilisation of religion, and of a return to the Abrahamic roots of the Quraysh. As far as the Quraysh were concerned, this was a dangerous call that struck at the very foundations of time-honoured Qurayshi legitimacy.

The Charter then addressed each of Yathrib's tribes, regarding them as social blocs with obligations towards their members and affirming that they "keep to their tribal organisation and leadership, cooperate with each other regarding blood money, and ransom their captives according to what is amicable and just among the believers". The function of Yathrib's tribes was to tend to the needs of their members; the responsibility of paying blood money was communal and fell to all the members of the tribe; ransoming captives was also a communal responsibility. The second and third functions relate to the tribes to which a murderer or captive is affiliated. As a general matter of solidarity among all believers, the Charter refers to the settling of the debts of a debtor or providing an honourable living for the needy. After addressing Yathrib's tribes, the Charter states: "The believers shall not neglect to give aid to a debtor among them according to what is just in matters of ransom or blood money." This decisively affirmed a system of social welfare for the inhabitants of Yathrib, with clearly defined obligations and rights that covered the needs of all citizens in a respectable society.

The Charter then affirmed a legal principle that is critically important to the construction of a legal system that would ensure just citizenship, completely different from the tribal partisanship that brought only sorrow, retribution, and war to the people of Yathrib. Tribal partisanship meant extending uncritical support to a fellow tribe member, whether right or wrong. The new approach required action on the basis of justice and truth.

> And no believer shall make an alliance with a client of another believer to the exclusion of the latter.

> The God-conscious believers are against whoever of them acts wrongfully, seeks an act of injustice, or promotes sin, transgression, or depravity among the believers. They shall all unite against him even if he is the son of one of them.
>
> A believer will not kill a believer [in retribution] for a non-believer and will not aid a non-believer against a believer.
>
> Indeed, the protection of Allah is one; the least of them [i.e., the believers] is entitled to protection that is binding for all of them. The believers are each other's allies to the exclusion of other people.[127]

This was a significant transition that placed justice at the centre of daily affairs. The era in which the oppressor was protected by his tribe or extended family was over. Oppression, transgression, and sin were to be regarded as despicable traits, and all citizens were obliged to unite against them, so that equity and justice might be entrenched, and sedition and depravity eliminated.

The Charter continued by affirming political allegiance, outlining the political obligations and strategic relationships for the tribes of Yathrib, including the Jews. Allegiance applied to the community as a collective, and separate alliances were not countenanced. Providing assistance and defence were joint responsibilities of all members of the community.

> The Jews who join us will receive aid and parity [or favour]. They will not be wronged, nor will their enemies be aided against them.
>
> The peace of the believers is one; no believer will make peace to the exclusion of another believer in fighting in the path of Allah. However, [peace must be concluded] on the basis of equality and justice between them.
>
> In every expedition made with us, the parties take turns with one another.

127. Ibn Hishām, *al-Sīrah*, vol. 1, 602.

The believers exact full retribution for the blood of one another that is shed in the path of Allah.

Indeed, the God-conscious believers [undertake to] follow the best and most upright guidance.[128]

The Charter then moved from the general to the specific and made a firm and frank declaration about the Quraysh. It stipulated the need for a collective stance regarding interaction with the Quraysh, especially by the polytheists in Yathrib, who were party to the Charter, but who had not yet embraced Islam. "A mushrik (polytheist) will not grant protection to any property or to any person of the Quraysh, nor will he intervene between a person [from the Quraysh] and a believer [in regards to the property or the person]."

The text then discussed rules for settling disputes between people and holding them accountable, especially for the crime of murder, an issue that often resulted in conflict and retaliation. The murderer would be personally and individually responsible for his crime and would face punitive retribution for his actions. The tribes of Yathrib would not be permitted to grant refuge, assistance, or support to the perpetrator of a crime. The tribe's role would relate to matters of social welfare that ensured the stability of society. Intervention in matters solely on the basis of tribal solidarity was strictly forbidden and stood in clear contradiction to the articles of the Charter; they deserved Allah's curse and wrath, in this world and the hereafter.

When evidence has been established that someone has wrongfully killed a believer, he is liable to be killed in retaliation, unless the kin of the victim is satisfied [with blood money]. All the believers are united against him, and it is not permissible for them not to act against him.

It is not permissible for a believer who affirms what is in this Charter and believes in Allah and the Last Day to support a murderer or give him shelter. The curse and wrath of Allah on the Day of Resurrection will be on whoever supports him or gives him shelter, and neither repentance nor ransom will be

128. Ibn Hishām, *al-Sīrah*, vol. 1, 503.

accepted from him.[129]

Since dispute inevitably requires arbitration, the Charter stipulated that the arbitration institution would be a single legislative authority, the law of Allah the Sublime, and a single judicial authority, the Prophet (ﷺ). "Whatever you differ about shall be referred to Allah, the Honoured and Almighty, and Muḥammad (ﷺ)." This effectively suspended all inherited methods of legal arbitration, such as the arbitration of soothsayers, the practice of al-Munāfarah (arbitration debates), drawing lots, and other methods that were prevalent among the pre-Islamic Arabs.

The Charter prescribed joint fiscal responsibility in times of war, and specifically mentioned the Jews, since they did not usually fight—except if Madinah was attacked by a foreign army, which would make fighting obligatory for all. In all cases, the Jews had an obligation to spend their wealth in support of the war effort. "The Jews bear expenses along with the believers as long as they continue at war."

The Charter then discussed in detail the relationship between the Believers and the Jews. "The Jews of Banī 'Awf are a community alongside the believers; the Jews have their religion and the Muslims have theirs. This applies to their clients and themselves. But whoever does wrong or sins, brings evil only on himself and his household." The Charter acknowledged that the Jews had their own established religious authority and that they were a community alongside the Muslim community, that is, that they were bound together by the Charter. This joint affiliation to the community of Madinah did not, however, negate the right of Jews to have their own religious affiliation; Muslims had their religion and Jews had theirs. Each side was entitled to make their religion the authority in their private affairs and among themselves and their clients. In a case where an individual committed a specific crime, his sin would not fall on all the adherents of his religion or on his tribe. This again confirmed that the measure of citizenship was justice and equality, without consideration for religion and tribal affiliation. This text, which specifically mentions the Banī 'Awf, applied to all the Jewish tribes, which were then mentioned in greater detail. The Charter

129. Ibn Hishām, *al-Sīrah*, vol. 1, 503.

then specified the Muslim relationship with the Jews and stipulated that none of the Jews could permanently relocate from one place to another except with the permission of the Prophet (ﷺ). It also prescribed a collective responsibility to protect Madinah. "They undertake to aid each other against whoever attacks the people of this Charter."

In the document's conclusion, its main articles are succinctly reaffirmed.

> Between them is goodwill and sincerity. And righteousness is easier than sin. A man will not act unjustly toward his ally, and assistance will be extended to anyone who is wronged.
>
> The Jews bear expenses along with the believers as long as they continue at war.
>
> The valley of Yathrib is consecrated [as a sanctuary] for the parties to this document.
>
> The protected neighbour is like one's self, as long as he does not harm or act treacherously.
>
> No protection may be granted without the permission of the parties to this [Charter].
>
> Whenever there is a murder or dispute between the people of this Charter from which evil is feared, the matter is to be referred to Allah, the Honoured and Almighty, and Muḥammad, Allah's Messenger. Allah demands the most pious and righteous fulfilment of this document.
>
> No protection will be granted to the Quraysh nor to whoever supports them.
>
> [The parties to this treaty] undertake to aid each other against whosoever attacks Yathrib.
>
> If [the Jews] are called to an agreement, they will accept it, and if they call for the same, it is incumbent upon the believers to

> accept it, except if someone makes war on account of religion. Each group is responsible for its own obligations [in this clause].
>
> The Jews of al-Aws, their allies, and they themselves have the same standing as the parties to this Charter, with the truest fulfilment with regard to the parties of this Charter [all parties are equal and equally accountable]. Verily, righteousness is easier than sin, and he who violates [the Charter] does so only against himself. Allah demands the truest and most righteous fulfilment of what is in this Charter.
>
> This document will not intervene to protect an unjust man or a violator of a pledge. He who goes out is secure, and he who stays in Madinah is safe, except he who acts unjustly or in violation of the pledge. Allah is the Protector of him who is righteous and God-conscious, and so is Muḥammad, Allah's Messenger.[130]

With the building of the mosque, the cementing of brotherhood, and the proclamation of the Charter, the legislative, social, and bureaucratic foundations of Madinah were completed. Ibn Isḥāq commented on these steps, reflecting the spirit that was prevalent in Madinah at the time.

> When Allah's Messenger (ﷺ) was settled in Madinah, his Muhājīrūn brothers had gathered around him, and the Anṣār had resolved their issues, Islam became established. Prayer was instituted, zakāh [compulsory wealth tax] and fasting were made obligatory, legal punishments were enacted, the boundaries of permissibility and prohibition were enforced, and Islam was entrenched among the people. It was in this corner of the land of the Anṣār where they made a homeland and [established] faith.[131]

In the space of less than ten months, the Prophet (ﷺ) had laid the foundations of a new society and, with unimaginable speed, the new society began to crystallise. The finest of Madinah's elite embraced Islam, the migration of Muslims from Makkah was completed, and a

130. Ibn Hishām, *al-Sīrah*, vol. 1, 504.
131. Ibn Hishām, *al-Sīrah*, vol. 1, 508.

new spirit prevailed, manifesting in a religious, intellectual, and social unity that had never before been experienced by the Arabs. The Prophet (ﷺ) transformed this energetic potential into tangible accomplishments. What became Madinah had previously been no more than a few villages spread across the plains, including Qubā', Yathrib, Rātiḥ, al-Sunaḥ, and Ḥusaykah. Islam united them and encouraged people to develop the abundant and fertile land. The result was an increase in development and, through immigration, in the population size.[132]

The Prophet (ﷺ) directed the Muslims to establish new markets, encouraged them to engage in trade and to control the levers of economic power, and inspired them to learn to read and write. They also learnt to be meticulous and virtuous, while congregational prayer gave them a sense of discipline and collective consciousness. They competed among themselves in serving the common good, and the spirit of sacrifice and redemption was entrenched in their very beings. In all this, the Prophet (ﷺ) stood over them, teaching, directing, and leading, and the Qur'ān continued being revealed, giving the new society a rejuvenated strength, broadening its outlook, and changing its perceptions. They became bound to a sublime message and were repeatedly prompted to reflect on the dominions of heaven and earth.

132. See Mu'nis, *Tārīkh Quraysh*, 324.

CHAPTER SEVEN

The Prophetic strategy in Madinah

"Permission is [hereby] given to those against whom war is made [to fight back], because they have been wronged. And verily Allah is most able to give them victory" (Qur'ān 22:39).

The Prophet (ﷺ) was acutely aware that a prerequisite for the Islamisation of the Arabian Peninsula was the Islamisation of the Quraysh; this, therefore, became the foundation of his strategy in Madinah. While the Quraysh were a relatively small tribe, they remained the most influential in the peninsula, with the longest reach. Qurayshi men enjoyed extensive influence, had a great deal of contact with the outside world, and were able to accumulate the kind of acumen, experience and diplomatic skills not found in other tribes. This soft power influence made the Quraysh a formidable opponent and a serious obstacle to the spread of Islam.

In addition, the Quraysh still controlled Makkah, the home of the Holy Sanctuary, which was regarded as sacred by all Arabs. The sanctuary was regarded as Allah's sanctuary and as the destination of the pilgrimage, the place where seasons were determined and markets convened. From Makkah, caravans departed for the north and the south, transporting merchandise, correspondence, and news. Makkah was the economic and religious centre of the Arabian Peninsula and absorbing it within the Islamic sphere of influence was, therefore, the primary strategic objective of the new political entity in Madinah. Without Muslim control over Makkah, the Islamisation of the Arabian Peninsula could not be achieved.

The Prophet (ﷺ) was also well aware that the Quraysh were propped up by two central pillars: trade and the Holy Sanctuary. The Qur'ān alerted the Muslims to this fact from the beginning of the Prophetic mission, and Surah Quraysh (Qur'ān 106) remained firmly rooted in the Prophet's (ﷺ) mind. It was an important strategic tool for understanding the sources of the Quraysh's power. The Prophet (ﷺ) understood from that surah that the Quraysh's trade pacts and its caravans were the lifeblood of its growth. Furthermore, the Holy Sanctuary, "which fed them against hunger and made them safe from fear" (Qur'ān 106:4), was the most important source of Qurayshi legitimacy.

The readings of the Prophetic compass regarding the Quraysh were explicit from the very beginning in Madinah. We saw that, as the Prophet (ﷺ) laid the foundations of Madinan society, he built the Muslim Quraysh—comprising the Muhājīrun—while simultaneously making the polytheistic Quraysh a common enemy to all Madinah. The Charter prohibited the people of Madinah from dealing with the Quraysh or their caravans, and it strongly emphasised the prohibition on granting them assistance and support. The Prophet's (ﷺ) strategic objective was thus clear: to pressure the Quraysh to either embrace Islam or surrender.

This objective was realised in two phases. Initially, the Muslims addressed the first pillar of Qurayshi power: trade. This was done by destabilising the Qurayshi economy through disruptions of their caravan trade routes. In the second phase, the second pillar of Qurayshi power was engaged: their control over the Holy Sanctuary. The Treaty of al-Ḥudaybīyyah, which followed the Battle of the Trench, forced the Quraysh to concede formal recognition to the Muslims as an independent power.

By studying the Prophet's (ﷺ) actions from his arrival in Madinah until the end of the Battle of the Trench, we can conclude that every expedition, battle, or agreement that was undertaken in that period accorded with the strategy of pressuring the Quraysh, wearing them down and besieging them. From this perspective, these expeditions, battles, and alliances may be viewed as links in a single chain, each joined to the next, and all serving the same strategy.

Beginnings of the Madinan Pact

The Prophet's (ﷺ) strategic initiatives were always decisive, swift, and well-planned. He launched eight expeditions and raids over a one-year period, just six months after his Hijrah; the first was Ḥamzah ibn 'Abd al-Muṭṭalib's expedition to Sayf al-Baḥr, and the last was 'Abdallah ibn Jaḥsh's expedition to Nakhlah on the outskirts of Makkah. All these expeditions conveyed the same message: Madinah was a sovereign entity, its sovereignty was powerful, and it could be asserted and protected. It was clear that Madinah had become a player that could not be taken for granted, and that it would reset the balance of forces in the Ḥijāz by redefining Madinah's sovereign sphere. Instead of being an isolated settlement preoccupied with its internal squabbles, Yathrib had become a closely integrated entity with a well-defined sovereign sphere of influence that was regionally secure, and which would expand to encompass Yathrib's neighbouring regions and reach the shores of the Red Sea.

The expedition that the Prophet (ﷺ) deployed a few months after the Hijrah confirmed this strategy. With thirty men, Ḥamzah ibn 'Abd al-Muṭṭalib departed for Sayf al-Baḥr on 2 Ṣafar 2 AH / June 623 to intercept a Qurayshi caravan.

> [The caravan was] coming from the Levant and heading for Makkah. The caravan was under the leadership of Abū Jahl and comprised 300 Makkan riders. The parties met and lined up for battle, but Majdī ibn 'Amr, an ally of both parties, walked between them. He continued to walk from one side to the other until the people settled and Ḥamzah withdrew and returned to Madinah with his companions. Abū Jahl and his companions continued to Makkah.[133]

This expedition aimed to send a message to the Quraysh, and it was delivered clearly and strongly. Abū Jahl, for one, knew exactly who Ḥamzah was, and he knew the strength of his blow. He might still have been suffering the effects of the facial fracture that Ḥamzah had given him when he found out that Abū Jahl had cursed his nephew Muḥammad (ﷺ). Knowing that he could do nothing to Ḥamzah, the Qurayshi leader told the men of Banī Makhzūm: "Leave Abū 'Umārah for, by Allah, I cursed his nephew with a most vile curse."[134] Abū Jahl's stupidity had been the direct cause of Ḥamzah's announcement of his

133. Al-Wāqidī, *Kitāb al-Maghāzī*, vol. 1, 9.

134. Ibn Hishām, *al-Sīrah*, vol. 1, 292.

conversion to Islam.

Word of Ḥamzah's expedition reached not only the Quraysh, but also the coastal tribes through whose territory the Quraysh's caravans passed; in particular, the Juhaynah tribe heard of the incident. The Juhaynah leaders knew that they would soon face difficult choices. In terms of their trade pact with the Quraysh, the latter paid them a tax for protecting their caravans from bandits, allowing them safe passage through Juhaynah territory and on into the protection of the next tribe, until they reached their destination. However, Juhaynah was also an ally of Yathrib, and its territory fell within Yathrib's sphere of influence. Some Juhaynah clans had even fought in the Bu'āth War on the side of the Khazraj and Banī Qaynuqā'. They also had trade links with the people of Yathrib, especially since Yathrib's sea access was through the Yanbu'[135]port, which lay within Juhaynah's territory. This was the context for the actions of Majdī ibn 'Amr, a Juhaynah elder, when he intervened between the Muslims and the Quraysh and prevented them from fighting.

The Prophet (ﷺ) would soon strengthen his alliance with the Juhaynah, invite their leaders to visit Madinah, reward them, and praise their leader Majdī ibn 'Amr. Soon thereafter, Islam would enter the homes of Juhaynah leaders. The Muslims thus benefitted from those Juhaynah who had embraced Islam, and they strengthened their relations with Juhaynah to such a degree that the Quraysh lost confidence in their protection, increasing their fears regarding the safe movement of their caravans along the coastal route. The Prophet (ﷺ) won over Majdī ibn 'Amr with messages of assurance and praise. Al-Wāqidī relates:

> When Ḥamzah returned to the Prophet (ﷺ), he informed him of Majdī's intervention and that they believed he had acted fairly with them. Majdī's delegation visited the Prophet (ﷺ), and he gifted them garments and treated them with kindness. Referring to Majdī ibn 'Amr, the Prophet said: "He did not know [that he] was of a blessed disposition and way." Or, he said: "judicious in judgement".[136]

135. The main port used by al-Madīnah al-Munawarah (Madinah).

136. Al-Wāqidī, *Kitāb al-Maghāzī*, vol. 1, 10.

The Prophet (ﷺ) also won over another leader, Kashd al-Juhanī, by granting Yanbu' to one of his sons as a fief. Kashd will be mentioned again in the discussion on the Battle of Badr, where his hosting of two of the Prophet's (ﷺ) companions played a critical role in the gathering of intelligence about Abū Sufyān's caravan.

Less than a month after the Sayf al-Baḥr expedition, the Prophet (ﷺ) launched a second expedition, this time under the leadership of 'Ubaydah ibn al-Ḥārith. He sent sixty riders with him to Rābigh. They confronted Abū Sufyān ibn Ḥarb in a caravan comprised of 200 individuals. The parties launched arrows at each other; Sa'd ibn Abī Waqqāṣ became the first Muslim to have shot an arrow in Islamic history. However, the two sides dispersed without engaging in battle. It is clear that the objective of this expedition was the same as the previous one, and that the message conveyed to Abū Jahl was not a random event. A month after Abū Jahl, Abū Sufyān was being taught the same lesson. The purpose of the expedition was not to engage in battle. Al-Wāqidī narrates that Sa'd ibn Abī Waqqāṣ had said to 'Ubaydah, the expedition leader: "If we were to follow them, we would have them, since they turned away in fear."[137] However, 'Ubaydah did not heed this comment and the Muslims returned to Madinah.

The third expedition was led by Sa'd ibn Abī Waqqāṣ, less than a month after the previous one. It aimed to confront a Qurayshi caravan at al-Kharrār, close to al-Juḥfah and Rābigh, the land inhabited by the Khuzā'ah tribe. The Khuzā'ah had an old alliance with 'Abd al-Muṭṭalib, the Prophet's (ﷺ) grandfather, and their alliance with the Prophet (ﷺ) was a continuation of that relationship.

The Prophet (ﷺ) himself led the fourth raid in the month of Rabī' al-Awwal in the second year of the Hijrah. This was his first campaign, so called because the Prophet's (ﷺ) biographers refer to a raid led by him as a campaign (ghazwah), and one led by someone else as an expedition (sirīyyah). The target was al-Abwā'a, north of Rābigh. The outcome was that "he made peace with the Banī Ḍamrah, who were from the Kinānah tribe, on condition that they did not make constant [demands] on him or assist anyone against him. He then signed an agreement with

137. Ibn Hishām, *al-Sīrah*, vol. 1, 292.

them and returned."[138]

The agreement that the Prophet (ﷺ) signed with the Banī Ḍamrah, and his strengthening of the alliance with Juhaynah and Khuzā'ah, show that he was, in a calculated manner, laying the foundations for a new pact with the coastal tribes. This pact demanded a reciprocal relationship in which benefits would be accrued by both parties. The Muslims wanted assurances that the neighbouring tribes would not assist the Quraysh and hoped that their new allies would act in disrupting Qurayshi trade routes. The agreements also served the interests of these tribes by ensuring that they were safe from any aggression from Madinah, which had begun to play a greater role in the region, and by ensuring that their trade relations with the Madinan markets were secured and accessible.

Two months later, the Prophet (ﷺ) led a group of his companions in pursuit of a Qurayshi caravan led by Ummayah ibn Khalaf, accompanied by 100 men, and driving 2,050 camels. The Prophet (ﷺ) returned safely "and did not encounter any deceit".

Shortly after returning to Madinah, the Prophet (ﷺ) again mobilised his forces, this time in pursuit of Kuraz ibn Jābir al-Fahrī,[139] who had led a raid on some Madinan pastural lands. The Prophet (ﷺ) and his companions followed Kuraz until they reached Badr, giving this campaign the name "the First Badr".

By contrast, the 'Ushayrah Campaign, in the month of Rabī' al-Awwal in the first year of the Hijrah, involved a relatively large number of Muslims. Al-Wāqidī estimated the number was between 150 and 200. They, too, tried to ambush Abū Sufyān's caravan as it headed to the Levant, but were unable to overtake it. This was the same caravan that the Muslims would again attempt to ambush on its return from the Levant, and because of this the Battle of Badr would take place. Al-Wāqidī's narration about Makhramah ibn Nawfil, who was with Abū Sufyān's caravan, suggests that the Prophet (ﷺ) had probably spent some time on the coast, during which he had engaged the tribes, especially the Juhaynah. Al-Wāqidī narrates from Makhramah:

138. Al-Wāqidī, *Kitāb al-Maghāzī*, vol. 1, 12.

139. He would later embrace Islam wholeheartedly and lead an expedition for the Prophet (ﷺ). He was killed by the polytheists on the day of the Conquest of Makkah.

> When we got to the Levant, we caught up with a man from [the tribe of] Judhām and he informed us that Muḥammad had set an ambush for our caravan upon our departure and had left it in place, awaiting our return. He had entered an alliance with the people of the route and made peace with them. We departed in fear, afraid of the surveillance, and sent Ḍamḍam ibn 'Amr [ahead of us] when we departed the Levant.[140]

We saw how the Prophet's (ﷺ) strategy of building alliances with the people of the coastal areas had progressed from the first expedition led by Ḥamzah ibn 'Abd al-Muṭṭalib. His military and diplomatic activities were careful and calculated, which ensured that he always had the element of surprise on his side. This can be inferred from an incident narrated by 'Amr ibn al-'Āṣ, who had also accompanied the caravan.

> When we were in al-Zarqā'a, in the region of Ma'ān in the Levant, about two leagues from Adhriā't, and we were descending towards Makkah, we met a man from [the tribe of] Judhām. He said, "Muḥammad and his companions were lying in wait for you at the beginning." We responded, "We were not aware." He said: "He waited for a month and then returned to Yathrib. You were concealed on the day that Muḥammad lay in wait, but he is now sure to confront you and is counting down the days. Be wary of [the safety of] your caravan and consider your situation carefully. By Allah, I do not see [you sufficient] in number, either in [terms] of weapons and horses, or in fighting companies." They then agreed to dispatch Ḍamḍam [al-Ghaffārī], who was in the caravan, [to go ahead of them and summon help]. The Quraysh had earlier passed him along the coast with his flock of camels and had hired him for twenty mithqals.[141]

Nakhlah opens a new era

We leave Abū Sufyān and his caravan as it was preparing to return

140. Al-Wāqidī, *Kitāb al-Maghāzī*, vol. 1, 28.
141. Al-Wāqidī, *Kitāb al-Maghāzī*, vol. 1, 28.

to Makkah and move back to Madinah, where we find that the Prophet (ﷺ) has mobilised for what would be the last excursion before the Battle of Badr. The raid, unique in both form and purpose, was named the Nakhlah expedition. An examination of the details of the expedition shows that its objective was to reach as close to Makkah as possible, in order to measure the levels of activity of the Quraysh and to assess their state of preparedness. It was essentially an intelligence-gathering exercise, not a military offensive. Because of the sensitivity of the expedition, the Prophet (ﷺ) took unprecedented security measures; he even ensured that none of the participants were aware of their destination. Eight Muhājīrun were selected, with 'Abdallah ibn Jaḥsh as their leader. The Messenger of Allah (ﷺ) gave 'Abdallah ibn Jaḥsh a letter and ordered him to proceed along the Najd road. He was to open the letter only after two days. When 'Abdallah opened the letter, he found the Prophet's (ﷺ) instructions to proceed to the middle of Nakhlah, which was on the road between Ṭā'if and Makkah.

The selected destination was close to Makkah, on the Ṭā'if road, not on the Qurayshi caravan routes to the Levant. The Quraysh usually regarded this route as safe, since it was well-travelled and full of activity, because of burgeoning trade and social relationships between Makkah and Ṭā'if. Targeting this route would be regarded as a dangerous escalation, and the Quraysh would realise that they were no longer safe in their own homes or in their immediate sphere of influence. The expedition would represent a massive escalation.

Although the Prophet (ﷺ) had not commanded the expedition to engage with the Quraysh, events played out in a manner that led to fighting, making it the first encounter of its kind between the Muslims and the polytheists. The expedition encountered four polytheists travelling in a caravan. The members of 'Abdallah's group initially managed to conceal their identities; some of them had shaved their heads to give the impression that they were on their way to perform the 'umrah (lesser pilgrimage). When the polytheists had been deceived, the Muslims attacked. The polytheist 'Amr ibn al-Ḥaḍramī was killed by an arrow and two others were captured. The fourth person fled, and the Muslims confiscated the caravan containing wine, cured hides, and raisins from Ṭā'if.

The situation was made more serious by the fact that the clash occurred on the last day of the month of Rajab, one of the consecrated months when fighting was prohibited by both polytheists and Muslims. Some members of the expedition assessed that the polytheists were about to enter the precincts of the Sanctuary and felt that it was therefore imperative that they be attacked before. Some of them said:

> If you left these people this evening, they will enter the Sanctuary and will be protected from you, but if you fought them, you would be fighting them in the consecrated month. The group was thus ambivalent and had doubts about launching an attack. They then convinced themselves to act, to kill whoever they were able to, and to take their possessions.[142]

Ibn al-Ḥaḍramī's killing at the hands of the Muslims and the confiscation of the group's property was a clear violation of the sanctity of the consecrated month, which the Prophet (ﷺ) also respected. The Quraysh took advantage of the violation and launched a vicious propaganda campaign against the Prophet (ﷺ). They announced: "Muḥammad has violated the consecrated month. He drew blood and took people's possessions [even though] he used to respect and glorify [the sacred months]."[143]

It is certain that the Prophet (ﷺ) had not ordered the expedition to fight—whether in the consecrated month or in any other month. He had, rather, ordered them to gather intelligence on the Quraysh. When the expedition returned to Madinah, the Muslims were shaken by their actions, and they were reprimanded. "Madinah was boiling like a cauldron." The Prophet (ﷺ) also condemned their actions and refused to accept any of the booty. The Muslims became extremely apprehensive, until the following verse of the Qur'ān was revealed:

> They ask you concerning fighting in the sacred month. Say: "Fighting therein is a grave (offence); but preventing access to the path of Allah, disbelieving in Him, preventing access to the Sacred Mosque, and expelling its people are even graver offences in the sight of Allah. Persecution is worse than killing."

142. Ibn Hishām, *al-Sīrah*, vol. 1, 603.
143. Al-Wāqidī, *Kitāb al-Maghāzī*, vol. 1, 16.

They will not cease fighting you until they make you revoke your faith, if they can." (Qur'ān 2:217).

This revelation reminded the Muslims that the polytheists had blocked the Muslims from the path of Allah, rejected Him, had denied the Muslims access to the Sacred Mosque, and had expelled them from the Mosque even though they were most entitled to it. The polytheists had thus already transgressed the principle of sanctity of the Sacred Mosque and had violated the right of all people to take refuge in it in peace and security. These actions, the revelation pointed out, were no less severe than fighting in the sacred month, because persecution and oppression were worse than killing someone. It was true that there was to be no fighting during the consecrated month, but the Sacred Mosque was also sanctified, and the Quraysh had transgressed this sanctity first. These verses ended the heated debates in Madinah.

With this revelation, the Muslims breathed more easily, and the Prophet (ﷺ) took possession of the caravan and the two captives. The Quraysh, meanwhile, had sent a representative to ransom the captives. However, one of the captives, al-Ḥakam ibn Kaysān, sincerely embraced Islam and remained in Madinah. The other, 'Uthmān ibn 'Abdallah, returned to Makkah and died there as a disbeliever.

In a practical sense, this expedition marked the beginning of offensive operations and was a precursor to the great Battle of Badr. This was also the first time that the Muslims had captured booty; 'Amr ibn al-Ḥaḍramī was the first person that the Muslims had killed; and 'Uthmān ibn 'Abdallah and al-Ḥakam ibn Kaysān were the first captives taken by the Muslims.

This phase, with its four expeditions and four campaigns, as well as the Prophet's (ﷺ) alliances with the Juhaynah and Ḍamrah tribes, heralded the beginning of a new era. The Muslim expeditions—with small numbers of people, rapidity of action, and firm discipline—established a new secure region and a new political pact stretching from Madinah to the Red Sea, descending along the coast from Yanbu' in the north to Rābigh in the south, and from Madinah to the outskirts of Makkah. This restructured regional order fulfilled its purpose: to announce to the Quraysh, Khuzā'ah, Juhaynah, Ḍamrah, Ghaffār, and all the other tribes of Kinānah, Qaḍā'ah, and Ghaṭafān that Madinah was in a commanding position, that it was the most important player, and that everyone had to engage it on the basis of this new reality.

The Qurayshi Pact that had made Makkah an influential role-player with regional and international powers had been destabilised, and the Madinah Pact had emerged and was beginning to take shape. The dominant and traditional forms of relationships in the region were no longer under the monopoly of the Quraysh; its regime had become insecure. After this point, there was no longer security for the Quraysh's caravans. More importantly, the Quraysh's prestige and dominance had been undermined, and the tribes saw that it had been destabilised. The various tribes sought only to serve their own interests, and began, therefore, to reconsider their options and alliances. The manner in which they engaged the new player increased the Quraysh's anxiety.

Qurayshi leaders were taken aback by the speed with which the new Madinah reality had established itself. In record time, within a year and a half, Madinah had become a central player and was leading all initiatives. This surprising turn of events upset the Quraysh's monotonous rhythm and lazy inactivity. Its leaders stood confused by this new reality and Madinah's innovative security approaches, but they did not understand the lesson that it presented to them. The Quraysh, with its ancient institutions, fossilised thinking, and arrogant leadership, believed that it was capable of uprooting the new player or deterring it by employing the traditional methods of brute force and aggression. Its leadership pushed it to act irresponsibly, and, for this, Makkah would pay a high price. The New Madinah would defeat the Old Makkah, and the Arabs would find themselves confronted by an unprecedented strategic miracle. A new centre of power was deploying a prodigious youthful force, imbued with a creative faith arising from the desert sands of their peninsula.

CHAPTER EIGHT

Leadership crisis in Makkah

"Leave Me with the one who I created alone, and to whom I granted abundant wealth, and sons by his side, and for whom I made [everything] easy" (Qur'ān 74:11-14).

While Madinah fashioned its political and social consensus and system of governance, and as its expeditions spread out across the Hijaz with deliberation and courage, Makkah was in the grip of a paralysing leadership crisis. The main cause of the paralysis was the difficult leadership transition from the Alliance of the Allies to the Alliance of the Scented; more specifically, it was the transition from the Banī Makhzūm to the Banī 'Abd Shams. These two clans rarely agreed on anything, following on ancient tensions between them. The obvious cause for the leadership crisis, shortly after the Prophet's (ﷺ) Hijrah, was the death of al-Walīd ibn al-Mughīrah, the leader of the Banī Makhzūm, head of the House of Assembly, and the oldest of the Qurayshi elders.

The Makkans had generously conferred many attributes on al-Walīd, such as "The Just". He was extremely wealthy, and, during the pilgrimage season, he usually sacrificed ten camels a day. He was also a prime mover behind the vicious campaign against the Prophet (ﷺ). It was he who had suggested that the Prophet (ﷺ) be maligned as a "sorcerer" when the Quraysh had sought ways to denigrate him during the pilgrimage season. In response, Allah had revealed a few verses of the Qur'ān (74:11-14) that referred to him: "Leave Me with the one who I created alone, and to whom I granted abundant wealth, and sons by his side, and to whom I made [everything] easy."

Al-Walīd died at the age of ninety-five, three months after the Prophet's (ﷺ) Hijrah. His death and his last wish created a massive problem for the Quraysh. On his death bed, al-Walīd issued three tasks to his three sons: Khālid, Hishām, and al-Walīd.

> I charge you with three decrees. Do not fail to carry them out. My blood [was spilt] by the Khuzā'ah; do not let it go uncompensated. By Allah, I know that they are innocent, but I fear that you may be spoken of badly because of it after this day. My usurious profit is with the Thaqīf; make sure that you claim it. My dowry is with Abū Uzayhar al-Dawsī; do not allow it to be lost to you.[144]

Al-Walīd's last testament was disastrous for the Quraysh, coming at a time when it was in desperate need of good relations with the Khuzā'ah, Thaqīf, and Daws.

The incident with Khuzā'ah had occurred when al-Walīd had been walking in a market, dragging his robe behind him. It hooked onto an arrow made by a craftsman from the Khuzā'ah tribe. The arrow scratched his calf and, seemingly, reopened an old wound, causing it to fester, which in turn led to his death. Al-Walīd held the Khuzā'ah responsible for his death and wanted his sons to claim blood money from the tribe. His problem with the Daws tribe resulted from his marriage to the daughter of Abū Uzayhar, the Daws leader. When he was alone with her, he asked, "Who is more noble, your father or me?" She replied, "My father, because he is the leader of the people of al-Surāt and the Arabs mobilise under his banner. You, on the other hand, are the leader of your father's people, which includes some who challenge you in status."[145] Al-Walīd responded by slapping her. She screamed and her family rescued her, after which she returned to her tribe. Al-Walīd then demanded her dowry be returned, but the Daws refused. He wanted his sons to retrieve the dowry. To the Thaqīf, he had granted a usurious loan. They had paid back the capital but not the accumulated interest. He tasked his sons with retrieving that outstanding interest. Al-Walīd's testament typified the pre-Islamic mentality that was obsessed with vengeance and bloated with pride.

For the Muslims, Al-Walīd's last words created an excellent opportunity. When the Banī Makhzūm began carrying out the late elder's instructions, the Quraysh found itself in an antagonistic position with three neighbouring tribes, at a time when the Prophet (ﷺ) was

144. Al-Baghdādī, *al-Munammaq fī Akhbār Quraysh*, vol. 1, 192.
145. Al-Baghdādī, *al-Munammaq fī Akhbār Quraysh*, vol. 1, 192.

preparing to harass the Quraysh and disrupt its trade routes.

Khuzā'ah refused to pay al-Walīd's blood money, and tensions between the two sides escalated. They exchanged panegyric poetry—which was the equivalent of today's media statements—condemning each other. The animosity subsided after an agreement was reached for the blood money to be paid in instalments. It was significant that the Khuzā'ah poetry insulted the Banī Makhzūm and praised the Banī 'Abd al-Muṭṭalib, the consequence of an ancient alliance between the Khuzā'ah and 'Abd al-Muṭṭalib ibn Hāshim, the Prophet's (ﷺ) grandfather.

The return of the dowry that was demanded of the Daws tribe escalated tensions for months without any resolution, and it finally exploded into bloody conflict. The Daws leader, Abū Uzayhar, was linked to the Banī 'Abd Shams through alliances and marriages: Abū Sufyān was married to 'Ātikah, the daughter of Abū Uzayhar, and 'Utbah ibn Rabī'ah was married to her sister Zaynab. Abū Uzayhar was thus related to two leaders of the Banī 'Abd Shams through marriage. The relationship was such that Abū Uzayhar visited Abū Sufyān during the Dhī'l Majāz market and was hosted in the Qurayshi leader's house. Al-Walīd's sons murdered him while he was under Abū Sufyān's hospitality, which was perceived as a huge insult to the Banī 'Abd Shams and led to tensions between them and the Banī Makhzūm. However, Abū Sufyān, who was known for his balanced temperament and preference for pacification over escalation, managed to end the conflict. He knew that such a battle would be catastrophic for the Quraysh, especially since the incident occurred just after the Battle of Badr, during which many senior Qurayshi leaders had been killed, and its leadership was now in Abū Sufyān's hands. If he allowed the internal situation in Makkah to descend into a clash between two leading houses, the Banī 'Abd Shams and the Banī Makhzūm, his leadership would collapse, and the Quraysh's unity would dissolve.

The Muslims followed these events with great interest and worked to deepen the divisions. The Prophet (ﷺ) asked Hassān ibn Thābit, Madinah's 'media spokesperson', to compose poetry to incite the Alliance of the Scented against the Alliance of the Allies in Makkah.

The Alliance of the Scented comprised five clans: the Banī ‘Abd Manāf (including the Banī ‘Abd Shams), the Banī Asad, the Banī Zahrah, the Banī Taym, and the Banī al-Ḥārith. The Alliance of the Allies comprised the Banī Makhzūm, the Banī ‘Abd al-Dār, the Banī Jumaḥ, the Banī Saham, and the Banī ‘Adī.

Hassān's poetry incited for Abū Uzayhar to be avenged, and he humiliated Abū Sufyān, accusing him of cowardice and incapacity.

> The people on both sides of Dhī'l Majāz rose one morning,
>
> But [Abū Sufyān] Ibn Ḥarb's protected guest in al-Mughammas did not.
>
> Hishām ibn al-Walīd draped you in his robes;
>
> Wear them out and make new ones like them later.
>
> He got what he wanted from [killing] him and achieved infamy,
>
> But you became flaccid and utterly useless.
>
> If the elders of Badr had been present,
>
> The people's sandals would have been red with freshly shed blood.
>
> The farting donkey did not protect the one he was bound to defend,
>
> And Hind did not avert her father's shame.[146]

Abū Sufyān's son Yazīd was so upset by these verses that he gathered the youth of the Banī ‘Abd Manāf and mobilised the Alliance of the Scented, who congregated and armed themselves, while Yazīd's father was away from Makkah. When the Alliance of the Allies saw this, they

146. Hind's father was killed in the Battle of Badr. Hassān's implication here is that her father would be ashamed that she was married to a coward such as Abū Sufyān.

also gathered and prepared to fight. Abū Sufyān was hastily summoned, and when he reached Makkah, he stood between the two parties that were on the verge of fighting.

> He saw that the banner was being hoisted by his son Yazīd, who, together with his allies from the Alliance of the Scented, was clothed in armour. Abū Sufyān snatched the banner from his son's hand and struck his helmet with it, breaking the banner. He said: "May Allah disgrace you! Do you want the Quraysh to fight against each other over a man from [the tribe of] al-Azd? We will give them the blood money, if they will accept it." He then shouted at the top of his voice: "O People, behind us, gloating, stands our enemy [Muḥammad (ﷺ)]. When we settle what is between us and him, we can settle what is between us and you. Every one of you should return to his home." They dispersed and the matter was resolved. When Abū Sufyān was informed of Hassān's poetry, he retorted: "Hassān wants us to fight each other over a man from Daws. By Allah, how contemptible his thoughts are."[147]

The de-escalation did not resolve the Quraysh's problem; the Daws still felt severely insulted by the murder of their leader. Hassān continued to compose verses inciting Daws to seek retribution. The tribe later launched a raid against the Quraysh, killing forty of its men. Daws continued to monitor and raid Qurayshi caravans, since the Quraysh's trade route to Yemen passed through their territory. The Quraysh finally capitulated and were forced to pay a tax of one dinar for every camel load that entered and exited Daws' territory. This tax continued to be paid until Islam was victorious and the Prophet (ﷺ) suspended all pre-Islamic arrangements.

If we examine the leadership situation in Makkah from from the death of al-Walīd until the Battle of Badr, we find that the leadership of the House of Assembly did not go to 'Utbah, the leader of the Banī 'Abd Shams, because the Banī Makhzūm's agenda, which was to fulfil al-Walīd's final testament, dominated events in Makkah. This effectively meant that the Banī Makhzūm took over the leadership of the Quraysh

147. Al-Baghdādī, *al-Munammaq fī Akhbār Quraysh*, vol. 1, 203.

since they were responsible for implementing the final testament of its deceased leader. The greatest beneficiary of this situation was Abū Jahl (‘Amr ibn Hishām), al-Walīd’s nephew and heir to the Banī Makhzūm. As expected, he was supported by the other clans of the Alliance of the Allies, since handing authority over to ‘Utbah meant handing the leadership over to the Alliance of the Scented, which was the last thing that the Alliance of the Allies wanted, especially the Banī Makhzūm and their leader Abū Jahl.

The relationship between Abū Jahl and ‘Utbah ibn Rabī‘ah was tense. Many written sources show that the two men were always on opposite sides. In addition to the inherited tribal partisanship that characterised the Banī Manāf and the Banī Makhzūm, and the Banī Makhzūm’s ancient hatred for the entire Banī Quṣay, the two men were also of very different temperaments. ‘Utbah ibn Rabī‘ah was recognised for his cunning, calm disposition, as well as his dismissal of provocation, while Abū Jahl was sharp-tongued, boorish, and moody. The two men continually disagreed on the management of the Quraysh’s affairs; their greatest disagreement would be on full display during the Battle of Badr.

CHAPTER NINE

The decisive moment

"Remember when Allah promised that one of the two (enemy) parties would be yours, you wished that the unarmed one should be yours. But Allah willed to establish the Truth by His words, and to cut off the roots of the unbelievers" (Qur'ān 8:7)

The Prophet's (ﷺ) strategy for state-building and propagating his message had the project of tackling the Quraysh at its core because the Islamisation of the Arabian Peninsula would be incomplete without the Islamisation of the Quraysh and the conquest of Makkah. The Prophet's (ﷺ) strategic actions from the time of his arrival in Madinah until the conquest of Makkah in 8 AH were all links joined in a single chain, strengthening each other in the service of this central objective.

The Prophet's (ﷺ) strategic actions—his every action or pronouncement issued in the context of Madinah's political and military relationships with its surrounding environment—consistently focused on achieving specific objectives. These actions included military deployments such as expeditions and campaigns, as well as relations between Madinah and the various tribal and political entities, whether allies or opponents. They also included the media discourse emanating from Madinah. It included the Prophet's (ﷺ) direct pronouncements, statements of the conveyors of his messages and his military commanders, and positions expressed by poets who spoke on behalf of Madinah, such as Hassān ibn Thābit, 'Abdallah ibn Rawāḥah, and Ka'b ibn Mālik.

To gain a deeper understanding of the essence of the Prophet's (ﷺ) strategy, we will examine strategic events in the period from the Hijrah to the conquest of Makkah as links in a continuous chain. His expeditions, envoys, and campaigns were not arbitrary responses, but well-considered manoeuvres in the service of the primary objective: the Islamisation of the Quraysh and the conquest of Makkah. His alliances with the tribes that inhabited the regions along the Quraysh's trade routes, like Juhaynah, Ḍamrah, and Khuzā‘ah, were critical for the development of Madinah's security sphere, and to entrench the siege of Makkah. The Prophet's (ﷺ) poets' inciting the Daws tribe against the Quraysh to avenge the killing of their leader not only worsened the Quraysh's predicament, but also inclined Daws toward the Prophet's (ﷺ) alliance. Similarly, the small-scale military campaigns against the bedouins of Najd and the desert tribes such as Ghaṭafān, Tamīm, and Sulaym were no more than attempts to avoid the security threat that they represented, and to protect Madinah from their hostility, thus allowing the Muslims to remain preoccupied with their primary objective. Furthermore, leaving an elite group of the Prophet's (ﷺ) companions in Abyssinia, despite the possibility of a safe destination in Madinah, was intended to strengthen regional ties to put pressure on the Quraysh and to tighten the siege on it.

We can also understand internal developments in Madinah within the framework of this primary objective. The Prophet (ﷺ) adopted an internal strategy that was founded on unity and the full integration of the different elements of Madinah. The Muslims showed restraint toward the provocations of the hypocrites so that people would not say: "Verily, Muḥammad is killing his companions." They wanted to ensure that internal cohesion in Madinah would not break down; if it did, it would have occupied the Muslims with marginal struggles. Even relations with the Jews, whether in Madinah or at their large trade centre in Khaybar, were conducted in a calculated manner, since this related directly to the balance of forces in relation to the central objective.

The road to Badr

The road to Badr began with the Sayf al-Baḥr expedition led by Ḥamzah ibn ‘Abd al-Muṭṭalib about a year after the Hijrah. The Sayf al-Baḥr raiding party comprised thirty Muhājirūn men tasked with confronting a Qurayshi caravan on the coastal trade route between Makkah and the Levant. Several military expeditions targeting Qurayshi caravans followed. At the same time, the Muslims forged alliances with the coastal tribes, until the Nakhlah expedition. This expedition caused great consternation for the Quraysh since it happened on Makkah's doorstep. It targeted a small Qurayshi caravan returning from Ṭā'if. Ibn al-Ḥaḍramī was killed and two Qurayshis were captured. This happened on the last day of the month of Rajab, one of the consecrated months.

Thus, the period between Ramaḍān 1 AH and Rajab 2 AH witnessed a gradual escalation that included eight military expeditions. All of them had clear and specific objectives, but fighting was not the goal. Several objectives were met in this period, the most important being the disruption of the Quraysh's trade. Trade does not thrive in an environment of risk, and the repeated raids on caravans began shaking the confidence of the Qurayshi traders in their trans-desert economy, creating fear and sending a message to the coastal tribes that Madinah had become the new broker of security in the region. It was therefore in these tribes' interest to reach an understanding with the Muslims, and to be wary of dealing with the Quraysh, because that would anger Muḥammad (ﷺ) and the Muslims. This resulted in a situation where Qurayshi caravans were subjected not only to a direct security threat from Muslim raids but would also have to cross the lands of people whose sincerity they could no longer trust; they could not be assured that these tribes would provide adequate protection for their caravans.

The pact that had characterised the Quraysh's relations with other parties in the region and beyond was profoundly shaken, and a new Madinah Pact (Īlāf Madinah) began representing an alternative to that of the Quraysh. Like the Qurayshi Pact, the Madinah Pact also comprised a set of agreements and understandings with various parties that made Madinah the broker of security in the region and the centre that could guarantee safe trade.

The eight expeditions fulfilled another objective for the Muslims: they helped shape the new Madinan society strategically. Madinan brigades were constantly travelling, expeditions were being prepared, and military operations were being planned. Associated with this was the training, discipline, planning, fore-knowledge of conditions on the routes, assessment of consequences, and the capacity to make the correct decisions. In Madinah, a seed was planted that would grow to meet the aspirations of its people. Despite their various tribal and social affiliations, they evolved from focusing mainly on their internal divisions to gazing at an ever-expanding horizon. The new Madinah environment transcended the mindset of the Bu'āth War and its cycles of retribution. The conflict between the Aws and the Khazraj had ended, as had plots between tribal leaders and the fear of bedouin raids on farms and livestock.

Madinah was born, and with it emerged a new direction and a confident communal personality. Instead of living in the shadow of fear and anxiety, Madinah's influence and prestige was expanding outwards, encompassing large regions, and setting in motion a powerful force with the capacity to mobilise instantly across the desert and to strike fear in the hearts of its enemies.

The new Madinah was in no way like the old withdrawn and isolated Yathrib. It had become a centre for advancement and communication, and a place of training and organisation. The year leading up to Badr was alive with vigorous military and psychological preparation. Muslim soldiers participated in eight military training expeditions in one year, with multiple targets, thus boosting their fighting readiness and enriching them with broad experience in surveillance and countermeasures. It was, therefore, not unexpected that, on the day of the Battle of Badr, the polytheists would be caught unawares by an extremely disciplined and organised army that moved as a single integrated unit. The Qurayshi army, on the other hand, still operated in the traditional manner, as disjointed units bloated by pride and arrogance, gathered around conceited leaders, and they rushed into the fray in a disorderly fashion.

The caravan, the caravan

All the works of sīrah suggest that the immediate reason for the Battle of Badr was a desperate rescue message from Abū Sufyān after he was overcome by the fear of being attacked by the Muslims on his caravan's return from the Levant to Makkah. He knew that the Prophet (ﷺ) had marched with 200 fighters to intercept his caravan on its initial journey from Makkah to the Levant in a campaign the Muslims called Dhī'l 'Ushayrah. Muslim forces had, however, been unable to intercept the caravan. Because Abū Sufyān suspected that they would try again on his return, he made enquiries about their movements. The reports he received confirmed his fears, especially when he reached the territory of the Juhaynah tribe. He knew of Juhaynah's close relationship with Madinah, and he realised that his suspicions were justified.

The Prophet (ﷺ) had deployed two of his companions to Juhaynah: Ṭalḥah ibn 'Ubaydallah and Saī'd ibn Zayd. They stayed with Kashd al-Juhanī in al-Nakhbār and gathered intelligence on the caravan. Abū Sufyān learnt about their presence and asked Kashd al-Juhanī if he had seen any of Muḥammad's (ﷺ) spies. Kashd replied: "I seek Allah's refuge! How can Muḥammad have spies in al-Nakhbār?" Abū Sufyān remained unconvinced. We earlier mentioned al-Wāqidī's account, from Makhramah ibn Nawfal, about the report Abū Sufyān had received from a man from the Judhām tribe, and the fear that had gripped the people in the caravan before they had left the Levant. Abū Sufyān realised that, for the Quraysh to be able to mobilise in a timely manner, he had to immediately summon help. He was afraid of being caught off guard and trapped by the Muslim army. He ordered Ḍamḍam ibn 'Amr to rush to Makkah for assistance. Ḍamḍam entered Makkah dramatically, ripped his shirt in the front and back, cut off the ears of his camel, and shouted: "O People of Quraysh, O Progeny of Lu'ay ibn Ghālib, the caravan, the caravan! It has been intercepted by Muḥammad and his companions! Salvation! Salvation! By Allah, I do not believe you will reach it [in time]!"[148]

The mood in Makkah had already been tense after the Nakhlah expedition and after the Muslims had intercepted several caravans the previous year. Abū Sufyān's caravan was the most important annual Qurayshi caravan. It included 1,000 camels and had a total value of 50,000 gold dinars. Most of the Quraysh owned a share in the caravan and they could not risk losing it. As a result of Ḍamḍam's dramatic performance and plea for rescue, the entire Quraysh took up arms and headed out to save the caravan.

Abū Sufyān did not wait for the Muslim attack; he took countermeasures to avoid a confrontation. He changed his route, taking

148. For the full account, see: Ibn Hishām, *al-Sīrah*, vol. 1, 609.

care to avoid places where the Muslims could be stationed, and he ordered the caravan to increase its pace. These steps ensured that the caravan managed to escape attack.

The Quraysh had mobilised in three days and headed out with a force of over 1,000 men. Once Abū Sufyān had passed the danger point, he sent a message informing the Quraysh that the caravan was safe and suggested they return to Makkah. "Your caravan is safe," his message read, "so do not expose yourselves to a fight against the people of Yathrib. There is no gain for you from this. You marched to protect your caravan and your wealth, and these have been saved by Allah."[149]

Abū Sufyān's message did not, however, convince the polytheists to return to Makkah, primarily because of Abū Jahl's psychological and leadership crisis. Abū Jahl had appointed himself leader of the Quraysh after his uncle al-Walīd had died, and he was presented with the opportunity to exhibit his assertiveness, determination, and rage. Haughty and inflexible, he took an extreme position, urging the Makkans to prepare for battle and inciting them to continue marching.

A dispute then broke out between Abū Jahl and 'Utbah ibn Rabī'ah over the leadership of the army. 'Utbah was the leader of the Banī Shams and was the most senior person in the Quraysh after al-Walīd's death, both in age and in rank. This qualified him to lead the Quraysh. However, Abū Jahl, leader of the Banī al-Mughīrah, neither listened to nor obeyed 'Utbah and unwaveringly continued with his plan.

'Utbah, who was Abū Sufyān's uncle and the father of this wife Hind, wanted to heed Abū Sufyān's message and return to Makkah. He justified a withdrawal by arguing that Makkah had been left without any warriors, and that the Banī Bakr—who the Quraysh had been battling—might exploit the opportunity and attack the city. It was vulnerable, he said, and the only residents left were women and children. Abū Jahl rejected this argument and viciously attacked 'Utbah, accusing him of cowardice and weakness, and alleging that 'Utbah did not want to fight because his son had embraced Islam and was in the Muslim army. The accusations infuriated and severely provoked 'Utbah. Consistent with pre-Islamic norms of honour, he decided to continue with Abū Jahl in

149. Al-Wāqidī, *Kitāb al-Maghāzī*, vol. 1, 43.

order to prove the accusations false.

Historical accounts indicate that many Quraysh leaders—led by the two sons of Rabīʻah, ʻUtbah and Shaybah, and including Umayyah ibn Khalaf, Ḥakīm ibn Ḥizām, Abū al-Bukhtarī, ʻAlī ibn Umayyah ibn Khalaf, al-ʻĀṣ ibn Munabbih, and Abū Lahab—had been ambivalent about leaving Makkah to fight the Muslims. However, Abū Jahl had successfully provoked them, with the support of al-Nuḍar ibn al-Ḥārith and ʻUqbah ibn Abī Muʻīṭ. These were the three henchmen of the Quraysh.

The polytheist army was thus wracked with indecisiveness and imbalance in its leadership structure, resulting in the lack of a clear vision and purpose. A famous comment by Abū Jahl indicates that the purpose of the campaign, as far as he was concerned, was propaganda rather than strategic action, and careful planning was therefore not necessary.

> No, by Allah! We will not return until we reach Badr and the Arabs hear about us and our march. We will spend three days at Badr, slaughtering camels, providing food, drinking wine, and we will have female singers [entertaining us] with music, so that the Arabs will forever acknowledge our prestige.[150]

The state of chaos drove two Qurayshi clans, the Banī Zahrah and the Banī ʻAdī, to abandon Abū Jahl and the others and to return to Makkah. The Banī Zahrah's withdrawal helps us to comprehend the Qurayshi mindset. The clan's ally and a senior tribal leader, al-Akhnas ibn Sharīq, advised them to withdraw because there was no convincing reason to continue. He passionately addressed his people.

> O Banī Zahrah, Allah has saved your caravan and your wealth, and your companion Makhramah ibn Nawfil has survived. Indeed, you came out to protect him and your wealth. Muḥammad is, after all, one of you, a son of your sister. If he turns out to be a prophet, you will be most happy with him, and if he turns out to be a liar, it is better if someone else kills him rather than you killing your nephew. Withdraw, and let any

150. For the full account, see: al-Wāqidī, *Kitāb al-Maghāzī*, vol. 1, 44.

> cowardice associated with the withdrawal fall on me. There is no need for you to march out without any gain, not for what this man [Abū Jahl] says. He will destroy his people and is quickly corrupting them![151]

They obeyed him since he commanded much respect among them.

The reason for al-Akhnas reaching this conclusion is revealed in an earlier exchange between him and Abū Jahl. Al-Akhnas asked Abū Jahl his opinion about the verses of the Qur'ān they had heard being recited by the Prophet (ﷺ).

> He entered the home of Abū Jahl and asked: "O Abū Ḥakam, what is your opinion regarding what you hear from Muḥammad." [Abū Jahl replied:] "We and the Banī 'Abd Manāf competed over status. They provided food [to the people] and we provided food; they showed humility and we showed humility; they gave generously and we gave generously. It was such that, if we saddled up, we were like two racing horses. They [then] said, 'We have a prophet among us who receives inspiration from the heavens.' How can we [ever compete] with that? By Allah, we will never pledge faith to him or believe him." Al-Akhnas stood up and left.[152]

Al-Akhnas had realised then that Abū Jahl's dispute with the Prophet (ﷺ) was the result of clan rivalry between the Banī Makhzūm and the Banī 'Abd Manāf. On the march, he believed that Abū Jahl's decision to continue the march to Yathrib was no more than a reflection of this rivalry for the leadership of the Quraysh. From a tribal perspective, the Banī Zahrah could gain nothing from this dispute. They were, in fact, closer to the Prophet (ﷺ), since his mother was from their tribe. Therefore, they had no reason to participate in other people's battles. Thus, al-Akhnas's advice to them was sound. He went further, providing a justification for their withdrawal so that Abū Jahl could not force them to stay. He said he would fall from his camel and feign sickness, at which point they should claim that he had been bitten by a snake. Thus, when the army advanced, they should delay and remain by his side on

151. al-Wāqidī, Kitāb al-Maghāzī, vol. 1, 44.
152. Al-Bayhaqī, *Dalā'il al-Nubūwwah*, vol. 2, 206.

the grounds that they could not leave him until they knew whether he would live. Once the army had departed, they would return to Makkah. They acted on this plan and were soon on their way back. The Banī Zahrah contingent was not large, probably around 100 warriors. The Banī 'Adī, the clan to which 'Umar ibn al-Khaṭṭāb belonged, had also returned to Makkah after receiving Abū Sufyān's message that the caravan was safe. Thus, with the removal of the Banī Zahrah and Banī 'Adī, the reduction in the number of Qurayshi forces was significant.

War consultation

Back at the Muslim camp, the Prophet (ﷺ) and around 300 of his companions, accompanied by seventy camel riders and horsemen, pursued the caravan. When Abū Sufyān had escaped, the Prophet (ﷺ) had been informed of the Qurayshi forces marching on Madinah. He convened a consultative meeting as he frequently did on matters of public importance, especially concerning war. This meeting, however, was exceptionally important; the Prophet (ﷺ) wanted to determine whether the Anṣār would stand by him in battle. Although the Second Pledge of 'Aqabah included an undertaking by the Anṣār to protect the Prophet (ﷺ) in Madinah, this confrontation would take place outside Madinah and was therefore not covered by that commitment. The Prophet (ﷺ), therefore, wanted to ensure that the Anṣār would fight alongside him.

During the meeting, Abū Bakr spoke eloquently. Thereafter, 'Umar spoke:

> O Messenger of Allah. By Allah, it is the Quraysh and its honour [that is at stake]. They have never been disgraced since achieving honour, nor have they submitted to faith since they disbelieved. By Allah, they will never surrender their honour; they will fight you, so [let us] rise [to this challenge] and be prepared.[153]

Others then spoke, all from the Muhājirūn. The Prophet (ﷺ),

153. al-Wāqidī, Kitāb al-Maghāzī, vol. 1, 48.

however, wanted to hear from the Anṣār. He said directly: "Speak to me, O people." Only then did the leader of the 'Aws, Sa'd ibn Mu'ādh, speak. "I respond on behalf of the Anṣār," he said. "It seems, O Messenger of Allah, that you want our response." The Prophet (ﷺ) replied: "Indeed." Sa'd said:

> We have pledged our faith to you and have believed in you. We bear witness that everything that you have come with is the truth, and we have given you our covenants and our pledges to listen and to obey. Proceed, O Prophet of Allah. By the One who sent you with the truth, if you took us to the ocean and you plunged into it, we would plunge in with you; not a single man would remain behind. Engage with whoever you please and ignore whoever you please. Take from our wealth whatever you please; that which you take from our wealth will be more loved than that which you leave behind. By the One in whose hand is my soul, I have never travelled along this path before and have no knowledge thereof, but we are not indisposed to encountering our enemy tomorrow. We are steadfast in war, true when [armies] meet, and perhaps Allah will show [you our qualities] that will please your eye.[154]

The Prophet (ﷺ) then responded: "Go forth with the blessings of Allah. Allah had indeed promised me one of the two parties. By Allah, it is as if I am looking at the end of [those] people."

A pertinent question arises at this point: If the Prophet (ﷺ) had decided to retreat to Madinah when he heard about the Quraysh's march to Badr, would the polytheists have continued their march to confront him in Madinah? It seems clear from the various accounts in the sīrah that the Quraysh's goal was to reach Badr. It was the season when they usually organised their markets, which were visited by people from various tribes. The markets were the best places for announcing news that would be transmitted across the desert. Abū Jahl's goal was propaganda; he wanted to reach Badr and hold a huge festive party, thereby communicating to the Arabs that the Quraysh was still powerful and still deserved prestige and respect. This was his desire; fighting the

---

154. al-Wāqidī, Kitāb al-Maghāzī, vol. 1, 49.

Muslims did not seem to be a clear objective, if events in the confused Qurayshi camp were the yardstick to judge their intentions.

For his part, the Prophet (ﷺ) had resolved to confront them, as was clear from discussions in the consultative meeting and from the comments of his companions. These indicated that the Muslims were preparing for a military confrontation, not a propagandistic show of strength. This conclusion was affirmed by the polytheists' surprise when they learnt of the arrival of the Prophet's (ﷺ) army at Badr.

Al-Wāqidī provides an important insight into the mood in the polytheist camp when the Quraysh learnt about the arrival of the Muslim army.

> Allah's Messenger (ﷺ) descended into the valley of Badr on Friday evening, seventeen days into the month of Ramaḍān. Dispatching 'Alī, Zubayr, Sa'd ibn Abī Waqqāṣ, and Basbas ibn 'Amr to search for water, he pointed to the small mountain of Ẓurayb and said: "I hope that you receive news at the well at al-Ẓurayb." They set out towards Ẓurayb, where they found Qurayshi water bearers watering their animals. Some of them fought the Muslims but most fled. One of those who fled was 'Ujayr. He was the first person to bring news to the Quraysh about Allah's Messenger's (ﷺ) [arrival]. He shouted: "O Progeny of Ghālib! Ibn Abī Kabshah and his companions have taken your watering hole!" The camp was agitated and angered by the news he had brought.
>
> Ḥakīm ibn Ḥizām said: "We were in one of our tents roasting camel meat when we heard the news. We left our food as we met with others. 'Utbah ibn Rabī'ah saw me and said: 'O Abū Khālid, I do not know of anyone who proceeds in a stranger manner than we do. Our caravan was rescued, yet we come to a people in their own territory, rising against them… The matter was settled but the one who is not obeyed has no say; this is the curse of Ibn al-Ḥanẓalīyyah [Abū Jahl]. O Abū Khālid, do you fear that the people will plot against us?' I said: 'I do not [believe] we are safe from that.' He responded: 'What is [your]

> opinion, O Abū Khālid?' I said: 'We keep watch until morning, then you can see who is behind you.' 'Utbah said: 'This is [a good] opinion!' So we kept watch until morning. [When] Abū Jahl [saw us, he] asked: 'What is this? This must have been by 'Utbah's order. He was disinclined to fighting Muḥammad and his companions! This is surprising. Do you think that Muḥammad and his companions can attack your gathering? By Allah, I will move over to one side with my people and no one will guard over us.' He then moved to one side and the skies rained down on him. 'Utbah then said: 'This is indeed petulance.'''[155]

This account illustrates the Quraysh's surprise at the Muslims' arrival. They were in a state of confusion, choking on their food and concerned about their safety. They were forced to take precautionary measures while the arrogant leader continued to be in denial about the news: "Do you think that Muḥammad and his companions can attack your gathering?" He believed that large numbers and a noisy celebratory atmosphere would intimidate the Muslims and deter them from any confrontation. By this point, it had become clear that the Prophet's (ﷺ) march to Badr was part of a carefully considered initiative. It followed his decision, which was strengthened by the consultation council and especially by 'Umar's belief that, since the Quraysh would fight the Muslims at some stage, it would be better for the Muslims to take the initiative.

Al-Wāqidī's account also points out how the conflict between 'Utbah and Abū Jahl quickly escalated to insults, name-calling, and accusations. The Qurayshi forces lacked a unified leadership, and Abū Jahl's de facto leadership was not official; he was self-appointed rather than chosen through consensus. It is also evident that Abū Jahl was unable to properly appraise the situation because his arrogance prevented him from believing the reports he had received. He was heedless even though he had strayed and had made a decision based on ego rather than careful assessment. 'Utbah ibn Rabī'ah had been marginalised and deprived of a voice. As he himself said, "The one who is not obeyed has no say."

155. al-Wāqidī, Kitāb al-Maghāzī, vol. 1, 50-51.

Liberation in confronting seclusion

The Qurayshi camp was characterised by disputes, insults, cruel leadership, a lack of goals, and a tense atmosphere. By contrast, the Muslim camp acted with coordination, respect, an appreciation of counter-opinions, and a sense of camaraderie. While a senior leader like 'Utbah ibn Rabī'ah was unable to express his opinion to a boorish and stubborn leader, a young man from the Anṣār, al-Ḥubāb ibn al-Mandhar, stood before the Prophet (ﷺ), the supreme military commander, and questioned—with deference and respect—his choice of the camp's location.

Was this the Prophet's (ﷺ) personal assessment, al-Ḥubāb asked, or was it revelation from Allah that could not be opposed? When the Prophet (ﷺ) responded that it was his opinion and that "war is deception", the twenty-four-year-old al-Ḥubāb, who was not a leader of his people, responded frankly: "This is not a good spot to set up camp!" Because he knew the terrain and location of Badr's wells, he proposed that the Muslims relocate their camp so that the wells would lie within their camp. This would give them an advantage, he argued, allowing them to access water whenever they wanted, while preventing the enemy access to it. He also proposed that the wells that were not within their camp should be covered so that the Quraysh would not be able to draw water from them. The leader listened to the proposal of his foot soldier, accepted it, and implemented it without debate or consideration of military hierarchy.

In another incident, the Muslim soldiers were standing in formation while the Prophet (ﷺ) inspected the ranks. When his eyes fell on a soldier standing out of step, he pushed him back into line with a stick that he was holding. The young Anṣārī, Sawwād ibn Ghazīyyah, who was not a leader or a senior figure, told the Prophet (ﷺ) and supreme military commander: "You've hurt me! By the One who has sent you with the truth, grant me recompense." The Prophet (ﷺ) exposed his midriff and asked Sawwād to extract his retribution. Instead, the young man leant forward and kissed the exposed area. When the Prophet (ﷺ) asked him to explain, he said that he had come to battle and did now know whether he would survive. If he were to die, he said, he wanted his final act to be his skin touching that of the Prophet (ﷺ).

Such narrations are usually found in accounts about the Prophet's ethics (ﷺ) and of his companions' love for him. However, this narration provides other perspectives on to the military context and the mindset of the Muslim army. Consider the scenario of soldiers in a state of high alert, preparing to imminently confront the enemy, with the commander inspecting his troops. In this situation of extreme discipline and vigilance, the commander noticed a soldier who was out of line and pushed him back into position. This was a normal and expected occurrence in military life, and a commander acting in this way would simply be carrying out his duty. In this case, however, the soldier claimed to be hurt by the push and demanded retribution. Although unusual in a military situation, the soldier found the courage to speak against his commander, who was maintaining discipline at a critical time. Even more unusually, the commander found the soldier's complaint to be valid and deserving of response. There is also no report that other soldiers who witnessed the incident protested or reprimanded Sawwād. It was as if his complaint was not extraordinary.

In both this incident and the one in which al-Ḥubāb ibn al-Mandhar suggested a re-arrangement of the battlefield, the seniority of the Prophet (ﷺ) and commander of the army did not prevent him from accepting the suggestion or demand of an ordinary soldier. We may conclude that the Prophet (ﷺ), as commander, had already planted the seeds of freedom in the hearts of his companions, granted them the necessary confidence to boldly express their opinions, and made them partners in the management of public affairs. They were, therefore, neither ambivalent nor cowardly; if a commoner had an opinion that would serve the interests of the Muslims, he approached the commander and advised him accordingly. The commander was not opposed to listening to advice and acting on it if he found it to be useful. Such an attitude opens wide horizons for renewal and innovation and ensures that the community is not trapped in fixed frameworks or ancient methodologies.

At Badr, there were a little more than 300 Muslim soldiers, while the polytheists were more than thrice that number. However, the qualitative difference between the two armies was huge. The battle was not a confrontation between 1,000 and 300; rather, it was between the old and confused on one side, and the young and steadfast on the other. It was between a previous era whose time had lapsed, and a present that was being born.

Birth of the new and collapse of the old

By late afternoon on 17 Ramaḍān 2 AH / 13 January 624, silence had descended on Badr. The battle was over, and the polytheists had suffered a resounding defeat.

The list of names of the Quraysh who had been killed was astounding. The seventy dead included leaders of the main Qurayshi clans, and some of their most valiant and senior figures. Among the casualties were Abū Jahl and his brother al-'Āṣ ibn Hāshim; 'Utbah ibn Rabī'ah, his brother Shaybah ibn Rabī'ah, and his son al-Walīd ibn 'Utbah; 'Uqbah ibn Abī Mu'īṭ; Umayyah ibn Khalaf and his son 'Alī; Abū al-Bukhtarī ibn Hāshim; al-Nuḍar ibn al-Ḥārith; Munabbih ibn al-Ḥajjāj and his sons, al-'Āṣ and al-Ḥārith, as well as his brother Nabīh ibn al-Ḥajjāj; Ḥanẓalah, the son of Abū Sufyān; Nawfil ibn Khuwaylid, the brother of the Prophet's (ﷺ) wife Khadījah; and Abū Qays ibn al-Walīd ibn al-Mughīrah, Khālid ibn al-Walīd's brother. The battle had decimated the Qurayshi leadership and had emptied the House of Assembly of its members. The clan that had lost the most was the Banī Makhzūm. Twenty-four of their members had been killed, including their arrogant leader Abū Jahl ('Amr ibn Hishām ibn al-Mughīrah). The leaders of the Banī Jumaḥ and the Banī 'Abd Shams, Umayyah ibn Khalaf and 'Utbah ibn Rabī'ah respectively, were also killed.

Another seventy people had been captured, including Suhayl ibn 'Amr; the Prophet's (ﷺ) cousin 'Aqīl ibn Abī Ṭālib; the Prophet's (ﷺ) uncle al-'Abbās ibn 'Abd al-Muṭṭalib; the Prophet's (ﷺ) son-in-law al-'Āṣ ibn al-Rabī'; Muṣ'ab ibn 'Umayr's brother Abū 'Azīz ibn 'Umayr; Abū Jahl's brother Khālid ibn Hishām ibn al-Mughīrah; Khālid ibn al-Walīd's brother al-Walīd ibn al-Walīd ibn al-Mughīrah; and 'Abdallah ibn Ubay ibn Khalaf.

Compared to the wars that had been raging at the time between the Persians and Byzantines on the peripheries of the Arabian Peninsula, Badr was a small battle. However, its strategic and symbolic significance overshadowed those epic battles. It was, after all, the first military encounter in which a single unified Muslim entity had participated. The Muslims represented the society of Madinah as a united body, even though some were Qurayshi Muhājirūn and others Anṣār from the Aws and Khazraj tribes. The ummah (community) of Madinah had officially been declared the year before, when the Prophet (ﷺ) adopted the Madinah Charter. It described the Muslims of the Muhājirūn and Anṣār as a single nation distinct from other people. This ummah forged in blood a unity and a common struggle (jihād).

The Muslims came together as equals to confront a common enemy, and the Qurayshi Muslims fought together with the Aws and Khazraj against the Qurayshi non-Muslims. Badr could therefore be considered the birth of the Muslim ummah as a single trans-tribal entity. Badr was the announcement of the birth of this new entity. News of the Quraysh's defeat soon spread across the peninsula. Those who had referred to the Muslims as a handful of migrants fleeing from Makkah were forced to take notice, re-evaluate that impression, and discover that the story had other dimensions that deserved reflection.

Following its resounding defeat and the great humiliation to which it had been subjected, the non-Muslim Quraysh were faced with the most difficult moment of their existence. The result of the battle had been the opposite of the goal that had been set by the now-deceased Abū Jahl. The Arabs had indeed heard about the Quraysh's march, as he had hoped, but they also heard about the Quraysh's defeat, the deaths of its leaders, and the capture of members of its elite. The reputation of the Quraysh had been gravely damaged. The Quraysh would have to travel to Madinah, one family member after another, to ransom their captives, and hand over wealth to the Muslims while depleting the Quraysh's wealth.

The Muslims emerged from the battle with minimal losses; fourteen fighters had been martyred. The believers were overjoyed with Allah's help at Badr, in fulfilment of the Qur'ān's promise a few years earlier in the opening verses of Surah 30 (The Romans). The Byzantine (Eastern Roman) victory in the first important battle against the Persians occurred two months after the Muslim victory. The Muslims triumphed in Badr on 17 Ramaḍān / 13 January 624, and Heraclius's victories against the Persians began on 24 March 624. The Byzantine emperor would win the decisive victory at Nineveh three years later. These were two major simultaneous transformations in the balance of forces. One represented the beginning of the collapse of the old, and the second represented the birth of the new. The number of Byzantine victories over the Persians would increase, but both were ageing empires, one weaker than the other. Even though Constantinople would be victorious, it would emerge from the war extremely fatigued. Its parallel on the Arabian Peninsula crafted a different narrative. The defeat of the Quraysh began at Badr, and the conquest of Makkah would occur a few years later. Thereafter, the young and powerful conquering force would emerge from the depths of the desert, march in the direction of two exhausted empires, overtake them, and move beyond them with incredible speed.

From this perspective, Badr represented the beginning of the end of both the Quraysh *and* the international powers, as well as the launch of the global Islamic force. This is why Allah refers to Badr as "Yawm al-Furqān" (the "Day of the Criterion" or the "Decisive Moment").

Benefiting from Badr

The Muslim victory created a new strategic reality in the Hijaz. As news of the Badr victory spread across the peninsula and, with it, news of the new Madinah force, the Islamic presence became a challenge that could no longer be ignored.

Before Badr, the alliances and relationships of the Quraysh with neighbouring tribes were not the best. We saw how the coastal tribes, such as Juhaynah and Ḍamrah, began inclining toward the Prophet (ﷺ), and we can speculate that the reactions of these tribes to the Muslim victory at Badr would have been positive. They would have been reassured that their decisions to conclude agreements with the Prophet (ﷺ) were correct and would keep them secure. The news was also welcomed by the Khuzā'ah, who were not on good terms with the Quraysh. Their historical dispute with the Quraysh over the Holy Sanctuary had been passed from generation to generation. The Khuzā'ah had also had an ancient alliance with 'Abd al-Muṭṭalib, which was respected and upheld by his grandson Muḥammad, the Messenger of Allah (ﷺ). The Hawāzin, the largest of the Qays 'Īlān tribes, still remembered the Fijār Wars they had fought against the Quraysh and had not held the latter in high regard. The Banī Bakr ibn Wā'il had many scores to settle with the Quraysh, and the Daws tribe was waiting for an opportunity to avenge the murder of its leader by the Banī Makhzūm. Similarly, the Banī Bakr were also waiting for the opportunity to exact their revenge. Although the Thaqīf tribe had maintained good relations with Makkah for trade purposes, they too did not fully agree with the Makkans. The Quraysh thus would have to confront the Prophet (ﷺ) alone.

Other bedouin groups, such as the Sulaym, Ghaṭafān, Tamim, and certain powerful Najdi tribes were too far away and were not directly involved in the struggle between Makkah and Madinah. Their only interest was raiding and exploiting fleeting opportunities. Unless it brought them booty, they did not maintain permanent strategic alliances or fixed relationships. These tribes previously raided on the outskirts of Madinah, pillaging and fleeing. However, soon after Badr, the Prophet (ﷺ) launched expeditions and campaigns to pursue them and push them away from Madinah.

After Badr, the internal situation in Madinah became a priority for the Prophet (ﷺ) and demanded much of his attention. Not everyone in Madinah had entered Islam; some inhabitants had maintained their polytheistic beliefs. Certain individuals from this group continued to harm the Muslims through incitement, propaganda, animosity, and lies. Some had also sided with Makkah, such as a group affiliated to the Aws and led by Abū 'Āmir al-Rāhib. The Muslims referred to him as al-Fāsiq (the Profligate). He migrated to Makkah with fifty followers and later fought alongside the polytheists at the Battle of Uhud.

However, the Hypocrites (al-Munāfiqūn) were a greater threat than the polytheists; they outwardly manifested Islam, joined the Muslims in prayers, made a show of affection for the Prophet (ﷺ), but secretly plotted against the Muslims. They were also allies of the Quraysh and provided them information about developments in Madinah. They were, thus, a security threat that had to be monitored.

The third bloc in Madinah was the Jewish tribes. There were several of them in the city, ten of which had been mentioned in the Charter. Three Jewish tribes, all partners in the Charter alliance, stood out as the most important and influential in the unfolding events: the Banī Qaynuqā‘, the Banī al-Naḍīr, and the Banī Qurayẓah. The Charter recognised the right of Jews to practise their faith, but also conferred obligations on them as citizens. The most important of these was the obligation to join other inhabitants in defending Madinah if it was attacked, and not to ally with or assist the Quraysh. They were also obligated to uphold the legal system that the Charter defined, and to accept the Prophet's (ﷺ) arbitration of disputes. While the Jews may not have adopted a warm and friendly attitude toward the Muslims, they did uphold the provisions of the Charter, except for the Banī Qaynuqā‘.

The Prophet (ﷺ) was extremely careful in determining his security and strategic priorities. He understood that the three main Jewish tribes together constituted a significant force in terms of numbers and resources, many times stronger than the Muslim army. Each tribe possessed around 700 warriors, as well as fortresses and sanctuaries. They were also much wealthier than the Aws and Khazraj. Together, their economic, human, and technical capacities represented the greatest threat to the Islamic presence in Madinah, and a plan was needed to address this threat.

Rebellion in Madinah

Of the three Jewish tribes mentioned, the Banī Qaynuqā‘ was the strongest and wealthiest. Its members were merchants and goldsmiths who hosted their market in their private fortress and possessed homes in Madinah. They were also the only Jewish tribe that was allied to the Khazraj; the Banī al-Naḍīr and the Banī Qurayẓah were allied to the Aws. The latter alliance did not attract any suspicion because most Aws leaders were young and had embraced Islam. Their loyalty to the

Prophet (ﷺ) was beyond question.

However, the Banī Qaynuqā‘ alliance with the Khazraj warranted careful reflection and was the cause for great concern, because their most important ally from the Khazraj was ‘Abdallah ibn Ubay ibn Sallūl, the leader of the Hypocrites and the Prophet's (ﷺ) most dangerous enemy in Madinah. Within Madinah, then, were two converging parties, each of which had its own reasons for its enmity toward the Muslims. If they were able to unite, they could upset the internal balance of forces in the city. With good reason, the Muslims anxiously monitored this alliance. Indeed, the military-economic bloc represented by the Banī Qaynuqā‘ and the citizens' bloc represented by the hypocrites would become the greatest challenge to confront the Muslims in Madinah. Strategic considerations demanded that an initiative be developed to rapidly confront and dismantle this threat. The Banī Qaynuqā‘ felt confident enough in their strength to want to publicly express their enmity toward the Prophet (ﷺ) and the Muslims, in flagrant violation of the letter and spirit of the Madinah Charter. Their hostility became more intense after Badr, especially with Ibn Sallūl's provocation and promises of support. To address the issue, the Prophet (ﷺ) convened a meeting with the Banī Qaynuqā‘ leaders. Ibn Hishām's account gives us a sense of the mood of the meeting.

> Regarding the deliberations with the Banī Qaynuqā‘, Allah's Messenger (ﷺ) gathered them in the Banī Qaynuqā‘ market and told them: "O Community of Jews, be wary of Allah's wrath as He sent it down on the Quraysh. Embrace Islam, for you know that I am a prophet sent by Allah. You find this written in your book and in Allah's covenant with you." They responded: "O Muḥammad, you seem to think that we are [like] your people! Do not be deceived that you have encountered a people with no knowledge of war, and that you can take advantage of them. By Allah, if we were to fight against you, you will learn that we are [strong] people."[156]

We do not have a full account of what transpired in the meeting, but these extracts are sufficient to understand the tense environment. The

156. See: Ibn Hishām, *al-Sīrah*, vol. 2, 47.

Prophet (ﷺ) warned the Banī Qaynuqā' to cease their provocations and to respect their agreement with the Muslims, or to face a wrath similar to that encountered by the Quraysh. His invitation to them to embrace Islam was not an act of imposition but of good counsel. They, of course, had the right to refuse, since the Madinah Charter gave them the right to practise their faith unimpeded.

The response from the Banī Qaynuqā' was charged and extremely hostile, suggesting that their intention was not to contain the crisis but to escalate it. This is why they spoke about war and claimed that they were more powerful than the Quraysh who, they said, were ignorant of war. Thus, the Banī Qaynuqā' leaders asserted, they were more able than the Quraysh of defeating the Muslims.

With the situation having reached the point where war was openly posited by a party inside Madinah against the legitimate authority, it was clear that the community faced a major crisis that could not be ignored. If the Prophet (ﷺ) ignored their threats, he would be acknowledging that they had the right to form a military force in opposition to Madinah's collective defences. This would be a blatant dismantling of the foundations of the defensive and political system, akin to stripping the Prophet (ﷺ) of his legitimacy as the supreme commander and of his role as the arbiter of disputes. The Madinah Charter was clear on this point: "And whatever occurs between the people of this Charter in terms of any incident or dispute that could lead to corruption, [such matters] will be referred to Allah the Most Sublime and to Muḥammad the Messenger of Allah."

In this charged atmosphere, the Banī Qaynuqā again provoked the Muslims, resulting in the Prophet (ﷺ) besieging them. A Muslim woman had entered their gold market to purchase some goods. While she sat with a goldsmith, a few men accosted her, but she managed to rebuff them. However, one of them tied the end of her robe so that the robe was stripped away when she stood up and her body was exposed. The woman screamed for help. A Muslim man came to her rescue and killed the Jewish man responsible. A group of Jews then gathered and killed the Muslim man. Thereafter, they barricaded themselves in the fortress.

If the incident had occurred under normal circumstances, it would have been a matter for a judicial process, since the Charter held all perpetrators individually liable for their actions. Furthermore, no party was allowed to aid a criminal on the basis of tribal affiliation. The Charter's provision on this read: "And the believers will withdraw their hands from all among them who rebel, or seek to aid in wrongdoing, sin, hostility, or corruption among the believers, and their hands will be collectively upon such a person, even if he was the son of one of them."[157]

The Banī Qaynuqā', however, decided to stand with the Jewish killer without resorting to the Charter. They threatened the use of arms and circumvented the judicial authority of the central leadership, thus contravening the Charter, the foundational constitution of Madinah. They were, therefore, dealt with as a rebellious party that had to be punished. This was also to serve as a deterrent to anyone else who might act in a similar manner.

With 700 warriors, the Muslims besieged the Banī Qaynuqā' fortress. The Banī Qaynuqā' also had 700 warriors, according to the most accurate estimates. The Muslims maintained the siege for fifteen days, until it was agreed that the tribe would be expelled from Madinah, their wealth and weapons confiscated, and on condition that they left with their families.

The Banī Qaynuqā''s alliance with the Khazraj did not benefit them. The Prophet (ﷺ) dealt with the matter with great insight and wisdom. Because 'Abdallah ibn Ubay ibn Sallūl, as a Khazraj elder, regarded himself as the pillar of the alliance, the Prophet (ﷺ) mandated another Khazraj elder, 'Ubādah ibn al-Ṣāmit, one of the first Anṣāris to embrace Islam, to resolve the matter of the Banī Qaynuqā'.The Prophet's (ﷺ) message was clear: if Ibn Sallūl was to hide behind the Banī Qaynuqā's alliance with the Khazraj, another Khazraj elder was prepared to enforce the settlement and expel them. Ibn Sallūl was thus unable to exploit the Banī Qaynuqā' issue or present it as a matter of tribal honour and mobilise the tribe behind him.

A conversation between Ibn Sallūl and 'Ubādah ibn al-Ṣāmit is

157. Ibn Hishām, *al-Sīrah*, vol. 1, 602.

illustrative of the clash between the old tribal mentality and the new conviction of faith.

> 'Abdallah ibn Ubay told 'Ubādah ibn al-Ṣāmit: "Have you absolved yourself of your promise to your allies? Of that which they have in their hands, what do they [share] with you?" He reminded 'Ubādah of their joint experiences. 'Ubādah replied: "Abū al-Ḥubāb, the hearts have changed and Islam has erased the [old] treaties. By Allah, you are insisting upon a matter whose consequences you will see [only] tomorrow."[158]

The Banī Qaynuqā' went into exile in Adhra'āt in the Levant. No one came to their aid, neither the Khazraj nor the other Jewish tribes. This was an important lesson in the decisiveness required for dealing with the unity of the fledgling political entity in Madinah.

Two decisive and important incidents occurred in Madinah within one month. The first was the resounding victory at Badr, which put the people of the surrounding areas on notice that the balance of forces had changed. The second was the resoluteness in implementing the Madinah Charter. It placed people inside Madinah on notice that the central authority would not tolerate rebellion.

Messages to the bedouins

The second project after the Badr victory addressed the bedouins of Najd who sought opportunities to raid Madinah. The Prophet (ﷺ) led three military campaigns against them. The first was against the Banī Sulaym and Ghaṭafān in what was known as the Battle of Qarqarat al-Kudr, in which 200 of the Prophet's (ﷺ) companions participated. The Muslims pursued the enemy and took 500 camels as booty without any fighting. The second campaign was against a band from the Banī Tha'labah and warriors from Ghaṭafān at Dhī Amr. The Muslim army, 450 strong, stormed these groups and forced them to disperse into the mountains without any fighting. The third campaign occurred when the Banī Sulaym tried to mobilise its forces to march on Madinah. The

158. Al-Wāqidī, *Kitāb al-Maghāzī*, vol. 1, 179. He meant that Ibn Sallūl was holding firmly to an issue, the results and consequences of which would soon be known.

Prophet (ﷺ) led an army of 300 to a place called al-Fur' and, as in earlier campaigns, the bedouins were consumed by fear and dispersed into the mountains.

The common factor in these three campaigns was that the Prophet (ﷺ) led them himself. He gave them high priority because the danger posed by these tribes was real and decisive action was required. Significantly, the number of Muslim warriors involved was not small; 450 were present in the Dhī Amr Campaign, a bigger army than the one that fought at Badr. That no fighting occurred during these campaigns indicates the level of fear that had spread amongst the bedouins after Badr; as soon as they heard of the Prophet's (ﷺ) march against them, they fled.

The Prophet's (ﷺ) strategy of rapid pre-emptive strikes achieved its goal of halting the harm that these tribes posed to Madinah. The tribes were kept at bay until the Battle of the Trench, when the Ghaṭafān joined the Quraysh in a final attempt to strike at the Muslims.

CHAPTER TEN

Abū Sufyān's tenure

"I do not oppose the Quraysh. I am a man from it, and its deeds are my deeds too."[159]

The Battle of Badr marked the most important transformation of the Quraysh since the Immoral Wars, but its impact was worse and its effect more profound. The Immoral Wars had been more confined, and the Quraysh had emerged victorious; Badr, however, resulted in a complete rout of the Quraysh. This defeat manifested in three perilous outcomes: the killing of most of the leaders of the House of Assembly, the disgrace and shame brought upon the Quraysh and the damage to its reputation among the Arabs, and the worsening of the trade blockade that was imposed on Makkah.

Most of the Quraysh's elders and leaders were killed at Badr, the three most prominent being Abū Jahl, the leader of the Makhzūm tribe; 'Utbah ibn Rabī'ah, the leader of the Banī 'Abd Shams; and Umayyah ibn Khalaf, the leader of the Banī Jumaḥ. These leaders had previously administered Qurayshi affairs. Abū Jahl was known for his rashness and volatility, 'Utbah was the counterbalance to Abū Jahl, and Umayyah ibn Khalaf was Abū Jahl's most important ally.

Another problem for the Quraysh was that its two main alliances—Alliance of the Allies to which Abū Jahl and Ummayah belonged, and Alliance of the Scented led by 'Utbah ibn Rabī'ah—were also afflicted by grave losses in their leadership ranks. Moreover, the fatalities included several other leaders from various Qurayshi clans. None of the clans—except the Banī Zahrah and the Banī 'Adī, which had withdrawn before the battle—had escaped without loss.

159. Al-Wāqidī, *Kitāb al-Maghāzī*, vol. 1, 181.

The biggest winner

In this tense, almost leaderless, climate, all eyes turned to Abū Sufyān. He had suffered a personal loss with the death of his first-born son Ḥanẓalah, but, in terms of Qurayshi politics, he stood to gain, since the leadership hierarchy was completely open to him, at least in this phase. Three outcomes of Badr worked in Abū Sufyān's favour. First, he had been able to save the caravan; second, he had advised the Quraysh to return to Makkah and not to march to Badr; and third, the Banī Makhzūm, the greatest rival of the Banī 'Abd Manāf, were weakened due to the deaths of many of its leaders. They had lost a total of twenty-four men. It was clear that Abū Sufyān was the logical choice to lead the Quraysh, and he was comfortably able to take control.

Ṣakhar ibn Ḥarb ibn Umayyah ibn 'Abd Shams, also known as Abū Sufyān, was granted the leadership of the Quraysh and Kinānah by default; everyone turned to him after Badr, since he had been the leader of the caravan that had resulted in the war. Furthermore, many Qurayshis believed that the wealth of the caravan could provide the means for revenge and reclamation of their honour.

Ibn Sayyid al-Nās narrates in *'Uyūn al-Athar*:

> When… Abū Sufyān ibn Ḥarb had returned to Makkah with his caravan, he was approached by 'Abdallah ibn Abī Rabī'ah, 'Ikramah ibn Abī Jahl, Ṣafwān ibn Umayyah, and other men from the Quraysh whose fathers, brothers, and sons had been killed on the day of Badr. They addressed Abū Sufyān and the other Qurayshis that [had a share] in the caravan: "O People of Quraysh, verily Muḥammad has wronged you and killed the best amongst you. Now assist us with this wealth to make war against him so that we may perhaps exact revenge from him for those we have lost." And they obliged.[160]

Of the three individuals who led the delegation to Abū Sufyān, two were young men from the Banī Makhzūm. 'Abdallah ibn Abī Rabī'ah ibn al-Mughīrah was Abū Jahl's cousin and 'Ikramah was Abū Jahl's

160. Ibn Sayyid al-Nās, *'Uyūn al-Athar fī Funūn al-Maghāzī wa Shamā'il al-Siyar* (Beirut: Dār al-Qalam, 1993), vol. 2, 5.

son. The third was Ṣafwān ibn Umayyah ibn Khalaf, a youth leader of the Banī Jumaḥ. These two tribes were central in the Alliance of the Allies. We will soon see how Ṣafwān ibn Umayyah began to doubt Abū Sufyān's leadership abilities. After the Battle of the Trench, these doubts sparked a leadership struggle that resulted in the collapse of the Quraysh in face of Prophetic leadership.

Using the caravan's wealth to equip the next Qurayshi army automatically put Abū Sufyān in the leadership seat. That explains his enthusiasm for the proposal. Ibn Sa'd explains:

> When the polytheists returned from Badr to Makkah, they found the caravan with which Abū Sufyān ibn Ḥarb had arrived in front of the House of Assembly. The Qurayshi nobles told Abū Sufyān: "It would please us if you were to use the profit of this caravan to equip an army to confront Muḥammad." Abū Sufyān replied: "I am the first to agree to this, and the Banī 'Abd Manāf are with me." They then sold it [in exchange for gold]. [The caravan comprised] 1,000 camels and goods to the value of 50,000 dinars. [The Qurayshi nobles] thus returned the capital investment to the owners of the caravan after deducting their profits. They made a profit of one dinar for every dinar [invested]."[161]

The responsibility of leading a wounded society that was overwhelmed with bitterness, anger, and calls for revenge was no small matter. The situation was worsened by the reputational damage to the Quraysh among the Arabs. Other Arab tribes viewed the routing of the Qurayshi army at the hands of a force one-third its size as extremely humiliating. In a society that valued bravery and sanctified strength, the reputation of the Quraysh had been battered by the worst shock in its history. Its leaders had been killed, its warriors had fled the battlefield, the very foundations of its prestige were shaken, and its trade was disrupted. Abū Sufyān had, therefore, to take urgent steps to mitigate the impact of the defeat.

He implemented three measures that supported his new leadership.

161. Al-Nās, *'Uyūn al-Athar*, vol. 2, 5.

The first was propagandistic and morale-boosting, through exercising patience, not despairing, and displaying a spirit of defiance. In dramatic style, he "swore an oath that water would not touch his head until he led a campaign against Muḥammad in Madinah".[162] The second measure was to make a show of his strong resolve. He decided to punish the Banī Zahrah for withdrawing from the Badr army despite his also having suggested that the Quraysh should withdraw. He thus withheld the Banī Zahrah's capital investment in the caravan, even though the investment of all others was returned, as had been agreed by the Qurayshi leadership. By withholding the Banī Zahrah's share, Abū Sufyān wanted to exhibit his adherence to the Qurayshi consensus, even though it differed from his opinion. He often said, "I do not oppose the Quraysh. I am a man from it, and its deeds are my deeds."[163] His third measure was quick military action that would bestow on him what he desperately needed: the image of a decisive military leader. This resulted in the Flour (al-Suwayq) Campaign. Ibn Hishām and al-Wāqidī both discuss Abū Sufyān's first military initiative. Al-Wāqidī narrates:

> When the polytheists returned to Makkah from Badr, Abū Sufyān [swore] to desist from oiling [his hair] until he extracted revenge from Muḥammad and his companions. He marched with 200 cavalrymen (according to al-Zuhrī) or forty cavalrymen (according to Ibn Ka'b). They proceeded along the al-Najdīyyah [desert pathway] and arrived at the Banī al-Naḍīr at nightfall. They knocked [on the door] of Ḥuyay ibn Akhṭab to ask him about the Prophet (ﷺ) and his companions, but Ḥuyay refused to admit them. They then called on Salām ibn Mishkam. He hosted them, served wine to Abū Sufyān, and informed him about the Prophet (ﷺ) and his companions. Abū Sufyān departed at dawn and passed al-'Urīd, where he saw a man from the Anṣār in his fields, accompanied by his hired hand. He killed the man and his worker and burnt down two houses and their crops. He announced this as a fulfilment of his oath and then fled, fearing he would be pursued. When the [news of the incident] reached Allah's Messenger (ﷺ), he mobilised his companions, who marched out in pursuit. Abū

162. Al-Wāqidī, *Kitāb al-Maghāzī*, vol. 1, 181.
163. Al-Wāqidī, *Kitāb al-Maghāzī*, vol. 1, 202.

> Sufyān and his companions hid [their tracks] and discarded their food rations—sacks of flour. The Muslims gathered these sacks as they passed. This campaign was called the Flour (al-Suwayq) Campaign for this reason.[164]

A military force of 200 (or forty) men could not have been aiming to eradicate the Muslims or to break their strength, an endeavour that would require a much greater military effort. Abū Sufyān's objective was, instead, to reinforce the perception that the Quraysh was serious about revenge, and to strengthen his leadership. He was a businessman chosen by fate to occupy the highest leadership position in a very charged climate. A hit-and-run raid was appropriate to fabricate an image for a new leader. He needed to project decisiveness, strength, and sharpness rather than his business image of flexibility, a preference for negotiation and stability, and an aversion to military action.

Considering the pitiful outcome of this expedition, or "aggression" as Ibn Hishām called it, it was certain that many Makkans, especially the youth, would not see it as fulfilling the promise of decisive military leadership. For many, it proved the opposite. The raid produced a meagre outcome: the killing of two Anṣār men and the burning down of two houses and some crops. These were acts of minor sabotage, not decisive military action that Abū Sufyān could be proud of. Ṣafwān ibn Umayyah, who later led the opposition against Abū Sufyān, referred to the Flour Campaign as proof of Abū Sufyān's inability to lead.

Although the military adventure was unsuccessful, Abū Sufyān's contact with the Jews was an important indicator for understanding his strategic orientation. As a trader, his skill in building alliances was more accomplished than his skill in leading armies. The fact that he visited the Banī al-Naḍīr and met with Salām ibn Mishkam, their leader and supervisor of their wealth, highlights this point. Salām was a wealthy man who likely had trade ties to Abū Sufyān. The visit also proves that Abū Sufyān understood the importance of the Jewish tribes in his battle with the Muslims. They were useful both as sources of information and as potential allies. Furthermore, they could help destabilise the alliance that the Prophet (ﷺ) had forged with the Jews through the Madinah

164. Al-Wāqidī, *Kitāb al-Maghāzī*, vol. 1, 181.

Charter. Though Abū Sufyān's attempt failed because the Banī al-Naḍīr feared negative repercussions just two months after the expulsion of the Banī Qaynuqā', there was little doubt that Abū Sufyān's strategic flirtation with the Jews would become beneficial later, as seen in the alliance during the Battle of the Trench.

Ṣafwān makes his move

In the following years, the influence of Ṣafwān ibn Umayyah continued to increase each time that Abū Sufyān made an error or fell short in fulfilling his leadership duties. The dispute between the two men escalated, culminating in Abū Sufyān being overthrown after the Battle of the Trench. Three young and energetic individuals—Ṣafwān, 'Ikrimah ibn Abī Jahl and Suhayl ibn 'Amr—then took over the reins of leadership. Ṣafwān attained prominence after his failed attempt to break the economic boycott on Makkah, a pressing problem that affected all the city's inhabitants. Ṣafwān knew that, had he found a solution to the boycott, he would have won great influence among the Quraysh.

The established trade routes between Makkah and the Levant were no longer safe, creating a serious problem for the Quraysh, most of whose trade, especially that to Gaza, had no alternative route.[165] There were three routes to the Levant from Makkah.[166] One was the al-Tahāmī Route that ran parallel to the coast, but it was inaccessible to the Quraysh because of the coastal tribes' alliance with the Prophet (ﷺ). The second route ran from Makkah to Madinah then north to Khaybar; and the third was the Tabūk Route, from Makkah to Madinah then to Tabūk. The latter two routes could not be used, because they passed through Madinah. There was, therefore, no other option for the polytheists except to attempt passage through untested routes. Ṣafwān's proposal was to initially follow the Tabūk Route, then to veer off to the east, away from Madinah, and to then take the Najd Route that passed through the Najd wilderness and deserts. This was an unfamiliar route that would require experienced guides.

165. Al-Wāqidī, *Kitāb al-Maghāzī*, vol. 1, 200.
166. Sāmī al-Maghlūth, *al-Atlas al-Tārīkhī li Sīrat al-Rasūl* (Riyadh: Dār al-'Ubaykān, 2004), 126.

Attempting this new route became necessary after the Quraysh sustained huge losses due to the suspension of their trade. Al-Wāqidī's account of what would become known as the al-Qaradah Campaign is helpful to understand the Qurayshi context at the time.

> The Quraysh were warned against travelling on the Levant route, and they were afraid of Allah's Messenger (ﷺ) and his companions. Ṣafwān ibn Umayyah said: "Muḥammad and his companions have impeded our trade. We do not know what to do with his companions who do not leave the coast. The people of the coast have made peace with them, and their common folk have joined him. We do not know which route to take, and if we remain stationary, we will drain our capital while we are in our homes. We have no way to use it. We used to invest it in trade to the Levant in the summer and to the land of Abyssinia in the winter." Al-Aswad ibn al-Muṭṭalib told him: "Detour away from the coast and take the Iraq route." Ṣafwān responded: "I am not familiar with it." Abū Zam'ah offered: "I will introduce you to the most knowledgeable guide who travels this route with his eyes closed, if Allah so willed." Ṣafwān asked: "Who is he?" Abū Zam'ah replied: "Furāt ibn Ḥayyān al-'Ijlī. He has mastered [this route] and travelled it." Then Ṣafwān said: "That's it, by Allah!" He sent for Furāt and told him: "I want to go to the Levant, but Muḥammad has impeded our trade since the route of our caravans goes [through] his [territory]. I want to [use] the Iraq route." Furāt replied: "I will guide you along the Iraq route. It is not frequented by any of Muḥammad's companions. The route [goes through] the lands of Najd and the wilderness." Ṣafwān said: "This is what I need. As for the wilderness, we are now in winter and our need for water these days is little." Ṣafwān ibn Umayyah prepared [a caravan] and dispatched Abū Zam'ah with it, along with 300 mithqals of gold and silver ingots. He also sent Qurayshi merchants with their wares. 'Abdallah ibn Abī Rabī'ah, Ḥuwayṭab ibn 'Abd al-'Uzza, and [other] men from the Quraysh went with. Ṣafwān took a large amount of money, silver ingots and utensils valued at 30,000 dirhams. They departed from Dhāt 'Irq.[167]

167. Al-Wāqidī, *Kitāb al-Maghāzī*, vol. 1, 197-198.

This quote presents Ṣafwān ibn Umayyah's assessment regarding the strategic reality after Badr. The Quraysh's trade was overcome by paralysis because most of the coastal people had entered an alliance with Muḥammad (ﷺ), and the Muslims had scouts permanently watching the coastal route. The Quraysh had previously habitually used the coastal route. The Najd route was familiar to only a few of them. Ṣafwān's assessment was correct: if the status quo persisted, the Quraysh would deplete their capital and would collapse economically. They would lose their status and other Arabs would join the Madinah Alliance. Therefore, a solution was needed that allowed the Quraysh to avoid the coastal route. The solution was the use of the Najd route that crossed the desert from Makkah in a northeasterly direction, avoiding Madinah and passing through the Najd wilderness. They believed—incorrectly—that Najd was far from the Prophet's (ﷺ) surveillance. They did not know that he had already been patrolling the area because of his three military expeditions and that the tribes in the area were also in a state of panic and fear. The Prophet's (ﷺ) scouts had been dispersed to monitor the movement and gatherings of the bedouins, as well as the travel routes and their tributaries.

The Quraysh had no option but to revive the Najd route. A caravan set out from Makkah carrying a huge quantity of Ṣafwān's silver and the merchandise of other traders. The Prophet (ﷺ) heard about the caravan and ordered Zayd ibn Ḥārithah, leading 100 warriors, to intercept it. Zayd's forces confronted the caravan in al-Qaradah, northeast of Madinah. This encounter occurred six months after Badr. The people accompanying the caravan fled, and the Muslims claimed it as booty. When the spoils were divided, it was discovered that the total value of the caravan was 100,000 dirhams. A huge part of the wealth of the Quraysh was lost and, with it, their last hope of breaking the siege that the Muslims had imposed on their trade. The Quraysh became even more desperate to act against Madinah, avenge the Badr defeat, and attempt to break the siege on its trade. Qurayshi leaders began preparing for Uḥud.

CHAPTER ELEVEN

Uḥud – Lessons in crisis management

"Indeed, those of you who turned back on the day the two hosts met, it was Satan who caused them to slip, because of some of their actions. And surely Allah has pardoned them. For Allah is Most Forgiving, Most Forbearing." (Qur'ān 3:155)

The Quraysh's preparations for the Battle of Uḥud were more thorough than their preparations for Badr. Badr had taught them many lessons, the most important of which was that they should not fight alone. They therefore built a broader Makkan alliance that incorporated the Aḥābīsh (the coalition of marginalised groups in Makkah), other clans from the mother tribe, the Kinānah, and from the Thaqīf. They also contacted their allies in neighbouring Tuhāmah, to which they dispatched poets and messengers to incite people and encourage them to join the coming military effort. These poets included Abū 'Izzah 'Amr ibn 'Abdallah and Masāfi' ibn 'Abd Manāf, both from the Jumah tribe, as well as 'Amr ibn al-'Āṣ and Hubayrah ibn Abū Wahb. They achieved moderate success. The mobilisation continued until "the Quraysh came out with [all] their strength, goodwill, and weaponry, with their Aḥābīsh allies, the Banī Kinānah clans that deferred to them, and the people of Tuhāmah".[168] Their combined forces swelled to 3,000 fighters, including 100 from Thaqīf; a large amount of weaponry was collected, as well as 200 horses and 3,000 camels. Women also joined the effort to boost the morale of the soldiers and to encourage them to stand firm.

Abū Sufyān's wife, Hind bint 'Utbah, was among these women. She sought revenge for her father, uncle, and brother, and wanted to murder the Prophet's (ﷺ) uncle, Ḥamzah ibn 'Abd al-Muṭṭalib, in retribution. Ḥamzah was the most prominent and distinguished Muslim warrior and was greatly beloved by the Prophet (ﷺ). Hind was not the only person seeking Ḥamzah's head, however. Jubayr ibn Muṭ'im also sought to avenge the killing of his brother Ṭa'īmah ibn 'Adī by Ḥamzah. He offered an Abyssinian slave, Waḥshī, his freedom if he were to kill Ḥamzah.

168. Ibn Hishām, *al-Sīrah*, vol. 2, 61.

Al-Wāqidī narrates that news of the new Qurayshi army reached the Prophet (ﷺ) through a secret letter from al-'Abbās ibn 'Abd al-Muṭṭalib. It was carried by a man from the Ghaffār tribe, which was sympathetic to the Prophet (ﷺ) because of the years-long effort of Abū Dhar al-Ghaffārī to spread Islam among his people. Also, a delegation from the Khuzā'ah tribe—allies of the Prophet (ﷺ)—had passed the Qurayshi army when it had been four days' march from Makkah. The Khuzā'ah delegation was led by 'Amr ibn Sālim al-Khuzā'ī, who appraised the Prophet (ﷺ) of what they had seen. The Prophet (ﷺ) was not surprised by the news from these and other sources. Makkah's preparation for war over the few months preceding these reports was not a secret. However, reports that the Qurayshi army was already on the march spurred the Prophet (ﷺ) to do what he always did in such circumstances: he sought counsel from his companions.

A consultative meeting was convened with the Muslim community in the Prophet's (ﷺ) mosque, and a discussion ensued about the best strategy to employ in confronting the enemy. The Muslims realised that the Qurayshi army would be much larger and more organised than the one at Badr. They also knew that revenge would be a strong motivator and would make the polytheists more united and more zealous. Two strategies were proposed at the meeting.

The first was for the Muslims to entrench themselves within Madinah, which was protected by natural cover on two sides. Called al-Ḥarrah, the volcanic landscape was difficult terrain for any army to traverse. Moreover, the Banī Qurayẓah had fortresses dotted along the third side, leaving only a single side from which the enemy could attack the city. This strategy would require the Muslims to take up defensive positions within the neighbourhoods of the city, allowing all citizens to participate in raining down arrows on the invaders from their rooftops, thus making it difficult for the attackers to gain ground and costing them many casualties.

The second proposal was for the Muslims to confront the enemy outside the city. Two justifications were provided for this proposal. The first involved morale. If the Muslims were to barricade themselves in the city, the Quraysh and Najd tribes would think of them as cowards and thus perceive them as weak. This would incite the enemy further and expose the Muslims to future attacks. The second justification was that many of those who had been unable to participate in the Battle of Badr saw this as an opportunity to gain some of the glory that had earlier eluded them.

The Prophet (ﷺ) supported the first proposal and argued that it would force the polytheists to camp outside the city. If they attempted to storm the city, the Muslims would resist from their rooftops and homes, making the enemy's progress perilous. ʻAbdallah ibn Ubay ibn Sallūl shared this view. However, the younger companions and a few others who had not participated in Badr argued for a confrontation with the polytheists outside the city. This would give them the opportunity to fight, as was given to those before them at Badr. Some senior companions such as Ḥamzah ibn ʻAbd al-Muṭṭalib and Saʻd ibn ʻUbādah also supported this option. They argued that remaining in the city would convey a message of weakness and would make the enemy more confident. ʻAbdallah ibn Ubay ibn Sallūl rejected this opinion and argued:

> O Messenger of Allah, we used to fight in the city in the times before Islam. We gathered the women and children in these fortifications and left stones with them. By Allah, the young boys sometimes spent a month gathering stones in preparation for our enemy. We ringed the city with fortifications so that it would be like a fortress from every side. The women and children pelted [the enemy] from the top of the fortifications and high houses, and we fought the enemy with our swords in the streets. O Messenger of Allah, our city has remained intact and has never been penetrated. Whenever we marched out [to confront] an enemy, we were overcome with affliction; whenever they attacked us in the city, we were always able to severely injure them. So let them come, O Messenger of Allah. If they persist, they will walk into the worst of traps, and if they withdraw, they will withdraw in despair and defeat without having achieved anything. O Messenger of Allah, obey me in this matter and know that I have learnt this lesson from my elders and those of my people who have insight. They were indeed a people of war and experience.[169]

169. Al-Wāqidī, *Kitāb al-Maghāzī*, vol. 1, 209.

The matter generated heated debate and many participants vociferously supported the position of the youth. Al-Wāqidī provides lengthy accounts of the meeting, quoting the views of many companions, including Khaythamah Abū Sa'd ibn Khaythamah, who argued in favour of marching out of the city. Using emotionally charged language, he pleaded for the opportunity to confront the enemy and attain martyrdom in the path of Allah.

> O Messenger of Allah, the Quraysh have spent a lot of time gathering their forces, summoning Arabs from the desert and their allies from the Aḥābīsh. They will come to us with cavalry and riding camels until they reach our domain. And they will try to besiege us in our fortified abodes. They will then return without suffering any casualties. That will make them bolder, and they will launch raids against us and harm those of us who live on the periphery [away from the city centre]. They send out spies to monitor us and to damage our crops. This will also embolden the Arabs around us until they [also] consider [attacking us], since they saw that we did not march out [to confront the Quraysh].
>
> Let us expel them from our midst and perhaps Allah will grant us victory. This is Allah's way, as far as we are concerned. The alternative is martyrdom. I did not participate in the Battle of Badr, even though I was keen to do so. I contributed through the participation of my son. His arrow left [the bow] and he attained martyrdom, but I was the one who was keen on martyrdom. I saw my son in my sleep last night. He was in the best of conditions, indulging in the fruits of jannah (paradise) and strolling along its rivers. He told me: "Catch up with me and accompany me in jannah for I have found what my Lord had promised to be true!" By Allah, O Messenger of Allah, I awoke with a desire to accompany him in jannah. I have grown old, my bones have become frail, and I desire to meet my Lord. Call on Allah, O Messenger of Allah, to bestow martyrdom upon me and to allow me to join Sa'd in jannah."[170]

Ibn Khaythamah was indeed granted martyrdom in the Battle of Uḥud.

---

170. Al-Wāqidī, *Kitāb al-Maghāzī*, vol. 1, 212-213.

The Prophet (ﷺ) did not support the youths' proposal. His opinion was reinforced by a dream in which he had seen himself inserting his hand into a coat of armour, which he interpreted as representing Madinah. However, the opinion of the youth was enthusiastically backed up and got majority support. The Prophet (ﷺ) upheld the majority view. Some companions, after some reflection, regretted having argued against the Prophet (ﷺ) and asked him to make the final decision about which strategy to employ. He, however, had already decided to abide by the majority view and had already donned his armour. He gave them glad tidings of victory if they were to remain steadfast. This was a trait of the Prophet's (ﷺ) leadership: if he took a decision, he put his faith in Allah and unhesitatingly proceeded to implement the decision with full confidence and determination.

Meanwhile, the Madinah debate about whether to fight from within the city or outside it was reflected in deliberations among the leaders of the polytheist army. Abū Sufyān speculated that the Muslims would remain entrenched in their stone fortresses and homes, which would make an invasion of Madinah very difficult. He expressed concern that, if the Muslims stayed in the city, the polytheists would encounter great problems in the battle. Safwān ibn Umayyah responded that the best counter would be to destroy Madinah's economy by cutting down its palm trees and burning its palm groves. If the Muslims decided to fight outside the city, the Quraysh believed, the larger, better equipped, and highly motivated Makkan army, driven by a desire for vengeance, would emerge victorious.

The Prophet (ﷺ) dispatched scouts to monitor the movements of the Quraysh army. One scout was al-Ḥubāb ibn al-Mundhar, the companion who had advised him to take control of the wells at Badr. The Prophet (ﷺ) asked him, in secret, to assess the progress and strength of the Qurayshi army and report back to him. He was told that, if the army was small, he should address the Prophet (ﷺ) publicly so that the people would hear the news, but that if the army was large, he should inform the Prophet (ﷺ) privately to ensure that it would not upset the Muslims. When al-Ḥubāb returned, he drew the Prophet (ﷺ) aside and informed him that the army comprised 3,000 warriors, 200 horses and 700 armoured warriors. The Prophet (ﷺ) confirmed with him that there were women in the camp and noted that the women's role was to incite the fighters. He had received this information earlier but had wanted al-Ḥubāb's confirmation. He asked al-Ḥubāb not to mention the women, then said: "Allah is sufficient for us, and He is the best disposer of affairs. O Allah, with You I engage and with You I attack."[171]

The Prophet (ﷺ) called for general mobilisation and readied the Muslims for battle. He donned his war apparel, consisting of armour, headgear, helmet, and breastplate that covered his head, part of his face, his shoulders, chest, and arms. He and his army then marched to an area outside Madinah called al-Shaykhayn, where they set up camp. The Prophet (ﷺ) gave the youth permission to participate in a warriors' parade, but he sent those who were too young or unprepared to fight back to Madinah. He delegated various duties to the different brigades and appointed a leader for each one.

The next morning, after spending the night at al-Shaykhayn, about 1,000 Muslim warriors marched to Uḥud. However, 'Abdallah ibn Ubay ibn Sallūl withdrew with a third of the army and returned to Madinah. He was angry, he said, that the Prophet (ﷺ) had not heeded his advice to fight from inside Madinah. He repeated: "He obeyed young boys and disobeyed me." As a result of Ibn Sallūl's action, only about 700 warriors remained with the Prophet (ﷺ). The Muslims did not pay much attention to Ibn Sallūl's withdrawal. A withdrawal of some forces before a battle was better than them if they later disrupted the camp, especially if they participated and were defeated.

The Prophet (ﷺ) arranged the columns of fighters for battle according to conventional practice, from right to left. He presented the banner to Muṣ'ab ibn 'Umayr from the Banī 'Abd al-Dār tribe, the traditional bearers of the Quraysh's banner. The duty of carrying the banner was symbolic; the carrier was required to keep it hoisted at all times to encourage the soldiers.

The Quraysh's banner was also to be borne by members of the Banī 'Abd al-Dār. Abū Sufyān suggested that he take it from them, saying he feared that it would be dropped during the battle. He hoped to incite them with his request. Leaders of the Banī 'Abd al-Dār vehemently

171. Al-Wāqidī, *Kitāb al-Maghāzī*, vol. 1, 208.

refused, and they raised angry voices in defence of the banner, as Abū Sufyān had hoped.

The polytheist army was more organised than at Badr. While at Badr it had no unified leadership, in Uḥud it had one leader: Abū Sufyān. At Uḥud, there was no dispute about its objective; the army was motivated by revenge for its defeat at Badr and the Quraysh stood united. The army was organised into military units with field commanders. The most important component was the cavalry, comprising 200 cavalrymen led by Khālid ibn al-Walīd. The cavalry was an offensive force, suited to striking and retreating and to speedy interventions. It was to be decisive in the coming battle. The Muslims had no cavalry worth mentioning.

After assessing the battlefield, the Prophet (ﷺ) chose to position the Muslims with Mount Uḥud behind them and to strengthen the army with suitable defences. Fifty archers were positioned on a hillock overlooking the battle, with specific instructions to defend their position and not to withdraw under any circumstances. Whether the Muslims were victorious or were defeated, the archers were to hold their positions. The Prophet (ﷺ) had calculated that the enemy's cavalry distinguished it from the Muslims, but its threat could be reduced by arrows. Without this archer cover, the Muslim rear would be exposed, and the enemy could attack them from two directions.

The battle initially favoured the Muslims, and their attack disrupted the polytheist ranks, creating confusion. The archers successfully contained the polytheist cavalry and camels. Their position overlooking the battlefield meant that the cavalry was within range of their arrows. The polytheist army was in chaos, and they began to lose ground; the Muslims charged forward in pursuit.

Disorder in the Muslim ranks

At this very moment, when victory seemed to be within the Muslims' grasp, a major disruption within their ranks led to disastrous consequences. Many archers, whose position on the hillock was crucial to maintaining the upper hand, believed that the battle had swung decisively in favour of the Muslims and abandoned their posts to invade the battlefield and claim a share of the spoils. This, despite the admonitions of their unit commander, who reminded them of the Prophet's (ﷺ) instructions. The Quraysh's astute military leader Khālid ibn al-Walīd was watching the battlefield, hoping to attack the Muslims from the rear. He noticed the breach and seized the opportunity to join the fray by killing the ten archers who remained on the mountain and then attacking the Muslim army from the rear.

This sudden manoeuvre created massive confusion and fear in the Muslim ranks. Disorganised by the sudden turn of events, many Muslims fled, battlefield configurations collapsed, and it became impossible to direct an army whose command-and-control structure had crumbled. Al-Wāqidī noted: "The Muslims did not have a single raised banner, nor any collective [action in unison]. The polytheist forces thrust them back and forth in the valley; they randomly came together and separated, and no one was able to command them."[172] In the midst of this confusion, someone called out that Muḥammad (ﷺ) had been killed. This created even more chaos and despondency. The Muslims were grief-stricken, their spirits collapsed, and some of them dispersed into the mountain passes or returned to Madinah.

News of the Prophet's (ﷺ) "death" effectively ended the battle. The Muslims dispersed, and Abū Sufyān focused on attempting to establish whether Muḥammad (ﷺ) had been killed. Accompanied by 'Āmir the Profligate, the Qurayshi leader began checking the bodies. Around that time, the Prophet (ﷺ) and a small group of his companions hastened to ascend Mount Uḥud, where they found a crevice in which to hide from the polytheists' attacks and fortified themselves there. Fourteen Muslims who had defended the Prophet (ﷺ) after he had fallen and injured his face and forehead joined him. Only when they were safe from the clutches of the polytheists did they call out that the Prophet (ﷺ) was not dead. More Muslims then joined the group, enlarging it to more than thirty.

The first day of the battle ended with a dialogue between Abū Sufyān and 'Umar ibn al-Khaṭṭāb.

---

172. Al-Wāqidī, *Kitāb al-Maghāzī*, vol. 1, 238.

Unable to find evidence to support Ibn Qami'ah's claim that he had killed Muḥammad (ﷺ), Abū Sufyān then saw the group of Muslims on the mountain and addressed them. Ibn Hishām's account of this episode is very informative about Abū Sufyān and the battle.

> When Abū Sufyān ibn Ḥarb wanted to leave, he turned to the mountain and shouted at the top of his voice: "You have done well. War has its ups and downs; a day [for you] and a day [against you]. Hubal is most sublime!" Allah's Messenger (ﷺ) instructed, "Stand up, O 'Umar, and respond to him." 'Umar responded: "Allah is the Most Sublime and the Most Majestic! There is no parity. Our dead are in heaven and yours are in the fire!" After 'Umar's response, Abū Sufyān called out: "Come down here, 'Umar!" Allah's Messenger (ﷺ) told 'Umar: "Go and see what he wants." 'Umar went down and Abū Sufyān pleaded: "I implore you, O 'Umar: have we killed Muḥammad?" 'Umar replied, "By Allah, you have not! He is listening to you right know." Abū Sufyān said, "I regard you as more truthful and trustworthy than Ibn Qami'ah."... Abū Sufyān then shouted out: "Some of your dead have been mutilated. By Allah, this neither pleases me, nor does it anger me; I have neither prohibited it nor ordered it." As Abū Sufyān and his companions were departing, he called out: "[Our next] engagement with you is at Badr next year." Allah's Messenger (ﷺ) told one of his companions: "Say: 'Yes, it is a [fixed] appointment between us and you.'"[173]

In his major biographical dictionary *Siyar 'Alām al-Nubalā'*, Al-Imām al-Dhahabī described Abū Sufyān as "one of the most cunning of Arabs, a person of sound opinion and honour".[174] At the end of the battle at Uḥud, Abū Sufyān was reproachful, relying more on careful consideration than on valour. This stands in stark contrast to Abū Jahl's impulsiveness and arrogance, which had resulted in the Quraysh's decimation at Badr. Abū Sufyān would, however, pay a high price for his invitation to confront the Muslims again. The Prophet (ﷺ) knew this, which was why he immediately accepted the offer. Abū Sufyān

173. Ibn Hishām, *al-Sīrah*, vol. 2, 93-94.

174. Al-Dhahabī, *Siyar 'A'lām al-Nubalā'* (Cairo: Dār al-Ḥadīth, 2006), vol. 3, 406.

probably issued the invitation to convince his army that he would lead them to another, even more decisive, victory. He understood that the outcome at Uḥud would not change the balance of forces as long as the Prophet (ﷺ) was still alive and in control of Madinah. For the Muslims, Uḥud was simply a temporary setback.

However, this episode raises the important question of why Abū Sufyān did not attack Madinah when the Muslim army had fallen into disarray. What motivated him to accept a partial victory and to return to Makkah?

Biographies of the Prophet (ﷺ) say that, after the exchange with Abū Sufyān, the Muslims deliberated over the possibility of a polytheist attack on Madinah. The Prophet (ﷺ) therefore wanted to ascertain the route of the Qurayshi army. If it returned to Makkah, that would be better for the Muslims, but if it attacked Madinah, he would fight them.

> Abū Sufyān and his companions began departing, but Allah's Messenger (ﷺ) and the Muslims grew concerned that the polytheists would attack Madinah and kill the children and women. Allah's Messenger (ﷺ) told Sa'd ibn Abī Waqqāṣ: "Give me a report on the people. If they have mounted their camels, they are heading for Makkah; but if they have mounted their horses, they intend to attack Madinah. By the One in whose hand is my life, if they march on Madinah, I will chase them and I will fight them."
>
> Sa'd said: "I endeavoured to pursue them and told myself that if I saw anything that I feared, I would take the news back to the Prophet (ﷺ). I followed their tracks and found that they had reached al-'Atīq. I was [positioned in a spot] from where I could observe them. They were riding their camels and had not mounted their horses, so I told myself that they were returning to their homes. They stopped for a while in al-'Atīq and deliberated about approaching Madinah, but Ṣafwān ibn Umayyah told them: 'You gained a victory over the people. Now go on your way and do not enter the city while fatigued. You have the victory, but you do not know what lies ahead for

you. You fled on the day of Badr and, by Allah, they did not pursue you and accepted their victory.'"

Allah's Messenger (ﷺ) said: "Ṣafwān stopped them."[175]

Ṣafwān was correct. There were several reasons that the decision to retreat and not enter Madinah was sound. The Quraysh could claim that they had won the battle and had killed enough Muslims to have achieved their goal of avenging Badr. Were they to have attacked Madinah, they would have raised the conflict to a new level, with no certainty as to the outcome.

The situation in Madinah was not entirely secure. Ibn Sallūl and his allies had abandoned the impending battle and had returned to Madinah, and not only were the Jews not keen to defend the Prophet (ﷺ) and his companions, they were hoping for their defeat. Nevertheless, the tribal relationships of both groups with the rest of Madinan society remained intact. The Banī al-Naḍīr and the Banī Qurayẓah remained allies of the Aws. Furthermore, the other inhabitants of Yathrib—whether Hypocrites or polytheists—would not accept the occupation of their city and the humiliation, loss of honour, and fear for their children associated with it. The Madinah Charter obligated all the city's tribes, including the Jews, to defend it should it be attacked. ("And together [they have to] stand up to whoever attacks Yathrib.") They were not obligated to fight alongside the Muslims outside Madinah, which was their reason for not participating in the Battle of Uḥud. Thus, if the Quraysh were to attack Madinah after Uḥud, the Jewish tribes and 'Abdallah ibn Ubay ibn Sallūl's followers, who had withdrawn from the battle, would be obligated to defend the city. The Muslims who had fled after the battle would also all rise again to defend Madinah. If the fighting were to take place in the city's residential areas and streets, it would ultimately be extremely costly for the Quraysh. They therefore withdrew, satisfied with the victory already achieved.

After the polytheist army withdrew, the Muslims returned to the battlefield to collect their dead. They were shocked at having lost seventy fighters. Even more shocking was the mutilation of the martyrs' bodies. The Qurayshi fighters had given full vent to their savagery,

175. Al-Wāqidī, *Kitāb al-Maghāzī*, vol. 1, 298.

severing noses and ears and disembowelling their victims. The most grotesque sight for the Muslims was the corpse of Ḥamzah ibn 'Abd al-Muṭṭalib. After he had been killed by Waḥshī's spear, Hind bint 'Utbah had slit open his belly with her dagger and chewed a piece of his liver to quench her anger.

Many people had targeted Ḥamzah, but Hind had transgressed all ethics, customs, and traditions. Perhaps it was her actions from which her husband Abū Sufyān had tried to dissociate himself when he had told the Muslims: "Some of your dead have been mutilated. By Allah, this neither pleases me, nor does it anger me; I have neither prohibited it nor ordered it." The Quraysh had violated the customs of war that were familiar to the Arabs, and, by custom, the same treatment could be meted out to them by the Muslims or anyone else in future.

Transcending adversity

The Battle of Uḥud took place on 7 Shawwāl 3 AH / March 625. It is not necessary to present all the details here; the narratives in any work of sīrah will provide sufficient insight. They portray a day of tribulation and deep sorrow, in which the Muslims experienced the first such trial. It is obvious that the battle would have serious consequences. This context demanded that the leader must exercise impeccable, visionary, and transformational leadership, and to help the people transcend adversity.

The Prophet (ﷺ) always took the initiative and did not allow the enemy to determine developments. However, he was also human and was also affected by the sorrow and exhaustion that afflicted his people. Uḥud weighed heavily on him. He had sustained seven wounds to his face, head, knees, and shoulder, and he was overcome by tremendous grief over his uncle Ḥamzah's death. A difficult night in Madinah followed the difficult day at Uḥud. The next day, he resolved to expel the negative mood of the previous day from all of Madinah, so that he could continue the war and write its final chapter.

At dawn, his heralds called out, urging the Muslims to prepare to march. However, only those who had fought on the previous day were allowed to join the mobilisation. Many warriors had sustained injuries, but all responded to the call. The army fell in behind its leader in pursuit of the Quraysh, to strip it of its pride and the moral victory with which it would have returned to Makkah.

The Prophet's (ﷺ) decision to pursue the polytheists was a strategic necessity. First, because there remained a risk that the Quraysh might attack Madinah and exploit the Muslim losses at Uḥud. Second, if the final outcome of Uḥud was negative for the Muslims, it would be a significant change of fortune that their opponents inside Madinah could exploit. Third, it would weaken their status and aura among the Arab tribes. The Prophet (ﷺ) was therefore determined that the Uḥud episode must end positively, and, to that end, he pursued the Quraysh.

The Prophet (ﷺ) marched to Ḥamrā' al-Asad, twenty kilometres south of Madinah, where his forces camped. The polytheists were only around twenty-five kilometres away, camped in a place called al-Rūḥā'. Meanwhile, the Quraysh forces had begun discussing the possibility of returning and attacking the Muslims. They realised that, even though they had killed seventy Muslims, this did not represent a decisive victory. The Prophet (ﷺ) and his senior companions were still alive, Madinah was still under their control, and the economic blockade against the Quraysh would continue. There was growing agreement that they had an opportunity for another attack.

It fell to a man from the Khuzā'ah tribe, Ma'bad ibn Abī Ma'bad al-Khuzā'ī, to undertake the task of dissuading the Quraysh. The Khuzā'ah would emerge as faithful advisors and allies of the Prophet (ﷺ).

Ma'bad was not a Muslim, but, being from the Khuzā'ah, he was not pleased by the Quraysh's victory. He was on his way from Madinah to Makkah when he encountered the Prophet (ﷺ) at Ḥamrā' al-Asad. The Prophet (ﷺ) asked him to dissuade the Quraysh by making them fearful of the Muslim army. When Ma'bad caught up with the Quraysh at al-Rūḥā', Abū Sufyān asked him what he had seen on his way. Ma'bad replied:

> Muḥammad and his companions are pursuing you with an army the likes of which I have never seen before. They are

burning [with rage]. Those who had stayed behind on the day that you clashed have joined him, as they are regretful over their absence. They bear a kind of hatred toward you that I have never seen before.

Abū Sufyān responded: "Woe to you! What are you saying?" Ma'bad continued: "By Allah, I believe that you should depart [so speedily] that I see the backs of your horses." Abū Sufyān said: "By Allah, we have agreed to attack them and exterminate whoever remains." Ma'bad responded: "I certainly advise you against that."[176]

Ma'bad had planted the seeds of fear in the hearts of the Quraysh, painting a dangerous scenario wherein all the people of Madinah, those who had participated at Uḥud and those who had not, were pursuing the Qurayshi forces, desperate for revenge. The Quraysh understood the importance of rage and its capacity to mobilise. Revenge was a tribal obligation, even in cases where there were religious differences between members of the tribe. The Quraysh also knew that most of the people killed at Uḥud had been from the Anṣār. Only six Muhājīrun had been killed. The Anṣār, both Aws and Khazraj tribes, both Muslim and Hypocrite, would not pardon the Quraysh for spilling the blood of their sons. By tribal custom, blood was valued above all else.

The Prophet (ﷺ) had ordered his warriors to burn a large number of fires that night and to exaggerate their activity in the camp so that the camp might be seen from afar and its noises might be heard at a great distance. Some reports say that more than 500 fires were lit that night.[177] To the Quraysh, this bustle confirmed what Ma'bad ibn Abī Ma'bad al-Khuzā'ī had told them, that the Muslim army was much larger than the one they had encountered at Uḥud. They therefore decided to continue their return to Makkah, be satisfied with a moral victory, and to hasten their departure to prevent the Muslim army overtaking them. When the Qurayshi forces began their march to Makkah, al-Khuzā'ī sent a message to the Prophet (ﷺ) with the news. The Prophet (ﷺ) tarried for three days at Ḥamrā' al-Asad to confirm the Quraysh's departure before returning to Madinah.

176. Ibn Hishām, *al-Sīrah*, vol. 2, 102.
177. Al-Nās, *'Uyūn al-Athar*, vol. 2, 54.

Lessons in difficulty and ease

Every experience or action has consequences. They might sometimes be negative, but there is no such thing as absolute difficulty. In fact, difficulty is accompanied by or contains within it ease, as is mentioned in Allah's book. "So, verily with difficulty there is ease. Verily, with difficulty there is ease" (Qur'ān 94:5-6). If a person reflects on his difficulties and is able to draw lessons and morals from them, ease will emerge thereafter. "After difficulty, Allah will grant ease" (Qur'ān 65:7). Every affliction encompasses both positive and negative aspects. An exceptional leader is able to maximise the positive and minimise the negative.

For the Muslims in Madinah, the positive consequences of Uḥud were that they learnt valuable lessons and derived good counsel and benefit from it. They learnt that divine laws were impartial. If they wanted victory, they had to meet the prerequisites for its attainment, including objective analysis, comprehensive preparation, decisive planning, and strict discipline. They realised that there were three reasons for their disaster at Uḥud. The first related to their psychological makeup, the second to battlefield discipline, and the third to Madinah's internal context.

Emotional justification should not be the most important element in military decision-making. The decision to confront the enemy outside Madinah was taken in an emotionally charged atmosphere and inserted non-objective considerations, rather than strategic thinking, into the decision. Further, many companions who had not participated in Badr desired to attain the same status and reward as their peers at Badr. This allowed emotion to trump strategic calculation.

Another psychological factor related to the temperament and ego of the Arab warrior, who was obsessed with proving his bravery and personal valour, even if it contradicted objective battlefield considerations. Therefore, many companions felt that confronting the enemy outside the city would give the impression that Muslims were unafraid and courageous, rather than cowardly. They also felt that remaining in the city would convey a message of weakness, which did not fit the image of the brave Arab warrior.

It is true that remaining in the city might indeed have given such an impression to the polytheists, but it would have been only temporary. Victory in battle and halting the onslaught would quickly wash away such sentiments. The effects of the bitterness of defeat, despair, and loss that the enemy would taste would be longer-lasting than fleeting outpourings of emotion.

Psychological and emotional calculations based on faith are important in determining the balance of forces because they can strengthen the warrior. However, they should not be preeminent in the military decision-making process. This should be influenced more by considerations such as preparation, the number of warriors, military parity, and battlefield geography. The Muslims quickly learnt this lesson after Uḥud. Their decision-making criteria certainly changed by the time they engaged in the next battle.

This is not to suggest that the consultative mechanism used was changed, compromised, or regarded as not useful. Rather, it was stabilised and reinforced. The leader did not claim that the outcome of the consultation for Uḥud had been incorrect or invalid. There is no record of the Prophet (ﷺ) reprimanding any of his companions who had supported the strategy of fighting outside Madinah. He also did not resolve that the future responsibility for deciding on matters of war would be solely his, or his with the assistance of a select group. The opposite was the case. After Uḥud, the Qur'ān lauded and reinforced the mechanism of consultation and advised the Prophet (ﷺ) to continue consulting on matters affecting the public: "It was by the mercy of Allah that you dealt gently with them. Had you been harsh and hard-hearted, they would have dispersed and left you. So pardon them, ask (Allah's) forgiveness for them, and consult them about affairs." (Qur'ān 3:159).

The Muslims thus collectively learnt from their mistakes. The entire community was elevated in the process, and there was no entrenchment of unilateralism in decision-making. They institutionalised consultation in a manner that valued innovation and transcended the ordinary. We will see later how consultative deliberations at the Battle of the

Trench led to a great victory. In that battle, the Prophet (ﷺ) adopted an innovative proposal to construct a trench. The idea was proposed by Salmān al-Fārsī, who was not an Arab noble, during a consultative assembly. His was the best idea that was proposed, and the Muslims adopted it, resulting in a military masterstroke and a strategy that would lay the foundation for a new phase of victory and conquest.

The second failure at Uḥud related to the structure of the army and the discipline of the warriors on the battlefield. Most accounts of the battle attribute the defeat at Uḥud to a single cause: the archers' failure to obey the clear commands of the supreme commander. By abandoning their posts on the hill, the archers exposed a huge vulnerability in the Muslim rear and offered the polytheists an opportunity to convert the battle from defeat to victory. While this reasoning is correct, it does not sufficiently account for all the weaknesses on the battlefield.

The problem began before the archers had abandoned their posts. Soon after the battle had begun, when the Muslims had realised that victory was at hand, they had rushed to gather the spoils, not waiting for the commander's instructions or considering the military state of play. They had acted unilaterally, and when the archers saw their brothers gathering the spoils, they too rushed down to claim their share. The lack of discipline afflicted most of the military formations on the Muslim side and manifested in the desire and rush to claim the war booty. After Uḥud, the question of the spoils of war was dealt with at its root. It was decided that all the booty would be handed over to the supreme commander, who would divide it according to a set formula.

There is no doubt that the archers' abandoning their posts was the decisive factor in exposing the Muslims' rear flank, and in the collapse of the army. The organisational knot of the army had been undone, and every individual was left to their own devices. Some fled toward Madinah, some sat and waited, and some fought on alone and without support. Nonetheless, by itself, the archers' surrendering their position would not have led to the Muslim defeat—if the other military formations had maintained their discipline. The Arab warriors had not fully grasped the importance and workings of a hierarchical military structure. Arabs idolised bravery, zeal, chivalry, retribution, and, above all else, individual valour. Military organisation in the form of disciplined units under a single command, orderly fighting without disruptions and individual initiative, and a discipline that prevented impulsive actions was not the norm in their battles.

While the army might have had formations on the left, right, and middle, as well as tribal banners under which they fought, this structure was not immutable; it was regarded as flexible and could be changed by individuals as they desired. Warriors fought as individuals and would advance or retreat based on personal assessment. This problem was, however, resolved after Uḥud. The new structure was not based on the contributions of individual warriors but on discipline, the hierarchical ordering of the different formations, clear duties for the various military units, and disciplined collective action. This restructuring proved its effectiveness during the conquest of Makkah. On that occasion, Abū Sufyān stood amazed before the well-organised and disciplined army, the likes of which the Arabs had never seen.

The third reason for the Muslim defeat was the desertion of 'Abdallah ibn Ubay ibn Sallūl with a third of the army before the battle had begun. This had a negative psychological and strategic effect on the army. The Prophet (ﷺ) strove to remedy the problem immediately after the battle. He dealt with those who had contravened the Madinah Charter, especially the Hypocrites and the Jewish tribes, in an unprecedented and decisive manner.

Containing the fallout

Every war has consequences; the consequences of Badr were positive because it had resulted in an overwhelming victory. The Prophet (ﷺ) had used the victory as an opportunity to strengthen the foundations of the state and its security architecture and to implement the Madinah Charter. Uḥud, on the other hand, had dangerous strategic consequences. The Muslims would need a full year to contain its fallout and to manage the crises that resulted.

The strategic challenges that arose after Uḥud were both external and internal. The external challenges manifested in the increasing danger posed by the bedouins and their audacious targeting of Madinah. The Najd and other tribes sought any opportunity to attack the Muslims. They believed that the Muslim loss at Uḥud provided them an opportunity to attack, pillage, and ransack Madinah at their whim. However, the Prophet (ﷺ) dealt with this danger immediately and swiftly; he launched pre-emptive attacks on enemy territory before the danger reached Madinah. The other internal strategic challenge related to the role of the Hypocrites and the Banī al-Naḍīr and Banī Qurayẓah Jewish tribes within Madinah. The Prophet (ﷺ) knew that they were thrilled with the Uḥud events. Their elation alerted him that precautionary measures were necessary to ensure that they would not consider acting on their sentiment. These threats—internal and external—remained active in the period between the Battle of Uḥud and the Battle of the Trench.

Confronting post-Uhud threats

Three months after Uḥud, the Prophet (ﷺ) received news of several clans of the Banī Asad ibn Khuzaymah planning to attack Madinah, following an abominable custom that they regarded as praiseworthy: to raid, pillage, and capture hostages. A conversation between them was conveyed to the Prophet (ﷺ). It reflected the mood and intentions that characterised that difficult period. During the conversation, one of the interlocutors had said:

> We [should] march on Muḥammad's home and attack his periphery, at their pasture outside Madinah. We should travel on horseback since our horses were well grazed in the spring, and on trained camels so that we will not be overtaken with our booty. If we encounter some of them, we are prepared for war, as we have horses and they have none, and we have the best of camels, which are as good as horses. The [Muslims] have been stricken by calamity, for the Quraysh recently claimed many causalities from them. They cannot fight for long.[178]

This report revealed their intention to attack the city's periphery,

178. Al-Wāqidī, *Kitāb al-Maghāzī*, vol. 2, 566.

especially the camel pastures and farms. They also knew that the Muslim army possessed no horses, which were necessary for swift attacks and retreats. That the Banī Asad possessed horses would, they believed, enable them to launch a speedy raid. If they were forced to confront a contingent of Muslims, they would be able to deal with it. However, their assessment of the Muslims' psychological state was incorrect. They believed that the Muslims had been overcome by a major affliction and would not be able to recover for a long time. This was incorrect. The Muslims had managed to quickly rekindle their fighting spirit and to overcome the pain and sadness of Uḥud.

When the Prophet (ﷺ) learnt about the planned attack, he sent a contingent of 150 warriors, led by Abū Salamah ibn 'Abd al-Asad, to attack the Banī Asad ibn Khuzaymah gathering before they mobilised their forces. Abū Salamah took them by surprise, scattered them, and returned to Madinah with booty. The Prophet (ﷺ) dispatched another detachment a few days later, after he discovered that a group from the Hudhayl tribe, led by Khālid ibn Sufyān al-Hadhalī, was preparing to attack Madinah. The Prophet (ﷺ) instructed 'Abdallah ibn Unays to assassinate Khālid preemptively. 'Abdallah returned to Madinah eighteen days later, having completed his mission.

A painful betrayal

The Prophet (ﷺ) often welcomed delegations from the various tribes in Madinah, proffered them warm hospitality, and invited them to Islam. Among his visitors after Uḥud was a leader of the Banī 'Āmir, Abū al-Barā' 'Āmir ibn Mālik, also known by the title Malā'ib al-Asinnah. The Prophet (ﷺ) invited him to embrace Islam. Even though he did not, he expressed some interest and suggested that the Prophet (ﷺ) send a delegation of Muslims with him to teach Islam to his clan. The Prophet (ﷺ) agreed, especially since he knew of the status of Abū al-Barā' among his people and knew that he would provide the necessary protection for the Muslims. The Arabs respected the custom of tribal protection extended to a guest. It deserved particular respect in this instance, since the one offering protection was advanced in age and of a high status.

The Prophet (ﷺ) asked forty young companions who were devoted to studying and memorising the Qur'ān to accompany Abū al-Barā' to the Banī 'Āmir base in Najd. Abū al-Barā' was true to his word and announced to the Banī 'Āmir that they should not be hostile to his guests. Everything went well until one of his nephews, 'Āmir ibn al-Ṭufayl, who was known for his boorishness and obscenity, rebelled against his uncle and incited the Banī 'Āmir to kill the Muslims. When he was rebuffed, he sought help from the 'Usayyah, Ra'il, and Dhakwan branches of the Sulaym tribe. The Dhakwan—comprising about 100 individuals—responded to his call, surrounded the Muslims at a water well called Ma'ūnah, and massacred them.

At the same time, another Muslim delegation of six persons was dispatched to the 'Uḍal and al-Qārah tribes, at their request, to teach them Islam. The Muslims were, however, betrayed by these two tribes in a gathering of the Hudhayl tribe at a well called al-Rajī' on the Hijaz road. They surrounded the Muslims and informed them that they would not kill them, but intended to sell them to the Quraysh. The young companions refused to surrender. Four were killed and two—Zayd ibn al-Dathannah and Khubayb ibn 'Adī—were taken prisoner. Ṣafwān ibn Umayyah bought Zayd and promptly murdered him to avenge the death of his father Umayyah ibn Khalaf. An ally of the Banī Nawfal bought Khubayb ibn 'Adī and killed him in retribution for his father. News of the murders of Zayd and Khubayb spread widely, especially among the people of Makkah who had witnessed the bravery of the young men and their love for the Prophet (ﷺ). Just before Zayd was murdered:

> Abū Sufyān asked Zayd: "I beseech you in Allah's name, O Zayd, would you not like Muḥammad to be in your place so that we may strike off his head, while you remain with your relatives?" Zayd replied: "By Allah, I would not like Muḥammad, wherever he is, to be pricked by a thorn while I sit with my kinsfolk." Abū Sufyān said: "I have not seen anyone who loves another person in the way that the companions of Muḥammad love Muḥammad."[179]

Khubayb also displayed tremendous bravery. He asked his

179. Ibn Hishām, *al-Sīrah*, vol. 2, 172.

executioners to allow him to perform two cycles of prayer, and he prayed very quickly. He said that he did not want his tormentors to claim that he had lengthened his prayer because he was afraid of death. When they hoisted him up to crucify him, he looked at them and said: "O Allah, take note of their number, kill them in different places, and do not let any of them survive." His words had such an impact on observers that Abū Sufyān shoved his son Mu'āwiyyah to the ground so that he would not be struck by Khubayb's prayer.

The Muslims were greatly saddened by these two incidents. The incidents at the wells of Ma'ūnah and al-Rajī' also contained two critical lessons for the Muslims. They were forced to take more serious precautions and to be prepared to face the betrayal of the bedouins. The non-Islamic environment respected only strength, and when the Bedouins felt weak, they became hostile and were prone to betrayal. There was, therefore, no option for the Muslims but to stand firm, build their capacity, and strengthen any weaknesses. The most important weakness confronting the Muslims at the time was the internal front in Madinah.

Expulsion of the Banī al-Naḍīr

Members of the Jewish tribe of Banī al-Naḍīr were among those who incited against the Muslims and had strong ties with the Quraysh. Abū Sufyān ibn Ḥarb had visited Salām ibn Mishkam, a Banī al-Naḍīr leader, and the two had spent time together after the Battle of Badr, which was a violation of the Madinah Charter. The Banī al-Naḍīr continued their intelligence collaboration with the Quraysh and their incitement of the Quraysh against the Muslims. They also sent information about the Muslims and their vulnerabilities to the Qurayshi leadership.[180] The Banī al-Naḍīr repeated the mistake of the Banī Qaynuqā'. Deluded by the Muslims' setback at Uḥud, they increased their intelligence-gathering activities. Meanwhile, they joined other parties that were also looking for an opportunity to attack the Prophet (ﷺ).

The direct cause of the Banī al-Naḍīr being expelled from Madinah

180. Al-Nās, *'Uyūn al-Athar*, vol. 2, 70.

was their attempt to assassinate the Prophet (ﷺ). Historians recount that the Prophet (ﷺ) sought their assistance to pay the blood money for two men of the Banī ʻĀmir tribe who had been killed by ʻAmr ibn Umayyah al-Ḍamarī, the sole survivor of the Maʻūnah Well massacre. He had encountered the two men on his return to Madinah. On being informed that they were from the Banī ʻĀmir, he killed them. ʻAmr was not aware that his victims had been in Madinah and had been granted protection and hospitality by the Prophet (ﷺ). When he reached Madinah, he informed the Prophet (ﷺ) about his action. The Prophet (ﷺ) decided to pay blood money in expiation for their slaying. The Banī al-Naḍīr were allies of the Banī ʻĀmir, and it was, therefore, not unexpected that the Prophet (ﷺ) would seek their assistance in the matter. He visited them with some of his companions. The Banī al-Naḍīr leaders pretended to agree to facilitate the payment. While the Prophet (ﷺ) sat beside a wall waiting for them, they decided to assassinate him by dropping a rock on his head. The Prophet (ﷺ) learnt about the plot and hurried back to Madinah.

He sent a messenger to inform the Banī al-Naḍīr that, since they had broken their covenant, they were required to leave Madinah. They could take their wealth but not their weapons. However, they refused and barricaded themselves in their citadel, hoping that ʻAbdallah ibn Ubay ibn Sallūl and the Banī Qurayẓah would assist them. They waited in vain for thirteen days, until finally acceding to the Prophet's (ﷺ) ruling; they left Madinah for Khaybar. Yet even there they posed a danger, and they would play a pivotal role in planning the confrontation at the Battle of the Trench.

With the departure of the Banī Qaynuqāʻ and the Banī al-Naḍīr, Ibn Sallūl had lost two crucial allies. His hostile activities were therefore reduced to mere verbal pronouncements without any concomitant action. He spread rumours and made promises, but was incapable of any practical action. The Prophet's (ﷺ) response to him and the other Hypocrites was containment. This strategy won over those among the Anṣār who had supported him and maintained Madinah's unity. His strategy in dealing with the Banī Qaynuqāʻ and the Banī al-Naḍīr had been different, since they had initiated hostile action and had been implicated in seditious activities. They had contravened their covenant with the Prophet (ﷺ) and were severely punished.

The Second Badr and Abū Sufyān's dilemma

One year after Uḥud, the mood in Makkah was very different. The Qurayshis had quenched their bloodlust by their revenge killing of seventy of the Prophet's (ﷺ) companions. They had also crucified Zayd and Khubayb and mounted their corpses on Makkah's walls. However, they knew that these actions had not changed the facts on the ground. The Prophet (ﷺ) and the Muslims survived, their influence on the coast was intact, and traffic on the Najd caravan route was non-existent. The Quraysh's trade had been suspended, leaving them in a financial crisis and a state of despair.

As the date for the agreed-upon confrontation with the Muslims approached, one year after Uḥud, the atmosphere in Makkah was tense. The expectation of another battle, following Abū Sufyān's challenge to the Muslims at the end of the Battle of Uḥud to meet them a year later at Badr, had been accepted on their behalf by 'Umar ibn al-Khaṭṭāb. The year was almost over and, with the Badr appointment almost upon them, the Quraysh had to decide their course of action. They were not excited at the prospect of fighting, and the mood in Makkah began turning against Abū Sufyān. Many people felt that his promise had involved them in an unjustified endeavour.

Abū Sufyān's promise of another engagement had been a serious error. It seemed to many in Makkah that his enthusiasm at Uḥud had clouded his judgement. He had committed himself to a battle that was so far in the future that it gave the Muslims ample time to prepare themselves. However, the commitment had been made, and as the time for the confrontation approached, the Quraysh found themselves ill prepared.

Abū Sufyān realised that he had landed himself in a quandary, and that he needed to escape without being accused of cowardice. His strategy was to try to convince the Muslims to renege on the agreement. In pursuance of this strategy, he used misinformation to try to scare the Muslims into failing to present themselves at Badr. He sought the assistance of Na'īm ibn Mas'ūd, a trader from the Ashja' branch of the Ghaṭafān tribe, who carried merchandise and news between Makkah and Madinah. Na'īm was known to both sides due to his frequent visits to the two cities. Abū Sufyān recruited him to scare the Muslims by misinforming them about the Quraysh's numbers and strength. Confiding in Na'īm, he said:

> I feel that I should not march [to Badr], but I would be displeased if Muḥammad does so and I do not. That will make the Muslims even more audacious. For them to stay away is better than for me to do so. Go to Madinah and tell them that we are a great force that they cannot overpower. You will get twenty camels from me in return. I will pay them to you through the hand of Suhayl ibn 'Amr.[181]

Upon his arrival in Madinah, Na'īm began spreading his rumours, assisted by the Hypocrites, who said that Muḥammad (ﷺ) would not be able to best the Qurayshi army. The rumours influenced some Muslims into opining that they should not go to battle. However, Abū Bakr al-Ṣiddīq and 'Umar ibn al-Khaṭṭāb told the Prophet (ﷺ):

> O Allah's Messenger (ﷺ), verily Allah supports His Prophet and honours His religion. We promised the people a meeting; we do not want to [dishonour the appointment] and allow our actions to be regarded as cowardice. Let us go forth and keep the appointment. By Allah, there is much good in this.[182]

The Prophet (ﷺ) was pleased by the suggestion and announced his departure for Badr. "By the One in whose hand is my life," he said, "I will march even if no one marches with me." The Prophet (ﷺ) and his companions prepared themselves, marched to Badr, and awaited the enemy. Na'īm ibn Mas'ūd had failed in his mission and forfeited the camels that Abū Sufyān had promised.

Abū Sufyān's attempt to avoid the battle through deception had failed. To protect the image of the Quraysh and his image as a leader, he was left with no choice but to face the Muslims. When he asked the Makkans to join him, they did so reluctantly. Most were angry about the predicament in which he had landed them. When he realised that the reluctance might

181. Al-Wāqidī, *Kitāb al-Maghāzī*, vol. 1, 385.
182. Al-Wāqidī, *Kitāb al-Maghāzī*, vol. 1, 386.

lead to rebellion or, worse, defeat, he returned to Makkah and blamed the drought for his change of heart. Ibn Isḥāq narrates:

> The Prophet camped for eight nights waiting for Abū Sufyān. Abū Sufyān marched with the people of Makkah until he reached Majannah, in the al-Ẓahrān region. Some say he reached 'Usfān before deciding to return. He said: "O people of Quraysh, only a fertile year is suitable for you. A year [when] you can graze on the [foliage of] trees and drink [the] milk [of your camels]. This is a year of drought, so I am turning back. You too should turn back." They all returned. The people of Makkah then called them the "Flour Army" (Jaysh al-Suwayq). The people [mockingly] said: "Verily, you marched out drinking flour."[183]

The real reason for Abū Sufyān's reluctance was not the drought nor a lack of supplies. A sound understanding of the situation necessitated cancelling the battle. His comment to Na'īm ibn Mas'ūd—"I feel that I should not march"—suggested that he had assessed that he might sacrifice the symbolic victory at Uḥud. Abū Sufyān knew that the Uḥud victory had been costly. Although the Quraysh had been united in their desire for retribution, they had initially been losing the battle. Were it not for the intervention of Khālid bin al-Walīd and his cavalry, the Quraysh would have been defeated. If the desire for revenge was the main motivation of the Qurayshi warriors at Uḥud, Abū Sufyān must have asked himself: What would be their motivation at the second Badr encounter?

By contrast, the Muslims had an additional motivation to fight. They were yearning for another confrontation to exact revenge for their loss at Uḥud. It is clear that, were a clash to take place, it would have been between a lethargic party that was unenthused and unmotivated for a fight, on the one hand, and another that was fully prepared and had impatiently been waiting for a whole year for the battle. There was a real possibility that the Qurayshi army would be defeated. For Abū Sufyān, another clash was too much of a gamble and could restore the balance of power to what it had been prior to Uḥud.

He must also have wondered what the strategic objective of another confrontation at Badr might be. If the first Badr clash was to defend the

183. Al-Ṭabarī, *Jāmi' al-Bayān*, vol. 2, 559.

Quraysh's trade interests, and Uḥud was to restore Qurayshi honour after the Badr defeat, what could possibly be the objective of a second battle at Badr? If the objective was to destroy the Muslims, it was unrealistic, since the Quraysh had been unable to do so on their own. If the objective was to strike at the Muslim capacity to disrupt the Quraysh's trade caravans, this too was unrealistic, since the Muslims needed only a few raiding parties and a few soldiers to capture caravans. A new military confrontation might even result in the Muslims tightening their economic blockade on Makkah.

For these reasons, Abū Sufyān was justified in his hesitation to march to Badr, and for using the drought and lack of supplies as an excuse. It was even worth the risk of handing the Muslims another moral victory and undermining his leadership status in Makkah.

Ṣafwān exploits the opportunity

The Quraysh's embarrassment at their failure to arrive at their promised meeting in Badr, or "Yellow Badr", as it was called, was a symptom of its general malaise and reflected the breakdown in its leadership structure. The discontent of Ṣafwān and his youth cohort with Abū Sufyān was escalating.

Abū Sufyān's personality inclined toward avoiding direct confrontation. He favoured caution and diplomacy, based on his cross-border trade experience and the profit and loss calculations with which he was familiar. It was expected that this would be interpreted as ambivalence and weakness by the more zealous sectors in Makkah, especially the youth, who had attained a greater role and had become more active after the deaths of the elders. The most prominent of this generation were three individuals, two of whose fathers had been killed at Badr: Ṣafwān ibn Umayyah and 'Ikrimah ibn Abī Jahl. The third was Suhayl ibn 'Amr. Khālid ibn al-Walīd's fortunes also rose after Uḥud; he was, after all, the man who had achieved the victory, and he was from a respected lineage. 'Amr ibn al-'Āṣ was the most cunning and experienced of this generation. He achieved fame a decade earlier when the Quraysh had deployed him to try to convince the Negus to expel the

Muslims who had migrated to Abyssinia.

Among these young leaders, Ṣafwān ibn Umayyah had the greatest gravitas and influence on Qurayshi decision-making, second only to Abū Sufyān. He represented the hard-line faction against Abū Sufyān, who was being accused of indecisiveness and leniency. An important psychological factor influenced Ṣafwān's position. His father, Umayyah ibn Khalaf, leader of the Banī Jumaḥ tribe, and his brother, 'Alī ibn Khalaf, had both been killed at Badr. Moreover, Ṣafwān's uncle, Ubay ibn Khalaf, had been slain at Uḥud. Harsh words had been exchanged between Ṣafwān and Abū Sufyān, and they had many differences; these intensified after Uḥud.

The tension escalated after the second Badr incident. Ṣafwān blamed Abū Sufyān for promising to confront the Muslims at a second Badr. "By Allah," he told Abū Sufyān, "I warned you against promising [to meet] these people [again]. They have acted boldly toward us and have seen that we did not show up. It is only weakness that held us back from them." Later, Ṣafwān would be active in the decision to proceed with the Battle of the Confederates, when he would again oppose Abū Sufyān's position. On that occasion, Ṣafwān addressed the Quraysh and encouraged them to accept the Banī al-Naḍīr's invitation. "O People of the Quraysh, you have made a promise to those people [Banī al-Naḍīr] regarding this situation [the upcoming Battle of the Confederates], and they have departed from here with that understanding. Be faithful to them so that this is not like the time when we had promised Muḥammad a Yellow Badr and did not keep our promise. That made them even bolder. I had disapproved of Abū Sufyān's promise at that time."[184]

The leadership tussle in Makkah, the general feeling that the Quraysh were losing the initiative to the Muslims, and the Quraysh's perception that they were in danger of losing their trade, all contributed to the Quraysh favouring the enthusiasm of the youth over the indecisiveness of the elders. The Quraysh thus followed the drums of war and the dreams of victory. They chose confrontation, which they hoped would be final and decisive, and they again began considering an invasion of Madinah.

184. Al-Wāqidī, *Kitāb al-Maghāzī*, vol. 1, 442.

CHAPTER TWELVE

Preparing for the final confrontation

"When they came at you from above you and from below you" (Qur'ān 33:10).

The Prophet (ﷺ) knew that the Qurayshi leaders were still seeking a solution to their problems. He therefore expected that an alliance would imminently be formed of the parties that felt disadvantaged by the Madinah Pact and its security domain. The alliance would include, he believed, the Quraysh and its supporters, the Jews of Khaybar (including the Banī al-Naḍīr), and various bedouin Arabs. He also knew that the strategic objective of the Quraysh and the Khaybar Jews was the extermination of the Muslims. However, those in the third group—the bedouin Arabs—were driven by utilitarian interests. The Prophet (ﷺ) began preparing for this confrontation with a sudden mobilisation northward, aiming to weaken the desert bedouins and the Jews of Khaybar.

North for the first time

The Quraysh's failure to arrive for the promised second Badr confrontation alerted the Prophet (ﷺ) to the fact that the Makkans were either not ready or were incapable of facing the Muslims on their own. This encouraged him to invest in expanding Madinah's sphere of security further into the north of the peninsula. This would be the first time that he was to head north and reach the outskirts of the Levant, specifically Dūmat al-Jandal.

Madinah's security domain had gradually expanded in the previous five years. In the first year, it had expanded westward towards the coast, then north along the coast from Yanbu', and south along the coast to Rābigh. The Prophet (ﷺ) then established a security sphere to the south and east of Madinah, using military campaigns and expeditions that targeted Najd and the tribes south of Madinah, such as Sulaym.

After the (aborted) Second Badr, he expanded northward, exploiting the Quraysh's lethargy and its apprehensiveness over any confrontation. Six months after the Second Badr, in Rabīʿ al-Awwal 6 AH / June 627, he led a unique military expedition that mobilised 1,000 warriors. The target was Dūmat al-Jandal, an important trade centre that hosted a large market, which was located in the north of the peninsula. Most of the inhabitants of this agricultural region were from tribes belonging to the Quḍāʿah tribal confederation.

At first glance, this expedition might seem anomalous, since Dūmat al-Jandal was 450 kilometres from Madinah, and it took fifteen days to reach. Moreover, it was in the far north, and to reach it from Madinah one had to cross territory under the control of the Khuzāʿah and Asad tribes that were still hostile toward the Muslims. Furthermore, Khaybar—which was only ninety kilometres north of Madinah—was also hostile to the Muslims and had become even more so after the Banī al-Naḍīr's exile. However, with careful analysis and reflection of the context within which this expedition occurred, any keen observer of the Prophet's (ﷺ) strategy will be amazed by his wisdom and astuteness. The northward expansion was crucial for two reasons. First, it was a pre-emptive strike at the northern tribes. Second, it isolated Khaybar from the northern region in anticipation of it being conquered by the Muslims.

Why the northern tribes?

The Quraysh were not the only tribe affected by the Prophet's (ﷺ) trade embargo on Makkah. Many of the Najd and Quḍāʿah tribes along the trade routes were also harmed in two ways. First, the Quraysh Pact had granted some tribes income through the provision of protection services, which were suspended due to the embargo, and, second, Qurayshi caravans had sustained the livelihoods of these tribes, selling them animal hides and other products and buying from them various commodities, such as weapons and clothing. The trade routes had formed an integrated system that had benefited the Quraysh and the other tribes.

However, the Najd route had been suspended since the Muslims gained control of Madinah. When Ṣafwān ibn Umayyah tried to circumvent

Madinah, he was attacked by Zayd ibn Ḥārithah's raiding party, and his caravan was confiscated. The Najd trade route was then completely abandoned. This is what convinced some tribes, including the Quḍā'ah in Dūmat al-Jandal, to respond by disrupting Muslim trade, which had already been expanding northward. These tribes then began considering an attack on Madinah. The Prophet (ﷺ) decided to pre-empt such actions and to eliminate the threat by penetrating the security domain of Khaybar and the Ghaṭafān tribe. He wanted to test their military capacity while simultaneously weakening their fighting spirit.

The road to Dūmat al-Jandal was long and passed through the territory of hostile tribes. The mission, therefore, was highly secret and disciplined. The army's destination was not announced beforehand, and they marched at night and hid themselves by day. When the Muslims reached Dūmat al-Jandal, most of the tribes had dispersed and spread out in the mountains. The Prophet (ﷺ) camped for a few days while he dispatched small units to intimidate anyone who might think of attacking Madinah. The Muslims would visit Dūmat al-Jandal again later, with a brigade led by 'Abd al-Raḥmān ibn 'Awf.

On their return, the Muslims passed through the territory of the Fazzāzah, a large clan of the Ghaṭafān tribe, and entered a peace agreement with 'Uyaynah ibn Ḥuṣn, the Fazzāzah leader. With several thousand followers, 'Uyaynah was a bedouin chieftain accustomed to raiding and pillaging. The Muslims referred to him as "the idiot who is obeyed", but this did not deter the Prophet (ﷺ) from reaching an understanding with him. One article of the agreement granted the Fazzāzah permission to graze their livestock in an area about sixty kilometres from Madinah. Previously, during droughts, the Fazzāzah and other Ghaṭafān tribes had raided farms around Madinah. The Prophet (ﷺ) wanted to regulate the relationship with them by restricting the geographical area within which they were allowed to operate.

The second objective of the Dūmat al-Jandal expedition was more long term. Khaybar was the richest city in the Arabian Peninsula, and was a trade, agricultural and industrial centre with powerful military capacity. It had a fortified citadel that could not easily be penetrated by attackers. Historical sources differ about its military capacity. Some say the city had 4,000 warriors, others put the number as high as 10,000. It also produced unique, high-quality weaponry.

Most importantly, Khaybar was the capital of the Ghaṭafān tribe and its many clans, the most important of which were the Ashja'a, Aslam, and Fazzāzah. They were migratory bedouins who constantly moved camp. They regarded Khaybar as their trading centre and developed enduring and beneficial relationships with it and its people. These relationships would soon develop into a strategic alliance leading up to the Battle of the Trench. The city was transformed into the heart of hostility towards Madinah. Among those who incited the Ghaṭafān to declare war against the Prophet (ﷺ) was Abū Rāfi' Salām ibn Abī al-Ḥaqīq, who reserved a great deal of wealth for anyone who fought against the Muslims. After the expulsion from Madinah, the Banī al-Naḍīr arrived in Khaybar and immediately contacted the Quraysh and the Ghaṭafān to form an anti-Muslim alliance.

The Prophet (ﷺ) knew that a confrontation with Khaybar was inevitable, but he wanted to delay it, because Makkah was still the priority. Khaybar would be dealt with after Makkah had been neutralised.

The Dūmat al-Jandal expedition forestalled Khaybar's seeking assistance from the northern tribes and reinforced its isolation. It also announced that Muḥammad (ﷺ) had the capacity to conduct military and political manoeuvres near the lands of Caesar and Khosrow, which, in the eyes of the Arabs, was extremely significant.

The accord with the Fazzāzah served a similar purpose: to draw it closer to Madinah and alienate it from Khaybar. The relationship between the Muslims and 'Uyaynah ibn Ḥuṣn would soon benefit the Prophet (ﷺ). During the Battle of the Trench, the Prophet (ﷺ) negotiated with him and al-Aqra'a ibn Ḥābis, convincing them to withdraw from the confederates' alliance.

Tri-partite alliance and delusions of power

Some 10,000 warriors came together in a tripartite alliance that was unprecedented in the Arabian Peninsula. The Quraysh brought its leadership, the Ghaṭafān its thousands of warriors, and the Khaybar Jews their wealth and aptitude for planning. This was the first alliance of its kind in the armed confrontation between the Muslims and their enemies; it was an army the likes of which the Arabs had never seen, but one that was more fragile than it appeared at first glance.

This alliance was a deviation from the tribal custom that prohibited a tribe from entering an alliance with another tribe against one of its own affiliates. Yet, in this case, the Quraysh allied with other tribes against Muḥammad ibn 'Abdallah (ﷺ), a descendent of the ancient Hāshimī clan of the Quraysh. The Prophet (ﷺ) and most of his Muhājirūn followers were from the Quraysh. They had established what might be described as the "Muslim Quraysh", and the "Disbelieving Quraysh" departed from tribal custom to oppose them. The latter had failed at Badr, were unable to change the balance of forces after Uḥud, and were now extending a hand to the Ghaṭafān. The Quraysh resorted to this alliance because its leaders were acutely aware that the Muslim problem had escalated and that they were incapable, on their own, of stopping it.

Even though the Quraysh and the Ghaṭafān shared a common lineage, having both descended from Muḍar, they had their own unique traits. The Quraysh held itself in high regard and felt that it was superior to all other Arab tribes. They were the people of the Sanctuary, the custodians of the Ka'bah, initiators of the trade pact, and the masters of Makkah, the mother of Arab villages. They were, effectively, rulers of the Arab Peninsula and the richest of the Arab tribes. Importantly, they had the strongest relationships with powers in the surrounding environment. Their contact extended to the Arab regions and the neighbouring kingdoms in Persia, Byzantium, and Abyssinia. Their trade caravans traversed the desert in summer and winter, amassing wealth, forging relationships, gaining experience, and developing an understanding of current affairs in the rest of the world. The Quraysh were thus proud of themselves and of their status.

The Ghaṭafān, on the other hand, were comprised of several clans of migratory bedouins who inhabited the eastern Arabian Peninsula. Their tribal heritage was immersed in bedouin culture. They had not developed in the same manner as the Quraysh and did not enjoy anything close to the status of the Quraysh. Moreover, they were poverty-stricken. Since they depended on pastoralism and raiding for their livelihoods, they were immersed in a violent tribal culture founded on war and retribution. The war between the ʿAbs and Dhubyān tribes was probably one of the biggest and longest Arab wars, in which these two Ghaṭafān clans fought for about forty years in what became known as the Dāhis wa al-Ghabrā'a War. The two rivals were finally reconciled through the mediation of Haram ibn Sinān and al-Ḥārith ibn ʿAwf. This destructive war, which ended shortly before the Prophetic mission began, left the Ghaṭafān weakened and weary, and they tried to revitalise themselves through raiding and accumulating booty.

The Quraysh-Ghaṭafān alliance was unique, but utilitarian. The Ghaṭafān sought to amass booty and the Quraysh sought to strengthen themselves with a mercenary army after they had failed to overcome the Muslims by their own strength.

The third component in the tripartite alliance was the Khaybar Jews. After the Banī al-Naḍīr were expelled from Madinah to Khaybar, they began communicating with the Quraysh to launch a well-planned campaign with a large army. The Banī al-Naḍīr contributed financially and in planning, and through an important strategic element: their relationship with their cousins, the Jews of the Banī Qurayẓah, who were still in Madinah.

The three parties were disparate in their military strength. The Quraysh were the origin and backbone of the alliance. They worked tirelessly, mobilising the Kinānah and their allies, which totalled 3,000 warriors (or 4,000, according to some accounts). This suggested that they had put their full weight behind the endeavour and wanted to win decisively. This convinced the Ghaṭafān, Sulaym, and other tribes to quickly join the alliance.

The Quraysh's role does not diminish the importance of the Ghaṭafān, which was larger in number and contributed 6,000 warriors. It also enjoyed a strong military reputation, after having clashed several times with the Muslims. Since they were bedouin tribes that subsisted on pastoralism and camel husbandry, raiding was common for them. This ensured that their warriors had developed a high degree of flexibility and a remarkable capacity to undertake hit-and-run operations. However, the Ghaṭafān were made up of various clans, each with its own leader, opinion, and objective.

The Banī al-Naḍīr did not have any significant military power, but actively contributed to building the alliance, especially through their leader, Ḥuyay ibn Akhṭab. He led a delegation of twenty tribesmen from Khaybar to Makkah to incite the Quraysh. He also met the leaders of the Ghaṭafān and convinced them to join the alliance. The Banī al-Naḍīr and the Khaybar Jews also played a huge role in financing the campaign. Ḥuyay ibn Akhṭab also attempted to convince the Banī Qurayẓah to break their pact with the Muslims and to join the alliance.

Contradictory motivations

All three components of the alliance were driven by their own motivations and objectives, and this disparity was a decisive factor in the outcome of the Battle of the Confederates, which ended in their disbandment and defeat. It is therefore necessary to critically examine the true motivations that drove the three parties so that we may see the cracks and understand their psychological and utilitarian impetuses.

Quraysh: Lifting the blockade and regaining its status

The Quraysh's participation in the Battle of the Confederates was motivated by an existential crisis; by targeting its trade caravans, the Muslims had imposed an economic blockade on Makkah. A few months after his arrival in Madinah, the Prophet (ﷺ) dispatched expeditions to attack Qurayshi caravans on the Levant route, followed by attacks on the Iraq and Yemen routes. This effectively besieged the Quraysh through an intelligence and military strategy. The Prophet (ﷺ) was thus able to strike at the heart of the Quraysh's strength and the source of its wealth and arrogance, robbing it of its role as the conduit for merchandise between the Levant, Iraq, and Yemen.

As a result, most Qurayshi caravans were suspended. When some were forced to change their routes, either during winter expeditions to Yemen or summer expeditions to the Levant, Muslim raiding parties intercepted them, spreading fear and panic among Qurayshi traders. With the persistence of the blockade, Makkan trade was devastated. By the fourth year after the Hijrah, the Quraysh concluded that, if the Muslims were not exterminated, Makkah would be on the path to utter economic collapse, which would further mean serious damage to its status and reputation. We earlier saw how Ṣafwān ibn Umayyah's had warned that the economic blockade posed a massive threat to Makkah. He had said, on that occasion:

> Muḥammad and his companions have impeded our trade. We do not know what to do with his companions who do not leave the coast. The people of the coast have made peace with them, and their common folk have joined him. We do not know which route to take, and if we remain stationary, we will drain our capital while we are in our homes. We have no way to use it. We used to invest it in trade to the Levant in the summer and to Abyssinia in the winter.[185]

The Quraysh's second strategic motivation for being part of the Confederates was its need to maintain its superior status among the Arabs, based on its control and maintenance of the Holy Sanctuary and the provision of water and sustenance to pilgrims. While these responsibilities were important and granted the Quraysh high status, they were not altogether bereft of economic benefit. The Quraysh had long managed to exploit their symbolic status for the purpose of attaining huge financial gain.

The Quraysh's social project and political ideology focused on tribe and lineage, in addition to the veneration of elders and ancestors, the pre-Islamic zeal for idol-worship, and political alliances. All of these emanated from tribal solidarity; the tribe formed the essence of Qurayshi identity. The Qurayshi view of society was thus one where concessions and privileges of the various tribes and clans was dependent on lineage. In such a worldview, the individual's existential

185. Al-Wāqidī, *Kitāb al-Maghāzī*, vol. 1, 197.

classification is predetermined and cannot be rejected—as with any racial classification. Such categorisation of people is inevitably unjust and robs the individual of an essential subjective humanity.

This arcane and closed Qurayshi identity faced a serious challenge from a new, vibrant, and open identity, which was attractive to some Qurayshis. The idolatrous Quraysh were unable to disparage the status of the Muslim Quraysh or their lineage, since they were the children of one of its main clans and from its leadership. Moreover, the Muslim Quraysh excelled over the idolatrous Quraysh by virtue of a noble calling, good morals, high resolve, and a tremendous capacity to connect with non-Qurayshi people through faith, even if the latter were clients or weak slaves who were demeaned, or individuals from distant countries.

The presence of the Muslim Quraysh in Madinah represented a serious and dangerous challenge that was intolerable to the idolatrous Quraysh. This was because the Muslims introduced a new system of values that forged bonds of brotherhood among people, regarded everyone as equal "as the teeth of a comb", broadened their horizons to transgress the limitations of tribe and its closed mindset, and embraced the vastness of a fraternity of faith that transcended colour, ethnicity, and lineage. Instead of interrogating its heritage and examining its shortcomings, the idolatrous Quraysh resorted to arrogant power supported by heritage and lineage. In this case, that approach took the form of armed confrontation that sought to exterminate the other.

During the five years of struggle between Makkah and Madinah, the Quraysh defended their economic position and status, but they failed to defeat the Muslims or to slow the spread of Islam. In fact, the military strength and political status of Muslims within this tribal milieu increased every day. Muslim raiding parties traversed the peninsula; their delegations were received by the different tribes with whom they had entered agreements; they promoted new values; and the tribes listened to their message and entered alliances with them. The marginal and passive role of Yathrib changed and was replaced by the active role of Madinah, bustling with a new religious, political, and economic energy, and damaging the image of Makkah's regional and economic status in the perception of the Arabs. The Quraysh required decisive action to exterminate the threat to

Makkah's economic security and leadership status.

However, a careful examination of events leading up to the Battle of the Trench reveals that the Quraysh were not enthusiastic about a decisive military confrontation with the Muslims. They sought only to preserve their trade interests and status among the Arabs. Not driven by a religious mission or moral ambition, they were, instead, preoccupied with pride and reputation. This was the kind of atmosphere prevalent in economic centres. They were also painfully aware of the courage of the Muslims and their military astuteness and boldness. The Quraysh were not a warmongering tribe, and disliked surprises. Circumstance had granted it economic abundance, the safety of its sanctuary, and a stable environment. Most of its military activities had been mere tribal skirmishes or brief battles that ended in tribal mediation. It never needed a standing army or to go to war to protect its territory. For the Quraysh, therefore, the Muslim military challenge was extraordinary, which is why some of their leaders preferred a strategy of containment and of limiting Islamic influence.

Ghaṭafān's objective: War booty

The Ghaṭafān tribe was part of the large northern Muḍar tribal confederation that was well known across the Arabian Peninsula. It had settled to the north of Yathrib and extended its presence into the heart of the Najd. Ghaṭafān was a powerful tribe that inspired fear in others. Decades before the coming of Islam, it had declared eight months of the year as sacred months, and other Arab tribes that interacted with it complied by respecting the sanctity of these eight months. Members of the Ghaṭafān freely roamed the desert safe in the knowledge that no one would confront them.

The Ghaṭafān had settled close to Madinah and were, therefore, in constant and direct contact with the Muslims. Yathrib had been an important trade centre for the migratory bedouins of the Ghaṭafān. When it became Madinah, the contestation between some members of the Ghaṭafān clans and Muslim herders over pastures and water wells caused disputes and skirmishes. In addition, the Ghaṭafān, when led by ‘Awf ibn Ḥārithah al-Marrī, had an alliance with the Quraysh and had aided them in the Immoral Wars. The cumulation of these factors served as a pretext for some Ghaṭafān clans to seek an opportunity to attack the Muslims of Madinah and to steal their livestock and other possessions. The Muslims, therefore, were always on guard to repel them; they also sent out armed detachments against them. The Prophet (ﷺ) led some of these expeditions.

The Ghaṭafān's participation in the alliance with the Quraysh and Jewish tribes was motivated purely by the interests of the tribe. Tempted by the promises of the Banī al-Naḍīr leader Ḥuyay ibn Akhṭab, they sought only to gain spoils of war. They did not have serious disputes with the Muslims, and from experience, it was clear that they and the Muslims were capable of reconciling, as had been the case with the Fazzāzah leader ‘Uyaynah ibn Ḥuṣn, when they had agreed to protect grazing land. The Prophet (ﷺ) later exploited this relationship to ensure that the Muslims were not betrayed at the Battle of the Trench.

The Jews' objective: Retribution

It is appropriate here to reflect on the situation with the Jews who were in the alliance and to examine their motivations. Jews had a strong presence in the Arabian Peninsula before Islam, and there were several Jewish tribal centres in cities on the main trade routes, including in Yathrib, Khaybar, Taymā'a, Fadak, and Wādi al-Qura. They had carved for themselves an eminent economic, political, and cultural status in Yathrib before the Hijrah. Through their economic prowess and artisanal and manufacturing capacities, they had constituted the economic centre of the Yathrib markets. Jews in Madinah had been recognised as the most skilful artisans and traders, and they had benefited from Yathrib's agricultural economy, acting as trade intermediaries marketing the city's farming products and sourcing the needs of its population. They also provided a usurious money-lending service to the people, taking back loans with large amounts of interest in the harvesting seasons. Through these very effective economic activities, their community had managed to amass a large fortune.

Politically, the three Jewish tribes had alliances with the two main groups in Yathrib: the Aws and the Khazraj. The Banī Qaynuqā‘ had entered an alliance with the Khazraj, while the Banī al-Naḍīr and Banī Qurayẓah were allied to the Aws. These alliances were not based on religious or ideological convergences but on the geographical proximity of the dwellings of these tribes to each other. The Aws had settled in the al-‘Awālī area, next to the Banī Qurayẓah and the Banī al-Naḍīr, while the Khazraj had settled at the lower end of the city, next to the Banī Qaynuqā‘.

The relationship between the Aws and the Khazraj had become dangerously strained just before the Hijrah, especially after the destructive Bu‘āth Civil War between them. The Jews, as an active minority, benefited from the state of conflict and achieved a strategic status and position. Their position was such that they had been able to crown the Khazraj leader and Jewish ally, ‘Abdallah ibn Ubay ibn Sallūl, as the king of the city; these aspirations were dashed when the Prophet (ﷺ) arrived in Madinah.

The three Jewish tribes were neither politically nor militarily united; the interests of each tribe were the most important consideration in their alliances. After the arrival of the Prophet (ﷺ), however, they quickly united in their enmity toward the new religion and felt threatened by the new prophetic and foreign leadership, and the civil accord it had managed to foster among all elements of society.

Initially, it seemed that the relationship between the Jews and the Muslim migrants would be positive. They were all People of the Book, followers of a revealed law who were surviving in an idolatrous environment, and the Jews had been announcing and warning the people of Yathrib of the coming of a prophet. However, they had decided on their relationship with the Prophet (ﷺ) immediately after having met him. Ṣafīyyah, the daughter of Banī al-Naḍīr leader Ḥuyay ibn Akhṭab, narrated how her father spoke, at the very outset, of the relationship between Muḥammad (ﷺ) and the Jews.

> I was my father's and my uncle Abū Yāsir's favourite child. There was never an occasion when I met them in the company of their other children that they did not pick me up instead of

> the others. Allah's Messenger (ﷺ) stopped in Qubā' on his way to Madinah and stayed with the Banī 'Amr ibn 'Awf. My father, Ḥuyay ibn Akhṭab, and my uncle, Abū Yāsir ibn Akhṭab, visited him at dusk and did not return until long after sunset. They returned fatigued and downcast, walking slowly. I ran to them as I usually did and, by Allah, neither of them turned to me due to their burdensome preoccupation. I heard my uncle Abū Yāsir asking my father Ḥuyay ibn Akhṭab: "Is he the one?" My father responded: "Yes, by Allah." Abū Yāsir then asked: "Do you know him and affirm [that it is] him?" Ḥuyay responded: "Yes." My uncle then asked: "What do you feel inside regarding him?" My father replied: "I feel hatred toward him, by Allah!"[186]

On the other hand, the Messenger (ﷺ) engaged the Jews who were well-intentioned and sincere. He tried to reconcile with them and wrote an agreement between him and them. He also included them in the Charter that managed the relationship between the Muslims, Jews, and other non-Muslims in Madinah. The Charter regarded the different Jewish tribes of Madinah as allies of the Muslims, in peace, war, and everyday existence, and as a united defence force.

From the Prophet's (ﷺ) perspective, building an alliance between the Jews and the Arabs of Madinah was necessary for stability in the new society. The Charter integrated the Muslims (Anṣār and Muhājirūn) into the fabric of Madinan society and entrenched their position on an equal footing with the traditionally established forces: the Aws, Khazraj, and Jewish tribes. However, the Prophet's (ﷺ) openness and his initiation of a strategic partnership that extended a hand to the Jews failed to convince them to be loyal to the new order in Madinah. They did not even bother to conceal their malicious intentions and doubts regarding the Prophet's (ﷺ) leadership, and they continued to incite crises and create difficulties.

Despite their other strengths, the Madinah Jews were politically and militarily weak because of their disunity. The total Jewish fighting force of young warriors numbered over 2,000, which is a respectable figure if we consider that the number of Muslim fighters was just over 300 at Badr, around 1,000 at Uḥud, and 3,000 at the Battle of the Trench.

186. Ibn Hishām, *al-Sīrah*, vol. 1, 519.

However, the Jews lacked a unified leadership and each tribe engaged with the Prophet (ﷺ) separately. Thus, when the Banī Qaynuqā‘ were expelled from Madinah in the second year after the Hijrah for having transgressed the provisions of the Charter, no one from the Banī al-Naḍīr or the Banī Qurayẓah assisted them. After the banishment of the Banī al-Naḍīr to Khaybar in the fourth year after the Hijrah, the Banī Qurayẓah, who were allies of the Aws and who lived in the eastern quarter of Madinah, were the only Jews remaining in the city.

The Banī Qurayẓah were hesitant to join the tripartite alliance that was planning for the Battle of the Confederates in the fifth year after the Hijrah. They were afraid of the consequences of breaking their covenant with the Muslims. However, Ḥuyay ibn Akhṭab, the leader of the Banī al-Naḍīr and the primary engineer of the alliance, pressured the Banī Qurayẓah leader, Ka‘b ibn Asad, insisting that the end of the Muslims was near. The Banī Qurayẓah finally gave in and broke the covenant with the Muslims.

> Ḥuyay knocked on his door but Ka‘b slammed it shut in his face. Ḥuyay continued to speak to him until he opened the door. Ḥuyay said: "O Ka‘b, I have come to you at the most honoured time and with an overflowing ocean. I have come to you with the Quraysh, their leaders and elders. I settled them at the point where the streams meet at Rūmah. I also come with the Ghaṭafān, their leaders and elders, who I have settled at the end of Naqmay, next to Mount Uḥud. They have pledged that they will not leave until we eradicate Muḥammad and whoever is with him." Ka‘b replied: "You have come to me at the lowest time with a cloud whose water has dried out. It thunders and [shoots] lightning but has nothing in it. Woe be unto you, O Ḥuyay. Just leave me be. I have not seen anything from Muḥammad other than honesty and devotion."[187]

Ka‘b's position was correct. Unfortunately, he did not remain steadfast to it. Ḥuyay persisted in trying to convince him until he wore down Ka‘b's resoluteness and, together with the rest of the Banī Qurayẓah, violated their covenant with the Prophet (ﷺ).

---

187. al-Nās, *'Uyūn al-Athar*, vol. 2, 88.

CHAPTER THIRTEEN

Upheaval

"In that situation the Believers were tried, and violently shaken" (Qur'ān 33:11).

A Khuzā'ah delegation informed the Prophet (ﷺ) about the Quraysh's mobilisation. As was his habit, the Prophet (ﷺ) convened a consultation council, and the same heated deliberations took place as those before the Battle of Uḥud. Should they move out of Madinah or fight in the city? This time around, however, the Muslims were much more open to alternative proposals. Uḥud had taught them to transcend typical, traditional ways of thinking. Salmān al-Fārsī suggested a novel idea: digging a trench around Madinah. He had learnt this stratagem from the Persians, who dug trenches when confronted by an invading enemy.

Madinah's geography was suited to this military tactic. The city was surrounded by three tracts of volcanic rock,[188] the Wabrah Tract in the west, the Wāqim Tract in the east, and the Southern Tract. This topography made Madinah virtually impenetrable to any army at that time. In addition, the Banī Qurayẓah's larger houses and fortresses provided barriers in some places and filled the gap between the Wāqim and Southern tracts. If the Muslims were to dig a trench in the north and northeast, Madinah could be turned into a fortified island that the enemy would be almost unable to breach.

With a sense of urgency, the Prophet (ﷺ) and the Muslims accepted Salmān's suggestion and hastened to implement it. To ensure that the trench would keep the enemy out, it was to be constructed approximately five kilometres long, three metres deep, and four metres wide, making it almost impossible for either cavalry or infantry to cross. Checkpoints would be spread across the length of the trench and Muslim fighters would intervene to prevent any breach. The Muslims completed the

188. These were long, outstretched elevations upon which there were a group of hills as well as stretches of flat land. They were called *al-Ḥarrah* in Arabic (meaning hot), because a large portion of their surface was covered by black volcanic rocks and stones, making it very hot in the summer.

excavation in fifteen days with digging equipment borrowed from the Banī Qurayẓah, who remained loyal to their covenant with the Prophet (ﷺ).

The excavation was an amazing achievement, characterised by precise organisation and great dedication to the task. Such an achievement required decisive planning and leadership, sharing of responsibilities, integration of work teams, and, above all, battlefield planning. The Arab tribes did not excel at these responsibilities. They were more accustomed to direct confrontations and one-on-one combat. That was precisely why the idea of the trench was ingenious, both innovative and a surprise to the enemy.

The Prophet (ﷺ) personally participated in the project, spreading a spirit of hope, giving glad tidings, making the Muslims recite poetry and rhymes, and helping them build a harmonious working relationship as they competed to complete the task. When the Muslims finished the digging, they had produced both a trench and a sand barrier. The sand that had been removed from the trench was piled high on the side facing Madinah, thereby acting as a barrier that protected the soldiers. Large amounts of stone and rock were then spread inside the trench to prevent any breach attempts.

The women and children also participated. They transported the rocks, linked the dwellings, and closed gaps so that Madinah was transformed into a single closed unit that was prepared for any emergency and ready to repel any attacker that might gain entry. Afterward, several strongholds were allocated as group shelters for the non-combatant women, children, and elderly. These were further fortified.

The Muslims harvested the barley and other crops at al-ʻIrd, an agricultural plain outside Madinah, and transported the crops and hay into the city so that the enemy's camels and horses would be deprived of fodder.

The Muslim army was 3,000 strong and was divided into well-organised military units with specific tasks. Some warriors were assigned guard duty, others were stationed at fixed points across the length of the trench, and yet others were grouped into small, mobile cavalry units to thwart any attempt to breach the trench during the day or at night. The Prophet (ﷺ) also appointed a mobile brigade of 200 warriors to patrol Madinah to ensure that it was not breached from other directions. The military organisation was tightly regulated, and the Muslims overcame the errors that had been committed at Uḥud. They had learnt discipline, collaborative work, and respect for leadership and the military command structure.

Trickery unknown to the Arabs

The Qurayshi army arrived on Tuesday, 12 Shawwāl 5 AH / 6 January 627[189] with 4,000 fighters of their own and from the Sulaym tribe, and 6,000 from the Ghaṭafān and Asad tribes. Shocked by the trench, they exclaimed, "By Allah, this is trickery unknown to the Arabs."[190] They had no option but to camp beyond the trench while they decided on a course of action. They had brought 1,000 horses and more than 1,000 camels, but they did not have extra fodder; all they had was what each fighter had carried with him, expecting, no doubt, a quick battle, after which they would be able to feed their animals. They were also unable to find grazing at al-ʻIrd and were in danger of watching their animals become emaciated and weak.

With Madinah besieged, the most precarious moment occurred when news of the Banī Qurayẓah's treachery began trickling into the Muslim camp. Allah's Messenger (ﷺ) immediately deployed two leaders of the Aws and the Khazraj, Sa'd ibn 'Ubādah and Sa'd ibn Mu'adh, to meet the Banī Qurayẓah and seek clarity on the matter. He asked them not to explicitly state their findings in front of the other Muslims if the news was true, but rather to "sing a tune"—to speak in a code that only he would understand. When the two Sa'ds met the Banī Qurayẓah, they found that the tribe had indeed broken the covenant. The two envoys tried to persuade them to return to the covenant, but they refused, insulted the Prophet (ﷺ), cursed the Muslims, and even threatened

189. The siege began on Tuesday, 12 Shawwāl 5 AH / 6 January 627 CE and was lifted on Saturday, 1 Dhu'l Qa'dah / 24 January, which was also the day on which the Banī Qurayẓah Campaign began.

190. Abū Muḥammad ʿAlī ibn Aḥmad ibn Saʿīd ibn Ḥazm, *Jawāmi' al- Sīrah* (Beirut: Dār al-Kutub al-'Ilmīyyah, Beirut), 150.

to attack the Muslims. The envoys returned and spoke of two tribes, 'Uḍal and al-Qārah, that had killed the Prophet's (ﷺ) companions at Bi'r Ma'ūnah, thus warning the Prophet (ﷺ) of the treachery. Allah's Messenger (ﷺ)

> wrapped himself up in his mantle when [news] of the treachery of Qurayẓah came to him. He lay down and remained in that position for a long time. It seemed that he did not want the Muslims to witness the anger or anxiety on his face. He then rose, gave glad tidings, and said: "Allah is the Greatest. Receive glad tidings, O gathering of Muslims, of Allah's conquest and victory."[191]

As news of Banī Qurayẓah's treachery spread, the Hypocrites exploited the opportunity to launch a campaign of suspicion and propaganda. The Muslims were extremely anguished because the result of Banī Qurayẓah's defection to the Confederates was that Madinah would be exposed from the lower end. The idolaters would be able to breach the city from the Banī Qurayẓah's residential areas, exposing the Madinan women and children to a massacre, since the Muslims did not have the military capacity to repel forces attacking from two different directions.

The Noble Qur'ān portrays this moment in verses rich with symbolism: "When they came at you from above you and from below you, your eyes became wild [with fear], and your hearts rose to your throats. And you made many assumptions about Allah." (Qur'ān 33:10).

Soon after the two envoys had returned to the Prophet (ﷺ), the Banī Qurayẓah began preparations for war. They sent spies to monitor the Muslim women and children who were sheltered in an elevated fortress. Ṣafiyyah bint 'Abd al-Muṭṭalib reported:

> A Jewish man walked past us and began circling the fortress. The Banī Qurayẓah had broken off their agreement with Allah's Messenger (ﷺ) and were now at war [with the Muslims]. There was no one between [the women and children] and them to protect us. Allah's Messenger (ﷺ) and the Muslims were in

191. Ibn Hishām, *al-Sīrah*, vol. 2. 222.

> the midst of their enemies and were unable to turn away from them if something were to befall us. I said, "O Ḥassān [ibn Thābit], this Jew, as you can see, is circling the fortress. By Allah, I do not trust that he will not expose us to the Jews who are after us. Allah's Messenger (ﷺ) and his companions are too preoccupied to [assist] us, so you go down to the Jew and kill him." Ḥassān replied: "By Allah, you know that I am not suited for that." I then prepared myself, took a heavy staff, and descended from the fortress toward his position. I beat him with the staff until I killed him. I then returned to the fortress and told Ḥassān: "O Ḥassān, go down to him and strip him of his possessions. The only thing that prevented me from doing so was that he is a man." Ḥassān replied: "I have no need to strip him of his possessions."[192]

When they heard that their spy had been killed, the Banī Qurayẓah probably believed that the fortresses were being protected by Muslim soldiers, even though the fortresses were completely isolated from them. Afraid, they did not deploy any more spies. They did, however, send supplies to the Confederate forces as proof of their alliance with them against the Muslims. The Muslims managed to capture twenty camel loads of supplies that were destined for the enemy.

To further strengthen security within Madinah, the Prophet (ﷺ) commanded two brigades, one comprising 100 men and the other 300, to continuously patrol the city at night, and to shout "Allahu Akbar" (Allah is the Greatest) as they were doing so, to intimidate the Jews within the city and thus prevent them from launching an attack. The Muslims also uncovered a plot by Ḥuyay ibn Akhṭab to facilitate the entry of 1,000 idolaters into the city via the Banī Qurayẓah district.

Breaking the enemy's ranks

The Prophet's (ﷺ) efforts to split the enemy alliance and spread discord within its ranks continued unabated. Exploiting the utilitarian motives of the Ghaṭafān tribe, he contacted its leader, 'Uyaynah ibn

192. Ibn Hishām, *al-Sīrah*, vol. 2. 228.

Ḥuṣn, with a generous offer: he would gift the Ghaṭafān the spoils that they sought without their having to risk the perils of an armed confrontation. If the Ghaṭafān were to agree, it would divide the tripartite alliance and the Muslims would attain an important strategic victory.

When the tribulations upon the people began to escalate, Allah's Messenger (ﷺ) contacted 'Uyaynah ibn Ḥuṣn ibn Ḥudhayfah ibn Badr and al-Ḥārith ibn 'Awf ibn Abī Ḥārithah al-Marrī, two Ghaṭafān leaders, and offered them one-third of Madinah's fruit harvest on condition that they and everyone with them would withdraw and [keep] far from the Prophet (ﷺ) and his companions. An agreement was discussed and a draft written up, but was not attested to or pursued in earnest.

When Allah's Messenger (ﷺ) wanted to implement the agreement, he sent for Sa'd ibn Mu'adh and Sa'd ibn 'Ubādah, informing them about the discussion and seeking their counsel. They asked him: "O Messenger of Allah, is this a matter that we prefer and have concluded, is it something that Allah has commanded and that we must do, or is it something that you have undertaken for us?" He said: "It is something I have undertaken for you. By Allah, I have only done this because I have seen that the Arabs have taken aim at you with a single bow and have come at you from all sides. I wanted to break their strength for you by some means." Sa'd ibn Mu'adh said: "O Messenger of Allah, we and these people associated partners with Allah and worshipped idols. We neither worshipped Allah nor did we know Him. They did not desire to eat [our] dates except by our hospitality or by buying them. Now that Allah has honoured us with Islam, guided us, and strengthened us with you, why should we give them our wealth? By Allah, we are in no need of this. By Allah, we will give them nothing other than the sword until Allah judges between us and them." The Messenger of Allah (ﷺ) said: "You [will have] what you ask for." Sa'd ibn Mu'adh then took the parchment and wiped off whatever was written on it. He said: "Let them come down upon us."[193]

193. Ibn Hishām, *al-Sīrah*, vol. 2. 223.

The fact that the Ghaṭafān had been willing to negotiate, and their leaders had agreed to accept one-third of Madinah's crops, was an important indication that they were tired of the long siege and were ready to accept a deal, even if it offered them less than what Ḥuyay ibn Akhṭab had promised. He had offered one year's yield of all Madinah's crops. Although the agreement with the Prophet (ﷺ) was not concluded, the talks succeeded in dividing the ranks of the alliance. News of the negotiations could not be kept secret, and it spread on both sides of the trench. It was also in the interests of the Muslims to leak the news, to undermine the confidence and trust between the allied parties.

The conversation between 'Uyaynah and al-Ḥārith when they returned to their camp shows that they had begun to comprehend the crisis they had created for themselves.

> Al-Ḥārith said: "By Allah, we don't think that we will attain anything from them, and the people have been made to see clearly! By Allah, I attended [the meeting] only under duress. We have no standing here. If the Quraysh come to know of what we have proposed to Muḥammad, they will know that we have forsaken them and are not supporting them." 'Uyaynah replied: "By Allah, that is how it is." Al-Ḥārith added: "We will not gain anything by endangering ourselves to help the Quraysh against Muḥammad. By Allah, if the Quraysh overcome Muḥammad, they will have exclusive dominion and will exclude the rest of the Arabs. I consider the affair of Muḥammad a victorious affair. By Allah, the Jewish scholars of Khaybar used to relate what they found in their books: that a prophet—who matches [Muḥammad's] description—will be sent from the Holy Sanctuary." 'Uyaynah said: "Indeed, by Allah, we did not come to help the Quraysh. If we ask the Quraysh for help, they will neither help us, nor will they leave their sanctuary. But I desired that we take the dates of Madinah, and that we be remembered for it, together with whatever we gain as booty, and helping our Jewish allies who brought us here." Al-Ḥārith said: "By Allah, the Aws and the Khazraj will accept only the sword. By Allah, they will fight for these date palms until there is not a man among them, the surroundings are barren, and the camels

> and horses are destroyed." 'Uyaynah added: "[Until] there is nothing [left]." When they reached their homes, the Ghaṭafān came to them and asked: "What happened?" They said: "The matter was not concluded. We saw a people with sharp insight, who will sacrifice themselves for their leader. We have been destroyed and the Quraysh have been destroyed. The Quraysh will disperse and will not even [get the opportunity to] speak to Muḥammad. Indeed, Muḥammad's anger will come down on the Banī Qurayẓah. When we turn away, he will pounce on them and besiege them until they give him whatever they possess." Al-Ḥārith said: "May they be destroyed. Muḥammad is dearer to us than the Jews."[194]

During these deliberations, the idolaters continued in their attempts, throughout the day and the night, to breach the trench with hit-and-run attacks by cavalry units. The Muslims held them back and fought them off with stones and arrows. Overcome by hunger, they nevertheless guarded the trench in shifts, in freezing weather. Units from the Banī Qurayẓah also tried to launch offensive actions against the Muslims, and the Hypocrites escalated their mischief by spreading rumours. The Muslims were, therefore, overcome by an unprecedented level of fear. Umm Salamah explained:

> [With the Prophet (ﷺ)] I witnessed scenes of fighting and fear: al-Muraysī'a, Khaybar, al-Ḥudaybiyyah, the Conquest of Makkah, and Ḥunayn. But none of them was as burdensome for Allah's Messenger (ﷺ), nor as fearsome for us, as the [Battle of the] Trench. It was as if the Muslims were [caught] in al-Ḥarajah [a tree with a lot of branches]. The Banī Qurayẓah threatened our children, Madinah was being guarded through the night, and the chanting of the Muslims could be heard until the sun rose.[195]

The Noble Qur'ān perfectly portrays the state in which the Muslims found themselves: "When they came at you from above you and from below you, your eyes became wild [with fear], and your hearts rose to your throats. And you made many assumptions about Allah." (Qur'ān 33:10).

194. Al-Wāqidī, *Kitāb al-Maghāzī*, vol. 2, 480.
195. Al-Wāqidī, *Kitāb al-Maghāzī*, vol. 2, 467.

The role of Nu'aym ibn Mas'ūd

Many works on the Prophet's (ﷺ) life mention the role of Nu'aym ibn Mas'ūd al-Ashja'ī. They narrate his account of how he caused dissension in the ranks of the allies by implementing an effective strategy for that purpose. His narration needs to be interrogated and analysed so that we may understand how the Prophet (ﷺ) was able to dismantle the Quraysh-Banī Qurayẓah alliance. Nu'aym's account, as related by al-Wāqidī, follows.

> The Banī Qurayẓah were people of nobility and wealth; we were an Arab people possessing neither date palms nor grapevines. We [possessed only] sheep and camels. I used to visit [Banī Qurayẓah leader] Ka'b ibn Asad and stay with them for days, drinking their beverages and eating their food. They then loaded [whatever] dates [I could carry] on my mount and I returned to my family. When the Confederates marched against Allah's Messenger (ﷺ), I marched with my people. I still followed my religion, and Allah's Messenger (ﷺ) was aware of this. The Confederates laid siege until [they were] overcome by drought and their sheep, horses, and camels were decimated. Allah, the Honoured and Sublime, then cast Islam into my heart. I concealed my Islam from my people and set out, sometime between the early evening (Maghrib) and late evening ('Ishā') prayers, to meet Allah's Messenger (ﷺ). I found him praying. When he saw me, he asked: "What has brought you here, O Nu'aym?" I replied: "I have come to affirm the truth [of your mission] and bear witness that what you have come with is the truth. Command me as you see fit, O Messenger of Allah, and, by Allah, whatever you command I will fulfil. My people are not aware of my Islam, nor are others." Allah's Messenger (ﷺ) said: "Subvert the people as much as you are able to." I said, "I will do so. However, O Messenger of Allah, I will speak untruths. So permit me this." He said: "Say what you deem appropriate; you are absolved thereof." [196]

The long narration continues. Nu'aym engaged the Banī Qurayẓah, it

196. Al-Wāqidī, *Kitāb al-Maghāzī*, vol. 2, 480.

says, and caused them to doubt the strength of the Quraysh's position. He thus sowed the seeds of uncertainty in their hearts. He then met Abū Sufyān and made him suspicious of the Banī Qurayẓah's stance, claiming that they had regrets about breaking their covenant with the Prophet (ﷺ). The alliance collapsed thereafter because the Quraysh asked the Banī Qurayẓah for hostages to prove their commitment.

This account inflates the role of a single person. The events of the Battle of the Trench—as this chapter shows—were too complex to be reduced to such a substantial role for one man. Its unfolding was a chain of surprises, fortifications, preparations, and negotiations. If there was a role for a single person, it would have been part of a process with many steps and many others involved, rather than just that one person, especially if that person was Nu'aym ibn Mas'ūd al-Ashja'ī, who had arrived with the Ghaṭafān Army.

There is another account, narrated by al-Zuhrī, that is more accurate, has a stronger chain of narration, and better describes the role of Nu'aym ibn Mas'ūd. It is narrated in 'Abd al-Razzāq al-Ṣan'ānī's *al-Muṣannaf*, on the authority of al-Zuhrī, who is regarded as an accurate narrator of the Prophet's (ﷺ) biography.

> As they were in that state, Nu'aym ibn Mas'ūd al-Ashja'ī came to them. He had been given amnesty by both sides as he had ingratiated himself with both. He said: "I was with 'Uyaynah and Abū Sufyān when the messenger from the Banī Qurayẓah [told them] to stand firm because we will go against the Muslims." The Prophet (ﷺ) said: "Perhaps we have commanded them to do so." Nu'aym could not keep a secret and left taking what the Prophet (ﷺ) said with him. 'Umar arrived and said: "O Messenger of Allah, if this is a command from Allah then proceed with it, but if it is your opinion, then [know] that the position of the Quraysh and the Banī Qurayẓah is weaker than this kind of thing that someone might say to you." The Prophet (ﷺ) commanded: "Return the man to me." So they brought him back. The Prophet (ﷺ) then told Nu'aym: "Look, whatever we said to you, you are not to mention it to anyone." But Nu'aym gave in to temptation. He went to

> ʻUyaynah and Abū Sufyān and asked them: "Have you heard from Muḥammad? He has said something, which may be true." They said, "No." Nuʻaym said, "When I mentioned the matter of Qurayẓah to him, he said: 'Perhaps we have commanded them to do so.'" Abū Sufyān said: "We will find out if this is a plot." He dispatched a message to the Banī Qurayẓah. The message said: "You have ordered us to stand our ground and said that you will turn against the Muslims. Give us hostages as [a reassurance]." They replied: "The Sabbath is upon us. We do not undertake any actions during the Sabbath." Abū Sufyān then said: "The Banī Qurayẓah are part of a plot." They then departed. Allah sent strong winds against them and cast fear into their hearts. Their fires were blown out, the harnesses of their horses broke, and they left, defeated without even having fought. That was when the following [verse] was revealed: "Allah was sufficient for the believers in battle. And Allah is All-Powerful, exalted in might" (Qur'ān 33:25).[197]

Al-Zuhrī's account is corroborated by another by ʻĀ'ishah.

> Nuʻaym was known for gossip. It was because of this that the Prophet (ﷺ) summoned and told him: "The Jews sent me a message asking if I would be satisfied with them if they gave me hostages from the leaders of the Quraysh and the Ghaṭafān. They said they will bring them to me so that I may kill them." Nuʻaym left the company of Allah's Messenger (ﷺ) and went to them to inform them of what he had said. When he left, Allah's Messenger (ﷺ) said: "Verily, war is deception."[198]

An objective analysis of the events of the day before the collapse of the alliance reveals that it was not achieved through Nuʻaym's efforts but because of the steadfastness of the Muslims and the Prophet's (ﷺ) decisive and careful planning. As the Prophet (ﷺ) stated, "Verily, war is deception."[199] It is clear that trust between the allies had already begun eroding. The Prophet (ﷺ) wanted to reinforce these doubts in his conversation with Nuʻaym ibn Masʻūd, who was known to be a

197. ʻAbd al-Razzāq al-Ṣanʻānī, *al-Muṣṣanaf*, (India: al-Majlis al-ʻIlmī, 1983), vol. 5, 367.
198. Al-Bayhaqī, *Dalā'il al-Nubūwwah*, vol. 3, 447.
199. Agreed upon, narrated by al-Bukhārī and Muslim.

gossip-monger. We may deduce from al-Zuhrī that Nu'aym had not yet accepted Islam, but had ingratiated himself with both sides. A bedouin, he was engaged in small-scale trade, which required his shuttling between Makkah and Madinah. He also had strong ties with Abū Sufyān. We saw earlier that Abū Sufyān had deployed him to misguide and sow seeds of fear in the hearts of the Muslims, so that they would not march out for the second encounter at Badr. Several sources also mention his links with the Jews, especially the Banī al-Naḍīr and the Banī Qurayẓah. It is likely that Nu'aym went to the Prophet (ﷺ) to get a sense of the Muslim reaction to the Banī Qurayẓah treachery, and the Prophet (ﷺ) provided him an ambiguous but intelligent response: "Perhaps we ordered them to do so." The Prophet (ﷺ) knew that Nu'aym could not keep a secret and would immediately spread the news, which is what transpired. Abū Sufyān had, from the outset, doubted the loyalty of the Banī Qurayẓah. When he received Nu'aym's news, he wanted to test the information and sent a messenger to request the Banī Qurayẓah to prove its fealty by providing hostages. They refused, using the Sabbath as an excuse. The differences between the two sides subsequently escalated and the alliance collapsed.

Who was besieging whom?

The month-long steadfastness and resolve of the Muslims, their political manoeuvring to dismantle the alliance—such as the Prophet's (ﷺ) negotiations with the Ghaṭafān leadership, the mounting cost of the siege for the allies, the hesitation of the Banī Qurayẓah to open the city's doors for the idolaters, and, finally, the freezing windstorm—were all reasons that led to the collapse of the morale of the alliance.

A huge army of 10,000 fighters, whose leaders thought that the battle would be a jaunt that would last a few days, was caught off guard and unprepared when confronted by a trench. They were forced to camp on barren land for close to a month, able neither to make progress nor to withdraw, out of fear of failure. To compound their difficulties, the Makkans, who were accustomed to their warm home climate, were subjected to a freezing winter.

We cannot regard an army that was subjected to such an impasse and was trapped in time as an army that had besieged the Muslims. Rather, this army was itself besieged. The Muslims were in their own city and fought on their own territory. Thus, no matter how prolonged the siege might have been, or how depleted their resources, they had no option but to remain steadfast. The alternative, defeat, would be devastating.

The alliance held on to the single hope that the Banī Qurayẓah would immediately enter the fray. However, the Banī Qurayẓah remained hesitant, and with good reason. They tried to justify their position by referring to the sanctity of the Sabbath and their inability to undertake any work on the day. This enraged Abū Sufyān, and he realised that he could not rely on them. Therefore, when Allah, the Praiseworthy and Sublime, sent a windstorm to the idolaters' camp during the night, Abū Sufyān swallowed the bitter pill of defeat and immediately decided to return to Makkah. His despair can be noted in the account in *Al-Ṭabaqāt al-Kubra.*

> Abū Sufyān said: "O People of Quraysh. You are not on firm ground; the mounts and livestock have been decimated; the environment is barren; and the Banī Qurayẓah have betrayed us. As you can see, we have suffered from the windstorm. Prepare to depart, for I am leaving." He sat on his camel, which was hobbled. He struck it so that it sprang up on three legs, and he did not remove its binding until it stood up. The people began departing, but Abū Sufyān remained until the camp was dismantled. [While this was happening,] 'Amr ibn al-'Āṣ and Khālid ibn al-Walīd formed a barrier with 200 warriors, in case they were attacked.[200]

"And Allah turned back the unbelievers in their rage, totally empty-handed. Allah was sufficient for the believers in battle. And Allah is All-Powerful, exalted in might" (Qur'ān 33:25).

200. Ibn Sa'd, *al-Ṭabaqāt*, vol. 2, 37.

CHAPTER FOURTEEN

A strategic coup

"From today we will invade them; they will not invade us. We will go to them."
(Prophet Muḥammad (ﷺ), Saḥīḥ al-Bukhārī)

The Battle of the Trench was a watershed event separating two eras in the history of Islam. Its outcomes upset the strategic balance that had prevailed from the time of the Hijrah. It irreversibly altered the balance of forces on the Arabian Peninsula and caused a massive shakeup of the political system. From a military perspective, the massive Confederate army was the largest in the history of the conflict between the Muslims and their enemies until that moment. It was also the most important political development because of the convergence of various tribes into an alliance against the Muslims. The failure of such a powerful alliance represented an unprecedented and decisive military and political defeats.

Quraysh beg

The Quraysh returned to Makkah defeated and broken, which hinted at the major political, economic, and administrative problems that Makkah was to face.

From a political perspective, the Quraysh's prestige was in tatters. Arab tribes began paying homage to the power of the Muslims and belittling that of the Quraysh. Furthermore, the Quraysh's alliance with the Ghaṭafān and the Jews collapsed; it had already begun deteriorating before Abū Sufyān had made the decision to withdraw from the Battle of the Trench. This is clear from his angry statements about the Jews after he had realised the Banī Qurayẓah's hesitancy. The Ghaṭafān's unilateral engagement with the Messenger (ﷺ) also damaged the confidence between it and the Quraysh. It is noteworthy that the decision to withdraw was Abū Sufyān's alone; the leaders of the Ghaṭafān and the Jewish tribes were not involved. This revealed a defective relationship between the leaders of the three allies.

The economic consequence was that there was no longer any hope of reopening the caravan routes between Makkah and the Levant and Yemen. Muslim troops immediately resumed attacks on the caravans and tightened the economic noose on Makkah. Within months, the Makkans began pleading with the Messenger (ﷺ), appealing to family ties to beg him to end the economic stranglehold that had exorbitantly inflated wheat prices. Ibn Isḥāq's account about the al-Yamāmah chief, Thumāmah ibn Athāl, is poignant and is illustrative of the condition of the Makkans after the Battle of the Trench. Ibn Isḥāq narrates on the authority of Abū Hurayrah:

> After Thumāmah ibn Athāl al-Ḥanafī confronted Allah's Messenger (ﷺ), he (ﷺ) prayed to Allah for dominance over Thumāmah. He had confronted Allah's Messenger [when he] was still an idolater and wanted to kill him. Still a pagan, Thumāmah entered Madinah as a pilgrim, raising suspicions. He was seized and brought before Allah's Messenger (ﷺ), who ordered him to be tied to a pillar of the mosque. Allah's Messenger (ﷺ) then asked him: "What's the matter, O Thumāmah? Has Allah gotten the better of you?" Thumāmah responded: "This is how it is, O Muḥammad: if you kill me, you will kill a kinsman; if you grant pardon, you will pardon one who is grateful; and if you ask for wealth, you will be given it." Allah's Messenger (ﷺ) left him. The next day, he passed by him and asked: "What's the matter, O Thumāmah?" He replied: "Very well, O Muḥammad. If you kill me, you will kill a kinsman; if you grant pardon, you will pardon one who is grateful; and if you ask for wealth, you will be given it." Allah's Messenger (ﷺ) [again] walked away. The poor among us said to each other: "What use do we have for Thumāmah's blood? By Allah, we would prefer a meal from a fat camel from his ransom than his blood." The next day, Allah's Messenger (ﷺ) passed by and asked: "What's the matter, O Thumāmah?" He replied: "Very well, O Muḥammad. If you kill me, you will kill a kinsman; if you grant pardon, you will pardon one who is grateful; and if you ask for wealth, you

will be given it." Allah's Messenger (ﷺ) said: "Release him. I have pardoned you, O Thumāmah." Thumāmah left. When he reached one of the walls of Madinah, he bathed, washed himself, and cleaned his clothes. He then went to Allah's Messenger (ﷺ), who was sitting in the mosque, and said: "O Muḥammad, before this time, there was no face that I detested more than your face, nor any religion that I detested more than your religion, nor any city that I detested more than your city. I then awoke, and there was no face that I loved more than your face, and no religion that I loved more than your religion, and no city that I loved more than your city. I declare that there is no deity except Allah, and I declare that Muḥammad is His servant and messenger. O Messenger of Allah, I had set out as a pilgrim while still a follower of my people's religion and I was incarcerated by your companions during my pilgrimage. Allow me to continue my pilgrimage. And may Allah's salutations be upon you." Allah's Messenger (ﷺ) allowed him to continue his pilgrimage after teaching him [how to perform it]. When Thumāmah reached Makkah, and the Quraysh heard him speak about Muḥammad's (ﷺ) mission, they said: "Thumāmah has abandoned his religion." He responded: "By Allah, I have not apostatised; I have submitted to Allah, have affirmed Muḥammad's [message], and I believe in him. By the One who holds Thumāmah's life, not a single grain will come to you from al-Yamāmah [in the countryside of Makkah] until Allah's Messenger (ﷺ) grants permission." When Thumāmah reached his home, he stopped all consignments to Makkah. The Quraysh fell on hard times… The Quraysh's sustenance[201] and beneficial [products] came from al-Yamāmah. When they started suffering, they wrote to Allah's Messenger (ﷺ): "We know that you advocate maintaining family ties. Thumāmah has cut off our sustenance and caused us harm. If you see fit to write to him and ask him not to come between us and our sustenance, then do so." Allah's Messenger (ﷺ) wrote to him: "Do not come between my people and their sustenance."[202]

201. This was wheat in general.
202. See Ibn Hishām, *al-Sīrah*, vol. 2, 638.

This detailed account illustrates that the Quraysh were desperate and were, therefore, forced to write to the Messenger (ﷺ), invoking their kinship ties. This was barely months after the Quraysh had besieged the Muslims in Madinah and had ignored their kinship bonds. The Noble Prophet's (ﷺ) acceding to the Quraysh's request sent a clear message to the people of Makkah: he was the giver and taker of their sustenance, and the Muslims were no longer marginal, isolated refugees who had left their wealth and property behind in Makkah. Moreover, the Makkans now saw the Prophet (ﷺ) as a generous and forgiving leader who did not remind them that they had cut kinship ties, or that, a few months earlier, they had gathered the tribes to exterminate the Muslims, even though their brothers and cousins were among the Muslim migrants.

The Prophet (ﷺ) did not react to their cutting of kinship ties by himself cutting ties. Rather, he ordered that the sale of wheat to the Quraysh be resumed. The Prophet (ﷺ) was most concerned with fulfilling his mission. He was a bringer of glad tidings, a warner, and a mercy to humankind. He also used the opportunity to build the foundations for a new relationship with the common people of Makkah. This was in preparation for the next phase, when they could accept him instead of the failed Qurayshi leadership. As we will see, the incident with Thumāmah was not an isolated one, but was instead part of an ongoing effort of the Messenger (ﷺ), after the Battle of the Trench, in his engagement with the Quraysh.

Within the Qurayshi leadership, Abū Sufyān found that his position was weakened and had become more unstable as a result of the defeat at the trench. The Islamic front was increasing in strength and capacity from one year to the next. The Makkan leadership, with Abū Sufyān at its helm, was helpless in the face of the Muslim threat and suffered one defeat after another. As a result, the influence of the second-tier leadership in Makkah began increasing. At the forefront of these emerging leaders was with Ikrimah ibn Abī Jahl, followed by Ṣafwān ibn Umayyah, Khālid ibn al-Walīd, 'Amr ibn al-'Āṣ, and others. Ikrimah had become leader of the Banī Makhzūm after his father's death at the Battle of Badr. This youth leadership did not, however, have a concrete plan of action, and they did not present any practical suggestions to change the course of the conflict and regain the initiative against the

Muslims. All they offered was populist statements aimed at mobilising the masses.

The Ghaṭafān withdrawal

The second component of the alliance, the Ghaṭafān, returned to the desert. They no longer posed a strategic danger to the Muslims and had no further major effect on the course of events. These migratory bedouin tribes were more concerned with pasturage and tribal alliances related to their migratory patterns. They made their living from raiding and plunder; their conflict with the Muslims was not an existential struggle. Nonetheless, the leaders of Khaybar made a tempting offer to the Ghaṭafān after the Battle of the Trench. The Jews of Khaybar offered the Ghaṭafān half of Khaybar's harvest if they provided them with the fighting capacity to repel the Muslims. However, the Ghaṭafān were hesitant. When they finally did agree, their participation was weak and too late.

Qurayẓah pay the price

The Khaybar Jews returned home after the dispersal of the confederates. However, Ḥuyay ibn Akhṭab accompanied the Banī Qurayẓah to their fortresses, fulfilling an oath he had made to himself. The leaders of Khaybar, which was a major economic power, realised that they had been strategically exposed by their conflict with the Muslims. They, therefore, began to reinforce their fortresses, and they contacted the Ghaṭafān tribes to negotiate a new alliance that would offer them some protection. The Banī Qurayẓah leaders were certain that they would face destruction for reneging on their covenant. They were correct; punishment was swift and arrived via the tongue of Sa'd ibn Mu'adh, the Aws leader. Being allies of the Aws, the Banī Qurayẓah chose Sa'd ibn Mu'adh as an arbitrator after the Muslims had besieged them. Sa'd ruled that their fighters must be put to the sword, their families enslaved, and their wealth divided among the Muslims. It was an unprecedented judgement, and it sent a message to the Arab tribes that a new era of power, initiative, and decisiveness had taken root in

Madinah, and that the fate of those who did not take their pledges to the Muslims seriously would be treated similarly to the Banī Qurayẓah.

The killing and capture of the Banī Qurayẓah is affirmed in the Qur'ān. "He brought those People of the Book who supported them down from their strongholds, and put terror into their hearts. Some of them you killed, and some you took captive" (Qur'ān 33:26).

Historians differ on the number of Qurayẓah men who were killed. Some say that 300 were put to the sword, others raise the number to 700, or even 900. Ibn Zinjawayh, author of the *Book of Wealth* (Kitāb al-Amwāl),[203] provides a much-reduced number of forty, based on a narration attributed to Ibn Shihāb al-Zuhrī. This question requires further research. There is a great disparity in these figures, and the issue requires more research and verification, like many other episodes in the Prophet's (ﷺ) biography that urgently need earnest study to uncover the realities and motives behind them. Considering its importance, researchers should dedicate time and energy to this effort; the Prophet's (ﷺ) biography is not only a legislative source, but also a source of inspiration. Muslims love their Prophet (ﷺ) and endeavour to emulate him, but most studies of his biography do not go beyond the transmission and repetition of earlier accounts. We desperately need a methodology to study it in depth, verify claims, and contextualise them.

New strategy

The Messenger (ﷺ) realised that the Confederates' defeat had created a new reality, and that the balance of military and political forces had begun shifting in the Muslims' favour. They were transitioning to a new era. Allah's Messenger (ﷺ) expressed the transition succinctly: "From today, we will invade them; they will not invade us." He knew that the idolaters were incapable of continuing their offensive campaign and had reached the pinnacle of their military and political strength at the Battle of the Trench. That campaign had failed at the military level, and, at the political level, caused their alliance's collapse. This collapse created a massive and unexpected strategic vacuum that neither the

203. Ḥamad ibn Mukhlad ibn Qutaybah al-Khurasānī Ibn Zinjawayh, *Kitāb al-Amwāl* (Riyadh: King Faisal Center for Research and Islamic Studies, 1986).

Quraysh nor the Ghaṭafān were able to fill.

It was impossible for the anti-Muslim alliance to be reconstituted after the devastating defeat at the Battle of the Trench, especially since the reputations of the Quraysh and the Ghaṭafān had been dealt a severe blow after the Banī Qurayẓah scandal. The Quraysh and the Ghaṭafān must have suffered terrible regret after hearing of the slaying of the Banī Qurayẓah. They had likely realised that their doubts about them had been wrong. The information that Nu'aym ibn Mas'ud had given them, that the Banī Qurayẓah had regretted breaking their covenant with the Prophet (ﷺ), had obviously been incorrect. They had been deceived by mind games, which was a major intelligence and political failure. Abandoning the Banī Qurayẓah and delivering them to the sword diminished their status in the eyes of the other Arab tribes. After that day, no one was bold enough to double-cross the Messenger of Allah (ﷺ) or to trust an alliance with the idolaters.

The Prophet (ﷺ) grasped the magnitude of the Confederates' defeat and knew the extent of the strategic vacuum that had been created by their failure. He also understood that the pagan and Jewish leaders were incapable of formulating a new vision and were preoccupied solely with mitigating the consequences of their defeat. The Prophet (ﷺ) seized the initiative by filling the vacuum and by shifting from a reactive to a proactive stance, from defensiveness to offensiveness. He had the option to invade, but also to propose a political alternative, which is the tactic he decided to pursue.

The major invasion

In terms of military activity, the period between Dhi'l Qa'dah 5 AH and Dhi'l Qa'dah 6 AH may be regarded as one of the busiest years in Madinah since the Prophet's (ﷺ) arrival. The Muslims implemented the excellent post-Trench offensive strategy of the Prophet (ﷺ): "From today we will invade them; they will not invade us." After the collapse of the Confederates' alliance at the Battle of the Trench and the liquidation of the Banī Qurayẓah soon thereafter, it was clear to the Muslims that their next objective was to strengthen Madinah's security domain and to reinforce control over three spheres: Khaybar, Najd, and the coast.

While Khaybar would be conquered after the Treaty of al-Ḥudaybīyyah, intelligence about its actions and communication with the Ghaṭafān and other hostiles suggested that it had begun preparations for military action against Madinah. The defeat of Khaybar, therefore, was a central strategic objective. The Najd region and its bedouins, who were gathering in different places to attack Madinah's periphery and steal livestock and crops, also posed a threat. The coast too needed to be safeguarded. The Quraysh had attempted to open gaps there after the Battle of the Trench, so that they might circumvent the siege and resume their trade activities.

The Prophet (ﷺ) organised fifteen military and security deployments in that one-year period, covering these three priority security spheres tightly and in an unprecedented manner. This period also witnessed a major escalation in the number and quality of military operations undertaken. A major shortcoming in the Muslim army was the small number of horses that it possessed. Horses were indispensable for an offensive strategy that was built on surprise and hit-and-run attacks. After the Battle of the Trench, the Prophet (ﷺ) dispatched several of his companions to Najd to purchase weapons and horses. They returned with vast quantities of both, which were distributed in Madinah. They then organised military training camps to ensure that the companions master military disciplines. This period also witnessed the formation of the first brigades comprised exclusively of warriors and young leaders, such as Zayd ibn Ḥārithah and Muḥammad ibn Musallamah, who patrolled the peninsula with speed and skill.

Khaybar: A Deferred target

The greatest strategic threat confronting Madinah in this phase came from Khaybar. The Muslims instituted various measures to contain and limit it, and the Prophet (ﷺ) began a limited escalation to intimidate Khaybar's people. The Muslims carried out two operations that targeted the two individuals who had led an incitement campaign against the Muslims. The first involved a team of six Muslims who infiltrated the home of Salām ibn Abī al-'Aqīq at night, killed him, and escaped without being detected. Thereafter, a detachment of thirty warriors led by 'Abdallah ibn Rawāhah killed Yasīr ibn Razām. Muslims also targeted Khaybar's allies to coerce them into breaking ties with it and leaving it isolated and vulnerable to being conquered.

In the meantime, Khaybar was communicating with numerous interlocutors in attempts to forge alliances and solicit assistance. Two of these were in the northeast: Fadak and Dūmat al-Jandal. They also reached out to Taymā', Wādī al-Qura', and the Ghaṭafān, their traditional ally. Al-Wāqidī narrates that the people of Khaybar had convened a meeting with their leader after they had received news of the slaying of the Banī Qurayẓah. They had been afraid and sought to find the best resolution.

> Afraid, the Jews asked Salām ibn Mishkam, "What is your opinion, O Abū 'Amr?" He replied, "What will you do with my opinion? You will not consider a single word of it." Kinānah responded: "This is not a time for admonition. The matter is obvious." Salām ibn Mishkam said: "Muḥammad has dealt with the Jews of Yathrib and is marching on you. He will descend on your homes and do to you what he did to the Banī Qurayẓah." They asked: "So what do you suggest?" He replied: "We must march out to him with whichever Jews of Khaybar are with us, they are a large number. We also call on the Jews of Taymā', Fadak, and Wādī al-Qura'. But we will not rely on any Arabs. You saw what the Arabs did to you during the Battle of the Trench after you had offered them Khaybar's dates. They broke their word, asked Muḥammad for some dates of the 'Aws and Khazraj, and abandoned you."[204]

The disintegration of their confidence in the Ghaṭafān is obvious. For those in Khaybar, the Ghaṭafān had disappointed them at the Battle of the Trench. Furthermore, as Ibn Mishkam describes them, they were mercenaries who could be bought with money and dates. They therefore had neither allegiance nor loyalty.

The Prophet (ﷺ) targeted the potential allies identified by Salām ibn

204. Al-Wāqidī, *Kitāb al-Maghāzī*, vol. 2, 530.

Mishkam. He dispatched a battalion of 100 warriors led by 'Alī ibn Abī Ṭālib to Fadak. Their goal was to intimidate the people of Fadak, diffuse their threat, and scare them sufficiently that they would terminate all communication with Khaybar. In the same month, Sha'bān/November, the Prophet (ﷺ) dispatched 'Abd al-Raḥmān ibn 'Awf at the head of a battalion of 700 warriors to Dūmat al-Jandal. This was the second time that the Muslims had targeted Dūmat al-Jandal; the first was during an expedition led by the Prophet (ﷺ) himself, before the Battle of the Trench. Abd al-Raḥmān ibn 'Awf's purpose was to develop enduring friendly relations with the Kalb tribe that was settled in Dūmat al-Jandal. 'Abd al-Raḥmān spent many days with them and invited them to Islam. Many accepted, including the Kalb's Christian king, al-Aṣbagh ibn 'Amr. 'Abd al-Raḥmān married the king's daughter, under the Prophet's (ﷺ) directive, and returned with her to Madinah. The Muslims thus strengthened their relationship with Dūmat al-Jandal and neutralised any danger it might have posed.

The Prophet (ﷺ) also dispatched two detachments led by Zayd ibn Ḥārithah to Wādī al-Qura'. The first was a reconnaissance squad comprising ten warriors. They were attacked by the people of Wādī al-Qura' and some were killed. The second squad was bigger, with more fighters. The direct cause of this expedition was an attack by some Wādī al-Qura' tribes on a caravan in which there were a number of Muslim traders. Muslim caravans had begun operating between Madinah and the Levant; they took advantage of the suspension of the Quraysh's trade and of the new security climate established by the Muslims.

The Ghaṭafān and the Najd tribes were targeted by five expeditions. The result was that their will to attack Madinah was broken and they became terrified. This occurred at the same time as the expansion of operations to the south to the Banī Sulaym, who had participated in the Confederates campaign with 700 warriors.

Quraysh's isolation intensifies

One strategic goal that was strengthened in this year was the tightening of the economic blockade on the Quraysh and the reaffirming of alliances with the coast. The Quraysh made numerous attempts to resume its caravan activity to the Levant. One of those caravans penetrated the Hijāz and crossed to the Levant, but it was attacked on its return by a Muslim force led by Zayd ibn Ḥārithah in al-'Ays. The Muslims confiscated everything that was in the caravan, including silver belonging to Ṣafwan ibn Umayyah, and they captured some of the men, including Abū al-'Āṣ ibn al-Rabī', the husband of the Prophet's (ﷺ) daughter Zaynab. The couple had been separated when Zaynab had migrated to Yathrib because her husband had refused to embrace Islam and remained in Makkah. When Abū al-'Āṣ reached Madinah, he sought Zaynab's protection. She announced that he was under her protection, which was then affirmed by the Prophet (ﷺ).

The Prophet (ﷺ) led an army of 200 warriors to the Banī Luḥyān, a clan of the Hudhayl tribe that had betrayed and killed six Muslims in Safar, 4AH / April 625, at the al-Rujay' water well. The Prophet (ﷺ) attacked them, but they dispersed into the mountains. He continued the expedition and marched on 'Usfān, which was seventy-five kilometres away from Makkah. He then dispatched two warriors to Kurā' al-Ghamīm, about 64 kilometres from Makkah, which was the closest point to Makkah that the Muslims had reached. The aim was to ensure that the Quraysh would hear of the expedition and become concerned and afraid for their future.

In a year of such outstanding military activity, we can be confident that the Prophet (ﷺ) had effectively exploited the victory over the Confederates. He secured Madinah and expanded its security domain in every direction. Even though Khaybar was not yet conquered, it was alienated from its strategic depth: isolated, vulnerable, and ready to be conquered by the Muslims. Nevertheless, the Prophet (ﷺ) remained primarily concerned with Makkah and his desire to get the Quraysh to embrace Islam. This had been the central objective governing his strategic praxis ever since his arrival in Madinah. The Quraysh were alone, isolated, and weak. Their leaders had lost all initiative and their strategy to exterminate the Muslims had failed. They had no allies and no negotiating positions when the Prophet (ﷺ) approached them as a pilgrim rather than as a conqueror. This not only astonished the Muslims, but it also surprised the Quraysh. One of the features of the Prophet's

(ﷺ) strategic praxis was that he often made surprise moves that placed him in a position where he dictated what options were available to the enemy. He then pressured them to choose the best option from the ones that he had determined.

Unlike other military leaders or conquerors who sought victory, domination, and to break the opponent at any cost, the Prophet (ﷺ) was first and foremost a messenger of Allah, and his mission was one of mercy to humankind. He was not interested in revenge, retribution, or in destroying and eliminating the Quraysh. He wanted them to have honour, dignity, and liberation under the banner of monotheism, the same banner under which Ibrāhīm had established the foundations of the Holy Sanctuary.

CHAPTER FIFTEEN

Emergence of the Islamic nation

"Verily We have granted you a manifest victory" (Qur'ān 48:01).

The Qur'ān drew attention to the various agreements that the Quraysh had successfully negotiated with neighbouring regional powers, forming, as a whole, the Makkah Pact. This reference occurred in the first days of revelation, in the chapter on the Quraysh. "For the pacts (of security) of the Quraysh. Their pacts [covering] their winter and summer journeys. Let them worship the Lord of this house Who provides them with food against hunger, and with security against fear" (Qur'ān 106:1-4).

These verses presented the Prophet (ﷺ) with one of the most strategic Qur'ānic directives regarding his interaction with the Quraysh. Allah draws his attention to the fact that the Quraysh's wealth and security were founded upon two pillars. The first was its trade pact and its accomplishments gained through open trade routes for its caravans. The second was the Holy Sanctuary, which granted the Quraysh a status that protected it from the threats that constantly faced other tribes. This chapter of the Qur'ān guided the strategy that the Prophet (ﷺ) developed to deal with the Quraysh, from the time of his Hijrah until the conquest of Makkah. The strategy was designed to unfold in two phases.

In the first phase, which began with the Hijrah and ended with the Treaty of al-Ḥudaybīyyah, the Muslims targeted the Makkan trade pact by establishing the Madinah Pact. They also targeted the Quraysh's alliances with the coastal tribes and attacked its caravans that passed through Najd. In this way, the Quraysh's summer and winter journeys were both disrupted, and Makkah was besieged economically. The first pillar of Qurayshi exceptionalism was thus shaken. The second phase of the strategy extended from the Treaty of al-Ḥudaybīyyah to the conquest of Makkah. During this phase, the Prophet's (ﷺ) strategy focused on the Holy Sanctuary, the second pillar of Qurayshi exceptionalism. The Prophet (ﷺ) astutely used the Quraysh's custodianship of the Holy Sanctuary as a cover to confront their obstinacy, which he ultimately broke during the Treaty of al-Ḥudaybīyyah, when he forced them to recognise the Islamic entity.

Freedom to enter the Sanctuary

The Arabs recognised the Quraysh as "the People of Allah and the Custodians of the Holy Sanctuary", but this came at a price. The Quraysh were not allowed to prevent pilgrims from visiting the Sanctuary, irrespective of whether they were allies or enemies. Ignoring this implicit obligation would undermine the Quraysh's legitimacy as the custodian of the Holy Sanctuary and would send a message to the Arabs that the Sanctuary was a political tool used by the Quraysh to punish or reward. No Arab would have accepted such behaviour. The Quraysh had many enemies and longstanding opponents, such as the Khuzā'ah, who had once themselves been custodians of the Holy Sanctuary. They had been expelled from Makkah by Quṣay when he had exerted Qurayshi control over the city. Other enemies included the Qays 'Ilān tribes and clans, and the Hawāzin, Thaqīf, Ghaṭafān, and Sulaym tribes that had fought the Quraysh during the Immoral Wars. The freedom to visit the Holy Sanctuary for pilgrimage was, thus, not a Qurayshi concession, but a binding agreement that had come about after wars and conflicts. The Arab tribes would never accept Qurayshi sovereignty over Makkah if it did not respect and protect this agreement, which might be compared, in the contemporary era, to the respect accorded to international law.

During the second phase of his strategy to deal with the Quraysh, the Prophet (ﷺ) invoked the principle of the freedom to visit the Holy Sanctuary, thereby casting the Quraysh into a major crisis. He decided that, in the month of Dhi'l Qa'dah, 6 AH, he would travel to Makkah as a pilgrim, carrying only a traveller's weapons, and accompanied by about 1,400 of his companions. They would perform the rituals required for such a journey: herding sheep and camels for sacrifice, wearing the pilgrims' garments (iḥrām), and raising their voices in prayer. The action would place the Quraysh in a quandary. If it allowed the Muslims to perform the rites, it would practically recognise their existence as a single independent entity and would therefore appear to the people as too weak even to turn Muḥammad (ﷺ) away, despite their being at war with him. However, if they refused, they would undermine their legitimacy as custodians of the Holy Sanctuary. The Quraysh understood the implications of this loss of legitimacy, and they feared it the most. The Muslims' journey to al-Ḥudaybīyyah presented the Quraysh with two difficult options; they would reject the first because of their arrogance, and the second would be rejected by all the Arabs. The Prophet (ﷺ) had effectively trapped them in a predicament from which there was no escape, and he knew it. He also knew that he was the only person capable of rescuing them from this quagmire because only he could provide a solution.

The Muslims travelled on their pilgrimage in a celebratory atmosphere. As they approached Makkah, there was a palpable feeling of the significance of closing in on their spiritual centre and the direction of their prayers. Five years after their prayer direction had been changed from Jerusalem to the Ka'bah, the Muslims were on their way to the Sacred Mosque, hoping to liberate it from Qurayshi paganism and return it to the monotheism of Ibrāhīm. Five years earlier, Allah, the Blessed and Sublime, had chosen a prayer direction for them that had pleased them and which they loved.

> We have seen you turning your face to the heaven. We will turn you to a qiblah (prayer direction) that will please you. Turn your face towards the Sacred Mosque. Wherever you (believers) are, turn your faces towards it (Qur'ān 2:144).

The Qur'ān also affirmed their right to Ibrāhīm's legacy. "Indeed, those who have the best claim of relationship with Ibrāhīm are his followers, this prophet, and those who believe. And Allah is the Protector of those who have faith" (Qur'ān 3:68). As the Prophet (ﷺ) travelled on his pilgrimage, he connected with the legacy of Ibrāhīm, the founding father, and not with the paganism of the Quraysh.

Some of the companions suggested that the Prophet (ﷺ) should bear arms: shields, spears, armour, and a helmet. Swords and daggers were generally carried by travellers, and they were not considered weapons of war. The Prophet (ﷺ), however, refused, and he insisted on carrying only travellers' weapons. The Muslims were stunned. They expected that the Prophet (ﷺ) had intended to conquer Makkah. It seemed an obvious course of action. Makkah was vulnerable and an attack was certainly possible. The Prophet's (ﷺ) strategy, however, was not to conquer Makkah by force, even though he had the capacity to do so and, if he did, victory would be guaranteed. While his companions expected him to enter Makkah as a conqueror, the Prophet (ﷺ) desired a solution that would be acceptable to both sides. This was a more prudent and far-sighted approach. Because he was a prophet and a mercy to humankind, he did not pursue victory at any cost. His goal was to get the Arabs and, after them, the rest of the world, to embrace Islam. The Arabs viewed the Quraysh with tremendous respect, and the Muslim Quraysh would be able to play a role in getting all the Arabs to embrace Islam. Furthermore, the Holy Sanctuary was sacred and inviolable, and a religion that was the inheritor of Ibrāhīm's monotheism could not begin its ascendency in Makkah with violence and bloodshed.

The Prophet's (ﷺ) gaze extended far beyond the conquest of Makkah. The conquest, for him, was an important step in the longer process of spreading the message to all Arabs, and then to the world. The conquest should therefore be an inauguration of a new age, carrying the necessary symbolism associated with that coming era. It should not just be a victory over the Quraysh, but a victory of the new and open-minded over the old and close-minded. It should be the veritable door through which all may enter, even those who had fought the Prophet (ﷺ) and expelled him from Makkah. The conquest, in the Prophet's (ﷺ) strategy, would be symbolic of a world exiting from a whirlpool of destructive conflict and entering one of gentle motion. He was thus in no hurry to conquer Makkah because the prerequisites of the conquest, as he understood them, had not yet been realised. We will later witness the stunning success of this strategy. However, on this occasion, the Prophet (ﷺ) insisted that he was just a pilgrim and that he did not like pilgrims to bear arms.

For the rest of the journey, the Prophet's (ﷺ) every action was intended to send a message to the Arabs, especially to the Quraysh, that his only objective was to perform the pilgrimage. He entered the state of ritual sanctity (iḥrām), donned the pilgrim's garments at the mosque in Madinah, and mounted his camel, al-Qaṣwā', for the journey. He ordered that the sacrificial animals be marked with special symbols that would indicate that they were to be sacrificed as part of the pilgrimage rituals. These were practices that were familiar to the Arabs and were recognised as rituals of the 'umrah (lesser pilgrimage) and the ḥajj (pilgrimage). It would therefore be clear to any observer that the Muslims had embarked on a pilgrimage. The Prophet (ﷺ) wanted it understood by everyone that he definitely had no intention to fight or to engage in any conflict.

As a precaution, he dispatched a squad of twenty warriors ahead of the pilgrims' procession to reconnoitre the route and secure it against any possible ambush or attack. He also sent Busar ibn Sufyān al-Khuzā'ī to Makkah as a scout, to gather information and get a sense of the Quraysh's reaction when the news of the Muslim procession reached them.

The procession passed through the territories of several tribes, including the Banī Bakr, Juhaynah and Mazīnah. Since not all were Muslim, members of the procession invited them to join. They all declined, claiming to be occupied, but later said: "Does Muḥammad want us to join his invasion of a people who are well prepared and have weapons and cavalry at their disposal? Muḥammad and his companions are camel eaters! Muḥammad and his companions will not be returning from this journey!"[205] They were soon to discover how wrong they were; the Prophet (ﷺ) and his companions would return with glad tidings of a manifest victory, even if they were mere camel eaters.

Makkah's new leadership

When news of the Muslim procession reached the Quraysh, they gathered in the House of Assembly to debate the matter. The Prophet's (ﷺ) prediction was realised, and his scenario began to play out. The

205. Al-Wāqidī, *Kitāb al-Maghāzī*, vol. 2, 574.

Quraysh compounded its predicament by not allowing the Muslims to enter Makkah. Their pride prevented them from making any concessions, no matter the cost.

They said: "He wants to come among us on pilgrimage with his soldiers. The Arabs will hear about this! That he has entered [Makkah] forcibly while there is war between us and him. By Allah, this will never be, as long as we have an eye that blinks! Forward your suggestions, decide, and delegate [this task] to those among you whose opinions are respected: Ṣafwān ibn Umayyah, Suhayl ibn 'Amr, and 'Ikrimah ibn Abī Jahl." Ṣafwān responded, "We never take a decision until we have consulted you. We suggest that we move 200 warriors, with a strong-willed leader, to Kurā' al-Ghamīm." The Quraysh said: "Your suggestion is good! Put 'Ikrimah ibn Abī Jahl [some reports say "Khālid ibn al-Walīd"] at the head of the cavalry." The Quraysh mobilised those who obeyed them from among the Aḥābīsh and took the Thaqīf with them. They appointed Khālid ibn al-Walīd at the head of the force. They positioned spies on mountaintops until they reached a mountain called Wazr'un Wazr'un. The ten spies were led by al-Ḥakam ibn 'Abd Manāf. They whispered to each other: "Muḥammad has done such and such!" until [the information] reached the Quraysh at [the valley of] Baldaḥ, where they had gone to with their women and children and set up tents and structures.[206]

Two important observations are pertinent here. First, the Quraysh's fundamental concern with allowing the Prophet (ﷺ) permission to enter Makkah was the harm it would do to their reputation. It would also be an implicit acknowledgement that they were unable to stop him and would result in a predicament. The second noteworthy observation is that the Quraysh's leadership had been handed over to the second generation of the Alliance of the Allies. That is why Abū Sufyān was not mentioned in the list of leaders who were delegated to study the issue and take the necessary action. The three names mentioned—Ṣafwān, 'Ikrimah, and Suhayl—were all Abū Sufyān's rivals and had accused him of negligence, especially after the resounding defeat at the Battle of the Trench. It is also possible that Abū Sufyān had realised that the three young leaders would be waging a losing battle, and, therefore,

206. Al-Wāqidī, *Kitāb al-Maghāzī*, vol. 2, 579.

voluntarily withdrew. However, it is more likely that he was marginalised by this group after the numerous criticisms of his leadership, including accusations of indecisiveness and failure. It is certain, however, that he was in Makkah, but was not heading the Quraysh. He is mentioned in an incident when ʻUthmān ibn ʻAffān visited him at his home in Makkah. It is also clear that the three energetic Qurayshi youth leaders were making the crucial decisions and directing events. The three persons in this new leadership structure were all from the Alliance of Allies, Makkah's party of power and wealth. Ṣafwān was the most prominent and the most engaging. He had taken several vociferous stances in the years leading up to the Muslim procession, mostly opposing Abū Sufyān. He had criticised Abū Sufyān at Uḥud when he had agreed to a second encounter at Badr, and again when Abū Sufyān had failed to keep his promise. He had also criticised Abū Sufyān's powerlessness and hasty withdrawal at the Battle of the Trench. Ṣafwān was keen to find ways to exterminate the Muslims; he represented the extremist faction of the Qurayshi leadership. He was also his father's heir, having taken over as chief of the Jumaḥ tribe after Umayyah ibn Khalaf had been killed at Badr.

ʻIkrimah ibn Abī Jahl al-Makhzūmī was faithful to his father's legacy. He also had his father's bad temperament and impatience. He and Ṣafwān together constituted an extremist duo. Suhayl ibn ʻAmr, by contrast, was more prudent, the most eloquent of the three, and the most cunning in terms of his political activities. After Suhayl had been captured during the Battle of Badr, ʻUmar ibn al-Khaṭṭāb had suggested to the Prophet (ﷺ) that his incisors be extracted so that his tongue would be corrupted, and he would be unable to orate. The Prophet (ﷺ) refused; he rejected the practice of maiming. He told ʻUmar: "Perhaps Suhayl will one day take a position that pleases you." The Prophet's (ﷺ) premonition was realised a few years later, when Suhayl delivered a speech in Makkah after the Prophet's (ﷺ) death.[207] He passionately encouraged people to remain committed to Islam, at a time when many Arab tribes were abandoning the religion.

207. The Prophet (ﷺ) passed away on Monday, 14 Rabīʻ al-Awwal 11 AH / 8 June 632.

The strategy of the three-person crisis committee was not innovative, but rather conventional. They wanted to exhibit brute force, which the Prophet (ﷺ) had expected. When one's enemy's reaction is predictable, one will have the final word in the planning and the containment of the threat, which is exactly what transpired in this instance. The Quraysh deployed cavalry under Khālid ibn al-Walīd. They camped on the outskirts of Makkah, but without any specific military objective. The Quraysh, exhausted and weak, had been abandoned by their allies and left to confront a young, organised, disciplined, and visionary force on their own. Military action in such an instance is simply an emotional reaction, not a strategic choice, something that the Prophet (ﷺ) understood very well.

Imposing a new reality on the ground

The Prophet (ﷺ) sent Busar ibn Sufyān to monitor the Quraysh. He travelled to Makkah, listened to their reactions, witnessed their preparations, and hastily returned to report to the Prophet (ﷺ) near 'Usfān. The Prophet (ﷺ) gathered the Muslims for a consultation, informed them of the Quraysh's mobilisation and of Khālid ibn al-Walīd's cavalry, and asked their opinion.

> The Prophet (ﷺ) said: "What do you think, O Muslims, about those who have mobilised their subordinates against us to prevent us from [entering] the Sacred Mosque? Should we proceed on our way to the Sacred House and fight whoever confronts us? Or should we go around those who have been mobilised against us and attack their people? [In that case,] if they follow us, we will have their necks, which Allah will slay. If they stand down, they stand down sad and dejected." Abū Bakr responded: "Allah and his Messenger know best. I feel, O Messenger of Allah, that we should continue on our path and fight whoever stops us from reaching the Ancient House."[208]

It must be pointed out that Abū Bakr was the companion who best understood the Prophet's (ﷺ) strategy and long-term objectives. This

---

208. Al-Wāqidī, *Kitāb al-Maghāzī*, vol. 2, 580.

was manifested again during the negotiations at al-Ḥudaybīyyah. The Muslims had two options available to them. They could either attack Khālid's detachment or proceed to Makkah as pilgrims, ignoring Khālid. Abū Bakr recommended the latter option, which aligned with the strategy that the Prophet (ﷺ) had already determined before he had left Madinah. He had planned that they would proceed with the pilgrimage and had no predetermined intention to fight. Others supported Abū Bakr's proposal and the Prophet (ﷺ) decided to accept it. However, he took precautions to avoid confronting Khālid's cavalry. He ordered that the Muslims follow a lesser-known path, hoping to reach the outskirts of the Sanctuary as quickly as possible. If they reached the Sanctuary, they would be safe and would have put the Quraysh in a bind that they would not be able to undo. It would be extremely embarrassing for the Quraysh to fight pilgrims who were intent on prayer within the sacred precinct. This was a preeminent strategic move that would embarrass the Quraysh, limit their options, and cast them in a predicament.

The Muslims reached al-Ḥudaybīyyah, about a day's march from Makkah. Part of al-Ḥudaybīyyah lies within the Sanctuary and part of it without. When they approached the borders of the Sanctuary, the Prophet's (ﷺ) camel knelt and refused to continue. The people said that al-Qaṣwā' had refused to continue. The Prophet (ﷺ) responded that it had not refused but had, in awe of the sanctuary, been held back by the One who had held back the elephant. He said: "By Allah, to whatever resolution the Quraysh invites me today, I will agree if it invokes the enjoining of kinship ties."[209] This was the Prophet's (ﷺ) first remark that alluded to the possibility of accepting a resolution that would avoid bloodshed and uphold kinship ties. However, the Qurasyhi leaders did not proffer such a proposal, leaving him to do so, and to push them to accept it.

Saving the Quraysh from their Predicament

When the Prophet (ﷺ) camped at al-Ḥudaybīyyah, he put himself within the grasp of the Qurayshi leadership, but they were at a loss about how to proceed. They knew only that they were in a predicament,

209. Ibn Hishām, *al-Sīrah*, vol. 2, 310.

and that they desperately needed a solution. A seasoned Khuzā'ī leader took the initiative to open communications between the two parties. The Khuzā'ah tribe was the Prophet's (ﷺ) ally. Budayl ibn Warqā'a led a Khuzā'ah delegation to meet the Prophet (ﷺ). Budayl was also close to the Quraysh and had a house in Makkah. An old man, Budayl had a son, Rāfi',who had accepted Islam and had been martyred during the Bi'r Ma'ūnah incident. Budayl spoke at length to the Prophet (ﷺ), trying to establish the purpose of the Muslims' journey. The Prophet's (ﷺ) brief and precise response was extremely significant.

> We have not come to fight anyone. Indeed, we have come only to circumambulate the Sacred House. However, we will fight anyone who stops us from doing so. The Quraysh have been debilitated and drained by the war. If they wish, I will grant them respite for a period in which they will be safe, [but] they should not come between us and the people. The people are more numerous than they are. If my case is put to the people, they have the choice to enter [Islam] as others have done, or to fight as they [now] seem to want to do. By Allah, I will persist with my mission until I am killed or Allah saves this mission of His![210]

The Prophet's (ﷺ) words conveyed important messages to the Quraysh. The first of these was that he had not come to fight, but to exercise his right to perform the pilgrimage. Second, that the Quraysh could not intimidate him by their mobilisation or other measures because he was aware of their desperate situation, their suspended trade, and their isolation. Drained and debilitated by the war, the Quraysh were not able to do anything against the Muslims. His third message was that there was before them a rational solution that would grant the Quraysh some respite and time to recuperate. In return, they had to agree to a truce in which both sides would suspend military operations for a fixed period, and the Prophet (ﷺ) would be allowed to invite people to Islam. He tried to convince them with logic, explaining that the truce was the best option because it would temporarily suspend the war between the Quraysh and the Muslims, which was in the interests of both parties. The doors of trade would again be opened for the Quraysh, allowing them

210. Al-Wāqidī, *Kitāb al-Maghāzī*, vol. 2, 593.

to flourish, and the Prophet (ﷺ) would continue his mission among the Arabs. They would either wage war against him or accept Islam. If the Arabs defeated the Prophet (ﷺ), this would accord with the Quraysh's wishes. However, if they embraced Islam, the Quraysh would be faced with two choices: either also to accept Islam, or to reject Islam and to continue fighting the Prophet (ﷺ). In the first instance, they would become the most prominent of the Arabs since they were the Prophet's (ﷺ) tribe. In the second, if they chose to fight the Prophet (ﷺ), they would have had time to recuperate, and to reconstitute their alliances.

The Prophet (ﷺ) concluded with his fourth message, a categorical affirmation that he had no intention to fight, but that the option to do so was still available if the Quraysh insisted on being obstinate, preventing him from performing the pilgrimage and rejecting the truce.

The Prophet's (ﷺ) address was balanced and logical, convincingly placed the issue within a practical context, made an attractive offer, and delivered a decisive warning. This was yet another example of the spirit of initiative that characterised the Prophet's (ﷺ) actions during this period. He took the surprise step of going on pilgrimage to the Qurayshi heartland, forcing them into a quandary. They were neither strong enough to prevent him from entering the Sanctuary, nor could they allow him to enter. He created their predicament and also offered a solution. The Prophet's (ﷺ) detailed offer was not one that any thinking person could easily dismiss.

This message, with all its consequences and implications, was directed not only to the Qurayshi leaders in the House of Assembly, but also to the masses in Makkah who suffered from the blockade more than the elite. In this phase, the Prophet's (ﷺ) messages were, in general, addressed to those beyond the Qurayshi leadership, which was clinging to its stubborn position; they were directed to the popular conscience, and presented convincing solutions to the masses.

Budayl addressed the House of Assembly but, because of their arrogance, the Qurayshi leaders placed no importance on his visit and asked him nothing about his visit to the Muslims. Their reasoning was that they had not tasked him with this responsibility. Further, he was from the Khuzā'ah tribe, which did not enjoy their confidence. However, 'Urwah ibn Mas'ūd al-Thaqafī, a leader of the Thaqīf tribe, happened to be in Makkah at the time, and he criticised them severely for ignoring Budayl's report. 'Urwah was a respected leader in Ṭā'if and had previously assisted the Quraysh. Since no one had accused him of entering a truce with Muḥammad (ﷺ), the Quraysh agreed, on his insistence, to give Budayl a hearing. Budayl conveyed the Prophet's (ﷺ) offer of a truce and explained its benefits for the Quraysh. However, they refused, mocking the offer.

'Urwah then suggested that the Quraysh delegate him to meet the Prophet (ﷺ) to confirm the details of the offer and to use the opportunity to examine the Muslim camp and assess their capabilities. For the Quraysh, 'Urwah was a more acceptable intermediary than Budayl. Therefore, the meeting at the House of Assembly agreed to his proposal. He became the second non-Qurayshi visitor to the Muslim camp, but this time, with an official mandate from them.

'Urwah addressed the Prophet (ﷺ) with threats. He claimed that the Quraysh had prepared and had gathered to fight the Muslims. If the Prophet (ﷺ) insisted on entering Makkah, he said, he would face two possible scenarios. The first was that he would be forced to attack his own people, which would be an unprecedented disgrace. The second was that the Prophet's (ﷺ) companions would abandon him and flee. 'Urwah then added insults to his repertoire, saying that he saw only the common rabble with the Prophet (ﷺ) and that he knew neither their faces nor their lineages.

Although Abū Bakr was usually a calm person who was never vulgar, he immediately intervened and swore at 'Urwah: "Suck al-Lāt's clitoris! Do you think we would betray him?" 'Urwah obviously knew Abū Bakr's stature and generosity, and he would not dare belittle his standing. 'Urwah could not forget that, many years earlier, he had been required to pay blood money for thirteen murdered people, and Abū Bakr had made a generous donation toward this fund. The debate continued, the discussion became more heated, and 'Urwah argued vociferously. The Prophet (ﷺ) said nothing more than he had already told Budayl ibn Warqā'a.

‘Urwah returned to the Quraysh and relayed his assessment of the atmosphere in the Muslim camp. He relayed his amazement at the discipline of the Prophet’s (ﷺ) companions, as well as their respect for and obedience to him. He told the Qurayshi leaders that he had visited the courts of Khosrow, Caesar, the Negus, and al-Muqawqas, but had not seen people who loved their leader as Muḥammad’s (ﷺ) companions loved him, and that he believed that they would sacrifice themselves for him if they met the Quraysh on the battlefield. He said most of the companions were young men who competed for the Prophet’s (ﷺ) pleasure, but that they were united. ‘Urwah proposed that the Quraysh accept the truce offer because they could not win a battle against the Muslims. Moreover, he said, the Muslims had arrived with the genuine intention of performing the pilgrimage and had brought sacrificial animals. He believed that they would perform the pilgrimage rites and depart. ‘Urwah’s assessment annoyed the Qurayshi leaders. They responded that, if anyone other than him had articulated such comments, they would have reprimanded him and cast aspersions on his character. An intelligent man, ‘Urwah ibn Mas‘ūd tried to provide the Quraysh wise counsel, but their leaders’ arrogance and rashness were obstacles to their accepting the advice. ‘Urwah embraced Islam after the Conquest of Makkah and returned to Ṭā’if with glad tidings of the new religion. He was later martyred by his own people.

The Quraysh then sent another envoy, this time from their own ranks. Makraz ibn Hafṣ was a harsh and treacherous man, known for his hatred of the Prophet (ﷺ). Nevertheless, he returned with an assessment similar to those of ‘Urwah and Budayl. The fourth envoy was an unusual choice. Al-Ḥulays ibn ‘Alqamah was the leader of the Aḥābīsh, the non-Qurayshi coalition of groups in Makkah. Theirs was an alliance of the marginalised and weak, and it included the general populace of Makkah, excluding the Qurayshi elite. There are many narratives about why they were called Aḥābīsh. They include the possibility that they took their name from al-Ḥabash, citizens of Makkah who were of Ḥabashi (Abyssinian) origin; that it was a reference to a mountain in Makkah; or because they “came together” (from the Arabic word Taḥabbashu). What is certain is that this group was not small. It was estimated to constitute about half of the Makkan population. The Qurayshi aristocrats did not regard them as equals but as second-class citizens. It is understandable, then, that the Aḥābīsh were less hostile to the Prophet (ﷺ) than the Quraysh; they had heard reports about his justness, tolerance, and equal treatment of his companions, and that he did not consider people's origins or skin colour as bases for judging them. Al-Ḥulays was probably a Christian.

When the Prophet (ﷺ) heard of his impending arrival at the Muslim camp, he told his companions that Al-Ḥulays was from a devout people who respected religious rites and aspired to draw close to Allah through worship. The Prophet (ﷺ) therefore ordered his companions to gather the sacrificial animals and herd them towards al-Ḥulays as he made his way to their camp, to evoke his religious sensibilities and to illustrate that the Prophet (ﷺ) was serious about performing the pilgrimage. When al-Ḥulays saw the herd and noticed that the sacrificial animals had become emaciated and weak due to the lack of fodder and to being penned for a long period, he shortened his visit and returned to Makkah.

The Aḥābīsh leader was enraged by the Quraysh's actions. The Muslims were in pilgrim garb, stuck outside Makkah for half a month so that their camels had become emaciated and their fur worn because of their long confinement. By what right, he asked himself, were pilgrims being prevented from entering the Ancient House to perform the circumambulation? The Qurayshi leadership insulted and derided him. "Sit down!" he was told. "You are but a bedouin who knows nothing." They displayed their disdain and disregard of his status. Al-Ḥulays became infuriated and threatened them with force.

> O People of Quraysh. By Allah, we did not pledge allegiance to you for this, nor did we enter an agreement with you for this. Are you blocking people who venerate Allah's house from entering it? By the One who holds the life of al-Ḥulays in His hand, you will not come between Muḥammad and what he came here for, or I will mobilise the Aḥābīsh to the last man.[211]

This response was an open threat from a person who was close to the Quraysh and their partner in Makkah.

The Prophet's (ﷺ) wisdom in winning over al-Ḥulays was to have

211. Ibn Hishām, *al-Sīrah*, vol. 2, 312.

a decisive impact on the outcome of the impasse at al-Ḥudaybīyyah. Unlike the envoys who had preceded him, al-Ḥulays represented the people of Makkah and had legitimacy among them. He was also guided by a sense of morality and was, therefore, trusted by his followers as someone who would not follow his vain desires or covet leadership. His understanding of the nature of the Muslims' visit immediately spread to the general population of Makkah. There was general support for his position that permission be granted to the Muslims to enter Makkah. The Makkans also seemed to support the Prophet's (ﷺ) offer of a truce with the Quraysh, believing that it would bring them relief.

'Uthmān's mediation

The Prophet's (ﷺ) strategy to create a split among the Makkans between the leadership and the general population was successful. The Quraysh were confused about how they should proceed, especially with the Aḥābīsh threatening civil war. The Quraysh's predicament intensified; they saw no possible solution except the Prophet's (ﷺ) truce proposal.

The Prophet (ﷺ) took the initiative to end the stand-off. For the first time, he sent an emissary to the Quraysh. Like Budayl, Khurrās ibn Umayyah was also from the Khuzā'ah tribe.[212] The envoy's lineage was an important consideration. Although they were allies of the Prophet (ﷺ), the Khuzā'ah also had covenants with the Quraysh and were their neighbours. The Quraysh would therefore not kill a person from the Khuzā'ah. The Prophet (ﷺ) dispatched Khurrās to officially inform the Quraysh that the Muslims' purpose was only pilgrimage and that they did not want to fight. However, the reckless Qurayshi leadership attacked him, and 'Ikrimah ibn Abū Jahl hamstrung the Prophet's (ﷺ) camel that Khurrās was riding. They wanted to kill the Khuzā'ī emissary, but the Aḥābīsh intervened and protected him. Previously regarded as simple masses, the Aḥābīsh now emerged as an active social group with influence and took a clear political stance. The Quraysh could no longer rely on them as an ally in a war against Muḥammad (ﷺ).

212. He was also an ally of the Banī Makhzūm and he lived in Madinah. He came with the Prophet (ﷺ) to al-Ḥudaybīyyah and accompanied him to Khaybar and on other expeditions thereafter. He died at the end of Mu'āwīyyah ibn Abī Sufyān's reign.

When the Prophet (ﷺ) was informed of the treatment that Khurrās had received, and of the Aḥābīsh's intervention, he knew that the Quraysh was dealing with a major split in Makkah, and it had become opportune to call for serious negotiations with them. His next envoy was a man from the Qurayshi aristocracy, from the central pillar of Qurayshi ancestry, the Banī 'Abd Manāf. He was 'Uthmān ibn 'Affān ibn Abī al-'Āṣ ibn Umayyah, an Umayyad Qurayshi with a stature that could not be ignored. 'Uthmān entered Makkah under the protection of his uncle Abān ibn Sa'īd ibn al-'Āṣ, both of them riding on Abān's stallion. 'Uthmān was warmly welcomed by the Makkan leaders and allowed to circumambulate the Sacred House. He, however, refused to do so until the Prophet (ﷺ) and the other Muslims were given the same opportunity. He then visited his cousin and fellow Umayyad, Abū Sufyān ibn Ḥarb. (In historical accounts, this was the first occasion on which Abū Sufyān's name is mentioned in relation to al-Ḥudaybīyyah.) There is an important signal in 'Uthmān's visit to Abū Sufyān. It afforded recognition to the traditional Qurayshi leadership rather than the reckless young leaders, especially after they had failed to resolve the crisis that had been gripping Makkah. Furthermore, it showed Muslim respect for Abū Sufyān's stature above that of anyone else. This signal, the Prophet (ﷺ) knew, would also be seen by the common people. In the days that followed, Abū Sufyān's status was reinstated and strengthened by each communication between the Quraysh and the Muslims.

After Abū Sufyān, 'Uthmān visited other Qurayshi leaders, explained the Muslims' objective, and tried to convince them to accept the truce proposed by the Prophet (ﷺ). His mission in Makkah included three days of intense dialogue and negotiations.

The three young leaders who comprised the crisis committee that had earlier been formed—Ṣafwān ibn Umayyah, 'Ikrimah, and Suhayl Ibn 'Amr—were unconvinced by the truce proposal and earnestly pursued the option of war. To ascertain the strength and readiness of the Muslims, they dispatched forty men with instructions to attack the camp with arrows and stones. However, the alert Muslim guards captured all forty and hauled them before the Prophet (ﷺ). He ordered their incarceration. A second group also attempted to attack the camp but was also captured. When the Quraysh learnt about the capture of their companions, they detained ten Muslims who had entered Makkah to visit their relatives; the Quraysh hoped to use them in a prisoner exchange.

Escalation for the sake of a solution

It had become clear to the Prophet (ﷺ) that the disputes within Makkah had reached a level where the Quraysh's decision-making capacity had been severely compromised and its ability to take a stance on the truce paralysed. Ṣafwān and 'Ikrimah continued to incite against a truce, while the Aḥābīsh and others pushed for it. Support for a truce spread in the House of Assembly, too, but it was conditioned on the Muslims returning to Madinah and not entering Makkah until the following year. For a splintered and paralysed Quraysh, it was difficult to reach a decisive position. The Prophet (ﷺ) realised that the situation required another initiative by him to stir the stagnant waters and break the impasse. It was not in the Muslims' interest to remain in al-Ḥudaybīyyah for an extended period, nor was it prudent to be absent from Madinah for a long duration. The city would be left vulnerable to attacks by bedouins or from Khaybar. A rapid resolution was urgent.

The Prophet (ﷺ) therefore acted in a way that terrified the Quraysh and pushed them to accept the truce: he asked the Muslims to pledge to fight to the bitter end. They lined up in disciplined ranks, in a sombre atmosphere, walked toward the Prophet (ﷺ) individually, shook his hand, and pledged their allegiance. This, the Pledge of al-Riḍwān, was done in full view of the Quraysh's spies. The Quraysh understood by this that the Prophet (ﷺ) was prepared to confront them, and they agreed to negotiate a settlement. They sent Suhayl ibn 'Amr—the most diplomatic member of the three-person crisis committee—to meet the Prophet (ﷺ). When he approached the Muslim camp, the Prophet (ﷺ) knew that the Quraysh were ready for a settlement. He told his companions, "Allah has eased your affairs."

Most biographical works attribute the Pledge of al-Riḍwān to a rumour that 'Uthmān had been killed. While rumours do tend to spread under such circumstances, the Prophet (ﷺ) was always careful to corroborate any reports that he received; he did not take decisions on war and peace based on hearsay. His network of spies in Makkah provided him with up-to-date information. However, in such circumstances, people do mix different reports and rumours and confuse the facts. Since several Muslims had entered Makkah to visit their relatives, rumours of 'Uthmān's murder could easily have been verified. It is, therefore, far-fetched that this was the reason for the Pledge of al-Riḍwān.

Moreover, al-Wāqidī states that the pledge was made when Suhayl and his two companions were still in the Muslim camp, and that they had been terrified by the Muslims' zeal as they stepped up to take the pledge. Suhayl would have denied any suggestion that 'Uthmān had been killed. Another account, also widely reported, is that the Prophet (ﷺ), after the other Muslims had pledged their support, put his right hand on his left and said that he would take the pledge on 'Uthmān's behalf because 'Uthmān was tending to a matter for Allah and His Prophet (ﷺ). This clarifies that, while the pledge was being taken, the Prophet (ﷺ) knew that 'Uthmān was alive and carrying out his mission.

There are two possible reasons for 'Uthmān's delay. The first, less plausible, possibility is that the Quraysh had incarcerated him and hoped to swap him and the other ten Muslims they had captured for the forty idolaters whom the Muslims had detained. This scenario is unlikely because 'Uthmān had entered Makkah under the protection of his cousin Abān ibn Sa'īd ibn al-'Āṣ, and Qurayshi custom would not allow this protection to be violated. Another, more plausible, explanation is that 'Uthmān's delay was related to a secret mission with which he had been tasked. Historical accounts show that 'Uthmān's mandate was not limited to negotiating with the Qurayshi leaders, but that he had a secret mission that required more time. This he carried out meticulously and covertly, unseen by the Quraysh.

'Uthmān reported:

> I then visited the believers, men and women who were oppressed, and I told them: "Indeed, Allah's Messenger (ﷺ)

sends you glad tidings of the [impending] conquest. He said: 'I provide you with cover so that faith does not disappear in Makkah.'" I saw a man and woman from among them sobbing until I thought they would die from joy because of what I had said. They then asked about Allah's Messenger (ﷺ), but kept the matter concealed, which was difficult for them. They told me: "Convey our greetings of peace to Allah's Messenger. Indeed, the One who brought him to al-Ḥudaybīyyah is surely able to bring him to the centre of Makkah.[213]

Groups of Muslims were living incognito in Makkah, and 'Uthmān had been tasked with secretly communicating with them. They were not a small number, and getting the message to them required a lot of time. We will discuss later how seventy men from among these Muslims left Makkah to join a military unit established by Abū Baṣīr in the coastal region. If the number of battle-capable men who left was seventy, the number of men not capable of fighting—as well as the women, children, elderly and incapacitated—must add up to large number. It was also a well-organised community that was able to communicate with their brethren outside.

When 'Uthmān contacted them, he emphasised that Islam would be victorious in Makkah. This gave them confidence, enthused their hearts, and contributed to the psychological war with the Quraysh. He also wanted to gain first-hand knowledge of their situation and to set up procedures to strengthen communication with them, since they represented a force inside Makkah that was committed to Islam. 'Uthmān's efforts helped make the situation inside Makkah even more unstable. The Aḥābīsh were threatening force, the spirits of the Muslims in Makkah were being lifted, and the Qurayshi leadership was divided and incapacitated. The Quraysh were left with no choice but to accept the Prophet's (ﷺ) offer of a truce.

Suhayl came to the Prophet (ﷺ) with an apology. He said that the group that had attacked the Muslim camp had not acted under instruction from the Qurayshi leadership, that they were imbeciles, and that the Qurayshi leadership was not pleased with their actions. He requested

213. Al-Wāqidī, *Kitāb al-Maghāzī*, vol. 2, 601.

their release, as well as the release of the second group. In exchange, the Prophet (ﷺ) asked for the release of the Muslims who were being held in Makkah. Suhayl agreed and wrote to the Quraysh, asking them to return the Muslims. This negotiation helped cool tempers and dissipate the tensions between the two parties.

In one tent with the enemy

Negotiations between the Prophet (ﷺ) and some of his companions on one side, and the Quraysh on the other, began in earnest after the prisoner exchange. The Qurayshi delegation comprised three persons: delegation leader Suhayl, Makraz ibn Ḥafṣ, and Ḥuwayṭab ibn ʻAbd al-ʻUzza.[214] Makraz was the radical in the delegation; Ḥuwayṭab was a wise elderly man who was highly regarded by his people.

This negotiation has been recorded as one of the most unique and distinguished events experienced by the Muslims. It has been reported in detail in the primary historical sources, reflecting the emotions, deliberations, frustrations, anger, and wisdom displayed by the Prophet (ﷺ). Sitting face to face with the enemy's leaders was extremely trying for the Muslims, forcing them into a psychological space that they had not previously inhabited. They had fought against the Quraysh in many battles and expeditions, and, barely a year earlier, the Quraysh had led the largest alliance in the history of the Arabian Peninsula against them, to exterminate them. Now, just six kilometres from the Kaʻbah, the only thing that prevented them reaching it was their leader's imminent order either to conquer Makkah or to continue with their pilgrimage. After waiting in the desert for three weeks for such an order, they found themselves sitting with the Quraysh and negotiating a return to Madinah without entering Makkah, and performing their pilgrimage only in the following year. The Muslims became increasingly anguished at this turn of events.

The negotiations included painful moments that left the Muslims dejected. The Quraysh's main goal was to ensure that the Muslims did not enter Makkah that year. This was the red line that they were

214. Suhayl and Ḥuwayṭab embraced Islam later, but accounts on Makraz vary, with most suggesting that he never converted.

unwilling to compromise on. Suhayl ibn ‘Amr insisted vehemently on this, causing the Prophet’s (ﷺ) companions to erupt in anger and to shout out their denunciation of the proposal. The Prophet (ﷺ) asked them to remain calm, and the negotiations continued. He also proposed certain conditions, the most important of which was that any Arab tribe that wanted to enter Muḥammad’s covenant should be free to do so, and whoever wanted to enter the Quraysh’s covenant should also be free to do so. He also proposed that the war between the Muslims and the Quraysh be suspended for ten years. These two points were extremely strategic. The first required the Quraysh to recognise, for the first time, the legitimacy of the Islamic entity. It was similar to an official recognition of the independence of the Islamic state and its ability to grant something akin to a “right of citizenship” to whomever it might desire. The Prophet (ﷺ) knew that his alliances with many tribes were insincere, since they also had interests that tied them to the Quraysh. But his proposal required the Quraysh to acknowledge that the declaration of such alliances would be legitimate, and that no one would need fear the Quraysh if they announced that they had entered an alliance with Muḥammad (ﷺ).

The second point would (temporarily) end the state of war between the Muslims and the Quraysh, allowing Islam to spread unencumbered. The message would be able to reach every corner of the Arabian Peninsula if people were protected from war, retribution, and conflict. Additionally, by neutralising the Quraysh, the Prophet (ﷺ) would dismantle the final obstacle to comprehensive peace, as well as economic and strategic security for the Islamic state. He would be free to deal with the remaining challenges in Khaybar, the northern parts of the peninsula, and with the Najd bedouins. When the Prophet (ﷺ) proposed the provision about the right of each party to build its own alliances, the Qurayshi delegation was afraid that this would mean that the people of Makkah could join the Prophet’s (ﷺ) alliance if they wished. The Qurayshi negotiators were also concerned that some of the Muslims who the Quraysh were incarcerating might escape to Madinah and seek refuge there.

They therefore stipulated that anyone from Makkah who fled to Muḥammad (ﷺ) must be sent back to the Quraysh and could not be accorded protection or residency in Madinah. However, the Quraysh would not be required to send back any person from the Muslim side who went to Makkah. Again, the companions felt that they were being deceived; they were infuriated and shouted out their protests. They believed that they were in the right and their enemies in the wrong. How, then, could they hand over to Allah's enemies the brothers and sisters who might seek refuge with them? These people would be abandoned, and their faith would be tested to the utmost.

Again, the Prophet (ﷺ) asked them to be calm, and he accepted the Quraysh's stipulation. Negotiations continued until every detail was settled. All that remained was for the agreement to be set down in writing, and for witnesses to attest to it. However, 'Umar ibn al-Khaṭṭāb could not contain himself. Overwhelmed by his emotions, he tried to prevent the agreement from being signed. He asked the Prophet (ﷺ): "Are you not truly Allah's Prophet?" "Are we not Muslims?" "Are they not idolaters?" To each question, the Prophet (ﷺ) responded affirmatively. 'Umar said: "So why do we give such little consideration to our religion?" The Prophet (ﷺ) responded: "I am Allah's servant and messenger. He will not let me stray." 'Umar persisted with his troubling questions. He then addressed Abū Bakr, who asked him to respect the Prophet's (ﷺ) decision. 'Umar was not the only one who was upset; most Muslims felt the same. 'Umar, however, was open about his feelings. Later, when relating the events of al-Ḥudaybīyyah, he said that he had never been overcome by doubt since accepting Islam except on that day.

Tribulations of the reconciliation

As they were preparing to write down the agreement, a Muslim man burst into the meeting. He had been held captive in Makkah, had escaped, and had fled to the Muslim camp. Abū Jandal, son of Suhayl ibn 'Amr, the head of the Qurayshi delegation, had escaped from his prison and, dragging his chains behind him, sought the protection of his Muslim brethren. His father immediately pounced on him and beat him in front of the Muslims. He told the Prophet (ﷺ): "We agreed that you will return whoever comes to you from Makkah; let's start with this one.

Return him to us!" The Prophet (ﷺ) responded that the document had not yet been written, but Suhayl retorted: "The agreement was already settled, and, by Allah, there will be no document drawn up between us if you do not return him." The Prophet (ﷺ) tried to dissuade Suhayl, but he refused, leaving the Messenger (ﷺ) with no choice but to acquiesce. Abū Jandal said: "O Muslims, am I being returned to the idolaters so that they may test my faith?" The Muslims were enraged and wept in response to Abū Jandal's plea. 'Umar again raised his voice, and demanded: "Are we not in the right? Are they not in the wrong? So why do we give such little consideration to our religion?"

Responding to the uproar from the Muslims, the Prophet (ﷺ) again asked Suhayl to release Abū Jandal; Suhayl again refused. Makraz ibn Ḥafṣ and Ḥuwayṭab then intervened. They offered Abū Jandal their protection, thereby ensuring that he would not be returned to his father's prison when they returned to Makkah. Allah's Messenger (ﷺ) then raised his voice and said: "O Abū Jandal, be patient and trust in Allah. Indeed, Allah will provide you and those with you relief and a way out. We have contracted an agreement with these people, and we have given each other promises. We do not renege on our promises."[215]

'Umar was not satisfied, and he walked beside Abū Jandal as his father led him away. He whispered:

> Be patient, Abū Jandal. They are but idolaters and the blood of one of them is [no more than] the blood of a dog. He is but a man and you are a man, and you have a sword. Verily a man may kill his father in Allah's path and, by Allah, if we were to encounter our fathers, we would kill them in Allah's path. Verily, it is a man for a man.[216]

'Umar continued inciting him to kill his father, but Abū Jandal refused, responding that he would be faithful to the command of Allah's Messenger (ﷺ). 'Umar returned to the Prophet (ﷺ) with a few others and asked him: "O Messenger of Allah, did you not tell us that you would enter the Sacred Mosque, take the Ka'bah's key, and stand on [the plain] of 'Arafah with the pilgrims? But neither our sacrificial

215. Ibn Hishām, *al-Sīrah*, vol. 2, 318.
216. Ibn Hishām, *al-Sīrah*, vol. 2, 318.

animals nor we have reached the Sacred House." Allah's Messenger (ﷺ) responded: "Did I say it would happen on this trip?" 'Umar replied: "No." Allah's Messenger (ﷺ) said: "You will surely enter it, and I will take the Ka'bah's key, and shave my head and your heads in the centre of Makkah. And I will stand on 'Arafah with the pilgrims!"[217]

A remarkable aspect about the Abū Jandal incident is that his brother, 'Abdallah ibn Suhayl, was also present at al-Ḥudaybīyyah in the Muslim camp. He had been one of the earliest converts to Islam and had migrated to Abyssinia. On his return to Makkah, Suhayl ibn 'Amr had incarcerated him. He went to Badr with his father, switched over to the Muslim side, and returned with the Muslims to Madinah. At al-Ḥudaybīyyah, he was a signatory to the agreement. This sent a poignant message to Suhayl ibn 'Amr. Even though he took back one of his sons, he should remember that he had attempted this previously with 'Abdallah, who was safely back with the Muslims. The day would come when Abū Jandal, like his brother 'Abdallah, would flee from Makkah. Ironically, less than two years later, Suhayl ibn 'Amr sought his son 'Abdallah's intercession on the day of the conquest of Makkah. He asked 'Abdallah to obtain the Prophet's (ﷺ) protection for him, which the Prophet (ﷺ) granted.

When the turmoil surrounding the Abū Jandal incident settled, the two parties began to draft the text of the agreement. The Prophet (ﷺ) dictated to 'Alī ibn Abī Ṭālib: "Write: 'In the Name of Allah, the Merciful, the Bestower of Grace'." Suhayl interjected: "We do not know 'the Merciful, the Bestower of Grace'. Write what we say: 'In Your Name, O Allah.'" The Prophet (ﷺ) agreed. 'Alī was about to continue writing, but 'Umar and others grabbed his hand and stopped him. Protests erupted, and the debate again became heated. However, the Prophet (ﷺ) signalled to 'Alī to write, "In Your Name O Allah". The Prophet (ﷺ) then continued dictating: "This is what was agreed upon by Muḥammad, Allah's messenger, and Suhayl ibn 'Amr." Suhayl again objected: "If I were to bear witness that you were Allah's messenger, I would not have fought you. Write your name and your father's name." Tempers flared again, but the Prophet (ﷺ) said: "I am indeed Muḥammad, the son of 'Abdallah." 'Alī then recorded it as such. The text was then drafted.

217. Al-Wāqidī, *Kitāb al-Maghāzī*, vol. 2, 609.

> In Your Name, O Allah. This is what was agreed upon by Muḥammad ibn ʻAbdallah and Suhayl ibn ʻAmr. They agreed to suspend the war for ten years. During this time, people will be safe, and the parties will restrain themselves from each other. There will be no cheating and treachery, and we will desist from attacking each other. Whoever wishes to enter Muḥammad's protection and covenant may do so, and whoever wishes to enter the Quraysh's protection and covenant may do so. Whoever comes to Muḥammad without the permission of his guardian will be returned to his guardian, and whichever of Muḥammad's companions comes to the Quraysh will not be returned. Muḥammad and his companions will turn away this year, and will, with his companions, return the next year. [When they return next year,] they will stay for three days. He will not enter [Makkah] bearing any weapons except the weapons of a traveller: swords and sheaths. Witnessed by Abū Bakr ibn Abī Quḥāfah, ʻUmar ibn al-Khaṭṭāb, ʻAbd al-Raḥmān ibn ʻAwf, Saʻd ibn Abī Waqqāṣ, ʻUthmān ibn ʻAffān, Abū ʻUbaydah ibn al-Jarrāḥ, Muḥammad ibn Maslamah, Ḥuwayṭab ibn ʻAbd al-ʻUzza and Makraz ibn Ḥafṣ ibn al-Akyaf.[218]

When they were done writing, Allah's Messenger (ﷺ) took the original document and Suhayl took a copy. Members of the Khuzāʻah tribe who were present immediately announced their entry into the Prophet's (ﷺ) protection. In response, those from the Banī Bakr who were present declared their entry into the protection of the Quraysh. The Banī Bakr and the Banī Khuzāʻah had long been enemies, had displayed extreme hostility to each other, and had been trapped in an unending cycle of retribution killings. Their allying with the opposing parties that had signed the agreement would not end their conflict.

Immediately, the Khuzāʻah announced that they had joined the Prophet's (ﷺ) alliance, and before the Banī Bakr responded, Ḥuwayṭab ibn ʻAbd al-ʻUzza whispered to Suhayl: "Your maternal uncles have become our enemies." He was referring to the fact that Suhayl's mother was from the Khuzāʻah. Suhayl responded: "They are just like everyone else, those of our relatives and flesh and blood who have entered

218. See Ibn Hishām, *al-Sīrah*, and al-Wāqidī, *Kitāb al-Maghāzī*, for full details.

[an alliance] with Muḥammad. These people have chosen a path for themselves. What should we do about it?" Ḥuwayṭab responded: "We should seek the aid of our allies, the Banī Bakr, against them." Suhayl said: "Be careful that the Banī Bakr do not hear this from you. They are a cursed people and may pounce on the Khuzā'ah. Muḥammad will then be angered by his allies and break the covenant between us and him." Ḥuwayṭab responded: "By Allah, you have supported your uncles on every issue." Suhayl said: "Do you think that my uncles are more honoured to me than the Banī Bakr? By Allah, whatever the Quraysh do, the Banī Bakr will do. And if the Quraysh assist the Banī Bakr against the Khuzā'ah, then I am but a man from the Quraysh, and the Banī Bakr are closer to me in terms of our lineage, even if those [the Khuzā'ah] are maternally linked. And from the Banī Bakr, those you know, we have positions that are not all good, like the day of 'Ukāẓ."[219]

The manifest victory in the reconciliation

When the two delegations had completed their task and the gathering had dispersed, the Muslim camp was overcome by extreme melancholy. The incident with Abū Jandal had been terribly painful. Furthermore, their profound hope and desire to perform the pilgrimage had been dashed. When the Prophet (ﷺ) ordered his companions to slaughter their sacrificial animals and shave their heads to terminate the state of consecration of the pilgrim (iḥrām), no one complied. Frustrated, he complained to his wife Umm Salamah. She suggested that he go out himself to slaughter his sacrificial animals and shave his head. If the people saw him doing so, she counselled, they would follow. The Prophet (ﷺ) took her advice, and the people followed his actions.

The herald announced their departure, and the procession began its return to Madinah. On their way, Allah revealed verses that affirmed the Prophet's (ﷺ) wisdom in concluding an agreement with the Quraysh. The Qur'ānic surah entitled "The Victory" was revealed. The Prophet's (ﷺ) face lit up as he recited it.

Indeed, We have granted you a manifest victory, so that Allah

219. Al-Wāqidī, Kitāb *al-Maghāzī*, vol. 2, 612.

may forgive you for your past and future sins, complete His favour upon you, and guide you to a straight path. And that Allah may help you with powerful help (Qur'ān 48:1-3).

'Umar asked, "Is this really a victory, O Messenger of Allah?" The Prophet (ﷺ) replied, "Did I not tell you so, O 'Umar?"

Since the Qur'ān refers to the Treaty of al-Ḥudaybīyyah as a "manifest victory", there can be no argument or doubt that it was indeed a manifest victory. Nowhere in the Qur'ān is the descriptor "manifest" used for any victory except in the context of al-Ḥudaybīyyah. It was a victory that had been attained without spilling blood or fighting, and its effects were to be far more comprehensive than any military victory. The Muslims were not accustomed to such a victory. Allah had previously granted them victories in battles and expeditions, but a victory attained through reconciliation was novel. They were obliged to view their affairs from a new perspective. The Prophet (ﷺ) who led them was not only a military leader, nor only a strategist, nor just a politician, but was a person who engaged in leadership, strategy, and politics with the utmost dedication to the task delegated to him from the heavens. Allah says about him: "Indeed, We have sent you [O Muḥammad] as a witness, as a deliverer of good news, and as a warner, so that you [people] may believe in Allah and His Messenger, support and honour him [the Messenger], and glorify Him [Allah] in the morning and evening" (Qur'ān 48:8-9). The focus was the message, with all its implications and consequences, and the message was conveyed using a methodology that differed from the norm in terms of relations between people and their enemies. Extermination, revenge, and retribution were unimportant. Anything that helped spread the message was a victory, and if the task of spreading the message was achieved without shedding blood or fighting, it was a manifest victory.

Some Muslims, including 'Umar ibn al-Khaṭṭāb, regretted their earlier doubts concerning the treaty, but Allah pardoned them and expressed His pleasure with them, so that they too could be pleased and receive glad tidings. "Indeed Allah was pleased with the Believers when they swore allegiance to you under the Tree. He knew what was in their hearts. And He sent tranquillity down to them, and He rewarded them with a speedy victory" (Qur'ān 48:18). The Qur'ān also focused their attention on the benefits that had accrued and would accrue to them because of the treaty.

> Allah has promised you many future gains, and He has hastened this gain for you. He has restrained the hands of people from you, as a sign for the believers, and so that He may guide you to a straight path. There are also other [future] gains over which you have no power, but which Allah has already decreed. And Allah has power over all things (Qur'ān 48:20-21).

Al-Ḥudaybīyyah, thus, was a "manifest victory" because it was the first of numerous achievements and victories, the most important of which were the many gains that the Muslims were to acquire soon thereafter. These would include the victory at Khaybar, the conquest of Makkah, and, thereafter, the forays beyond the Arabian Peninsula. It was important that none of the Muslims should feel that the treaty was accepted from a position of weakness. Allah therefore confirms in Surah Al-Fath that the Muslims had been capable of defeating the Quraysh had fighting broken out. "If the disbelievers had fought you, they would have taken flight, and they would have found neither a protector nor a helper" (Qur'ān 48:22). However, Allah's will was that Makkah should be conquered without fighting; it should be an honourable conquest in which the Quraysh were respected, and Muslim achievements were crowned by an atmosphere of forgiveness for which the nation could forever be proud.

Al-Ḥudaybīyyah and consultation

Regarding the Treaty of al-Ḥudaybīyyah, it is important to address an issue that might raise many questions: the role of consultation in public affairs. The Prophet's (ﷺ) habit was to consult his companions on important matters that affected society, such as those relating to war and peace. He usually accepted the outcomes of these consultations even if they were contrary to his opinion, as was the case with the Battle of Uḥud. However, at a superficial reading, this principle seemingly did not apply in al-Ḥudaybīyyah. Biographers of the Prophet (ﷺ)

repeatedly refer to companions such as ‘Umar ibn al-Khaṭṭāb and Sa‘d ibn ‘Ubādah as rejecters of the agreement. Furthermore, in the works of sīrah, it appears that most companions supported ‘Umar’s view. This apparent contradiction requires further interrogation.

The first observation is that, in the case of al-Ḥudaybīyyah, a Muslim consultative council had first been convened at ‘Usfān when the Muslims had heard that Khālid ibn al-Walīd was marching toward them. The Prophet (ﷺ) had consulted the Muslims about whether they should fight Khālid’s detachment or continue to Makkah. The majority opinion was to proceed on the pilgrimage and to fight only if attacked. This decision represented a strategic approach that would determine events until the end of this episode. The ‘Usfān consultation was not limited to the question of Khālid’s detachment; it was also an agreement on the very nature of this unique journey. Most companions understood that the journey to al-Ḥudaybīyyah was not a military expedition. Hence their support for the decision to continue without resorting to military action, except defensively. If this first consultation deemed military action to be unlikely and unnecessary, then the leader had been mandated to follow this strategic approach in deciding on the most appropriate way of engaging the enemy. The Prophet (ﷺ) chose to negotiate when the Quraysh were agreeable.

The second important observation is that most of the Muslims supported the Prophet’s (ﷺ) decision to proceed with the reconciliation treaty at al-Ḥudaybīyyah. The gathering there comprised of over 1,400 Muslims, including senior persons from the Muhājirūn and the Anṣār. Among them was Abū Bakr, ‘Alī, ‘Uthmān, Sa‘d ibn Abī Waqqāṣ, Ṭalḥah ibn ‘Ubaydallah, al-Zubayr ibn al-‘Awwām, ‘Abd al-Raḥmān ibn ‘Awf, al-Mughīrah ibn Shu‘bah, Jābir ibn ‘Abdallah, Zayd ibn Ḥārithah, and ‘Abdallah ibn Rawāḥah. ‘Umar and a few like-minded companions were not opposed to the principle of negotiation or the legitimacy of the agreement; their opposition was to the manner in which the Abū Jandal incident was handled and the fact that they had to return without performing the pilgrimage. These two matters greatly affected the companions, with some becoming emotional and openly expressing their anger. There is, however, no written record to suggest that most companions rejected the principle of entering an agreement, except for their hesitance to terminate their state of consecration.

This hesitance should be understood within its emotional context. This was a group of Muslims camped for weeks within the boundaries of the Sanctuary, close to the Ancient House, adorned in pilgrims' garments, and overcome with the fervour to enter the Sacred House and perform the holy rituals. After weeks of waiting, this zeal was dampened by their being told to return home and to postpone their pilgrimage for a year. This overwhelmed the Muslims with a profound despondency. It shocked them, and they clung to the hope that this matter would be revisited. However, they quickly proceeded to end their state of consecration when they saw the Prophet (ﷺ) shaving his head. His act confirmed the finality of the decision, and all the Muslims listened and obeyed.

The third point to remember is that most Muslims had granted the Prophet (ﷺ) an open mandate at al-Ḥudaybīyyah through the Pledge of al-Riḍwān. While it was a pledge to go to war, it was also a pledge of allegiance to the Prophet (ﷺ).

> The Prophet (ﷺ) requested that each person take their pledge according to whatever intention they held in their hearts. The first person to take the pledge was Abū Sinān al-Asadī. He said: "O Messenger of Allah, extend your hand so that I may take my pledge to you." The Prophet (ﷺ) asked: "What for?" Abū Sinān replied: "For whatever you desire." The Prophet (ﷺ) asked: "And what do I desire?" Abū Sinān replied: "Victory or martyrdom," and he pledged his allegiance. The people then came forward, and each one said: "We give you our pledge, which is the same as Abū Sinān's pledge."[220]

If they had all pledged to abide by whatever accorded with the Prophet's (ﷺ) desire, it meant that they had given him an open mandate. If we narrow the mandate to "victory or martyrdom", that formulation also includes the possibility of a treaty. The victory was not necessarily a military triumph, as the companions would learn not long after the agreement had been concluded. The Qur'ānic revelations

220. Al-Wāqidī, *Kitāb al-Maghāzī*, vol. 2, 603.

described al-Ḥudaybīyyah as a "manifest victory". The Pledge of al-Riḍwān thus encompassed every action that the Prophet (ﷺ) might deem appropriate in his dealings with the Quraysh, whether to go to war or to make peace.

Furthermore, despite the Muslims' understanding and aspiration that they were journeying to umrah, the general atmosphere was one of being on the edge of war. This expectation was strengthened the moment they were prevented from entering Makkah. But even before that, the fact that warriors were part of the procession, protecting the group, gave a sense that there was a possibility of war. In such circumstances, none of the Muslims would have expected that they would be consulted on every decision that the Prophet (ﷺ), as political leader and commander-in-chief, would make. Soldiers or officers who demand consultation on the battlefield would generally be regarded as being in breach of military discipline and of disregarding the command structure. Even if war was ultimately averted, al-Ḥudaybīyyah was a potential battlefield where a battle could easily and quickly have broken out.

The fourth noteworthy point is that, from the outset, the Prophet (ﷺ) had been clear in all his deliberations and statements that he was willing to accept any plan in which the Quraysh respected the sanctity of the Sanctuary, and that he had not come to Makkah to wage war. It should also be remembered that it was he who suggested a truce. His messages to the Quraysh about this were very clear, and all the Muslims in his delegation were privy to these correspondences. There is no record of any companion opposing this strategy. The opposition that later arose was not against the principle of a treaty, but about the details and form. 'Umar was incensed by the treatment of Abū Jandal, and by the deferment of the pilgrimage. These emotional and knee-jerk reactions had to be contained by the leader, and they had no impact on the strategic decision. 'Umar's objections cannot be construed as disobedience to the Prophet (ﷺ), nor were they a rejection of his leadership. This is proven by 'Umar's interaction with Abū Jandal when he suggested that he kill Suhayl. Abū Jandal asked, "Why don't you kill him?" And 'Umar responded, "Because the Prophet has prohibited us from doing so." Clearly, 'Umar deferred to and obeyed the Prophet (ﷺ) and his wishes, even at that very difficult and emotional moment.

The fifth important observation is that 'Umar ibn al-Khaṭṭāb and 'Alī ibn Abī Ṭālib were both among those who witnessed the signing of the treaty. Other witnesses included Abū Bakr and 'Uthmān, proving that all the senior companions had witnessed and approved it, despite any personal misgivings. This strengthens the conclusion that the objections were to certain details and processes related to the negotiations, and not to the agreement itself. This is understandable within the context of negotiations between two enemies who were meeting for talks for the first time. In such circumstances, there are bound to be moments when emotions would run high, dialogue would break down, and, even, the meeting might break up. Usually, after differences are resolved, delegates return to the negotiating table and continue the dialogue. The events at al-Ḥudaybīyyah were not different from this general pattern.

It is also necessary to reflect on the Prophet's (ﷺ) patience and tolerance, and the ability of his companions to express their opinions openly and freely without being influenced by fear or awe of him. Islam had liberated that generation from dependence on blind following and imbued it with the kind of motivation and confidence that would lead it to build a healthy and optimistic society that was committed to its mission. The victory of al-Ḥudaybīyyah was the beginning of the end of the faction of the Disbelieving Quraysh; it also signalled the imminent expansion of the Islamic state. After the Muslims had contained the Quraysh through a treaty, they needed to turn their attention to another pressing task: the conquest of Khaybar.

CHAPTER SIXTEEN

Khaybar – The last citadel

"Muḥammad is invading us? No way! No way!"

Khaybar was one of the richest and most fortified settlements in the Arabian Peninsula. Located in a rugged mountainous region surrounded by volcanic rocks, it was a fertile oasis with abundant water, verdant gardens, large date palm orchards, and fields of wheat and barley. Khaybar was situated on the trade route to the Levant and was used as the urban base of several tribes, including the Ghaṭafān, Asad, and Ṭayyī'. These were powerful and formidable tribes that were steeped in their bedouin ways. They depended on Khaybar for their livelihoods and frequented the town for trade and for their basic supplies. The conquest of Khaybar would have a direct impact on them since they would remain dependent on it, even if it fell under Muslim rule.

The town's Jewish inhabitants lived in several citadels, some of which were fortified due to their location high in the mountains. Khaybar comprised three villages, with eleven fortified citadels. Some citadels had wells and food silos that could sustain their inhabitants for lengthy periods. Some had underground tunnels and canals that allowed their inhabitants to exit the town in secret. Khaybar was described by the Quraysh and the Arab tribes as "the impregnable rural village of the Ḥijāz, well-supplied with people and weapons".

Al-Wāqidī's description suggests that Khaybar's inhabitants, the Quraysh, and many Arab tribes were sceptical of the Muslims' ability to conquer the town.

> The Jews of Khaybar did not think that Allah's Messenger (ﷺ) would invade it because of its impregnability, citadels, weapons, and numbers. Some 10,000 warriors went out each day, lined up, and chanted: "Muḥammad is invading us? No way! No way!" When the Prophet (ﷺ) was setting out for

> Khaybar, the Jews of Madinah advised: "By Allah, Khaybar is much stronger than you! If you were to see Khaybar, its citadels and its men, you would return before reaching your destination. [They have] fortified citadels high up in the mountains, with water always in abundance. Verily, in Khaybar there are 1,000 armoured warriors. The Asad and Ghaṭafān tribes cannot be stopped by any Arabs except them. And you [think] that you can withstand Khaybar?" They said such things to the Prophet's (ﷺ) companions, who responded: "Allah has promised His prophet that he would take them as booty."[221]

Although these were the discouraging words of the Madinah Jews, the Jews of Khaybar were deeply afraid. The story of a bedouin spy from the Ashja' tribe illustrates this fear. Spying for Khaybar, he had been captured and was brought before the Prophet (ﷺ). He told the Prophet (ﷺ):

> The people [of Khaybar] are terrified of you, overcome with fear and horror because of what you did to the Jews of Yathrib. The Jews of Yathrib had sent one of my cousins who they had found in Madinah. He had come there with goods he wanted to sell. They sent him to [Banī al-Naḍīr leader] Kinānah ibn Abū al-Ḥuqayq to inform him of your small number and your few horses and weapons. They told Kinānah: "Give [the Muslims] a true beating and they will flee from you. You will not be encountering a people who are good fighters. The Quraysh and the Arabs are pleased with his march on you, because they know about your many supplies, large number of weapons, and strong fortresses. The Quraysh and others with the same interests want Muḥammad. The Quraysh say, 'Khaybar will be victorious.' Others say, 'Muḥammad will be victorious.' If Muḥammad succeeds, it will be an eternal shame."[222]

The Prophet (ﷺ) marched to Khaybar with an army that included most of the people who had been with him at al-Ḥudaybīyyah. He left Madinah on Thursday, 11 Muḥarram 7 AH / 21 April 628, less than two

221. Al-Wāqidī, *Kitāb al-Maghāzī*, vol. 2, 637.
222. Al-Wāqidī, *Kitāb al-Maghāzī*, vol. 2, 641.

months after his return from al-Ḥudaybīyyah.[223]

Khaybar is 160 kilometres from Madinah, a distance that infantry could traverse in five days. The Jews of Khaybar knew that they would be the Prophet's (ﷺ) next target; they had long been a key centre for Muslim opposition forces, especially the Banī al-Naḍīr and some of the Banī Qaynuqā'. Furthermore, the Banī al-Naḍīr had played a critical role in building the confederate alliance. Khaybar was also the urban centre to which the Ghaṭafān, the other major partner in the tripartite assault at the Battle of the Trench, was linked.

Even before the Treaty of al-Ḥudaybīyyah, the Prophet's (ﷺ) forces had attempted to isolate Khaybar from its allies in Fadak, Taymā', Wādī al-Qura, and Dūmat al-Jandal. Two of their leaders had also been assassinated by Muslim units. That had foiled Salām ibn Mishkam's plan for a military alliance with the Jewish centres in Fadak, Taymā', and Wādī al-Qura, and to attack Madinah, which was his advice after the Battle of the Trench. They remained in their citadels, taking comfort in the strength and impregnability of their fortifications, until news reached them of the Prophet's (ﷺ) march on their town.

Their confidence in the bedouin Arabs had been shaken, especially after the Ghaṭafān had withdrawn from the Battle of the Trench. Nevertheless, they realised the need to seek the help of Ghaṭafān leader 'Uyaynah ibn Ḥuṣn. Having received the promise of half a year's harvest of Khaybar dates, he sent 4,000 fighters to the town. Historians estimate that 10,000 warriors had gathered at Khaybar, but this large number is likely exaggerated. It is unlikely that the number of Jewish warriors exceeded 3,000, which is still a large number. The number of Muslims at al-Ḥudaybīyyah was around 1,500. Khaybar's citadels made a conquest of the town difficult. However, the Muslim cavalry numbers had gradually increased to between 200 and 300 horses, which was a significant boost. The Muslims had spent part of the Banī Qurayẓah booty on horses that they had purchased from Najd, and the Prophet (ﷺ) had encouraged his companions to improve their equestrian skills. To encourage the procurement and use of horses in battle, he had also announced that every horseman would receive two extra shares of

223. The Prophet (ﷺ) returned from al-Ḥudaybīyyah on 6 Dhi'l Ḥijjah 6AH, which aligns with the period between 13 March and 10 April 628.

battle spoils—one for the warrior and two for the horse.

The Muslim strategy was to besiege the main citadels of the town and to prevent communication between them. The main military effort would be focused on one citadel at a time; once it was conquered, the focus would shift to the next one. The Prophet (ﷺ) also deployed a cavalry unit outside the fortress where the Ghaṭafān army was stationed. One night, a shout was heard outside the Ghaṭafān fortress, "O people of the Ghaṭafān, your families, your families. Help! Help!" Panic and confusion ensued in the Ghaṭafān ranks. Believing that the Muslims were raiding their dwellings in the desert, the Ghaṭafān abandoned their posts in the fortress and returned to their families, where they found that their homes were safe. When the Jews heard about the Ghaṭafān desertion, their spirits sank. Bewildered, their leader Kinānah ibn Abī al-Ḥuqayq said: "We were wrong about those bedouins. We marched with them, and they promised us victory, but they deceived us. By my life, had they not promised us their help, we would not have engaged Muḥammad in war."[224]

The Muslim siege began in the al-Naṭāh area because its citadels were located on high ground and their arrows harmed the Muslim warriors. The siege continued for a week. When the citadel was conquered, the offensive moved to other citadels. With each falling citadel, the Muslim zeal increased, while the commitment of the Jews weakened. In one citadel, the Muslims found useful siege weapons: a catapult and two armoured carriages. The catapult was used to hurl projectiles over the citadel walls. The wooden carriages were covered with animal hides under which fighters took cover from arrows and stones as they drew closer to the walls. This protected them as they attempted either to breach the walls or to burn the doors. The acquisition of these weapons made it easier to assault the remaining citadels.

Some citadels surrendered only after the Muslims blocked the water canals that supplied them. Some had secret tunnels that were used for exit and entry to compromise the siege. The Muslims gained substantial useful intelligence during the expedition. Important information was collected on enemy movements, the numbers of fighters, and the places

224. Al-Wāqidī, *Kitāb al-Maghāzī*, vol. 2, 651.

where supplies and weapons were stored. This is a clear indication of how the capabilities of the Muslim army had developed, and how it was able to broaden and improve its modus operandi.

After over a month of fighting and living under siege, Kinānah ibn al-Ḥuqayq agreed to a truce. His condition was that the Jews be allowed to continue applying their vast agricultural experience by tending to their farms. However, half of their harvest would be ceded to the Muslims. The Muslims confiscated many items from Khaybar, including books and parchments. The Jews informed the Prophet (ﷺ) that the parchments were copies of the Torah, and he returned them undamaged.

Khaybar was an important military experience that helped uplift the Muslim army, which had never fought in a battle as complicated and prolonged. They gained new experience in siege warfare and learnt the value of patience and perseverance. They also learnt to use new weapons, such as catapults and armoured carriages; trained to breach citadels and climb fortress walls; developed their intelligence tradecraft; utilised subterfuge to deceive the enemy; and employed propaganda and psychological warfare.

The campaign also resulted in the Arab tribes that had allied with Khaybar—such as the Ghaṭafān, Asad, and Ṭayyī'—deciding to yield to the Prophet (ﷺ). This is highlighted in a conversation between 'Uyaynah ibn Ḥuṣn al-Fizāzī, the Ghaṭafān chief, and al-Ḥārith ibn 'Awf, another Ghaṭafān leader. Within a short period, 'Uyaynah had both lost his Jewish allies and broken his covenant with the Prophet (ﷺ). Finding himself empty-handed, he was overcome by remorse. After 'Uyaynah returned to his family, wringing his hands, al-Ḥārith ibn 'Awf asked him:

> Did I not tell you that you would end up with nothing? By Allah, Muḥammad will be victorious over whoever is between the east and the west. The Jews used to warn us of this. I heard Abū Rāfi' Salām ibn Abī al-Ḥuqayq saying: "We are jealous of Muḥammad because of the prophethood, which is now no longer with the people of Hārūn [Aaron]. He is a prophet sent

> [by Allah], but the Jews do not obey me in this matter. At his hands, we will suffer two losses, one in Yathrib and the other in Khaybar." I asked Salām: "Will he possess all the world?" He replied: "Yes, by the Torah that descended upon Mūsa [Moses], but the Jews did not want to know what I said about him."[225]

The Khaybar expedition also delivered an economic victory. Although the fortresses had been forcefully conquered, they remained under the administration of their inhabitants. For this concession, the Muslims would receive half of all their harvests. Khaybar thus became Madinah's main supplier of dates, wheat, butter, and barley. This is the reason that the Khaybar conquest is regarded as Madinah's transition from poverty to plenty; its booty granted Madinah huge fiscal liquidity. Khaybar's annual payment to Madinah was over 40,000 loads of goods, where each load was around 160 kilograms. Madinah thus gained about 5,000 tons of dates, wheat, and barley annually.[226]

After Khaybar was subdued, the Muslims turned their sights to the three centres that fell within its security domain: Fadak, Taymā', and Wādī al-Qura. Most of the inhabitants of these towns were Jews. The Prophet (ﷺ) made peace with them on condition that they ceded half of their land to the Muslims. The former systemic Jewish influence, including economic influence, over the Arabian Peninsula thus ended, and the new centre of influence was undoubtedly Madinah.

---

225. Al-Wāqidī, *Kitāb al-Maghāzī*, vol. 2, 677.
226. Muḥammad Naṣrī Al-Ṣāyigh, *al-Sīrah al-Siyāsīyah,* (Beirut: Dār al-Fārābī, 2019).

CHAPTER SEVENTEEN

The Madinah Pact

"When the Truce was concluded, the war was suspended, and people were secure, they spoke to, met, and engaged each other in speech and debate. Any person with some understanding who was told about Islam embraced it. In those two years, the number of people who embraced Islam was as many as those who had embraced it before, or more."

(Al-Zuhrī)[227]

The conquest of Khaybar initiated a new era in the strategic and economic spheres, but without a significant loss of life. The Muslims lost fifteen lives, the Jews ninety-three. For the Muslims, there were tremendous strategic and reputational gains through the conquest of Khaybar—the Arab tribes finally realised that they had no power over Muḥammad (ﷺ) and his companions. After Khaybar, many people entered Islam, and tribal delegations poured into Madinah either seeking alliances or pledging allegiance.

The new era entrenched the Madinah Pact, the complex of relations and agreements that placed Madinah at the centre of a secure trade regime. It replaced the Makkan Pact of the past. Madinah's economic and security strength, and the alliances that the Prophet (ﷺ) had forged with the Arab tribes, opened the doors of cross-border trade. Caravans travelled in peace under the protection of the central authority in Madinah. They were not accosted by any Arab tribes, nor did they encounter any obstacles on their journeys.

By contrast, Makkah was unable to re-establish its pact. While the Treaty of al-Ḥudaybīyyah gave Makkah the opportunity to re-establish its trade status, and Qurayshi caravans securely resumed their journeys to Yemen and the Levant, the suspension of trade over the previous eight years had irreparably damaged Makkah's commercial position, and it had lost a major portion of its wealth and a number of its agents.

227. Ismā'īl ibn 'Umar Ibn Kathīr, *al-Bidāyah wa al-Nihāyah* (Damascus: Dār al-Fikr, 1986), vol. 4, 170.

It had become difficult for Makkah to compete with the emergent economic centre in Madinah.

Despite these successes, the Prophet (ﷺ) continued his military and intelligence activities, entrenching the new reality and expanding its range. He dispatched ‘Umar ibn al-Khaṭṭāb at the head of a military expedition to Turbah, east of Ṭā’if, in Sha‘bān 7 AH / 628, to monitor the activities of some clans of the Hawāzīn tribe. The Hawāzīn, along with the Thaqīf tribe, were allied to the Quraysh and very hostile to the Prophet (ﷺ). Therefore, assessing their activities was essential to determining the condition of the Quraysh. The Prophet (ﷺ) then dispatched expeditions to Najd to placate some clans of the Banī Murrah, and then to Mayfa‘ah in Najd’s western regions, from where attacks against Madinah were being launched.

We will take a closer look at Makkah and examine the changing circumstances in the city. Our focus will be on three important developments that reflected the reality in the city in the aftermath of al-Ḥudaybīyyah. These are the emergence of armed resistance against the Quraysh, the Muslims’ moral conquest of Makkah during their ‘umrah, and the leadership crisis in the Quraysh.

Armed resistance

The first incident of armed resistance against Makkah is associated with the Treaty of al-Ḥudaybīyyah, specifically related to the provision about any person fleeing from one side to the other. The clause had stipulated that if anyone from Makkah fled to Madinah, Muḥammad (ﷺ) would return that person to the Quraysh, and if anyone fled to Makkah from Madinah, the Quraysh were not obligated to send the person back. This clause had caused much anger among the Muslims during the Ḥudaybīyyah negotiations. Suhayl ibn ‘Amr had also invoked it to demand the return of his son Abū Jandal, who was then shackled, in the presence of the Prophet (ﷺ) and witnessed by many of the Muslims, causing much heartache and sorrow.

After the Prophet (ﷺ) had returned to Madinah, a fugitive from the Quraysh arrived to see him. 'Utbah ibn Usayd, also known as Abū Baṣīr, was an ally of the Banī Zuhrah tribe who had embraced Islam in Makkah. After his persecution by the Quraysh, he had fled to Madinah. Shortly after he arrived in Madinah, two Qurayshi emissaries followed and visited the Prophet (ﷺ) with a letter from al-Akhnas ibn Sharīq, the Banī Zuhrah chief. Al-Akhnas demanded the implementation of the agreement and insisted Abū Baṣīr be handed over to the emissaries so that he might be returned to Makkah. The Prophet (ﷺ) had no choice but to uphold the agreement. This was extremely painful for the Muslims, just as the surrender of Abū Jandal had been, especially when Abū Baṣīr addressed the Prophet (ﷺ): "O Messenger of Allah, are you handing me over to the idolaters who tempt me away from my faith?" Allah's Messenger (ﷺ) responded: "O Abū Baṣīr, we gave those people [our word], as you are aware, and treachery does not befit our religion. Indeed, Allah will grant you and those Muslims with you relief and a way out."[228]

The Prophet's (ﷺ) allusion to Allah granting Abū Baṣīr and the downtrodden Muslims like him in Makkah "relief and a way out" indicated that their situation could change, which is precisely the message that Abū Baṣīr seized on. On the return to Makkah, he killed one of his captors. The other fled to Madinah seeking the Prophet's (ﷺ) protection, with Abū Baṣīr in hot pursuit. When he reached Madinah, the Prophet (ﷺ) saw he was carrying the dead man's sword. Abū Baṣīr told the Prophet (ﷺ): "O Messenger of Allah, you have been faithful to your word and Allah has absolved you. You handed me over to those people. I resisted with my religious conviction and refused to have my faith tested or to be toyed with." Abū Baṣīr knew that when the Prophet (ﷺ) surrendered him to the Quraysh, it was to fulfil his al-Ḥudaybīyyah obligations. Since he had been handed over, but had escaped while outside the borders of Madinah, there was no obligation on the Prophet (ﷺ) to surrender him again. However, he also realised that he was unable to remain in Madinah, because that would violate the agreement. He had to find another place to which to migrate.

The Prophet's (ﷺ) response to Abū Baṣīr was a clever hint that the man immediately understood: "Woe be unto his mother. He would have

228. Al-Wāqidī, *Kitāb al-Maghāzī*, vol. 2, 625.

incited a war if he had men with him." Abū Baṣīr left Madinah and escaped to a coastal region that was on a Qurayshi trade route known as al-'Īṣ, where he established a resistance cell.

The suppressed Muslims of Makkah heard about Abū Baṣīr's activities and about the Prophet's (ﷺ) hint. Several fugitives who had been imprisoned by the Quraysh fled and joined Abū Baṣīr. One of them was Suhayl's son Abū Jandal. The group very quickly grew to seventy individuals. They made it their mission to harass the Quraysh, attack its caravans, and loot its merchandise. This created a serious security problem for the Quraysh; its caravans could no longer travel safely to the Levant. In desperation, Qurayshi leaders wrote to the Prophet (ﷺ) and requested a nullification of the surrender clause in the Ḥudaybīyyah Treaty. Appealing to him for the sake of Allah and on the basis of family ties, they asked him to shelter Muslims who went to Madinah. The Prophet (ﷺ) then sent a message to Abū Baṣīr's group and invited them to join him in Madinah. Sadly, the letter reached Abū Baṣīr when he was on his deathbed. He was buried in al-'Īṣ. However, Abū Jandal and the others settled in Madinah in peace and tranquillity, as if the surrender clause had never existed.

This incident illustrates the vastness of the strategies that the Muslims employed and the narrowness of the Quryash's perspectives. The Prophet (ﷺ) dealt with an extremely weighty psychological burden borne by the Muslims in a way that did not violate the treaty. Much credit for this is due to men such as Abū Baṣīr, Abū Jandal, and their companions. They were able to pick up on the Prophet's (ﷺ) hint and to execute a clever strategy that caused such harm to the Quraysh that they were forced to beg the Prophet (ﷺ) to nullify the surrender clause. These individuals represented a new generation that was open-minded, quick to seize the initiative, imbued with courage, and ready to stand up against an ancient and wobbly generation that was holding tightly to old ways founded on bigotry and narrow-mindedness.

The moral conquest

A year after the signing of the Treaty of al-Ḥudaybīyyah, on

7 Dhi'l Qa'dah 7 AH / 6 February 629, the Prophet (ﷺ) set off with 1,400 companions to perform the 'umrah (lesser pilgrimage), as had been agreed in the treaty. This became known as 'umrah al-qaḍā', a compensatory pilgrimage, performed in lieu of the one that had been abandoned a year earlier. As the treaty stated, the Muslims were to enter Makkah unarmed, and to spend no more than three days there.

The procession from Madinah was characterised by reverence, dignity, and order. The pilgrims' group was preceded by 100 warriors on horseback, kitted in full armour. Someone asked the Prophet (ﷺ): "O Messenger of Allah, why do you bear weapons, even though they stipulated that we enter the city with only travellers' weapons of swords and sheaths?" He replied: "We will not allow the cavalry to enter the sacred precinct. They will remain close; in case one of their mobs attack us, we will have weapons close by." It was said: "O Messenger of Allah, are we afraid that the Quraysh might do this?" The Prophet (ﷺ) remained silent and the procession advanced.

The Prophet (ﷺ) ordered Muḥammad ibn Maslamah to march with cavalry and weapons ahead of the military procession, and to get to Marr al-Ẓahrān, where a Qurayshi guard was waiting. Muḥammad ibn Maslamah informed them that the Prophet (ﷺ) would arrive there the next day. They quickly conveyed the news to Makkah. The Quraysh were shocked and afraid that Muḥammad (ﷺ) had decided to enter Makkah with weapons. "The Quraysh were [overcome] by fear. They said: 'By Allah, we have not caused any incident, and we are abiding by our written agreement and the stipulated time period. Why is Muḥammad invading us with his companions?'"[229]

When the Prophet (ﷺ) arrived at Marr al-Ẓahrān, he ordered the armed contingent to advance to Baṭn Ya'jaj, near the boundary of the sanctuary at al-Tan'īm opposite the al-Ḥudaybīyyah site. Makraz ibn Ḥafṣ, a signatory to the Treaty of al- Ḥudaybīyyah, and a group from the Quraysh met the Prophet (ﷺ) at Baṭn Ya'jaj. They told him: "O Muḥammad! By Allah, you have never been known—either as a youth or as an adult—to be treacherous. Yet you are entering the Sanctuary with weapons against your people, even though you had assured us that

229. Al-Wāqidī, *Kitāb al-Maghāzī*, vol. 2, 734.

you would not enter except with the arms of a traveller: swords and sheaths." Allah's Messenger replied: "We will not enter, except as has been stipulated."[230] The Qurayshis were relieved.

The Prophet (ﷺ) spent his three days in Makkah preparing for the coming conquest. When he entered the city, most of the Qurayshi aristocracy had left for the mountains because they had not wanted to witness his entry. The Muslims knew that, even though the Qurayshi leaders camped in the mountains, they closely monitored the Muslims and evaluated their movements. They therefore behaved with the utmost discipline and morality. The Prophet (ﷺ) ordered them to exhibit great energy and strength during the circumambulation and the running between the hills of Safa and Marwa. This was to quell a rumour that the Quraysh had spread that the Muslims had been weakened by a fever that had spread through Madinah. The arrangement of the Muslims in rows for prayer behind the Prophet (ﷺ) and their deliberate movements and reverence during the prayer also created a dignified and sublime impression that the idolaters had not encountered before. Every year, the Ancient House had been visited for pilgrimage by huge crowds from across the peninsula, but their circumambulation and efforts were ignorant rituals, surrounded by shouting and chaos. People circumambulated in a disorderly manner, some in the nude, in a frivolous, festive atmosphere with no reverence or piety. There was a huge contrast between that familiar scene and the reverent and pure Muslim expression of faith. In their interaction with the Muslims, the Makkans were also impressed by their trustworthiness and determination to honour their word.

The Quraysh realised their own weakness and Muḥammad's strength; nevertheless, he entered Makkah at the agreed time, and left at the agreed time, with neither disturbance nor delay. In their three days in the city, the Muslims neither accosted anyone nor caused any damage to any amenities. They also maintained their camp in a clean and organised way. The Makkans were left with the impression that they had interacted with a unique generation, and that Muḥammad (ﷺ) and his companions were truthful and acted out of kindness, and thus deserved respect. Many asked themselves how they could justify

230. Al-Wāqidī, *Kitāb al-Maghāzī*, vol. 2, 734.

continuing hostility toward, or fear of, the Muslims.

On the third day, Suhayl ibn ʿAmr and Ḥuwayṭab ibn ʿAbd al-ʿUzza led a Qurayshi delegation that visited the Prophet (ﷺ).

> Suhayl said: "Your time is up. Leave us." The Prophet (ﷺ) replied: "It [brings you no harm] if you were to leave me to prepare a wedding feast in your midst and cook food." The two Quraysh leaders said: "We have no need of your food; leave us. We call on you, O Muḥammad, by Allah and by the covenant that is between us and you, to depart from our land as three days have elapsed." The aggressiveness of Suhayl and Ḥuwayṭab angered Saʿd ibn ʿUbādah. He told Suhayl, "You lie, you motherless one. This is neither your land nor your father's land. By Allah, [Muḥammad] will not depart from here except by his own will and when he desires." Wanting to end the hostile exchange, the Prophet (ﷺ) told Saʿd ibn ʿUbādah: "O Saʿd, do not offend people who have visited us in our camp." He then ordered his bondsman Rāfiʿ to announce the departure of the Muslims and to announce to them: "No Muslim will spend the night here."[231]

The difference between the tolerance of the Prophet (ﷺ)—who was strong enough to subdue the Quraysh—and the abrasiveness of the Qurayshi leaders highlighted the condition of the Quraysh; they were overwhelmed by a mixture of anger, fear, and a lack of vision. The Prophet (ﷺ) had made a generous offer when he informed them that he intended to marry Maymūnah bint al-Ḥārith and suggested that he stay an extra day to organise a wedding feast. The Quraysh would have been invited to celebrate and share food with the Muslims. However, their response was typical of the haughtiness of pre-Islamic ignorance. The Prophet (ﷺ) thus respected the agreement, and his herald made the call to depart before sunset.

The Qurayshi leadership was undoubtedly anxious about the consequences of the compensatory pilgrimage. Their hearts were still filled with hatred, and they were unable to accept the new reality.

231. Al-Wāqidī, *Kitāb al-Maghāzī*, vol. 2, 740.

However, the other inhabitants of Makkah, the general population, the bondsmen, and the Aḥābīsh had mingled with the Muslims in the three days or had watched them from a distance. They were more balanced in their appraisal of the unique experience that allowed the parties to interact in a space other than the battlefield.

The compensatory pilgrimage was a psychological propaganda initiative that allowed the people of Makkah to internalise the idea that Muḥammad (ﷺ) and his companions were strong and organised and, despite this, maintained an ethical posture and a gentle disposition. The Quraysh were already familiar with the Muslim courage and fierceness in battle, but the ʻumrah gave them the opportunity to see another side of the Muslim personality, one that was revealed only in peacetime. For the Muslims, it had been pleasing to know that their enemies, who knew them only as strong and fearsome, had discovered that they were also noble, with elevated morals. The compensatory pilgrimage therefore represented the moral conquest of Makkah before the actual conquest, which was soon to follow.

Where is the escape?

By this time, the Qurayshi leadership was caught in a crippling crisis. Its three leaders—Ṣafwān, ʻIkrimah and Suhayl—were becoming increasingly reckless and anxious. Abū Sufyān was marginalised, and the other youth leaders were mired in confusion. This milieu of uncertainty was visible in the stories of three of the most prominent Qurayshi youth leaders who embraced Islam: Khālid ibn al-Walīd, ʻAmr ibn al-ʻĀṣ, and ʻUthmān ibn Ṭalḥāh. They were, respectively, the Qurayshi military leader, the head of Qurayshi diplomacy, and the doorkeeper (ḥājib) of the Kaʻbah. All three were children of senior Qurayshi leaders and were of high status, both because of their capacity and their lineage.

Khālid ibn al-Walīd had won the Battle of Uḥud for the Quraysh. Abū Sufyān had proposed that he wear special merit bracelets that would be made for him, and that wreathes be placed on his head, as the Romans did with their heroes. His father was al-Walīd ibn al-Mughīrah, a unique personality in Makkah, and the only leader who commanded total obedience. After al-Ḥudaybīyyah, Khālid had been stricken by doubt, which intensified after the pilgrimage. He was filled with despair and believed that the Muslims could not be defeated, especially after the Treaty of al-Ḥudaybīyyah had bestowed legitimacy on them. He stared at the Muslims from the hilltops as they circumambulated the Sacred House in peace and security during their compensatory pilgrimage. He then began to question the reason for his hostility. Khālid was surrounded by Muslims in his own household. Two of his brothers had already embraced Islam; al-Walīd ibn al-Walīd had embraced Islam after Badr, and Hishām ibn al-Walīd, Khālid's younger brother, in 4 AH / 625. Most recently, the Prophet (ﷺ) had married Khālid's maternal aunt, Maymūnah bint al-Ḥārith, and had invited the Quraysh to the wedding festivities.

With the rest of the Qurayshi aristocracy, Khālid had left Makkah during the compensatory pilgrimage. However, a letter from his brother, al-Walīd ibn al-Walīd, helped shape his thoughts about Islam. Khālid eloquently relayed his experience.

> When the Quraysh reconciled [with the Prophet (ﷺ)] at al-Ḥudaybīyyah, I asked myself: "What is left? Where should I go? To the Negus? He follows Muḥammad, and his companions are protected by him. Should I go to Heraclius? I will [have to] leave my religion for Christianity or Judaism and live with non-Arabs. Or do I stay in my home with whoever is left? I was in this state when Allah's Messenger entered Makkah for the compensatory pilgrimage. I had already left and did not see him enter. My brother al-Wālid ibn al-Walīd entered Makkah with the Prophet for the compensatory pilgrimage. He had asked for me but could not find me. He wrote me a letter: "In the Name of Allah, the Beneficent, the Merciful. I haven't seen anything stranger than your dissenting opinion of Islam. Your intellect is sharp. Can anyone afford to be ignorant of something like Islam? Allah's Messenger asked me about you. 'Where is Khālid?' he asked. I said: 'Allah will bring him.' He said: '[Can] one such as him be ignorant of Islam? If he were to place his defiance and earnestness with the Muslims against the idolaters, it would

be best for him. We would promote him above others.' I ask you to catch up with that which you have lost, dear brother, for you have lost many good opportunities." When his letter reached me, I was excited to leave, and my desire to embrace Islam had increased. I was [also] happy that Allah's Messenger had asked about me.[232]

'Amr ibn al-'Āṣ, like Khālid, was also anxious and fearful. He was the son of al-'Āṣ ibn Wā'il al-Sahamī, the Banī Saham chief. He too refused to remain in Makkah in anticipation of the Prophet's (ﷺ) entry and migrated to Abyssinia, to the Negus, who was an old acquaintance. The Negus encouraged him with beautiful words about Islam, which convinced him to travel to Madinah. Along the way, he met Khālid ibn al-Walīd. They arrived in Madinah together, accompanied by a third Qurayshi, 'Uthmān ibn Ṭalhāh, who, being the doorkeeper of the Holy Sanctuary, was also symbolically important. His ancestors had inherited the custodianship of the Ka'bah, which was now in his hands. When the Prophet (ﷺ) heard of their imminent arrival, he told his companions: "Makkah has thrown you a slice of its liver."[233]

The conversions of the three men greatly influenced the youth of Makkah. They were, after all, respected icons, and the most prominent members of the Quraysh to accept Islam since the Hijrah. Their conversions prompted Makkah to begin reconciling with the idea that some of its leaders would embrace Islam. Even though the three main leaders—Suhayl, 'Ikrimah and Ṣafwān—persisted in their arrogance and continued inciting and plotting against the Muslims, the general masses of Makkah gradually accepted the idea of a transition to Islam. After the important step that Khālid, 'Amr, and 'Uthmān took, there was no barrier preventing anyone else from embracing Islam.

The three leaders accepted Islam in the month of Ṣafar 8 AH. The Prophet (ﷺ) kept his promise to them. In a mere three months, Khālid was the head of the largest army known to the Muslims, the Mu'tah army. 'Amr was appointed to lead the Dhāt al-Salāsil expedition of 500 companions, including Abū Bakr, 'Umar, and Abū 'Ubaydah. One cannot but marvel at the Prophet's (ﷺ) capacity to evaluate talent and

232. Al-Wāqidī, *Kitāb al-Maghāzī*, vol. 2, 746-747.
233. An Arabic saying referring to its most valuable and highly-regarded men.

deploy the new Muslims according to their abilities, even though they had not yet learnt much of the Qur'ān or of religious practices. This facility for careful and strategic deployment undoubtedly made it easier for many others to enter Islam. It also transformed the Muslims into a powerful driving force that was unrestricted by the hierarchies of al-Jāhilīyyah (pre-Islamic era of ignorance). Claims of seniority were no longer considerations; all were welcomed, and their efforts and abilities were to guarantee them a place in the community.

The appointments of Khālid and 'Amr to senior leadership positions greatly affected the people of Makkah. Both the general masses and their leaders were satisfied that their future would be secure if they were to enter Islam. They would have no fear of being marginalised or ignored. This is always a major consideration for leaders who fear losing status and respect if they were to switch from one camp to another.

Unlike Khālid ibn al-Walīd and 'Amr ibn al-'Āṣ, 'Uthmān ibn Ṭalhāh had to wait for his appointment. After the conquest of Makkah, the Prophet (ﷺ) handed him the keys to the Ka'bah, thus confirming his and his progeny's custodianship of it. "Take it, O Banī Ṭalhāh," the Prophet (ﷺ) said, "forever and in perpetuity. It will not be taken from you except by an oppressor."[234]

The strategic coup

A little over a year after the signing of the Treaty of al-Ḥudaybīyyah, it was still bearing fruit. The Muslims were stronger militarily and economically than at any time before; they had conquered Khaybar and subdued most of their major rivals, especially the Ghaṭafān; they had entrenched their influence over the coast; and many Arab tribes had entered their alliance, either accepting Islam or just pledging their allegiance. Madinah had become a sought-after destination for those seeking new opportunities, strong alliances, and profitable trade. In contrast, there was a dangerous leadership split among the Quraysh. Senior leaders whose opinions had been respected, such as Abū Sufyān, were marginalised, while rash youngsters had taken the lead. The

234. Narrated by al-Ṭabarānī in *al-Kabīr* and *al-Awsaṭ*.

Qurayshi leadership was losing the capacity to take creative initiatives, resorting instead to foolish adventures such as the one that contravened the treaty. The Makkan leadership lacked strategic thinking, was steeped in the ignorance of the pre-Islamic ways, and was unable to take control even of Makkah. Oppressed Muslims of Makkah were slipping out of the city and heading for the coast, and from there they struck at the Quraysh's weakest point, its trade. The Quraysh were forced to seek the intercession of the Prophet (ﷺ) to end this threat. Even youth leaders from the Quraysh were fleeing to the Prophet (ﷺ). He welcomed them with open arms and placed them at the forefront of his companions.

Al-Wāqidī succinctly captured these developments in his description of the period after al-Ḥudaybīyyah.

> The war [between the Quraysh and the Muslims] had become an obstacle between the people; dialogue had been suspended, and there was only fighting when they met. When the truce was agreed, the war ended, and people became safe from each other. Anyone who spoke about Islam and had some understanding of it entered Islam. During the truce, even the most strong-willed idolaters [those who had committed idolatry and engaged in war] entered Islam, [such as] 'Amr ibn al-'Āṣ and Khālid ibn al-Walīd. Indeed, the truce held for twenty-two months before [the Quraysh] violated the agreement. In this period, [the number of] people who entered Islam was like [the number of those] who had entered it before then, or even more. Islam spread to all the lands of the Arabs.[235]

Ibn Isḥāq has a similar reference to the period after al-Ḥudaybīyyah. He narrated the account of al-Zuhrī.

> When the truce was achieved, the war was suspended, and people were secure, they spoke to each other, met, and engaged in speech and dispute. Whoever was told about Islam and had some understanding embraced it. In those two years, the number of people who entered Islam was as many as those who had entered it before, or more.[236]

235. Al-Wāqidī, *Kitāb al-Maghāzī*, vol. 2, 624.
236. Ibn Hishām, *al-Sīrah*, vol. 2, 322.

Ibn Hishām said: "The proof of al-Zuhrī's statement was that Allah's Messenger (ﷺ) marched to al-Ḥudaybīyyah with 1,400 men, according to Jābir, but then, two years later, in the year of the Conquest of Makkah, he marched with 10,000 men."

This was a major strategic coup in which the balance of forces shifted decisively from Makkah to Madinah, or, we might say, from the Makkan Pact to the Madinan Pact. It became clear to everyone that the new had indeed been born, and that the old was withering and fading away. The new was being led by the Muslim Quraysh; the old was being defended by the idolatrous Quraysh. It would be only a matter of time before this major transformation would be crowned with the official announcement of the death of the old. The announcement would bear a name that would be chosen by the Noble Qur'ān, and that would represent the decisive moment between two eras and two worlds: "Nasrun min Allah wa fatḥun qarīb" (Help from Allah and a speedy victory) (Qur'ān 61:13).

However, the Prophet (ﷺ) still faced one more critical task before the conquest: to focus his attention on the international balance of forces and carefully consider those developments. The conquest of the Arabian Peninsula could be fully achieved only within an international context that allowed for the persistence of the Islamic project after the conquest. This is precisely the task that he addressed in the months before the conquest.

CHAPTER EIGHTEEN

Addressing the new world

"Submit and be safe, Allah will give you your reward twice over" (from the Prophet's (ﷺ) letter to Heraclius)[237]

The major strategic revolution that overwhelmed the Arabian Peninsula unfolded in twenty-two months, in the period from the signing of the Treaty of al-Ḥudaybīyyah to the conquest of Makkah, from Dhi'l Qa'dah 6 AH / March 628 to Ramaḍān 8 AH / January 630. In the same period, another strategic revolution was playing out on the world stage. The global balance of forces was set to be transformed by developments in the Byzantine-Sassanid War that had been fought for three decades. The global powers were both exhausted and had used up all their resources. The Sassanid Persians were set to suffer the most massive defeat. On 12 December 628, after the Battle of the Trench and before the Treaty of al-Ḥudaybīyyah, the Byzantine emperor, Heraclius, defeated the Persian army near Nineveh in present-day Iraq. This was the most important and most decisive battle in the war and led to the resounding collapse of the Persian empire. After his victory at Nineveh, Heraclius marched to Ctesiphon, the Persian capital. The Sassanid emperor, Khosrow II, fled. Heraclius entered his reception hall and retrieved the Holy Cross that had been stolen by the Persians during their occupation of Jerusalem in 614. On 6 January 628, Heraclius demanded Khosrow's surrender. Instead, the Persian generals deposed and imprisoned Khosrow and appointed his son Shiruya the emperor on 25 February 628, around the time that the Prophet (ﷺ) was preparing to march to al-Ḥudaybīyyah. Kavad II, as the new emperor was called, was a bloodthirsty and impetuous youth who killed all his siblings to prevent them challenging his throne. He also ordered the imprisonment and assassinations of his father and several of his generals. The authority and prestige of the Sassanid empire crumbled, and it spiralled into civil war and bitter struggles over the throne. Kavad lived for only six months after ascending the throne; he died from the

237. Ibn Kathīr, *al-Bidāyah wa al-Nihāyah,* vol. 4, 265.

plague in September 628. He was, in reality, the last Persian emperor.

After the Persian military leader surrendered in July 628, Heraclius returned to Constantinople a victor and supervised the recapture of Upper Mesopotamia and the Levant from the Persians. On 14 September 629, he went to Jerusalem to return the Holy Cross to the Church of the Holy Sepulchre. This coincided with the time when the Prophet (ﷺ) wrote letters to several kings, including Heraclius.

After al-Ḥudaybīyyah, the Prophet (ﷺ) dispatched four emissaries to four kings: the Persian king Khosrow, the Byzantine king Heraclius, the Egyptian king al-Muqawqas, and the Abyssinian king Negus. These letters are extremely important because they were the first official communications between the political entity in Madinah and the key global political entities at the time. All the letters bore the same message: an announcement of the emergence of a new political entity and an invitation to embrace Islam and follow the Prophet (ﷺ). The Prophet (ﷺ) also addressed several regional leaders who exercised local power over specific regions, most of which fell under the authority of either the Byzantine or the Persian empires.

The Prophet (ﷺ) sent an emissary to the Baḥrayni king, al-Mandhar ibn Sāway. Historically, al-Baḥrayn had encompassed the Arab Gulf region in general and had been under Persian influence. The Prophet (ﷺ) also sent an emissary to Yemen, which was also under the Persian empire, and another emissary to al-Ḥārith ibn Shummar al-Ghassānī, the governor of the al-Balqā' region, which was under Byzantine influence. After the conquest of Makkah, the Prophet (ﷺ) sent an emissary to the two kings of Oman, Jayfar and 'Abd. Oman was also under Persian influence.

These diplomatic forays indicated that the Muslim political entity headquartered in Madinah had begun considering the lands that lay beyond its familiar security domain in the Hijāz, the Najd, and its surroundings. Such a consideration is proof that the Prophet (ﷺ) believed that the immediate security domain was secure, and that it was time to think about opening wider horizons. Entrenching Madinah's trade pact required moving beyond the traditional security domain.

In addition, the Prophet (ﷺ) carried a universal message and was obligated to convey it to the leaders of the world. This was necessary for Islam to become accessible to all the subjects or citizens of these countries.

A kingdom torn apart

The Prophet's (ﷺ) letter to Khosrow deserves special attention, particularly since it reached him when the Persian empire was collapsing and slipping into civil war. The Persian king was in a bad mood when the Prophet's (ﷺ) emissary called on him. Impetuously, he tore up the letter, angered by its introduction because it mentioned the Prophet's (ﷺ) name before the king's.

It is important to reflect on exactly which king received the letter. Biographies of the Prophet (ﷺ) state that the letter was sent to "Khosrow"; the Arabs referred to all Persian kings as Kisra (Khosrow), and even had a plural for the word: Akāsira. Ibn Kathīr noted this phenomenon:

> The Arabs used to call the Byzantine ruler of the Levant and Upper Mesopotamia "Caesar", the ruler of the Persians "Khosrow", the ruler of Abyssinia "Negus", and the king of Alexandria "Muqawqas". The disbelieving ruler of Egypt was called "Pharaoh" and the ruler of India was called "Ptolemy".[238]

However, historical records show that Khosrow was a proper name, not a title. Two Persians kings bore the name. The reign of Khosrow I was ending when the Prophet (ﷺ) was born; Khosrow II was his grandson. It was Khosrow II who ascended the throne in 602 and was killed on 28 February 628 / 16 Shawwāl 6 AH by his son Kavad after the Persian defeat at Nineveh.

The Treaty of al-Ḥudaybīyyah was signed in Dhi'l Qa'dah 6 AH / March 628, at least a month after the assassination of Khosrow II. Historical sources say that the Prophet (ﷺ) sent the letter, which was carried by 'Abdallah ibn Ḥudhāfah al-Sahamī, to "Khosrow" after al-

238. Ibn Kathīr, *al-Bidāyah wa al-Nihāyah*, vol. 4, 272.

Ḥudaybīyyah. Therefore, the letter must have been received by Kavad II, not by Khosrow Parvez, who was already dead.

Kavad II died from the plague on 6 September 628, six months after al-Ḥudaybīyyah. He was succeeded by his son Ardashir III, who was only seven years old. When two emissaries of the Persian governor of Yemen, Bādhān, arrived in Madinah, on instructions from the Persian emperor to capture the Prophet (ﷺ), he referred to the death of Kavad II, saying: "My Lord has killed your Lord." In another account, it is reported that the Prophet (ﷺ) said that if Khosrow were to die, there would be no khosrow after him, and he prayed that Allah should tear up the Persian kingdom as Kavad had torn up the letter of Allah's Messenger (ﷺ). Kavad was indeed effectively the last king of the Sassanid Persians. And Allah did indeed tear up his kingdom with wars from outside and from within, leading to the Islamic conquest of the Persian domains.

The collapse of the Persian empire caused a major strategic disruption of the international order. The empire that had prevailed for more than 1,200 years had been, at its height, the largest and strongest empire in the world. Its influence over the Arabian Peninsula was far beyond that of the Byzantines, and its collapse left a huge strategic vacuum that could not be filled by the victor. The Byzantines emerged from the war exhausted. Their strategic priority was to strengthen their grip over their closest neighbours in Upper Mesopotamia: the Levant, Egypt, and Armenia. Extending their domain eastward or southward was not an option because of a depleted treasury and a battle-weary army.

The Persian empire's collapse opened wide horizons for the spread of Islam in the lands that had been under Persian influence, especially al-Baḥrayn, Oman, and Yemen. The people of all three voluntarily embraced Islam after receiving invitations from the Prophet (ﷺ). He acknowledged the rule of the kings who ruled these provinces, and they joined the Madinah Pact. Al-Baḥrayn's king, al-Mandhar ibn Sāway, had been a Christian who converted to Islam. The two kings of Oman, Jayfar and 'Abd, both of whom were the sons of al-Jalandī ibn al-Mustakbir al-Azdī, also accepted Islam, as did the Persian governor of Yemen, Bādhān. All of them continued to fulfil their governance obligations under Islam.

The collapse of the Persian empire also prompted the Arab tribes in Iraq, who were mostly Christian, to ally with Madinah. Their relations with Ctesiphon quickly deteriorated after the Battle of Dhī Qār in 609. They were occupied and severely repressed by the Persians. After the fall of the Persians, these Arabs were liberated; the new message arrived at an opportune time to fill the vacuum. For the first time ever, they were introduced to a paradigm of governance that had emerged from Arab lands, but with a global message. These Arab tribes, therefore, snatched the message and quickly reconciled with the new power. Some of them embraced Islam while others remained Christian. All of them were delighted to be rid of their humiliating dependence on the two great empires and aspired to an era in which they would be able to build their own future without injury or coercion. They would also soon provide support to the Muslim armies that burst forth to finish off the aging empire and incorporate it into the Islamic nation.

Encountering the victor

Daḥīyah ibn Khalīfah al-Kalbī[239] the Prophet's (ﷺ) messenger, handed his letter intended for Heraclius to the governor of Busra, in what is now southern Syria, who sent it to Heraclius in the month of Muḥarram 7 AH, according to the sīrah sources.

Byzantine sources contain no reference to this letter, but Islamic sources are rich in detail about the manner in which Heraclius received it. These texts claim that it met with his approval and admiration, and that he was even on the verge of accepting Islam. They blame vehement protests from his priests and advisors for his reconsidering. The most famous narration about this states that Heraclius, when he received the letter, wanted to personally verify the Prophet's (ﷺ) character. He asked his subordinates to bring him someone who could provide more information. Since this event coincided with one of Abū Sufyān's trade visits to the Levant, his delegation was taken to Heraclius in Jerusalem. The king asked Abū Sufyān about the new religion, about the Prophet

239. He was one of the Anṣār and fought at Uḥud alongside the Prophet. He was known for his good looks and died during the reign of Muā'wiyah ibn Abī Sufyān.

(ﷺ), and about his relationship with his people. Abū Sufyān's account of the meeting is interesting.

> When we finally [appeared] before [Heraclius], he asked, "Which one of you is his closest relative?" I said, "I [am]." He said, "Come closer." He sat me down in front of him and asked that my companions be seated behind me. He told them, "If he lies, refute him." I knew that if I lied, they would not refute me, but I was a leader and a benefactor and was embarrassed to lie. I also knew that, at the very least, my companions would recount [the incident] to others, and would speak about me in Makkah, so I did not lie.
>
> He said: "Tell me about this man who has emerged from among you?" I was not very forthcoming about the matter and downplayed his mission. By Allah, he did not heed what I had said. He said, "Answer the questions I ask you concerning him." I replied, "Ask me whatever you please." He asked: "What is his lineage among you?" I said: "Pure, and from our midst in terms of lineage." He asked, "Was there anyone from his household who says what he claims? Someone [who he may] be imitating?" I replied, "No." He asked: "Tell me, did he have any possessions that you may have stripped him of, and he [therefore] came with this talk so that you may return his possessions?" I replied: "No."
>
> He said: "Tell me about his followers. Who are they?" I said: "Newcomers. The weak and the impoverished. No one from among the nobility and the people of lineage." He asked: "Tell me about those who keep his company. Do they love him and show him honour, or do they detest him and disobey him?" I replied: "No person who has joined his company has disobeyed him."
>
> Then he asked: "Tell me about the war between you and him?" I said, "Give and take. We [sometimes] have the upper hand, and he [sometimes] has the upper hand." He asked: "Tell me, does he deceive people?" I replied, "No, but we have not been with

him for a while, and we cannot guarantee that he has not been deceitful since."

By Allah, the king did not take heed. He [then] repeated the conversation to me. He said: "You claimed that he was of pure lineage. When Allah appoints a prophet, He appoints a person from amongst his own people. I asked you if there was anyone from his household who was saying what he claims, and whether he might be imitating that person, and you said no. I asked you if he had possessions that you may have stripped him of, and whether he might have come with this talk so that you may return his possessions. You said no. I asked you about his followers, and you claimed that they were newcomers, the weak and the impoverished. Such have been the followers of the prophets throughout time. I asked you about those who follow him, whether they love and honour him, or whether they despise and disobey him. You claimed that rarely does anyone who follows him disobey him. Such is the sweetness of faith, that once it enters the heart, it does not leave. I asked you about the war between yourselves and him, and you claimed that he sometimes has the upper hand, and you sometimes have the upper hand. Such is the war of the prophets, but they prevail in the end. I asked you whether he is deceitful, and you claimed that he was not.

If you were honest with me, then he will conquer everything that is under these two feet of mine. I wish that I were in his presence, for I would wash his feet." He then said: "Get back to your affairs."

I stood, struck my one hand against the other, and I said: "O servants of Allah, the matter of the son of Abū Kabshah[240] has become known far and wide, and the kings of the Banī al-Aṣfar[241] now fear losing power."[242]

240. By "the son of Abū Kabshah" he meant the Prophet (SAW); Abū Kabshah was the Prophet's great grandfather on his mother's side. Scholars explain that Abū Sufyān refers to a relatively unknown figure in the Prophet's lineage as a way of belittling him [tr].

241. The expression "Banī al-Aṣfar" was used in reference to the Byzantines [tr].

242. Ibn Kathīr, *al-Bidāyah wa al-Nihāyah*, vol. 4, 263-264.

This and similar stories about the circumstances under which Heraclius received the Prophet's (ﷺ) letter are oversimplified and reductionist. They portray Heraclius as an emperor impartially searching for the truth. This is far-fetched for kings and emperors in general, but especially so for Heraclius who, at that moment, was basking in the glow of an overwhelming victory and had just conferred on himself the new title of "King of Kings", which had been the title of the Persian kings. At this stage, his highest priority was to entrench his status as the leader of the Christian world. He reportedly walked barefoot to Jerusalem, in a procession reported all over Christendom, to return the Holy Cross and to reunite Christianity. It had been torn apart by sectarian conflict and doctrinal disputes related to the nature of Christ, and by massive inter-church battles across the empire. As a statesman, Heraclius wanted to quell the destructive religious disputes that had a negative impact on the integrity of his empire. It is therefore highly unlikely that he would have considered conversion to a new religion. In fact, even his alluding to it would have created huge and unnecessary problems for him.

Such accounts contribute to an incorrect assessment of the Byzantine position and reduce it to the person of Heraclius, even though we know that the Byzantine empire did not hesitate to go to war against the Muslims. The story of Abū Sufyān's encounter with Heraclius requires further research and reflection. It is immaterial whether this encounter happened or not. What is certain is that the Byzantine empire, the protector of Christianity and heir to the Roman empire, had just emerged victorious in a brutal global war and was entirely unconcerned with the new religion. It awakened from its slumber only after the onslaught of the conquering Muslim army that liberated the Levant, Egypt, and Upper Mesopotamia. A few years later, when Constantinople finally awoke to the reality of a new player, it was too late, and it would find itself in a conflict with Muslim armies that would span centuries.

Empires are normally focused on authority and wealth; they rarely pay attention to minor entities. They manipulate such minor role-players through intimidation or ambition but do not regard them as sources of truth or legitimacy. It was for this reason that Divine Wisdom decreed that the small remote town of Makkah should be the place where revelation descended, far from the gaze of emperors and kings. If the revelation had descended in Constantinople or Ctesiphon, the balance of forces, the interests of the state, and the authority of people would have been impediments in the path of the message. Alternately, these actors would have exploited the message for their own cause and turned it into propaganda and a mechanism of control.

Allah, the Most Sublime, had decreed that the message would be issued to the world at a decisive historical moment, when the world order had been disrupted and destabilised. Hence, Islam entered a world that had been cast into a major strategic vacuum. These circumstances allowed Islam, firstly, to entrench itself in a region far from the influence of the big players, and, secondly, to be disseminated globally when the international order had begun to shatter and its global stranglehold had begun to weaken.

If we are to comprehend the amazing speed at which Islam spread, it is necessary to have a broad view of the totality of these events. International contestation, the balance of forces, and trends in strategic and economic praxis are all important considerations to properly understand Islam's emergence, in a brief period, as a massive strategic force.

Mu'tah: A new horizon

The Mu'tah Expedition may be regarded as the opening of a new strategic horizon. Before Mu'tah, the Muslims had not fought imperial forces, nor had they opened a battle front beyond the security domain of the Arabian Peninsula. The immediate impetus for the Mu'tah Expedition was the murder of the Prophet's (ﷺ) emissary by a Byzantine functionary. The Prophet (ﷺ) had sent al-Ḥārith ibn 'Umayr al-Azdī as his envoy to the governor of Busra. Al-Ḥārith was, however, intercepted and killed by Sharḥabīl al-Ghassānī, a Byzantine official responsible for the lands of al-Balqā', in what is today Jordan, in the Levant.

When news of al-Ḥārith's murder reached the Prophet (ﷺ), he resolved that such an insult deserved to be responded to with action rather than silence. In terms of an ancient custom that applied globally, emissaries were not to be harmed. Madinah had become a recognised political entity that had dispatched emissaries to kings and princes. It had thus joined the global political community and expected to be treated with the appropriate respect. If the Prophet (ﷺ) were to ignore such an insult, Madinah's prestige would be shattered, and the Arabs—including the Quraysh—would be encouraged to disrespect the Muslims and, perhaps, to break their covenants and resume their hostility.

From his myopic perspective, Sharḥabīl ibn 'Amr al-Ghassānī did not believe that this diplomatic custom should apply to Madinah, an entity undeserving of such respect. Madinah, for him, was merely a settlement of a few Arab tribes that subsisted on farming and raiding. For Madinah to have the temerity to directly address kings and princes was criminal and deserved punishment. Its envoy did not deserve immunity and its presence was irrelevant to the authority of Byzantine officials, who were generally more arrogant than their political masters.

It must be borne in mind that, by this time, the Ghassanids had been weakened, and their dominion was crumbling. Until a few weeks before al-Ḥārith's murder, the entire Levant had been under Persian authority. Although Heraclius had vanquished the Persians at the beginning of 628, Persian forces began to withdraw only after Heraclius had signed the withdrawal agreement with the Persian general Shahrbaraz at Arabissus, near Cappadocia in today's Türkiye, in July 629.[243] This was two months before the Battle of Mu'tah. When the Byzantines returned, the Ghassanids carved out a marginal, inconsequential role for themselves. Sharḥabīl was a product of this trivial phase. He was not a Ghassanid leader, but a minor official who had arrived too late on the scene to create a reputation for himself; he thus sought to affirm his presence through violence and brutality.

From July to December 629, the Levant was in a transition between two eras: one, a broken Persian occupation; and the other, a revitalised Byzantine occupation, the withdrawal of Persian forces, and the redeployment of Byzantine forces. However, the Byzantine army had become fatigued after three decades of war. Byzantine sources maintain

243. Walter E. Kaegi, *Heraclius: Emperor of Byzantium* (Cambridge: Cambridge University Press, 2003), 185.

that the army was small, and that Heraclius had used small, highly trained units that were able to move quickly. In the Battle of Nineveh, he had led a force of only 30,000 soldiers, which had enabled him to penetrate to the centre of the Persian empire in a surprise strike that had unsettled the huge and slow Persian army.

Historians maintain that, by 629, the Byzantine army—spread across North Africa, Anatolia, Constantinople, the Balkans, Armenia, Upper Mesopotamia, and the Levant—comprised between 98,000 and 130,000 soldiers. Some put the number even lower, since Heraclius had discharged many soldiers due to the empire's inability to pay their salaries, and because they had become redundant with the end of the war. The number of Byzantine soldiers in the Levant was estimated at no more than 5,000 regulars, which is why the army relied on Arab tribes to protect the fronts, especially in the desert.[244]

Extraordinary army

The Muslim army deployed for the Mu'tah Expedition was extraordinary in two respects. First, with 3,000 warriors, it was the largest army mobilised by the Muslims by that point. While the number of warriors at the Battle of the Trench is also pegged at 3,000, that battle was in Madinah and the Muslim forces included almost all the fighting men. The Mu'tah mobilisation, on the other hand, was for deployment outside Madinah. Second, the destination was the most distant target yet; Al-Balqā' was more than 1,200 kilometres from Madinah. To make such a journey, the areas that would be passed had to be relatively safe to avoid surprise attacks and losses.

Moreover, the army would deploy to the periphery of the Byzantine empire, which was a brazen step that required caution and extreme vigilance. Considering this, the Prophet (ﷺ) took the unprecedented step of appointing three leaders for the army: a primary leader and two successors, in the event of the death of the main commander. The primary leader was Zayd ibn Ḥārithah, who would be succeeded by Ja'far ibn Abī Ṭālib if he were to be killed; and if he were killed, he, in

244. Kaegi, *The Byzantine Empire*, 39.

turn, would be succeeded by ‘Abdallah ibn Rawāhah. If ‘Abdallah were killed, the soldiers were to elect a successor by consensus.

The expedition's objective was to exact retribution from Sharḥabīl ibn ‘Amr al-Ghassānī, the murderer of the Prophet's (ﷺ) emissary. In other words, it was to be a disciplinary expedition that did not intend to confront Constantinople. It also did not intend to subdue al-Balqā' or the Levant. The expedition would send a message to the Arab tribes and Byzantine officials not to underestimate or disrespect the Muslims. The expedition was granted much importance by the Prophet (ﷺ) and the Muslims, and it was eagerly monitored by various Arab tribes. Its outcome would have a major impact on the balance of forces in the Arabian Peninsula.

The army camped at Ma‘ān, about 200 kilometres from its target. There, they learnt that Constantinople, in league with the Arab tribes of Lakham, Judhaymah, and Quḍā‘ah, had mobilised a massive force to confront them. Historical sources mention extremely exaggerated figures for the Byzantine mobilisation, some suggesting the number of 100,000 Byzantines and 100,000 Arabs. These figures are incorrect; the Byzantines did not have more than 5,000 regular soldiers in the Levant, and they relied on their Arab allies to keep the bedouin raids in check. The number of Byzantine soldiers is, therefore, definitely incorrect. The number of Arab fighters was also lower. They numbered more than the Byzantine soldiers, but not as high as 100,000.

Byzantine sources say that when Constantinople retook the Levant, it did not rely on the Ghassanids in al-Balqā' as it had previously done. Instead, it used a military force led by a General Theodore. He might have been Heraclius's brother Theodore, the leader of the Byzantine army that had fought the Persians. However, he also might have been some other commander. Theodore was accompanied by Arab warriors who had been protecting the empire's southern borders. The Greek name for this force means "Desert Guard Forces".[245]

The Byzantine historian Theophanes relates that Theodore had learnt about the Muslim expedition from a Qurayshi spy, and that skirmishes broke out between Theodore's forces and the Desert Guard

245. Kaegi, *The Byzantine Empire*, 39.

Forces on the one side, and the Muslims on the other. Three of the Muslim leaders were killed, and they fled thereafter.[246] It is unlikely that Heraclius—who was busy with the task of re-occupying the lands that the Persians had evacuated—or his main army participated in the battle. The confrontation at Mu'tah likely involved a few skirmishes between the Muslims and the Desert Guard Forces that continued intermittently for three days. Thus, stories of clashes between two armies, one of 3,000 and the other of 100,000 or 200,000 soldiers are wildly exaggerated. The argument that victory is from Allah, and that Allah assists the small group over the larger one is correct, but this refers to the balance of forces and the laws of engagement defined by the Qur'ān, not specifically to the Mu'tah expedition. Allah, the Most Sublime, determined this balance to be one-to-ten at the most, and one-to-two at the least.

> O Prophet, rouse the believers to fight. If there are twenty among you who are patient and persevering, they will vanquish 200. And if there are among you 100 [who are patient and persevering], they will vanquish a thousand of the disbelievers, for they are a people who do not understand. For now, Allah has lightened your [burden], for He knows that there is weakness in you. So if there are among you a hundred [who are] patient and persevering, they will vanquish 200. And if there are among you a thousand, they will vanquish 2,000, by Allah's permission. For Allah is with those who patiently persevere (Qur'ān 8:65-66).

To escape the confusion of numbers, however, it must be clear that the Byzantine army and its Arab allies constituted a much larger force than the Muslim army. When the companions reached the Ma'ān region, they consulted among themselves for two days about whether to continue marching and to confront the enemy. After much debate, the matter was decisively resolved by 'Abdallah ibn Rawāhah, an accomplished poet with a great deal of religious passion. He said:

> By Allah! O People. That which you dislike is what you marched here for and what you seek: martyrdom! We do not

246. Kaegi, *The Byzantine Empire*, 39.

> fight the enemy with resources, or strength, or numbers. All we fight them with is this religion that Allah has honoured us with. So go forth, and you will achieve one of two good things: victory or martyrdom![247]

The army continued until it reached Mu'tah, a small settlement located on the trade route that crossed into the Levant, which was famous for the manufacture of weapons. The Muslims confronted their enemy in Mu'tah, where skirmishes took place. The Muslims' first leader, the experienced fifty-five-year-old commander Zayd ibn Ḥārithah, was martyred here. The Prophet (ﷺ) had appointed him to head several military expeditions. The flag then passed on to forty-year-old Ja'far ibn Abī Ṭālib, the Prophet's (ﷺ) cousin, who attacked the enemy and was also martyred. Ja'far had joined the Prophet (ﷺ) at Khaybar a year earlier, after returning from his seventeen-year deployment to Abyssinia. He was succeeded by 'Abdallah ibn Rawāhah, an Anṣārī from the Khazraj tribe, who the Prophet (ﷺ) had appointed as his representative at the Pledge of 'Aqabah.

Considering the rapidity by which the three leaders were killed, it seems that they had all adopted the same strategy, which was to lead the army in an offensive attack on the enemy. Death or injury was almost certain in circumstances where the opposing army was superior in armaments and numbers. If we consider that thirteen Muslims were killed at Mu'tah, with the three leaders topping the list, it is clear that they had waged an offensive campaign, a mistake that was corrected by 'Abdallah ibn Rawāhah's successor.

After 'Abdallah's martyrdom, the army was temporarily leaderless, until the soldiers elected Khālid ibn al-Walīd, the accomplished Qurayshi commander who had accepted Islam only three months earlier. The Prophet (ﷺ) had not named him as one of the army's potential leaders, but his appointment was supported by most of the warriors. While surprising, the election shows that the popular Muslim consciousness was not superficial and accorded with the Prophet's (ﷺ) inclination to always appoint the most qualified person.

---

247. Al-Wāqidī, *Kitāb al-Maghāzī*, vol. 2, 760.

When Khālid took charge, he correctly assessed that a continuation of the attack would result in more deaths. He therefore decided to retreat. However, in such an unbalanced confrontation, retreat was also dangerous. He needed to execute a smart and strategic retreat. By rearranging the positioning of the different units, Khālid tricked the enemy into believing that Muslim reinforcements had arrived. He moved the left flank to the right and the right flank to the left and ordered the soldiers to stir up clouds of dust so that the enemy would think that there was a huge military mobilisation occurring. He hoped that, as a result, the enemy would not pursue the Muslims. They then gradually retreated and returned to Madinah.

News of the battle had reached Madinah and the people emerged to confront the army. They censured the soldiers, threw sand at them, and shouted, "You deserters! You fled from the path of Allah!" The situation became so serious that some fighters from Mu'tah isolated themselves in their homes and refused to even go to the prayers, fearing the censure and anger of the people.

However, the Prophet (ﷺ), who always rushed to raise people's spirits, decisively ended the deteriorating communal psyche through several actions. He described the soldiers "not [as] those who flee, but those who turn back, if Allah wills".[248] He also conferred on Khālid ibn al-Walīd the title "Allah's Unsheathed Sword" and dispatched the Dhat al-Salāsil Expedition to raise morale and reverse the negative sentiment.

The Prophet (ﷺ) realised that Khālid's decision to retreat was wise, and that, under the circumstances that the army had faced, it was the only viable approach. It is true that deserting a battle is a major sin, but this is only if a fighter unilaterally flees the battlefield to save himself, places his personal interests over the interests of others, and weakens the ranks and betrays his companions. However, Khālid's decision as the military commander was driven by the desire to protect the lives of all fighters. Furthermore, the objective of the encounter was not to defeat Constantinople and its allies, but to send them a warning. While this may not have been fully accomplished, it was no mean feat to retreat without incurring huge losses when confronting a massive army

248. Ibn Kathīr, *al-Bidāyah wa al-Nihāyah*, vol. 4, 265.

belonging to a victorious empire.

One outcome of Mu'tah was that Khālid ibn al-Walīd was able to introduce a new strategy to the Islamic military, based on hit-and-run tactics, and relying on flexibility, rapid mobilisation, and deception. Under Khālid's leadership, the Muslims would later utilise this strategy against the Persians and the Byzantines. Khālid was never defeated in any battle thereafter. His strategy at Mu'tah deservedly earned him the highest title in the army, "Allah's Unsheathed Sword".

Mapping the final act

A prominent trait of the Prophet's (ﷺ) leadership was that he did not allow any military or political campaign to be concluded on the enemy's terms. This was clear, for example, from his deploying the army after its defeat at Uḥud, and from his march on Ḥamrā' al-Asad the day after Uḥud. That had scared the Quraysh, whose fighters had fled. He was, thus, able to return to Madinah after regaining the prestige and reputation of the Muslims. After Mu'tah, the Prophet (ﷺ) decided to deploy 'Amr ibn al-'Āṣ with a detachment of 300 warriors to punish the Arab tribes that had fought alongside the Byzantines at Mu'tah. They marched to a watering hole called al-Salāsil, which was near the homes of the Quḍā'ah tribe, which bordered the Levant. When 'Amr saw that the balance of forces did not allow him to engage, he wrote to the Prophet (ﷺ) asking for assistance. The Prophet (ﷺ) deployed 200 Muslim warriors under Abū 'Ubaydah 'Āmir ibn al-Jarrāḥ. His force included senior companions such as Abū Bakr and 'Umar. They caught up with 'Amr's detachment and fought under his leadership. This, even though he and Khālid ibn al-Walīd had accepted Islam just four months earlier.

This expedition, which became known as the Dhat al-Salāsil Expedition, succeeded in striking fear into the hearts of the Arab tribes that had been loyal to Constantinople. The Muslim army returned to Madinah victorious. They had let the tribes know that the Prophet (ﷺ) had promised to punish anyone who allied themselves with the Muslims' enemies.

Byzantine sources mention a dispute that broke out between the Arab warriors of the Desert Guard Forces and Theodore. The Arabs had demanded that Theodore pay them the same salaries as that of the Byzantine conscripts, but he had violently dismissed and humiliated them, saying: "The Emperor pays his soldiers, and he does not have anything extra to throw to the dogs."[249] This enraged the Arab fighters, who then revolted against Byzantine authority. The Desert Guard Force collapsed, opening the possibility of the conquest of the Levant. Because of this incident, many of these tribes joined the Muslim army.

The Prophet (ﷺ) thus mapped the final act at the Battle of Mu'tah and its extension, the Dhat al-Salāsil Expedition. The latter limited the negative consequences of Mu'tah and restored the Muslim confidence in the army. However, the Quraysh did not get the message. Their leaders believed that the Muslims had been weakened by Mu'tah and that their capacity to fight had been reduced. This incorrect assessment resulted in the Quraysh making foolish decisions and violating the Treaty of al-Ḥudaybīyyah. In violation of the treaty, they provided military support to their allies from the Banī Bakr tribe, which had undertaken a surprise attack on the Khuzā'ah, the Prophet's (ﷺ) main ally.

249. David Powers, *Muhammad is Not the Father of Any of Your Men: The Making of the Last Prophet* (Pennsylvania: University of Pennsylvania Press, 2009), 84.

CHAPTER NINETEEN

The Great Conquest

"When comes the help of Allah and victory" (Qur'ān 110:1).

The conquest of Makkah[250] was the key objective that drove the political and strategic praxis of the Prophet (ﷺ) from the time that he migrated to Madinah. He was fully aware that conquering Makkah would be the decisive element needed to spread Islam across the Arabian Peninsula, because of the city's unique sacred status in the hearts of Arabs. Moreover, Makkah was the home of Abrahamic monotheism and the qiblah (prayer orientation) of the Muslims. It was thus logical that it should be their strategic qiblah as well.

The Prophet's (ﷺ) strategy of engaging the Quraysh was divided into two phases. The first extended from the Hijrah to the Battle of the Trench and sought to strike at the Quraysh's pact and trade. The second began at the Battle of the Trench and ended with the Treaty of al-Ḥudaybīyyah. Its goal was to challenge the Quraysh's legitimacy as custodians of the Sacred House. The first phase was characterised by the building of strong cells for the mission in Madinah, followed by the expansion of Madinah's security domain to include the coast, joining the tribes along the Quraysh's trade routes in an alliance with Madinah. Thereafter, the tribes that were loyal to the Quraysh along the desert routes were targeted. When the Quraysh realised the danger to their trade, they militarily confronted the Prophet (ﷺ) on three occasions: Badr, Uḥud, and the Trench. However, they failed miserably in their attempts to eliminate the Islamic threat. In fact, the economic siege that targeted them worsened. The Quraysh were further weakened and lost allies that had fought alongside them during the Battle of the Trench. The Quraysh were left isolated, exhausted, unable to take any initiative, and overwhelmed by leadership disputes.

250. The Prophet (ﷺ) departed from Madinah on Monday, 6 Ramaḍān 8AH / 27 November 629. He entered Makkah on Monday, 13 Ramaḍān / 4 December.

At this crucial juncture, the Prophet's (ﷺ) strategy shifted from siege and confrontation to peace and reconciliation. Al-Ḥudaybīyyah had blindsided the Quraysh. It had been consummately planned by the Prophet (ﷺ) and had forced the Quraysh into a crisis, leaving them helpless and uncertain about how to proceed. That was when the Prophet (ﷺ) presented them with a solution: a truce in which the parties would suspend war for a decade, the Quraysh would revive their trade routes, and they would further recognise the political legitimacy of the Muslim entity. In addition, whoever desired to enter an alliance with Muḥammad (ﷺ) was free to do so, and whoever wanted to enter an alliance with the Quraysh was also free to do so. Hence, the Khuzā'ah allied with Muḥammad (ﷺ) and the Banī Bakr with the Quraysh.

The Khuzā'ah were from the Azadīyyah tribal confederation and had an ancient pedigree. They had been the custodians of the Holy Sanctuary in Makkah before Quṣay ibn Kilāb stripped them of the honour and entrenched Qurayshi domination over Makkah. For generations thereafter, the Khuzā'ah felt that they had been wronged; therefore, they never enjoyed a good relationship with the Quraysh. Although not at war with the Quraysh, they also felt no affection for them. However, when the Prophet's (ﷺ) grandfather, 'Abd al-Muṭṭalib, had a dispute with his uncle Nawfal and sought the help of his maternal uncles from the Khazraj tribe, the Khuzā'ah saw in 'Abd al-Muṭṭalib a free-thinking and independent Qurayshi leader and decided to enter an alliance with him. This alliance was inherited by Abū Ṭālib. The Prophet (ﷺ) maintained the alliance, and his relationship with the Khuzā'ah continued throughout the Madinan period. The Khuzā'ah's admiration for the Prophet (ﷺ) increased exponentially when they saw how he challenged Qurayshi arrogance. They hoped he would vanquish them. They assisted his cause by corresponding with him, sharing information with him, and supporting him however they could.

When the Treaty of al-Ḥudaybīyyah was signed, the Khuzā'ah were able officially to declare their affiliation to Muḥammad's (ﷺ) alliance and, consequently, to benefit from his protection. The Banī Bakr were the Khuzā'ah's long-time rival. They were from the Kinānah tribal confederation and had joined the Quraysh, their maternal cousins.

Some Qurayshi leaders, such as Ṣafwān and ʻIkrimah, were unhappy with the Treaty of al-Ḥudaybīyyah. They bitterly witnessed the Prophet (ﷺ) skilfully harvest the fruits of the treaty over the next year and a half. He conquered Khaybar and other Jewish settlements in the north, broadened his alliances on the Arabian Peninsula in an unprecedented manner, spread Islam among the Arabs, establish the Madinah Pact that rivalled the Makkah Pact, and took over their markets and trade relations. It was difficult to see what benefit the Quraysh had gained from al-Ḥudaybīyyah. They did reclaim their trade routes, but were unable to regain their previous commercial stature. Furthermore, they lost allies daily while Muḥammad's (ﷺ) allies increased in number. Worse, the best of their youth were being lost to Islam and were migrating to Muḥammad (ﷺ), without the Quraysh being able to stop them or harm them, since the Treaty did not allow this after the article on returning migrants was nullified. The Quraysh were unsure about how to proceed and respond.

Ṣafwān and ʻIkrimah believed that the Muslims had been weakened after the Battle of Mu'tah, and wishfully thought that the strong tribes of the north, like the Quḍāʻah, Judhām, and Lakham, would attack Madinah. Such fantasies played on their minds and, with their imaginations running wild, they began to consider withdrawing from the treaty. They wanted to test the strength of the Islamic force by creating tensions between the Banī Bakr and Khuzāʻah. They therefore supported a Banī Bakr attack on several Khuzāʻah members at the watering hole of al-Watīr, sixteen kilometres southeast of Makkah. Twenty men were killed. In flagrant violation of the Treaty of al-Ḥudaybīyyah, Ṣafwān, ʻIkrimah, and some of their slaves disguised themselves and participated in the fighting. The intention of the two Qurayshi leaders was, seemingly, to use the incident as a test to monitor the consequences of the aggression and thus assess the Muslims' strength. If Muḥammad (ﷺ) were to respond actively, they would deny any involvement, but if his response was weak, they would consider how best to exploit the situation.

A few days later, the Prophet (ﷺ) received news of the attack from two sources: from Budayl ibn Warqā' al-Khuzāʻī and from a Khuzāʻah delegation led by renowned poet ʻAmr ibn Sālim. In an emotional poem, ‘Amr made a passionate appeal for assistance. The Prophet (ﷺ) responded, “You have the help [that you ask for], O ‘Amr ibn Sālim.”[251]

The Prophet (ﷺ) advised both Budayl ibn Warqā’ and ‘Amr ibn Sālim not to tell anyone about their respective visits to Madinah. He preferred that the Qurayshi leaders remain uncertain so that they might be unable to accurately assess the situation. The Prophet (ﷺ) correctly assumed that the young impetuous Qurayshi leadership had committed the act of folly without Abū Sufyān’s knowledge, and that they would seek his help to solve the problem when they realised the enormity of their error.

After news of the attack reached Makkah, several Qurayshi leaders, including al-Ḥārith ibn Hishām and ‘Abdallah ibn ‘Abī Rabī‘ah, confronted Ṣafwān, ‘Ikrimah, and Suhayl and castigated them for supporting the Banī Bakr and violating the agreement with Muḥammad (ﷺ). The leaders continued to criticise the younger men until the latter became remorseful and approached Abū Sufyān for advice. Abū Sufyān had known nothing about the affair, but he was forced into a position where he could not refuse to assist to resolve the problem, despite his anger and condemnation. Al-Wāqidī narrates Abū Sufyān’s response when a Qurayshi delegation asked him about a solution.

> By Allah, this is a matter that I did not witness, but cannot avoid. This problem has been placed on no one else but me. By Allah, I had not been consulted, and did not like what I was told! By Allah, Muḥammad will surely invade us if my suspicions are correct, and I am sure they are. I have no choice but to go to Muḥammad before he is informed of this, and discuss extending the truce and renewing the covenant.”[252]

Abū Sufyān in Madinah

Two days after he was informed about the issue, Abū Sufyān hastily made his way to Madinah, hoping to reach the Prophet (ﷺ) before the news. He met Budayl ibn Warqā’ returning from Madinah and asked

251. Ibn Hishām, *al-Sīrah*, vol. 2, 395.
252. Al-Wāqidī, *Kitāb al-Maghāzī*, vol. 2, 785.

him if he had visited Muḥammad (ﷺ). Budayl replied in the negative. However, being as astute and observant as he was, Abū Sufyān realised that Budayl had already informed Muḥammad (ﷺ) of the news. This increased his fear. Abū Sufyān knew that Makkah could not defend itself against Muḥammad (ﷺ), and that he had to do everything possible to resolve the problem. He decided not to discuss the incident, but to ask the Prophet (ﷺ) to strengthen the Treaty of al-Ḥudaybīyyah and extend its timeframe.

He decided that, when he met the Prophet (ﷺ), he would say that he had not been present at al-Ḥudaybīyyah and wanted to reinforce the agreement. The amended agreement, he would argue, would mark the beginning of a new phase, and the recent problem could be forgotten. When Abū Sufyān arrived, he told the Prophet (ﷺ): "O Muḥammad, I was not present at the Treaty of al-Ḥudaybīyyah. Let us strengthen the covenant and increase its time of implementation." The Prophet (ﷺ), much more astute than the Qurayshi leader, responded: "Did you do something?" The Prophet (ﷺ) directly asked him whether the Quraysh had violated the agreement, thus requiring them to ask for its extension. As if surprised by the question, Abū Sufyān responded, "[No, I seek] Allah's refuge!" Allah's Messenger (ﷺ) then told him: "We are committed to the period and the provisions we had agreed to on the day of al-Ḥudaybīyyah. We will not change or amend anything."[253] Abū Sufyān's strategy to extract a new agreement failed, and he realised that the Prophet (ﷺ) was fully aware of how the Quraysh had violated the agreement.

He decided that his only option was to plead for assistance from the Prophet's (ﷺ) companions and family. He began with his own daughter Umm Ḥabībah, the Prophet's (ﷺ) wife. She rebuffed him and reproached him for worshipping idols. He approached Abū Bakr to intercede with the Prophet (ﷺ), but he too refused. He found 'Umar even more hostile. His cousin 'Uthmān also refused the request, as did the Anṣār leader, Sa'd ibn 'Ubādah. Changing tack, Abū Sufyān appealed to Fātimah, the Prophet's (ﷺ) daughter, to publicly announce her protection of the Quraysh. He reminded her that her sister Zaynab had conferred similar protection on al-Āṣ ibn al-Rabī', and that her

253. Al-Wāqidī, *Kitāb al-Maghāzī*, vol. 2, 792.

protection had been confirmed by the Prophet (ﷺ). Fātimah told him that in such a matter no one could offer protection over that of Allah's Messenger (ﷺ). In desperation, anxiety, and despair, he asked her to send one of her sons, either al-Ḥasan or al-Ḥusayn, to announce their protection over the Quraysh. They were just young boys, she responded. In a similar manner, Abū Sufyān made his rounds among other Muslims for several days, hoping for a solution. His delay in Madinah sparked rumours in Makkah that the Qurayshi leader had abandoned his religion and accepted Islam.

Abū Sufyān's extended stay in Madinah gave him the opportunity to closely observe Madinan society, leading him to conclude that the Prophet (ﷺ) would undoubtedly be victorious in a confrontation with the Quraysh. Abū Sufyān was perceptive, and he knew that an ordered, disciplined, and prepared community was more than capable of effortlessly defeating the Quraysh. It was likely this realisation, arrived at during his visit, which caused Abū Sufyān to embrace Islam the day before Makkah was conquered, and to play an active role in Makkah's negotiated surrender, before any fighting could take place.

Abū Sufyān was unable to extract a promise from the Prophet (ﷺ) to renew the Treaty of al-Ḥudaybīyyah. All he was able to do was to follow the advice of 'Alī ibn Abī Ṭālib, who suggested that Abū Sufyān should present himself to the people of Madinah as the leader of the Kinānah tribal confederation and seek their protection. He stood up in the mosque and loudly announced that he sought the people's protection. He then told the Prophet (ﷺ): "I do not think you will deny me your protection." The Prophet (ﷺ) replied: "It is you who says that, O Abū Sufyān." It was a smart, noncommittal statement that did not oblige the Prophet (ﷺ) to recognise the protection plea, but did not deny it, either. However, his reply made the situation more confusing to Abū Sufyān, leaving him baffled about the Prophet's (ﷺ) intentions. Abū Sufyān then returned to Makkah, without having achieved anything during his visit.

When he reached Makkah, he heard the rumour of his conversion to Islam from his wife, Hind bint 'Utbah. The next day, to refute the rumour, he shaved his head in front of the idols Isāf and Nā'ilah and offered a sacrifice to them. He addressed the Quraysh on his visit, informed them that he had been unable to find a solution, and said that he had sought protection from the Muslims. They asked him if Muḥammad (ﷺ) had extended the protection, and he replied in the negative. The Qurayshi leaders mocked him and told him that Muḥammad (ﷺ) had "done nothing but make fun of Abū Sufyān".

Mass mobilisation

Immediately after Abū Sufyān's departure from Madinah, the Prophet (ﷺ) ordered his companions to prepare for travel, without indicating the destination. He ensured that news of his mobilisation did not spread, thus denying the Quraysh the opportunity to prepare for war. The Prophet (ﷺ) took several steps to conceal his plans and actions. He did not disclose his destination except to his closest companions, such as Abū Bakr, and asked them to also keep the matter under wraps. He instructed 'Umar ibn al-Khaṭṭāb to patrol all Madinah's entrances and to deploy guards at each. 'Umar ordered them to note anyone leaving Madinah, especially those heading for areas around Makkah, out of concern that they might carry the news of the Prophet's (ﷺ) mobilisation to the Quraysh.

"Do not allow anyone who passes you and who might look suspicious to [continue]. Turn them back. Keep back and question anyone who is heading for Makkah or its surroundings," 'Umar said.[254] Conflicting rumours spread, probably by design, that the Prophet (ﷺ) was preparing to march on the Levant, or on Thaqīf, or on the Hawāzin. The Prophet (ﷺ) also dispatched Abū Qatādah at the head of an eight-person team to Baṭn Iḍam, located between Makkah and al-Yamāmah, to make people think that this was his destination. All this was intended to turn people's attention away from the real destination, Makkah.

The Prophet (ﷺ) hoped to conquer Makkah without fighting, aware that such a great victory would be complete only if it was achieved without violence. It would not befit Makkah, with the Holy Sanctuary, the Ka'bah, and its symbolism in the popular Arab imagination, to

254. Al-Wāqidī, *Kitāb al-Maghāzī*, vol. 2, 796.

be conquered through a bloody spectacle. He also wanted to save the Quraysh the ignominy of a military defeat in which blood would be spilt and wealth looted; an honourable conquest would inaugurate a new era of peace. That is why it was necessary to keep the news of the mobilisation from the Quraysh for as long as possible. It would deprive them of enough time to gather an army, especially since they had, among them, impetuous leaders who would likely consider embarking on a foolhardy adventure.

However, open preparations were being made all over Madinah. There was mass mobilisation, as well as invitations sent to allied tribes, asking whoever believed in Allah and the Last Day to be present in Madinah in the month of Ramaḍān. Many Muslims were convinced that the Prophet's (ﷺ) destination was Makkah, but neither he nor his senior leaders openly declared the target, leaving the destination uncertain.

Ḥāṭib in the dock

The companions of the Prophet (ﷺ) were not all faultless. One companion, Ḥāṭib ibn Abī Balta'ah, wrote to the three Quraysh leaders—Ṣafwān, 'Ikrimah, and Suhayl—and informed them of the Prophet's (ﷺ) preparations. However, his attempt was discovered, and the letter was intercepted before it travelled far from Madinah. 'Umar ibn al-Khaṭṭāb was incensed by Ḥāṭib's spying, something that would be regarded as treasonous by any nation and would, in many instances, be punishable by death. The Prophet (ﷺ), however, considered several mitigating factors: that Ḥāṭib had been one of the earliest migrants, that he had participated in Badr and other battles, and that he had fought bravely at Uḥud. He believed in Allah and His Messenger, was one of those who had pledged his allegiance under the tree at al-Ḥudaybīyyah, and had acted as the Prophet's (ﷺ) emissary to al-Muqawqas. The Prophet (ﷺ) did not believe that he was a Qurayshi spy, but that he had faltered in a moment of weakness. Ḥāṭib was a Qurayshi bondsman (mawla) and not of an established lineage. He had family in Makkah and believed that, if he did a favour for the Qurayshi leadership, they would be in his debt, and he would be able to ask them to protect his family. Moreover, the letter had not reached its destination and Ḥāṭib had admitted his guilt.

Further, if the Prophet (ﷺ) had acceded to 'Umar's call for Ḥāṭib to be executed, he would have indicated to everyone that his camp was not united, and he had started killing his companions. A key element of the Prophet's (ﷺ) leadership and strategy was not to allow the appearance of weakness or division in the Muslim camp. He had previously forgiven people who had been responsible for actions worse than Ḥāṭib's, such as those of 'Abdallah ibn Ubayy ibn Sallūl, the leader of the Hypocrites in Madinah. At the time, the Prophet (ﷺ) had commented: "People should not say that Muḥammad is killing his companions." This policy had proven extremely effective in building a healthy society that was not burdened by fear and retribution, one that was responsible for its own unrighteousness. Such an approach did not prevent lapses and deviations, but it also did not allow them to prevail. It addressed such faults directly, checked them, and enhanced society's immunity against them in an atmosphere of civil peace and societal dialogue. Correct action was thus affirmed, shortcomings contained, and blood and property protected.

The great alliance

A prudent analysis of the Prophet's (ﷺ) strategy for the conquest of Makkah shows that he had resolved, first, to conquer it peacefully, and, second, to ensure that it would be a collective action of various Arab tribes. He wanted the maximum participation of Arab tribes, hence his call for everyone who had entered Islam to gather in Madinah. A quick glance at the tribes that had mobilised for the conquest of Makkah gives wonderful insight into the growth of the Madinah alliance after al-Ḥudaybīyyah. Significant tribes from the Muḍar confederation, which was very important in the Hijāz and Najd, had joined the alliance, and five of them would become so prominent that the Prophet (ﷺ) would regard them as the equals of the Anṣār and the Quraysh. He mentioned them by name: "Quraysh, Anṣār, Juhaynah, Mazaynah, Aslam, Ghaffār, and Ashja' are my bondsmen. They have no bond affiliation to other than Allah and his Messenger." The Quraysh mentioned here refers to the Muhājirūn from the Quraysh, or the Muslim Quraysh, not the idolatrous Quraysh.

The Juhaynah tribe had allied itself with the Prophet (ﷺ) from the first year of the migration. The alliance was necessary for harassing the Qurayshi trade routes along the coast. Some Juhaynah leaders, such as Kishd al-Juhanī, were important informants for the Prophet (ﷺ), which contributed to the success in the Battle of Badr. The Mazaynah, who lived near the Juhaynah, between Madinah and Makkah, played a similar role. The Ghaffār were from the Banī Ḍamrah confederation that had reconciled with the Prophet (ﷺ) in the first year of the Hijrah. Islam had spread among them through the efforts of Abū Dhar al-Ghaffārī. The Aslam tribe also reconciled with the Prophet (ﷺ) in the first year of the Hijrah, and many of its members embraced Islam. The relationships of all four Hijāzi tribes with Islam started early, soon after the Hijrah. The Ashja', a Najdi tribe from the Ghaṭafān tribal confederation, had been extremely hostile to Madinah. It had joined the Quraysh in the Battle of the Trench but began inclining toward the Madinah alliance after al-Ḥudaybīyyah, and Islam gradually took root among its people thereafter.

The alliance preparing for the conquest was not limited to these five tribes. Surprisingly, the Sulaym tribe also joined, contributing 1,000 warriors. Sulaym was known for its extreme hostility toward the Prophet (ﷺ) and its close relations with the Quraysh. The Muslims would not forget how Banī Sulaym had deceived the companions, massacred them at Bi'r Ma'ūnah, and confronted them in the Battle of the Trench. Sulaym's participation in the alliance was, therefore, a powerful indication of the growing strength of the Prophet's (ﷺ) alliance. It also alerted the Quraysh to the fact that its closest ally had abandoned it. Equally surprising was the participation of 200 fighters from Banī Bakr. Banī Bakr had, not long before, attacked the Khuzā'ah, prompting the violation of the treaty. However, Islam had entered some of their hearts, resulting in their joining the Prophet (ﷺ) and his march on Makkah.

Why a massive army

The army that assembled outside Madinah for the march to Makkah was 10,000 strong. It comprised 1,000 warriors from each of Sulaym and Mazaynah; 800 from Juhaynah; 400 from Aslam; 300 from each from Ashja' and Ghaffār; 250 from Banī Layth; and 200 Banī Bakr. The core and foundation of the army, however, was the Madinah contingent: 700 Muhājirūn warriors with 300 horses, and 4,000 Anṣār with 500 horses.

The Anṣār and the Muhājirūn were distinguished from everyone else by their impeccable order and full kit. They all wore armour, were fully armed, and they carried a variety of flags—including the Prophet's (ﷺ) Green Brigade banner. Their very presence generated awe. No earlier battle had witnessed this many well-equipped warriors from the Anṣār and the Muhājirūn. Previously, the largest Muslim army comprised 3,000 fighters, at Mu'tah. This raises an important question: Wasn't an army comprising 4,700 warriors from the Muhājirūn and the Anṣār incapable of conquering Makkah by themselves? Why did the Prophet (ﷺ) assemble such a massive force?

It is obvious that there was no military rationale for an army of 10,000; the Quraysh could have been defeated by a much smaller force. There were, however, other considerations for such a mobilisation of all who had embraced Islam. The first and most important consideration was that the Prophet (ﷺ) wanted to enter Makkah without using violence. A massive and impressive army that would affect people psychologically, appeal to their common sense, and convince the Quraysh that they had no option but to surrender was, therefore, an effective strategy. The usefulness of this strategy was illustrated in Abū Sufyān's later comment to the Quraysh to justify a surrender. He described the Muslim force as: "What no one has the power to overcome." In the Prophet's (ﷺ) calculation, if the army was so impressive that even thinking about fighting it would be regarded as insanity, the Quraysh would surely surrender, and the objective would be achieved; Makkah would be conquered without blood being spilt.

The second consideration was the Prophet's (ﷺ) cognisance of the importance of Makkah to all Arabs. That was the reason that the maximum number of Arabs should be part of its conquest. Makkah was the only city in the entire peninsula whose affairs were regarded as part of the general affairs of all the tribes. Thus, conquering it peacefully and with the participation of all Arabs would convey a clear message across all divisions: that a new era of tolerance had emerged, and that all Arab tribes had participants in the conquest and in the inception of the new era.

The third consideration was organisational and pedagogical. By assembling all Muslims into a single army under the Prophet's (ﷺ) leadership, he entrenched the concept of a single united ummah. The army gathered Muhājirūn, Anṣār, the tribes of Juhaynah, Ghaffār, Ghaṭafān, and Ashja', all standing side-by-side with a single objective and under a single leadership. It was poised to birth a nation that would transcend tribe, and it would be a united and disciplined force ready for organised collective action. No single tribe could act according to its own whims, which was the reason that they had been summoned to Madinah. From there, they marched together to al-Ṣalṣal, eleven kilometres from Madinah, where they camped. Zubayr was sent ahead with a vanguard of 200 cavalrymen and the brigade flags were distributed. These were all actions designed to reinforce the idea of a single army with a centralised, extra-tribal command structure, a notion that was unfamiliar to the tribes.

The future mandate of the army was the fourth consideration. Its mandate would not end with Makkah's subjugation. It would be engaged in battle immediately thereafter, against the Hawāzin and Thaqīf tribes, which had begun preparing for a confrontation when news spread of the Muslim march from Madinah. They feared that they, rather than Makkah, were the Prophet's (ﷺ) targets and began preparing in earnest. The Hawāzin deployed their spies to track the Muslims. One was captured, and he informed the Muslims that the Hawāzin were mobilising for war. The spy's statement provides insight into the angst of both the Hawāzin and the Quraysh.

> I am from the Hawāzin, from the Banī Naḍr. The Hawāzin deployed me as a spy. They told me: "Go to Madinah, meet Muḥammad, and inform us what he and his allies intend. Is he sending a delegation to the Quraysh or invading them by himself? We do not believe anything other than that he intends to invade them. If he marches or dispatches a delegation, follow

him until he reaches Baṭn Sarif. If he intends [to attack] us first, he will proceed to Baṭn Sarif until he reaches us; if he wants [to march on] the Quraysh, he will stick to the path."

Allah's Messenger (ﷺ) asked: "Where are the Hawāzin?" The spy replied: "I left them at Baqā'a. They had gathered their forces and were inciting the Arabs. They also asked the Thaqīf [for assistance] and the Thaqīf responded [positively]. I left the Thaqīf when they had gathered their forces and were on the move. The [Hawāzin] also sent [emissaries] to al-Jurash to acquire armoured carts and catapults. They are all marching to meet at the Hawāzin's gathering place." Allah's Messenger (ﷺ) asked: "To whom have they given the leadership?" He replied: "To their young [leader] Mālik ibn 'Awf." Allah's Messenger (ﷺ) asked: "And have all the Hawāzin responded to what Mālik invited them to?" He said: "Some serious and powerful people from the Banī 'Āmir have held back." The Prophet (ﷺ) asked: "Who?" He replied: "Ka'b and Kilāb." Allah's Messenger (ﷺ) asked: "What about the Hilāl?" He said: "Only a few of them have joined. I passed by your people [Quraysh] in Makkah yesterday. Abū Sufyān ibn Ḥarb spoke to them, and I saw that they were very angry with what he told them. They are scared and apprehensive."[255]

It was clear from the spy's report that a Hawāzin-Thaqīf alliance had been forged, and the Prophet (ﷺ) knew that he would have to fight them after he was done with Makkah.

At Makkah's door

The Muslim army covered the distance between Madinah and Makkah in nine days and reached Marr al-Ẓahrān, on Makkah's outskirts, on 12 Ramaḍān 629. The Quraysh had been dejected and anxious after Abū Sufyān's failure to renew the Treaty of al-Ḥudaybīyyah. They expected the Prophet's (ﷺ) wrath to be unleashed on them. They were undoubtedly following news of the Muslim march toward them.

255. Al-Wāqidī, *Kitāb al-Maghāzī*, vol. 2, 805.

Therefore, the claim by some commentators that they were surprised when the army arrived is not plausible. If news of the army had reached the Hawāzin, Thaqīf, and the neighbouring Sulaym, the Quraysh could not have been unaware of it.

Biographies of the Prophet (ﷺ) narrate that the Quraysh had sent Abū Sufyān as an emissary to the Prophet (ﷺ) with the instructions: "If you encounter Muḥammad, seek protection from him for us. But if you see weakness in his companions, declare war."[256] This statement reflects the psychological state of the Qurayshi leadership. On the one hand, they were terrified and sought the Prophet's (ﷺ) indemnity; on the other hand, they dared to imagine the possibility that the Prophet (ﷺ) could be weak, as they had believed after the Mu'tah incident. They therefore wanted Abū Sufyān to assess the Muslims' strength.

It is worth considering, however, which Quraysh Abū Sufyān was representing. It is clear from the general context that most inhabitants of Makkah had reconciled themselves to the possibility of a conquest. The Makkans had closely interacted with the Muslims during the compensatory pilgrimage, and, before that, the Treaty of al-Ḥudaybīyyah had opened a door for the exchange of merchandise and reciprocal visits. Most Makkans regularly received accurate news of events in Madinah, without the distortions of informants or the propaganda of the Qurayshi leadership. Even within the Makkan elite, there was a huge disparity in their positions. An extremist wing comprising people such as Ṣafwān ibn Umayyah, 'Ikrimah ibn Abī Jahl, Ḥuwayṭab ibn 'Abd al-'Uzza, and Makraz ibn Hafṣ wanted to terminate the treaty. Although not as radical, Suhayl ibn 'Amr supported their position. Other leaders, such as Abū Sufyān, al-Ḥārith ibn Hishām, 'Abdallah ibn Abī Rabī'ah, Ḥakīm ibn Ḥizām, Jubayr ibn Muṭ'am, and 'Itāb ibn Asyad had an opposing view and wanted to strengthen the treaty. The Prophet (ﷺ) was aware of the Qurayshi leadership's internal contradictions. When he reached the outskirts of Makkah, he said: "I deem four [of them] to be far from idolatry: 'Itāb ibn Asyad, Jubayr ibn Muṭ'am, Ḥakīm ibn Ḥizām, and Suhayl ibn 'Amr."[257] Such a statement, uttered on the doorstep of Makkah, was, undoubtedly, politically significant. It

256. Al-Wāqidī, *Kitāb al-Maghāzī*, vol. 2, 814.

257. Shams al-Dīn al-Dhahabī, *Siyar 'A'lām al-Nubalā'* (Cairo: Dār al-Ḥadīth, 2006), vol. 18, 302.

strengthened the hand of the Qurayshi moderates and encouraged them to accept the new reality.

The moderate leadership within the Quraysh, along with Budayl ibn Warqā', who was not Qurayshi but had significant influence in Makkah, had condemned the manner in which the extremists had managed the relationship with the Muslims, especially their support for the Banī Bakr against the Khuzā'ah, and their contravention of the treaty. The moderates thought it necessary to take the initiative and to salvage whatever could be saved by entering a surrender agreement that would grant protection to the people of Makkah and secure their lives, wealth, and possessions. Abū Sufyān was therefore chosen to lead a delegation that included Budayl ibn Warqā' and Ḥakīm ibn Ḥizām to make representations to the Prophet (ﷺ).

The Capitulation Delegation

Sīrah literature credits two men, al-'Abbās ibn 'Abd al-Muṭṭalib and Abū Sufyān ibn Ḥarb, who were accompanied by Budayl ibn Warqā' and Ḥakīm ibn Ḥizām, with making the greatest effort to reach an agreement for the peaceful entry of the Muslims into Makkah.

Al-'Abbās ibn 'Abd al-Muṭṭalib, the Prophet's (ﷺ) uncle and the chief of the Banī Hāshim, was a unique character whose biography raises a controversial question. He was the person who, at the Pledge of al-'Aqabah, had extracted assurances from the Anṣār to support and protect the Prophet (ﷺ). However, he had remained in Makkah, tended to the affairs of the Banī Hāshim, and fulfilled his duty of providing water to pilgrims. He participated in the Battle of Badr as part of the Qurayshi army. On that occasion, the Prophet (ﷺ) had asked his companions not to kill al-'Abbās. The Muslims had captured him, but he had paid a ransom for his freedom and had returned to Makkah, where he remained until the Prophet (ﷺ) marched on the city. He met the Prophet (ﷺ) at al-Juḥfah, 170 kilometres from Makkah, a few days before the conquest, as part of Abū Sufyān's delegation. The delegation hoped to negotiate a truce that would allow the Muslims to enter Makkah peacefully.

The historical controversy around al-‘Abbās relates to the date of his embracing Islam. Some historians believe that he had secretly become Muslim, with others in his household, while he was in Makkah, that he had participated in Badr under duress while on a secret mission to spy for the Prophet (ﷺ), and that he had been assisting the Muslims in Makkah who had kept their Islam hidden. In other words, he was the Prophet's (ﷺ) secret agent. This is likely an exaggeration of his role. It was probably concocted by the propaganda machinery of the Abbasid state more than a century later. The other view is that he embraced Islam at al-Juḥfah on the eve of the conquest. This is a longstanding dispute, with both sets of historians presenting their evidence. However, for our purposes, it is an irrelevant debate. What *is* important is that al-‘Abbās was the Prophet's (ﷺ) uncle and the chief of the Banī Hāshim.

His fondness for the Prophet (ﷺ) was renowned among the Quraysh. An illustration of this was al-Ḥajjāj ibn ‘Ilāṭ's report that, when al-‘Abbās had heard a rumour about the Prophet's (ﷺ) capture at Khaybar, he had collapsed into al-Ḥajjāj's hands and onto the ground, immobile. When he learnt that the rumour was false and that the Prophet (ﷺ) had conquered Khaybar, he expressed his joy in the presence of the Qurayshi elders. Thus, his support for the Prophet (ﷺ) was no secret, but we cannot say with certainty whether it was because of family ties or because of Islam. Nonetheless, the issue here does not pertain to when he embraced Islam, but to the strategic role that he played in ensuring the peaceful conquest of Makkah.

In general, the Quraysh elders did not trust al-‘Abbās, treated him harshly, and kept information from him. However, there was one Qurayshi elder who had a close relationship with him and was regarded as his intimate friend and drinking companion in the pre-Islamic days of ignorance; this was none other than Abū Sufyān, the leader of the Quraysh. Their relationship raises some interesting questions about Abū Sufyān, the cunning trader and shrewd politician. Did he not suspect that the Prophet (ﷺ) would march on Makkah after the al-Watīr watering hole attack? Did he not realise that Madinah, which he closely observed, was capable of defeating the Quraysh? Was Abū Sufyān, who travelled across the Arabian Peninsula and collected news from all over, unaware that the Arab tribes had joined Muḥammad's

(ﷺ) alliance, and that all the Quraysh's allies had abandoned them? If Abū Sufyān had ascertained all this beforehand, what would his view be about Muḥammad (ﷺ): the victorious prophet or a son-in-law and relative with whom he shared a common ancestry?

It is also noteworthy that the Prophet (ﷺ) had been lenient toward Abū Sufyān after the Battle of the Trench defeat, when he had been deposed by the younger Quraysh leaders. There were several positive indicators regarding the Prophet's (ﷺ) attitude towards Abū Sufyān. An important indicator was his marriage to Abū Sufyān's daughter, Umm Ḥabībah. He had sent his proposal with 'Amr ibn Umayyah al-Ḍamrī, to be conveyed to Umm Ḥabībah via the Negus. He later sent the same 'Amr ibn Umayyah al-Ḍamrī to Abū Sufyān to inform him of the marriage, the celebration, and the dowry that had been paid by the Negus. This had pleased Abū Sufyān tremendously, and he had described the Prophet (ﷺ) as "the stallion whose nose could not be struck", an Arabic expression that is used to praise a generous person.

Some Qur'ān commentators assert that verse 60:7 was revealed on the occasion of the Prophet's (ﷺ) marriage to Umm Ḥabībah. The verse reads: "Perhaps Allah will create affection between you and those who are your enemies. Allah is All-Powerful, Allah is most Forgiving, Most Merciful." They also comment that the marriage contributed to nudging Abū Sufyān towards Islam.

The Prophet (ﷺ) had also gifted 'ajwa dates, delivered by 'Amr ibn Umayyah al-Ḍamrī, to Abū Sufyān after al-Ḥudaybīyyah. He had asked for a gift of animal hides in return. Abū Sufyān, who traded in oil and animal hides, had obliged. Moreover, when Abū Sufyān had visited Madinah, he had not been met with hostility or bad behaviour from the Muslims. Even though they did not respond positively to his pleas to intercede with the Prophet (ﷺ), he remained safe and moved around the city in complete freedom, visiting many senior companions. Abū Sufyān's trip had been an opportunity to incline him to the Prophet's (ﷺ) alliance and to convince him that surrendering Makkah was not shameful and did not mean the end of the Quraysh. It is also significant that Ḥāṭib ibn Abī Balta'ah had written to Ṣafwān, 'Ikrimah, and Suhayl when he had wanted to inform the Quraysh about the Prophet's (ﷺ)

mobilisation, rather than to Abū Sufyān. This confirms that when Abū Sufyān had left Madinah, he had been certain that Makkah was on the verge of being conquered, and that he did not strongly oppose it.

Furthermore, al-'Abbās was not only the Prophet's (ﷺ) unofficial envoy in Makkah, but was also Abū Sufyān's intimate friend. They were also paternal cousins; one was the leader of the Banī Hāshim and the other the leader of the Banī Umayyah, and they were all part of the Alliance of the Scented, the Banī 'Abd Manāf faction that had been displaced from Makkan leadership in favour of the Alliance of the Allies. All these factors suggest that al-'Abbās probably communicated with Abū Sufyān about his diplomatic mission and its outcomes. This raises the question of whether it was a coincidence that al-'Abbās had met the Prophet (ﷺ) on the road three days earlier, or whether he knew of the Prophet's (ﷺ) march and wanted to clinch an agreement that would preserve Makkah's status.

Al-Wāqidī narrated that, when the Muslims reached Marr al-Ẓahrān, al-'Abbās rode the Prophet's (ﷺ) grey donkey around the camp at night, hoping to find someone that might inform the Quraysh that the Prophet (ﷺ) would enter Makkah. He wanted the Quraysh to try to reach an agreement with the Prophet (ﷺ) so that he would not enter using force. It can be assumed that al-'Abbās would not have done this without the Prophet's (ﷺ) knowledge, especially since it accorded with his strategy of entering Makkah peacefully. Moreover, al-'Abbās rode the Prophet's (ﷺ) donkey so that the guards and soldiers would know that he was on an official assignment. Thereafter, al-'Abbās accidentally met Abū Sufyān, Budayl ibn Warqā', and Ḥakīm ibn Ḥizām. They had gone to Madinah to verify the news and stood in awe before the huge gathering and the numerous campfires.

Al-Wāqidī narrates al-'Abbās's account of his ride around the camp.

> There was Abū Sufyān. I called out to him: "O Abū Ḥanẓalah!" And he replied: "Yes, Abū al-Faḍl," as he had recognised my voice. "What is the matter? [Shall] I offer my mother and father in ransom for you?" I said: "Woe be to you. Here is Allah's Messenger with 10,000 [warriors]." He said: "By my father and

> mother! What do you command? Is there any way out?" I said: "Yes. Ride on the back of this donkey, and I will go with you to Allah's Messenger. By Allah, if someone else encounters you before you meet Allah's Messenger, you will be killed."[258]

Al-'Abbās extended his protection to Abū Sufyān and they made their way to the Prophet (ﷺ). 'Umar ibn al-Khaṭṭāb reached the Prophet (ﷺ) before al-'Abbās and asked the Prophet's (ﷺ) permission to kill Abū Sufyān. Al-'Abbās, however, rescued him, and the Prophet (ﷺ) invited him to Islam. Abū Sufyān was hesitant; he bore witness that there is no god except Allah, but avoided witnessing that Muḥammad (ﷺ) was Allah's messenger. When al-'Abbās warned him that he might be killed if he did not accept Islam, he submitted. He then attempted, for the last time, to convince the Prophet (ﷺ) not to conquer Makkah.

> O Muḥammad, you have come with a mob—with people who we know and those who we don't know—to your kin and to your origin." Allah's Messenger (ﷺ) replied: "You are most oppressive and most vile. You violated the Treaty of al-Ḥudaybīyyah and you aggressively confronted Banī Ka'b in Allah's Sanctuary and safe place." Abū Sufyān said: "Woe be to you, O Messenger of Allah! If only you directed your scorn and machinations toward the Hawāzin who are not your near kin and are far more hostile to you." Allah's Messenger (ﷺ) said: "I hope that my Lord will gather all of that for me [direct my scorn and machinations towards the Hawāzin] through the conquest of Makkah, and will strengthen and honour Islam through it. I will defeat the Hawāzin, and I hope that Allah will grant me their wealth and offspring as booty. I seek all of that from Allah."[259]

After some hesitation, Abū Sufyān professed his Islam before the Prophet (ﷺ). Al-'Abbās asked the Prophet (ﷺ) to grant Abū Sufyān some standing before the people of Makkah. The Prophet (ﷺ) responded: "Whoever enters the house of Abū Sufyān is safe, whoever closes his door is safe, and whoever enters the mosque is safe."[260]

258. Al-Wāqidī, *Kitāb al-Maghāzī*, vol. 2, 817.
259. Al-Wāqidī, *Kitāb al-Maghāzī*, vol. 2, 816.
260. Al-Wāqidī, *Kitāb al-Maghāzī*, vol. 2, 818.

Al-'Abbās hosted Abū Sufyān for the night and accompanied him early the next morning to the valley through which the Muslim army passed in an impressive military parade, intended to convince Abū Sufyān that this force could not be defeated. He observed the Arab tribes flying their banners and flags. Whenever a brigade marched passed him, he asked about it and al-'Abbās responded. "This is Sulaym; this is Muzaynah; this is Ashja'; this is Juhaynah; this is Ghaffār;..." As the soldiers passed him, they shouted "Allahu Akbar" (God is the greatest) thrice, intending to leave a deep impression on Abū Sufyān. When the Prophet's (ﷺ) Green Brigade passed, covered in armour, with only their eyes visible, Abū Sufyān was struck with terror. He told al-'Abbās: "I have never seen such a brigade before and was not informed of it by anyone! Praise be to Allah. No one has the power or strength to overcome this! Your nephew's authority has become great overnight!" Al-'Abbās said: "Woe be unto you, O Abū Sufyān. It is not authority; it is prophethood." Abū Sufyān responded: "Indeed."[261]

This account by al-Wāqidī mixes actual events with exaggerations and imagined narratives that were introduced for the purpose of embellishment. It is, thus, inaccurate. It was narrated in this way during the rule of the Abbasid Dynasty to give al-'Abbās a position and stature above Abū Sufyān's.[262] Al-'Abbās is portrayed as the one who led Abū Sufyān to Islam and saved his life. It must be understood within the context of the struggle between the Abbasids and the Umayyads, a century after this incident. Al-'Abbās became the symbol of legitimacy and lineage for the Abbasid Dynasty; Abū Sufyān was the chief of the Banī Umayyah and is portrayed here as hesitant to embrace Islam, even under such difficult circumstances. According to this report, he agreed to accept Islam only after al-'Abbās threatened him, telling him that the alternative would be the sword. This would not have been acceptable, since there can be no compulsion in religion, and the Prophet (ﷺ) never coerced anyone into Islam, including those who were worse and more harmful than Abū Sufyān, such as Ṣafwān ibn Umayyah. As a prudent man, why would Abū Sufyān affirm that there was no god but Allah, but stop short of affirming that Muḥammad (ﷺ) was the messenger of Allah?

261. Al-Wāqidī, *Kitāb al-Maghāzī*, vol. 2, 822.

262. For more details, see the views expressed by Ḥusayn Mu'nis on the circumstances surrounding this account: Mu'nis, *Tārikh Quraysh*.

Moreover, in the period of just under a month that Abū Sufyān had been in Madinah and spent a great deal of time consulting Muslim leaders, no one insulted or spoke harshly to him. It is therefore strange that 'Umar ibn al-Khaṭṭāb would suddenly chase after him, sword drawn, to kill him, only for him to be saved by al-'Abbās, who, so the report says, placed himself in front of 'Umar and secured the Prophet's (ﷺ) protection for Abū Sufyān. Moreover, 'Umar could not have expected the Prophet (ﷺ) to allow him to kill Abū Sufyān if he beat al-'Abbās by a few paces.

All this must be regarded as exaggeration and as political exploitation of an historical event. The general context of the event, and our understanding of the Prophet's (ﷺ) methodology and wisdom in interacting with Abū Sufyān, cause us to dismiss these details as far-fetched. There is actually no inherent benefit in these fine details, except to create a dramatic and propagandistic atmosphere that detracts from the core message. Let us position the essential elements of these events within their general context.

New leadership in Makkah

The general context of the events that preceded Marr al-Ẓahrān and those that occurred on the eve of the conquest of Makkah indicates that an agreement had been reached between the Prophet (ﷺ) and the Makkan delegation comprising Abū Sufyān, Budayl, and Ḥakīm.

The most quoted historical narrative regarding this encounter focuses on the role of al-'Abbās and Abū Sufyān, with less prominence afforded to Budayl ibn Warqā' and Ḥakīm ibn Ḥizām. The agreement with the Prophet (ﷺ) was, however, concluded jointly by the three-person delegation. There were several reasons for this. Abū Sufyān was experienced and cunning, and he would not agree to be the sole representative of the Makkan capitulation, especially after he had been accused of accepting Islam during his extended visit to Madinah. Like any leader in such a position, he wanted to share the burden with others in order to protect himself. It is likely, therefore, that the sojourn of Abū Sufyān, Budayl, and Ḥakīm was not coincidental; they travelled together with the intention of securing a peaceful conquest.

These three also represented the majority popular opinion in Makkah. They were part of a leadership group that had begun to feel threatened by an extremist leadership. Their delegation represented the mood that had begun to develop in Makkah after al-Ḥudaybīyyah and the compensatory pilgrimage, and that strengthened after the truce violation. That mood culminated in the view among many Makkans that surrender was preferable to confrontation. Abū Sufyān and his two companions were deployed for this purpose—to secure terms for a surrender, and the delegation's visit was coordinated beforehand with al-'Abbās, who travelled before them to meet the Prophet (ﷺ) at Marr al-Ẓahrān.

Additionally, the delegation's composition was carefully considered, and each member had a specific task. Abū Sufyān's role has already been discussed. Budayl ibn Warqā' was a Khuzā'ah leader, of the tribe with the oldest affiliation with the Prophet's (ﷺ) alliance. Budayl, who owned a large residence in Makkah, was the Prophet's (ﷺ) ally and had a good relationship with the Quraysh. He had previously mediated between the Muslims and the Quraysh and had been the primary mediator at al-Ḥudaybīyyah. He had also been responsible for conveying the Prophet's (ﷺ) truce offer to the Quraysh. Budayl was an elderly man with an elevated status whose two sons had embraced Islam. He had also informed the Prophet (ﷺ) less than a month earlier that Ṣafwān and 'Ikrimah had violated the truce. Therefore, there was no better person to assist Abū Sufyān in ensuring a peaceful transition to Islam in Makkah.

Ḥakīm ibn Ḥizām ibn Khuwaylid was a Qurayshi leader from the Banī Asad tribe, part of the Alliance of the Scented. He was also a nephew of the Prophet's (ﷺ) first wife, Khadījah, and a cousin of al-Zubayr. Ḥakīm was known for his generosity, nobility, and rational temperament. He had been friends with the Prophet (ﷺ) and had taken positive stances regarding the Muslims in Makkah, including contributing to breaking the siege on the Muslims who had been besieged in Abū Ṭālib's valley outside Makkah. He had secretly sent them food and tried to negate the boycott declaration drawn up by the

Quraysh. Ḥakīm was very fond of the Prophet (ﷺ) and had regularly visited and communicated with him. Earlier, when the Prophet (ﷺ) had been approaching Makkah, he had praised Ḥakīm, and included him among the four persons he regarded to be too exalted for idolatry. His inclusion in the delegation certainly had increased its value.

The members of the delegation also had certain things in common. They all opposed the Alliance of the Allies, enjoyed the status and positions that qualified them to mobilise on behalf of Makkah, and had all previously communicated with the Muslims. They represented the moderate leadership that would take over from the extremist trio of Ṣafwān, ʿIkrimah, and Suhayl. If they had left the Quraysh in the hands of the extremists, a great disaster would have befallen Makkah. If the Prophet (ﷺ) were to enter the city by force, they would lose everything, as was the prevalent custom. The conqueror had the right to appropriate everything that belonged to the vanquished, including women and children as slaves. The Makkans had already seen how Khaybar had lost its wealth and farmlands when it had been conquered by force.

The visit of the Abū Sufyān delegation was, therefore, justifiable and planned. It was neither spontaneous nor accidental, and it helped resolve the leadership crisis in Makkah with the decentring of the extremists. Because these actions converged with the Prophet's (ﷺ) policies, he granted the three delegates a distinguished status and recognised their leadership. This recognition was reflected in the Prophet's (ﷺ) official pronouncement: "Whoever enters the house of Abū Sufyān is safe, whoever enters the house of Budayl ibn Warqā' is safe, and whoever enters the house of Ḥakīm ibn Ḥizām is safe."[263] The Prophet (ﷺ) did not specify only Abū Sufyān's house as a safe haven, but granted this privilege to the entire delegation. However, he knew that his pronouncement was symbolic; no one would have any need to seek shelter in anyone's home if they were able to enter their own homes or the mosque, or could lay down their weapons to secure protection for themselves, as per custom. More importantly, the Prophet (ﷺ) sought to bestow legitimacy upon the leadership of the three with his

263. Ibn Saʿd, *al-Ṭabaqāt,* the fourth category concerning those who accepted Islam during the Conquest of Makkah.

pronouncement, thus helping them to implement the agreement more easily.

This is corroborated by another of the Prophet (ﷺ)'s pronouncements. He allowed the spilling of the blood of two of the three extremists, Ṣafwān and 'Ikrimah, even if they were below the covering of the Ka'bah. This was because of their role in violating the treaty and fighting against the Khuzā'ah. Suhayl ibn 'Amr was not included on the wanted list because he had not fought against the Khuzā'ah, and because he was the most reasonable of the three. The Prophet (ﷺ) would soon pardon him, after his son 'Abdallah's intercession. Ṣafwān and 'Ikrimah were not killed, however. They had gone to ground for several days, but finally approached the Prophet (ﷺ) and asked for pardon, which he granted. On the morning of the conquest, however, they were placed on the wanted list of the new ruling authority while Abū Sufyān, Budayl, and Ḥakīm were accorded respect.

Fulfilling the task

When the delegation returned to Makkah, its members announced the terms of the surrender and the justifications for accepting it. Muḥammad's (ﷺ) army was strong, it could not be defeated, and there was no point in fighting, they said. They further announced that he would enter Makkah in peace, had granted everyone amnesty, and had guaranteed the protection of their wealth. In response, the extremists tried to incite popular opinion. They had the support of Abū Sufyān's wife, Hind bint 'Utbah, who was known for her extremist positions against the Prophet (ﷺ). Al-Wāqidī conveys the mood.

> Abū Sufyān addressed the people: "O people of Quraysh, woe be unto you! He has come with that over which you have no power! Here comes Muḥammad, at the head of 10,000 armed men in armour. Surrender!" They said: "May Allah deface you, emissary of the people!" The strongest response came from his wife Hind bint 'Utbah. She shouted, "Kill this emissary of yours. May Allah deface you, emissary of the people." Abū Sufyān responded: "Woe unto you. Do not be swayed by this woman.

I have seen what you have not. I have seen men and horses and weapons that none of you can overpower! Whoever enters the home of Abū Sufyān has amnesty, and whoever closes the door of his house has amnesty."[264]

The Makkans responded to the plea of Abū Sufyān and his companions; they dispersed into their homes and rejected the incitement of the extremist trio, which managed to gather only a few dozen supporters. This small group clashed with Khālid ibn al-Walīd's troops as they entered the city from the south.

The four battalions that entered Makkah had strict orders from the Prophet (ﷺ) not to fight. They were led by al-Zubayr ibn al-'Awwām, Khālid ibn al-Walīd, Abū 'Ubaydah 'Āmir ibn al-Jarrāḥ, and Sa'd ibn 'Ubādah. Three of them were from the Quraysh and the fourth—Sa'd ibn 'Ubādah—was an Anṣār leader. Caught up in the moment, and with a small measure of conceit, Sa'd blurted out, "Today is a day of slaughter. Today the Ka'bah will be defaced." Some Muslims feared that blood would be spilt. They reported his comment to the Prophet (ﷺ), who announced: "Sa'd lied. Today Allah will honour the Ka'bah."[265] In another narration, he is reported to have said: "This is a day of mercy, a day in which Allah will honour the Quraysh." The Prophet (ﷺ) then took the banner from Sa'd and handed it to his son Qays, ensuring that it remained in Sa'd's household.

The four battalions entered Makkah without needing to fight, except for the incident with Khālid's battalion. He tried to avoid the group that had responded to Ṣafwān and 'Ikrimah's call, but they engaged the Muslims aggressively and Khālid fought back. Most of the rebels fled, but twenty-four were killed. Abū Sufyān and Ḥakīm ibn Ḥizām shouted out, "O People of Quraysh, why are you killing yourselves? Whoever enters his house has amnesty; whoever lays down his weapons has amnesty." People rushed into their homes and shut their doors. They also abandoned their weapons in the streets, allowing the Muslims to gather them.[266]

264. Al-Wāqidī, *Kitāb al-Maghāzī*, vol. 2, 823.
265. Quoted in al-Bukhārī, *Kitāb al-Maghāzī*, Chapter: Where the Prophet (ﷺ) fixed the banner on the Day of the Conquest, (1: 1048), Ḥadīth no. 4280.
266. Al-Wāqidī, *Kitāb al-Maghāzī*, vol. 2, 823.

The Prophet (ﷺ) saw the shimmering of swords from a distance and asked: “What is this glimmer? Did I not forbid fighting?” He was told: “O Messenger of Allah, Khālid ibn al-Walīd was engaged in a fight. If he was not, he would not have fought.” Allah’s Messenger (ﷺ) said: “Allah’s Decree is [always] good.”[267] Ironically, Khālid, the leader of the battalion that clashed with the Quraysh, was the same person who had led the Qurayshi vanguard to stop the Prophet (ﷺ) at al-Ḥudaybīyyah.

A Victory without a defeat

Every victory has a counterpoint in defeat; every honour is matched by disgrace; and the confidence displayed by victors is always contrasted by the fear that shakes the will of the vanquished, except in the conquest of Makkah.

In every age until then, when conquerors entered a village or city, they destroyed it, humiliated its inhabitants, put them to the sword, looted, pillaged, and enslaved. In contrast, the Prophet’s (ﷺ) entry into Makkah was peaceful, efficient, and orderly. The vanquished knew that he was neither a malicious enemy nor a treacherous opponent, and they surrendered their city without fear or trepidation. They knew that the Prophet (ﷺ) would usher in a new era in which all people were equal, where everyone’s honour was guaranteed, and when the door to the future would be thrown wide open, even for those who had raised their weapons in the final skirmish at the gates of Makkah.

The Prophet (ﷺ) entered Makkah on his mount and bowed his head in humility before Allah, the Sublime, in gratitude for delivering on His promise and fulfilling His blessings. The Prophet (ﷺ) dismounted in the morning at a tent erected for him in the al-Ḥajūn area. He performed the ritual cleansing, prayed eight cycles of prayer, donned his armour, and placed a helmet on his head. He then called for his camel, al-Qaṣwā’, and mounted, with Abū Bakr beside him, and rode between the lines of people on opposite sides of the road. When he reached the Ka‘bah, he touched its corner with his staff and shouted out “Allahu

267. Al-Wāqidī, *Kitāb al-Maghāzī*, vol. 2, 826.

Akbar". The Muslims repeated his words in a roar that reverberated across Makkah, while the leaders of the idolaters looked on from the surrounding hilltops. The Prophet (ﷺ) then circumambulated the Sacred House on his mount, his camel being led by Muḥammad ibn Maslamah. The Prophet (ﷺ) ordered that the 360 lead-embellished idols that surrounded the Ka'bah be smashed. He completed his circumambulation, drank from the well of Zam Zam, and prayed at the Station of Ibrāhīm (al-Maqām). He then ordered that the largest deity, Habal, be destroyed, and he asked 'Uthmān ibn Ṭalḥah for the key to the Ka'bah. Entering it, he removed all the images from inside, including a portrait of Jesus and his mother Mary, and one of Abraham drawing lots. The Prophet (ﷺ) then performed two cycles of prayer inside the Ka'bah, grabbed hold of the Ka'bah's door handles, looked out at the people gathered before him, and addressed them.

> The Prophet (ﷺ) said: "Praise be to Allah, Who fulfilled His promise, granted victory to His servant, and singlehandedly defeated the confederates. What do you say? What are your thoughts?"
>
> They said: "We say that which is good, and we think that which is good. You are a noble brother and the son of a noble brother; you have the [power to] decree!"
>
> Allah's Messenger (ﷺ) responded: "Verily I say what my brother Yūsuf said: 'There is no blame on you today. Allah will forgive you; and He is the Most Merciful of the merciful!' [A reference to Qur'ān 12:92.]
>
> "Verily, every usurious act, or retributive act, or claim on wealth, or glorious deed from al-Jāhilīyyah (the pre-Islamic time of ignorance) is under these two feet of mine, except for the custodianship of the Sacred House and the provision of water for the pilgrims…
>
> "Verily, Allah has done away with the arrogance and the veneration of ancestors of al-Jāhilīyyah (the pre-Islamic time of ignorance). All of you are from Adam and Adam was from dust. The most honoured among you before Allah are those who are

the most conscious of Allah.

"Allah made Makkah sacrosanct the day that he created the heavens and the earth; it is a sanctuary by Allah's sanctity. It has not been open to transgression before me, nor will it be opened to transgression to anyone after me. It was not opened to me except for a part of the day... Do not frighten its animals or prune its shrubs. Its pickings are not lawful to any of you except the needy. Do not cut the herbage, except for the idhkhir [a pestilent shrub], for it is surely permitted...

"A Muslim is the brother of another Muslim, and all Muslims are brethren. The Muslims are like one hand against those who oppose them. Their blood is equal. The one furthest away from them responds to their call, and the one nearest gives them his covenant. The strong among them will protect the weak, and the affluent will support the needy. No Muslim will be killed for a disbeliever and no possessor of an agreement will be killed in the time stipulated by the agreement."[268]

The speech proceeded to outline some penal codes of Islam and abrogated certain practices from the pre-Islamic time of ignorance.

As the people of Makkah listened to the Prophet's (ﷺ) address, their apprehension was replaced by tranquillity. They felt safe in their homes, and they had just heard a pronouncement that ushered in a new era in which there would be no retribution and revenge, no usury, no vainglorious pride in lineage, and no unjust class domination. Makkah retained its sacrosanct status, and the Holy House retained its custodians. No favouritism was shown, even to the Prophet's (ﷺ) uncle al-'Abbās, the chief of the Banī Hāshim. The Prophet (ﷺ) returned the Ka'bah's key to the Banī 'Abd al-Dār, affirmed a system of justice in which all people were equal, provided for the poor from the wealth of the rich, addressed people's disputes, settled blood compensations, and ended whatever caused dispute and conflict. He accomplished it all in a few minutes, in a short speech that made it feel as if Makkah had been reborn, as if centuries of idolatry, oppression and isolation had been lifted from its shoulders, as if the city had reconnected with its

268. Al-Wāqidī, *Kitāb al-Maghāzī*, vol. 2, 835-836.

Abrahamic legacy, regaining its status as the destination for all, from every distant corner.

The emancipated

Those who embraced Islam on the day of the conquest became known as the emancipated (al-ṭulaqā'). The Prophet (ﷺ) ensured that they were introduced into the Muslim community and integrated into the nation of Islam. This was only to be expected from the Noble Prophet (ﷺ) regarding the general population of Makkah and their moderate leaders. It was surprising, however, how he dealt with the extremist leaders of the Quraysh. Just before the conquest began, he had issued orders for their elimination, but he later pardoned them, granted them amnesty, indulged them, and showed them kindness.

An account of Suhayl ibn 'Amr's conversion to Islam makes interesting reading.

> Suhayl ibn 'Amr said: "When Allah's Messenger (ﷺ) entered Makkah and cemented his victory, I rushed home and locked my door. I sent [a message] to my son 'Abdallah ibn Suhayl to seek Muḥammad's protection for me, for I truly believed that I would be killed. I began thinking about my past with Muḥammad and his companions and [realised] that no one had a worse record than I. I had confronted Allah's Messenger (ﷺ) on the day of al-Ḥudaybīyyah in a manner that no one had done before, and I was the one who had [insisted] what he should write. I was also present at Badr and Uḥud, and whenever the Quraysh made a move, I was with them."
>
> 'Abdallah ibn Suhayl approached Allah's Messenger (ﷺ) and asked: "O Messenger of Allah, [will] you grant my father your protection?" Allah's Messenger (ﷺ) replied: "Yes, he is protected with Allah's protection, so let him show himself." Then Allah's Messenger (ﷺ) told those around him: "Whoever meets Suhayl ibn 'Amr, do not look at him harshly. Let him come out [of hiding]. By my life, Suhayl truly has intelligence

> and honour, and someone like him [will not] ignore Islam. He has seen that [the position in which] he has been placed cannot benefit him." 'Abdallah informed his father of the pronouncement of Allah's Messenger (ﷺ). Suhayl said: "He was, by Allah, righteous during his youth and in old age." [However,] Suhayl still vacillated. He went to Ḥunayn with the Prophet (ﷺ) as an idolater but accepted Islam at al-Ji'rānah."[269]

Another of the extremist leaders who faced a death penalty was 'Ikrimah ibn Abī Jahl. He had fled to the coast and had hoped to board a ship to Yemen. His wife, Umm Ḥakīm, sought the Prophet's (ﷺ) protection for her husband. When the Prophet (ﷺ) assented, she travelled to 'Ikrimah and convinced him to return. When 'Ikrimah was close to Makkah, the Prophet (ﷺ) told his companions: "'Ikrimah ibn Abī Jahl comes to you as a believer and an immigrant. Do not curse his father, for verily cursing the deceased offends the living and does not reach the deceased." Before they reached Makkah, 'Ikrimah asked to have sexual intercourse with his wife, but she rejected him. She said: "Verily you are a disbeliever, and I am a Muslim." He responded: "Surely a matter that keeps you from me [must certainly] be of great importance." When the Prophet (ﷺ) saw 'Ikrimah, he jumped up from joy—even though he was not wearing his upper garment. Allah's Messenger (ﷺ) then sat down while 'Ikrimah remained standing before him with Umm Ḥakīm, who was veiled.

> He said: "O Muḥammad, this woman informed me that you granted me your protection." Allah's Messenger (ﷺ) replied: "She has spoken the truth; you are protected." 'Ikrimah asked: "To what do you invite, O Muḥammad?" He replied: "I call upon you to bear witness that there is no god but Allah, and that I indeed am the Messenger of Allah; that you perform the prayer and pay the zakāh (compulsory wealth tax) and do [such and such]," until he had outlined all the practices of Islam. 'Ikrimah said: "By Allah, you have not invited except to the truth and a matter that is good and beautiful. By Allah, before you invited to that, you were the most honest in speech and the most kind among us… Verily, I bear witness that there is no god

269. Al-Wāqidī, *Kitāb al-Maghāzī*, vol. 2, 846.

> but Allah, and I bear witness that Muḥammad is His servant and messenger." Allah's Messenger (ﷺ) was pleased. 'Ikrimah said: "O Messenger of Allah, teach me the best thing that I may say." He said: "You say, I bear witness that there is no god except Allah and that Muḥammad is His servant and messenger." 'Ikrimah asked: "And then what?" Allah's Messenger (ﷺ) said: "You say: I bear witness before Allah and before everyone present that I am a Muslim, a Muhājir and one who strives [in Allah's Path, a mujāhid]." 'Ikrimah repeated this, and Allah's Messenger (ﷺ) said: "Whatever you ask of me today that I [am able] to give to anyone, I will give it to you." 'Ikrimah said: "I ask you to seek forgiveness for me for every hostility with which I sought to harm you, or path [of enmity] that I set out on, or places I confronted you in, or [hurtful] words that I spoke to your face or in your absence." Allah's Messenger (ﷺ) said: "O Allah, forgive him every hostility with which he harmed me, and every path he set out on, seeking by that journey to extinguish your light. And forgive him for any insults that he inflicted on me, whether to my face or in my absence." 'Ikrimah responded: "I am satisfied, O Messenger of Allah. I swear, by Allah, O Messenger of Allah, that I will not spare any expense that I used to spend in blocking the path of Allah, except that I will spend twice as much in the path of Allah, nor fighting that I engaged in to block the path of Allah, except that I will exert twice the effort in fighting in the path of Allah."[270]

The third member of the extremist trio, Ṣafwān ibn Umayyah, had been the most hostile toward the Prophet (ﷺ). He had fled to al-Shu'aybah Port, close to present-day Jeddah. 'Umayr ibn Wahb sought protection for him from the Prophet (ﷺ).

> He said: "O Messenger of Allah, the leader of my people has taken flight and will fling himself into the sea, afraid that you will not grant him your protection. So [I ask you to] grant him your protection and let my mother and father be your ransom." Allah's Messenger (ﷺ) said: "I grant him my protection." 'Umayr then pursued Ṣafwān until he caught up to him and

270. Al-Wāqidī, *Kitāb al-Maghāzī*, vol. 2, 851-852.

informed him: "Allah's Messenger has granted you protection." Ṣafwān responded: "No! By Allah, I will not return with you until you bring me a symbol that I recognise." 'Umayr returned to Allah's Messenger (ﷺ) and told him: "O Messenger of Allah, I went to Ṣafwān, who was fleeing. He wanted to kill himself. I informed him that you had granted him your protection, but he said he would not return until I took him a symbol that he recognises." Allah's Messenger (ﷺ) said: "Take my turban." It was a garment that Allah's Messenger had wound around his head, a garment of ḥibrah [that was made in Yemen]. 'Umayr again went searching for Ṣafwān. He found him and showed him the garment. "O Abū Wahb, I have come to you from the best of people, the most affectionate of people, the kindest of people, and the most patient. His glory is your glory, his honour is your honour, his dominion is your dominion. Son of your mother and father, I remind you of Allah for [the sake of] your own soul." Ṣafwān replied: "I am afraid I will be killed." 'Umayr said: "He has invited you to enter Islam, if you are happy to do so. If not, he has granted you two months [respite], and he is the most faithful and the most gracious of people. He sent you his turban that he wore around his head. Do you know it?" "Yes," Ṣafwān replied. 'Umayr showed it to him. Ṣafwān said: "Yes, that is the one." Ṣafwān then returned [to Makkah]. When he reached Allah's Messenger (ﷺ), he was praying the 'Aṣr (mid-afternoon) prayer with the Muslims in the mosque. Ṣafwān asked: "How many times do you pray in the day and night?" 'Umayr replied: "Five prayers." Ṣafwān asked: "And Muḥammad leads them in prayer?" 'Umayr said: "Yes." When the Prophet (ﷺ) concluded [the prayer], Ṣafwān shouted: "O Muḥammad, verily 'Umayr ibn Wahb brought me your turban and claimed that you invited me to you if I was satisfied with a certain matter. And if not, then you will grant me two months [respite]." Allah's Messenger (ﷺ) said: "Dismount, O Abū Wahb." He responded: "No, by Allah. Not until you give me clarity." Allah's Messenger (ﷺ) said: "You will be granted four months." Ṣafwān dismounted.[271]

271. Al-Wāqidī, *Kitāb al-Maghāzī*, vol. 2, 853-854.

'Ikrimah accepted Islam immediately, but Suhayl and Ṣafwān remained polytheists for a while longer. This did not prevent the Prophet (ﷺ) from consulting them and borrowing weapons from Ṣafwān before the Battle of Ḥunayn. When the Prophet (ﷺ) had asked to borrow the weapons, Ṣafwān asked: "Voluntarily or coercively?" The Prophet (ﷺ) replied: "A loan for a period." The Prophet (ﷺ) had no need to borrow weapons from Ṣafwān; rather, he sought to soften his heart and to deal with him in a normal way so that Ṣafwān would feel that he was in the same trench as the Muslims.

Ṣafwān accepted Islam only after the Battle of Ḥunayn. He marched with the Prophet (ﷺ) against the Hawāzin and rode beside him after the battle. As the Prophet (ﷺ) marched, inspecting booty:

> Ṣafwān began to look intensely at a mountain pass full of cattle and sheep. Allah's Messenger (ﷺ) gazed at him and asked: Abū Wahb, do you like this mountain pass?" He said: "Yes." The Prophet (ﷺ) said: "It is yours, with everything in it." Ṣafwān replied: "No one would give this with such satisfaction other than one with the heart of a prophet. I bear witness that there is no god except Allah, and Muḥammad is His servant and messenger." He accepted Islam on the spot.[272]

The day of the conquest was a day of gracious pardon, without favour or reprimand. The Prophet (ﷺ) did not treat the people as if they were defeated and humiliated; he did not coerce them to seek pardon or forgiveness. He looked beyond all this; he pardoned men and women who had committed the worst transgressions against the Muslims and granted them amnesty. He opened the doors of Islam for them and allowed them to enter without compulsion or humiliation.

The Prophet's (ﷺ) policy to protect the honour of the Quraysh succeeded; Makkah maintained its covenant with the new religion. When some Arabs abandoned Islam after the death of the Prophet (ﷺ), the Quraysh stood firm. Suhayl ibn 'Amr addressed the people in Makkah much as Abū Bakr had addressed those in Madinah. He recited the verse:

272. Al-Wāqidī, *Kitāb al-Maghāzī*, vol. 2, 853-854.

> Muḥammad is no more than a messenger. Other messengers passed on before him. If he died or was killed, would you revert to your old ways? If anyone did so, he would not harm Allah in the least; but Allah will reward the grateful (Qur'ān 3:144).

Suhayl then said:

> Whoever worshipped Muḥammad, know that Muḥammad has died; and whoever worshipped Allah, verily Allah is alive and never dies. By Allah, verily I know that this religion will spread like the spreading of the sun from its rising to its setting; so do not let yourselves be swayed by this. The death of a prophet is a reality; but Allah is present, is living, and never dies. Islam will prevail as long as the heavens and the earth prevail.

Following his call, the people of Makkah stood firm in their faith. Suhayl went out fighting in the path of Allah until he attained martyrdom in the Battle of al-Yarmūk. His companion 'Ikrimah ibn Abī Jahl was martyred with Suhayl, after also fighting earnestly and sincerely in Allah's path.

A beautiful gesture of the Prophet (ﷺ) was to appoint 'Itāb ibn Usayd as the governor of Makkah. 'Itāb was a young man in his twenties, one of the "emancipated" who accepted Islam on the day of the conquest of Makkah. From the Banī Umayyah tribe, he was also Abū Sufyān's nephew. 'Itāb was appointed when the Prophet (ﷺ) marched to Ḥunayn. He remained Makkah's governor through the caliphates of Abū Bakr and 'Umar. He was known for his integrity and resolve.

The Prophet's (ﷺ) policy of pardoning his opponents had a long-term impact; it laid the foundation for the spread of Islam across the Arabian Peninsula and beyond. The Quraysh carried a huge share of the honour of spreading Islam eastward and westward. Their children and grandchildren conquered many lands, carrying the universal message to all people. The Prophet's (ﷺ) methodology of dealing with the Quraysh was clear, even in the days of difficulty, siege, and oppression. It was the same methodology that he had expressed when the Quraysh had injured him and pursued his small group of companions. He had, at that time, supplicated: "Lord, guide my people for they do not know." It is the same methodology that he had expressed after the worst torment he had suffered at their hands in Ṭā'if. He had prayed then that Allah would give them progeny who would worship Allah alone.

CONCLUSION

A new beginning, a brighter future

"This is only a reminder to the worlds. And you shall certainly know the truth of it after a while" (Qur'ān 38:87-88).

There is nothing more beautiful than basking in the shadow of the sīrah of the Prophet of Islam, Muḥammad (ﷺ). This experience and these moments of reflection bind Muslims firmly to the foundations of our self-perception, to our mission, and to our legacy of knowledge. In addressing today's political and strategic realities, we are in desperate need of the insights that may be derived from the life of the Prophet (ﷺ). These are the insights on which this book has attempted to shed some light.

In the twenty-first-century context, the domain of politics and strategy presents us with a serious challenge. Current methodologies for engaging public affairs—whether political, strategic, or economic—are fraught with problems. These methodologies, contending strands of which have become part of contemporary orthodoxy and have become globalised, have penetrated deeply into our epistemological consciousness, social structures, and systems of ethics and morality, and, in the process, they have limited our intellectual creativity and imagination. They have left generations with the impression that there are no alternative forms of thought,[273] and have thus struck at the heart of our ability to engage with our present or to imagine better futures. These intellectual onslaughts have belittled and undermined traditional and age-old understandings and worldviews, dismissing them as irrelevant and forcing everyone to engage within predetermined frameworks.

Between dreaming and confusion

The age that we live in is characterised by intellectual stagnation.

273. Former British prime minister Margaret Thatcher famously said, 'There is no alternative' when referring to her neoliberal antipoor economic policies. That sentence has developed its own acronym: TINA.

Methodologically, some of us still look to the past and see beauty in it. In reality, however, we live in the present and view it with contempt, and our gaze into the future reveals terrifying possibilities. Such perplexity can produce either a generation of dreamers or a generation of the confounded. The task before us is to encourage dreamers who will dare to imagine, and strive to create, a future that is a continuation of, and draws inspiration and lessons from, our glorious past. This book engages with, and provides pointers for, this task.

By focusing on the political and strategic aspects of the sīrah, it does not intend to spark a yearning to live in a beautiful past, nor does it aim to instigate veneration for certain actions and stances. It is, instead, an attempt to contribute to an epistemological methodology and an integrated approach that will help develop a new political and strategic consciousness for the present conjuncture.

To construct such a methodology, we must understand the spirit of the Prophet's (ﷺ) political praxis, grasp its objectives, and examine its purposes and consequences. Every sound methodology requires a source of knowledge, a higher purpose, and a methodical approach. This book sheds light on these aspects in the Prophet's (ﷺ) political and strategic praxis. To sketch the outlines of such a methodology, we first identify seven unique insights and characteristics about human consciousness that arise out of the actions of the Prophet (ﷺ) as a leader in the political, economic, and social domains. These insights are: the role of monotheism in the liberation of humanity; the manner in which revelation interacts with context; the importance of human responsibility; society as the repository of power and sovereignty; the role and responsibility of the individual; the need for rational and precise assessment; and the preference of engagement over conflict.

The liberatory praxis of monotheism

The objective behind every political and strategic action of the Prophet (ﷺ) was the liberation of human beings, collectively and individually, from the shackles of idolatry, ignorance, narrowness, and oppression. The foundation of the Prophetic message was monotheism (tawḥīd), which represents and aims for the complete emancipation of the human being from dependence on everything other than the Sublime and All-Powerful Creator. It was this idea that unleashed the massive and powerful stream of human consciousness that revealed the latent capacities of the Prophet's (ﷺ) companions and became a torrent that enabled them to transform a place and an age stagnated in pre-Islamic ignorance (jahīlīyyah) to the dynamism and vibrancy of Islam.

There is no better expression of this than the Qur'ān's Verse of the Throne (2:255), which provides the most wondrous illustration of Allah's sublime status, Allah's complete control over all existence, and Allah's absolute greatness.

> Allah: there is no deity but Him, the Ever Living, the Self-sustaining. Neither drowsiness nor sleep overtakes Him. All that is in the heavens and on the earth belong to Him. Who is there who can intercede with Him except by His permission? He knows what is before them and what is behind them, but they do not comprehend any of His knowledge except what He wills. His throne extends over the heavens and the earth; it does not weary Him to preserve them both. He is the Most High, the Tremendous.

It is no coincidence that this verse about God's Majesty is followed immediately by a verse affirming human freedom: "There is no compulsion in religion: the path of truth has become distinct from error" (Qur'ān 2:256). We have become accustomed to people in power—kings, rulers, military leaders, or business executives—inflating their reputation, praising their abilities and achievements, and, on the basis of this imagined superiority, granting themselves privileges, powers, and rights that others do not have or are deprived of. They are also wont to engage in authoritarian practices, to impose their decisions on others, and to coerce them into following their orders. By contrast, the All-Powerful and Sublime Creator granted human beings the freedom of belief immediately after the most poignant verse in the Qur'ān that celebrates His Greatness and All-Encompassing Power.

The interplay between revelation and context

The relationship between Allah's revelation and the context to which it was revealed, the transcendent and the prosaic, the eternal other-world and this temporal world, is the most troubling issue for contemporary Islamic thought. The Prophet (ﷺ) provided a solution for this problem. He derived his goals and objectives—as well as his reference point and the framework for his actions in this world—from revelation. It was the revelation of the Qur'ān that guided his and his community's actions. But his pursuit of the ideal did not deter him from engaging with the realities of his time, nor did it cause him to discard any appropriate means of influencing events. He engaged the prevailing context with the best available techniques and methods, and he utilised everything at his disposal to serve his mission—guided at all times by the revelation—as we observe on numerous occasions in his sīrah. His environment was the point of departure for his political and strategic actions, within the framework already provided by the Qur'ān.

This is evident, for example, in his seeking the protection of his uncle Abū Ṭālib, a polytheist, and his willingness to inherit the alliance with the Khuzā'ah tribe from his grandfather 'Abd al-Muṭṭalib. From his Qurayshi lineage, the Prophet (ﷺ) also inherited his status among the Arabs. He was open and positively inclined toward the just king of Abyssinia, and he communicated and maintained relations with his maternal uncles from the Banī al-Najjār in Yathrib. Furthermore, he allowed the two kings of Oman to retain their positions after their conversion to Islam, as he did for the king of al-Baḥrayn and the Persian governor of Yemen. In summary, he respected the prevailing custom and affirmed the tribal order as long as it helped fulfil his mission and did not fall foul of the Divine guidance that he had been given.

Human responsibility

The praxis developed out of the constant interplay between revelation and context highlights our third insight: the acknowledgement of human responsibility and its interaction with Divine Will. This matter, as much as it is a challenge to the contemporary Islamic consciousness, also challenged the companions and society of the Prophet (ﷺ). Being guided by revelation and by the Divine Will does not mean that the human being may be absolved from individual responsibility in public and societal affairs, be they political, strategic, social, or economic.

Revelation is the source of guidance, the sublime compass, the regulator of human objectives, and the inhibitor of certain destructive actions. In the life of the Prophet (ﷺ), revelation descended after specific events. It also proscribed certain actions and corrected others. It focused the attention of the Muslims on the implicit moral lessons underlying events, pointed out weaknesses, and braced them for the challenges and difficulties on the path. But it was people who then had to assume responsibility for their actions.

In the Prophetic methodology, the Prophet (ﷺ) assumed full responsibility for his engagement with contextual realities. He was responsible for his interpretation, understanding, assessment, engagement, and the resultant outcomes. That is why he used all necessary and available tools to fulfil his mission in the best way possible. He built alliances, mobilised armies, established intelligence networks, monitored responses, deployed emissaries, utilised the soft power of poets and public speakers, and built constitutional, legal, and consultative systems. All this was accomplished within an integrated context of planning and human action—very human endeavours. The Prophet (ﷺ) evaluated these plans and actions and if the outcome was not optimal, he drew lessons from the experience, corrected any shortcomings, addressed the consequences of any setback, and continued the march forward.

His sīrah foregrounds an integrated and pragmatic human praxis that can logically be grasped and practically justified, but which is regulated by a higher objective and a single goal: to liberate humanity from corrupt systems of bondage to a world in balance and justice.

Power is vested in the collective

The Prophetic methodology introduced a unique and universal technique to engage with power and wealth, politics and economics. In contemporary politics, power implies a veneration of strength, control of resources and wealth, and absolute sovereignty. The person or group in a position of power is usually driven by a desire to tyrannise to the point of self-deification, and to regard themselves as autonomous and independent of all others. In the effort to protect their own status, they belittle the status, honour, and dignity of others, negate others' identities, and turn them—or attempt to turn them—into submissive slaves or acolytes. This militates against the innate human nature of striving for freedom and autonomy from this world, and resistance to bondage. The Prophetic methodology opposed this notion of power; he conceptually and practically transformed the idea of power into a resource that belonged to the entire society rather than to select individuals or groups. In his model of society, people resolved matters through processes of consultation that then became binding on every individual, even if one or more persons had different views on the matter under consideration.

Similarly, in this model, wealth should remain firmly in the hands of the people as a whole "so that it may not circulate only among your rich" (Qur'ān 59:7). Even the Prophet (ﷺ) did not have the authority to spend from the people's wealth without their explicit approval. Islamic mechanisms such as zakāh (compulsory wealth tax), the proscription of usury, mandatory and formulaic distribution of inheritance, and the prevention of monopolies were successful in preventing social and economic domination of one person or group over others.

The impact of the notion of power vesting in the collective also had psychological and social consequences. While upholding the need for individual responsibility, it destroyed the idea of the individual as the centre and focus of life. The individualism that plagues the world today is a result of the system of capitalism that sees worth only in the individual's ability to produce, focusing on the smallest unit of society and making that person the most important factor. It is this individualism that encourages materialism and consumerism, destroying souls, economies, and damaging the earth, while making a small group of people wealthier and giving them greater control over the affairs of the world than ever before. In the Prophetic model, the individual's focus was society and its betterment. The reciprocal responsibility was that of the society to ensure the dignity and improvement of each individual member. The society as a whole was responsible for each person's well-being and development, and mechanisms such as zakāh were intended to ensure that society embraced and fulfilled that responsibility.It is no surprise, then, that the eleventh-century scholar, Ibn Ḥazm al-Andalusi, the imam of the Zahiri school, wrote in his *al-Muḥalla*:

A starving person might fight for his rights when necessary [to gain access to] the surplus food in someone's possession. If the starving person is killed [while claiming his rights], then his killer is subject to qiṣāṣ [just retribution], and if the one who is refusing [to share the food] is killed, he is cursed by Allah because he blocked a person from his rights. [In that case, the one who refused to share] is regarded as being from a rebellious group…[274]

> If a person dies of hunger in a town, its inhabitants are assumed to have killed him, and blood money should be taken from them."[275]

The individual's role and responsibility

The fact that power is vested in the collective does not, however, negate the responsibility of the individual. The Prophet (ﷺ) laid the foundations for a unique relationship between the individual and the project of social, political, and economic transformation. Every individual became a partner in this project, had ownership over it, and ardently believed in its importance. In this, the individual was driven by personal faith and commitment and was also secure in the knowledge that, in the fulfilment of this project, there was no preference for one person over another based on lineage, wealth, or authority. This relationship is what unleashed innovation and initiative among the companions. A bondsman could propose a meritorious idea that would be embraced by others of established lineages; a new convert might lead, politically or on the battlefield, those who had embraced Islam

274. Abū Muḥammad ʿAlī ibn Aḥmad ibn Saʿīd ibn Ḥazm, *Kitāb al-Muhallā bi'l Āthār,* vol. 4, 282, https://shamela.ws/book/767/1523#p1.
275. Abū Muḥammad ʿAlī ibn Aḥmad ibn Saʿīd ibn Ḥazm, *Kitāb al-Muhallā bi'l Āthār,* vol. 11, 186, https://shamela.ws/book/767/4736#p1.

at the beginning of the Prophetic mission; and a youth might express an opinion that differed from those who were more experienced, with the certainty that it would be seriously considered. Thus, a model was created that was unlike any other at the time, neither in the land of the Arabs nor anywhere else.

Rational assessment

A critical, and perhaps the most prominent, element of the Prophet's (ﷺ) political and strategic praxis was his rational, careful, and precise assessment of the balance of forces. This was the case at the interpersonal, inter-tribal and international levels, and included deliberations in military strategy, geopolitical analysis, and geographical assessment. The Prophet's (ﷺ) plans were not based on vain desires, wishful thinking, or emotional reactions. His situational assessments were always realistic, and his planning always practical. He considered the matters at hand in the manner that they presented themselves—not as emotion might dictate—and he went straight to the heart of the matter without bothering about irrelevant considerations.

With the Prophet's (ﷺ) leadership, the Muslims never fought an enemy that was at the peak of its strength. In such cases, his strategy was usually to occupy the enemy with other matters that would reduce its strength and exhaust it. Then, when the balance of forces had tipped in favour of the Muslims, he would exploit the opportunity. Every military or political step that he took was measured, well-timed, and followed a precise plan and schedule. In the terrain of battle in the peninsula, he used profound wisdom to engage (differently and separately) all four fronts: the coast, the desert, the north of the peninsula, and Makkah.

His seizing the initiative often surprised his opponents and forced them into reactive posturing. He keenly monitored all existing alliances; constantly received news to be analysed; pondered and reflected over regarding geopolitical, economic, and social events; and developed a rigorous understanding of the balance of forces. This gave him the ability to respond to various developments in the most appropriate manner. His engagement with the relevant role-players was always prudent and displayed tremendous flexibility. The Prophet (ﷺ) also developed precise insight into the global and regional balance of forces and used that insight to plan his strategy. For example, he invaded the periphery of the Levant only after the disruption of the global balance of forces and the weakening of its two major powers. Furthermore, he corresponded with the rulers of Oman, al-Baḥrayn, and Yemen only after they had been freed from the yoke of Persian hegemony.

Preferring engagement over conflict

Our final insight derived from the sīrah is that the Prophet (ﷺ) introduced a new methodology in political and strategic relations, favouring engagement (al-tadāfu‘) over conflict. Competition, contestation, and conflict were the main ways in which human beings resolved their problems and gained ascendency and control. Wars were thus the engines for empire-building and a deliberate means of attaining domination and wealth. This resonates in contemporary political and international relations theories; conflict and competitiveness remain central to shaping the modern international system. Following a different paradigm, the Prophet (ﷺ) introduced engagement as a preferable alternative. Engagement neither leads to, nor has as its goal, the destruction or elimination of one's opponents, the "other". It is more focused on interaction, pressure, and redirection in a manner that encourages the opponent to become a partner in the achievement of goodness. With engagement, the outcome can be positive, and everyone can benefit. Conflict, on the other hand, is a zero-sum game where one party is the victor and the other the vanquished.

A new global order

The recent history of the Islamic ummah has been characterised by crises, some of which have been strategic and some intellectual. We are now harvesting their bitter fruits and find ourselves struggling to survive in a tumultuous and extremely stressful world. Frustration with the present and pessimism over the future have overtaken the minds of generations of Muslims, especially Muslim youth.

Our current reality demands deep reflection—especially regarding political and strategic praxis. The political systems and regimes that exist today differ fundamentally from those at the time of the Prophet (ﷺ) and the Islamic caliphate. The modern state is altogether different from the "state" that had prevailed in that period. Moreover, globalisation—in its economic, diplomatic, political, legal, social, and technical dimensions—has created a paradigm for the modern state from which we cannot escape.

The question of engaging effectively with the present and the future conjunctures transcends politics and poses a much deeper and more comprehensive challenge. Our ever-changing realities impose practical and constantly evolving values that one must adopt or adapt to simply to be able to continue with daily life. Some people reject these impositions from a theoretical basis, to protect their own identities and values, but this often results in a dangerous schizophrenia that leads to a clash between one's ideals and the reality that confronts (or embraces) them. In their attempts to reconcile the two, they end up with anxiety, depression, and multiple personalities. There are numerous examples of this phenomenon in our daily lives, relating both to individuals and groups or communities. Many people live lives that are "modern" at work, in the streets, in the laboratories, in their financial transactions and educational interactions, but they hold on to inherited intellectual systems and theories in their homes, places of worship, and social structures because these, for them, have historical legitimacy.

Such a paradox is harmful, undermines one's cognitive and psychological balance, and is an obstacle to building a stable personality or community. Consequently, those who are afraid of the new or the modern attempt to deal with it in one of two ways. Some resort to a continuous feeling of sinfulness, pessimism, rejection of reality, and the absence of tolerance, which sometimes lead to extremism. Preeminent in the minds of such people is the need for constant battle against all that is new, coupled with nostalgia and attempts to reconstruct the present in the image of an inherited ideal. Some in this group even resort to violence in the attempt to reclaim that ideal. Others attempt to formalise their multiple personalities and the rupture between ideal and reality by compartmentalising their lives, with their practical and material existence being separated from their spiritual and theological existence. Their political and economic lives lie somewhere in between. Such a person might live for a period in spiritual isolation, divorced from practical life, and may seek personal salvation and psychological stability by turning to meditation or, for example, to Sufism. Their practical and material life, meanwhile, continues unaffected along its trajectory. Neither of these approaches is satisfactory in resolving this problem. Both the struggle to recreate the historical ideal and the attempt to formalise the split personality are doomed to fail.

The best solution is to harmonise one's intellectual and theoretical frameworks with the constantly changing current reality, and to craft a vision that can deliver a unified intellectual paradigm free of cognitive dissonance and double standards. This effort requires a deep awareness and careful analysis of the context along with a constantly evolving understanding of the ideal. Such an effort is possible only for minds that are, firstly, liberated from the prison of blind imitation that reflects the laziness of our minds and, secondly, willing to look deep into our traditions and history to learn lessons that will engage with the current context.

There is no reason to be afraid of the future, unless we reject its inevitability and shut ourselves off from it, preferring to live in the past. In this case, it will overwhelm us, even as we agonise over and try to revive the old. Suspending the future is an impossibility. People who are afraid of change continue to embrace certain cultural concepts and practices, even if they have become archaic and irrelevant, believing them to hold a certain sanctity that has been inherited from a pristine and beautiful past. For them, the problem is the present. They therefore place all the blame on the present and on the people living in this present, and they exhibit a hatred for the future and the degeneracy that they believe it will bring. More than anything else, what we need for the future is a psyche—individual and communal—that is balanced and confident and that offers stability and satisfaction, without deviating from the ethical and existential objectives that give life meaning and mission. We do not need a psyche that is fearful and fortifies itself with immobility, and our identity should not be based simply on a perceived version of history while ignoring the present.

We must consider identity a dynamic awareness that grows, develops, and matures, rather than as a fixed, foundational category. Change does not necessarily mean a compromising of one's identity, except if one regards identity as stagnant. Whether change is for better or for worse depends on, and is a consequence of, our interaction with it. We are not required to acclimatise or submit to change but to understand and engage it, so that we may strengthen good values and keep all evil inclinations in check.

The sīrah and the future

Ever since the colonialist interventions in Muslims lands, and their engagement with—and, often, assault on—the Islamic intellectual tradition, particularly toward the end of the colonial era, the predominant approach of Muslims seeking to liberate themselves from the yoke of colonialism and the imposition of capitalism has been to search for one or another foreign ideology or path that could serve as references in their liberatory struggles. This attempt by nations and communities that had previously been oppressed to liberate themselves using the ideologies and tools of their oppressors' culture and paradigm is something that afflicts not only Muslims. Sections of elites in all postcolonial societies have resorted to such attempts, which included the importation—and sometimes attempts to localise—different forms of nationalism, liberalism, communism, and so forth. It is clear that these attempts have failed and, in some cases, have left our societies worse off. True liberation will come from a serious attempt at digging deeply into our own traditions, epistemologies, and methodologies to unearth the liberatory spirit within them so that our struggles for justice might be authentic, indigenous, and suited to our environments.

For Muslims, this process must necessarily include an interrogation of the sīrah and probing its relevance to our struggles in our contexts. This book, with one eye on contemporary challenges, is an attempt to do exactly that in the political and strategic fields. It discusses the experiences of the first community of Muslims, revealing the tools that they used, guided by Allah's revelation and Allah's Messenger (ﷺ), to address the challenges that they confronted. While the challenges today are vastly different from those that faced the Prophet's (ﷺ) community almost fifteen centuries ago, the methodology that he developed remains relevant, as is clear from the seven insights discussed earlier.

The onslaught against justice and human dignity has become globalised, and the response and resistance to it, too, should be globalised. The challenges facing humanity are gargantuan: from the poisoning of our livelihoods through climate change, to the deliberate impoverishment and under-development of entire communities and nations of people (while a small elite benefits from the misery of the majority), to genocidal programmes in some places, to the deprivation of basic freedoms in almost all societies across the world.

These challenges require us to join with those who share our values. The differences between the various nations and peoples are no longer as they were in the past. The future is no longer a private space that small communities can mould as we see fit. We must look toward a single human destiny that must be built by the broadest coalition of people seeking justice, to ensure that the future will be one that will benefit all, not just a privileged elite. The values of justice, freedom, and inclusivity do not concern Muslims alone; they are shared concerns among the majority of human beings. It is therefore necessary that we find allies everywhere, and that we rebuild our alliances on the basis of common human values. Only then will we truly have been faithful to the message of our Prophet (ﷺ), which is directed at all humanity; only then will we have perfected good morals; and only then will we have struggled against corruption and depravity on earth. In the Qur'ān, the struggle against corruption is often twinned with the process of setting matters aright.

Our struggles against injustice, then, must also include a programme for the construction of a more just future for all people. Only when the solid structures and institutions of the powerful begin to shake and crack will the marginalised and weak around the world find new opportunities to advance, and to liberate themselves from the yoke of injustices that have accumulated over centuries. The strategic approach of the Prophet of Allah (ﷺ) provides us with critical markers for the way forward.

We ask Allah for guidance and steadfastness.

All praise is due to Allah, Lord of all that exists.

Glossary

Aḥābīsh: A coalition of the marginalised social groups of Makkah

al-Anṣār: Madinan allies

al-Fāsiq: The Profligate

al-Ḥijābah: Maintenance of the Ka‘bah

al-Ḥums: The Sanctified People

al-I‘tifār: Literally meaning "polluted by soil," but practically suicide by starvation

al-Jāhilīyyah: Pre-Islamic era of ignorance

al-Liwā'a: The Brigade

al-Mu‘allaqāt: Hanging odes

al-Muhājirūn: Makkan émigrés

al-Mujīrūn:The Protectors

al-Munāfarah: Tribal form of litigation or arbitration

al-Munāfiqūn :The Hypocrites

al-Rifādah: Food Provisioning

al-Siqāyah: Water Supplying—for supplying pilgrims with water and milk

Dār al-Nadwah: The House of Assembly

Ghazwah: Campaign, i.e. a military excursion led by the Prophet (ﷺ) himself

Hadīth: The speech, actions, and condonations of the Prophet Muḥammad (ﷺ)

Ḥājib: Doorkeeper of the Ka'bah

Ḥajj: Pilgrimage

Ḥaramīyūn: Sanctified

Hijrah: The Prophet's (ﷺ) migration to Yathrib (Madinah)

Ḥilf al-Aḥlāf: Alliance of the Allies

Ḥilf al-Fuḍūl: Alliance of the Virtuous

Ḥilf La'qat al-Dam: Alliance of a Lick of Blood

Ḥilf al-Muṭayyībīn: Alliance of the Scented

Ḥurūb al-Fijār: Immoral Wars

Iḥrām: The state of ritual sanctity. Also, the pilgrim's garments.

Īlāf Madinah: The Madinah Pact

Īlāf Quraysh: The Quraysh Pact

Mawālī (pl.), *Mawla* (sing): Clients, client—someone who has entered into a client alliance with a tribe that takes them under its wing and provides them with tribal protection and cover.

Qiblah: Prayer direction

Ṣaḥīfat al-Madinah: Charter of Madinah

Sīrah (al-Sīrah al-Nabawiyya): The biography of the Prophet (ﷺ). From the root word which means to travel (sārah), it refers to the journey of the Prophet's (ﷺ) life. The sīrah is generally regarded by Muslims as not just a historical or biographical account but as normative, and therefore a model for emulation.

Sirīyyah: Expedition, i.e. a military excursion led by a Muslim leader other than the Prophet (ﷺ) himself.

Tawḥīd: Monotheism

Ummah: Nation or community

'*Umrāh*: Lesser Pilgrimage

'Umrah al-Qaḍā': Compensatory pilgrimage

Zakāh: Compulsory wealth tax

References

Arabic Sources

1. Al-'Asqalānī, Shihāb al-Dīn Abū al-Faḍl Aḥmad ibn Nūr al-Dīn 'Alī ibn Muḥammad ibn Ḥajar. *Al-Iṣābah fī Tamyīz al-Ṣaḥābah.* Vol. 13. Beirut: Dār al-Kutub al-'Ilmīyyah, 1994.

2. Al-Baghdādi, 'Abd al-Qādir. *Khizānat al-Adab.* Vol. 1. 4th ed. Cairo: Al-Khānjī Library, 1997.

3. Al-Baghdādī, Abū Ja'far. *Kitāb al-Munammaq fī Akhbār Quraysh.* Vol. 1. Beirut: 'Ālam al-Kutub, 1985.

4. Al-Balādhurī, Aḥmad ibn Yaḥyā. *Ansāb al-Ashrāf.* Vol. 1. Beirut: Dār al-Fikr, 1996.

5. Al-Bayhaqī, Abū Bakr. *Dalā'il al-Nubūwwah.* Beirut and Cairo: Dār al-Kutub al-'Ilmīyyah and Dār al-Rayyān li al-Turāth, 1998.

6. Al-Bukhārī, Muḥammad ibn Ismā'īl. *Ṣaḥīḥ al-Bukhārī.* Damascus: Dār Ibn Kathīr, 2002.

7. Al-Būṭī, Muḥammad Sa'īd Ramaḍān. *Fiqh al-Sīrah al-Nabawīyyah.* Damascus: Dār al-Fikr, 1991.

8. Al-Dhahabī, Shams ad-Dīn. *Siyar 'A'lām al-Nubalā'.* Vol. 18. Cairo: Dār al-Ḥadīth, 2006.

9. Al-Ghazālī, Muḥammad. *Fiqh al-Sīrah.* Cairo: Dār al-Shurūq, 2000.

10. Al-Ḥamawī, Shihāb al-Dīn Yāqūt ibn 'Abdallah. *Mu'jam al-Buldān.* Vol. 3. Beirut: Dār Ṣādir, 1993.

11. 'Alī, Jawwād. *al-Mufaṣṣal fī Tārīkh al-'Arab Qabl al-Islām.* Beirut: Dār al-Sāqī, 2001.

12. Al-Jawzīyyah, Ibn al-Qayyim. *Hidāy'ah al-Ḥiyāra' fī Ajwibah al-Yahud wa al-Naṣāra'*. Makkah: Dār 'Ālam al-Fawā'id, 2008.

13. Al-Maghlūth, Sāmī. *al-Aṭlas al-Tārīkhī li Sīrah al-Rasūl.* 3rd ed. Riyadh: Dār al-'Ubaykān, 2004.

14. Al-Nīsābūrī, Muslim ibn al-Ḥajājj. *Ṣaḥīḥ Muslim.* Edited by Muḥammad Fu'ād 'Abd al-Bāqī. Beirut: Dār Iḥyā' al-Turāth al-'Arabī, 1954.

15. Al-Qurṭubī, Muḥammad ibn Aḥmad al-Anṣārī. *Al-Jāmi' li Aḥkām al-Qur'ān.* 2nd ed. Cairo: Dār al-Kutub al-Miṣrīyyah, 1964.

16. Al-Ṣan'ānī, 'Abd al-Razzāq. *Al-Muṣannaf.* Vol. 5. 2nd ed. India: al-Majlis al-'Ilmī, 1983.

17. Al-Ṣāyigh, Muḥammad Naṣrī. *Al-Sīrah al-Siyāsīyah.* 2nd ed. Beirut: Dār al-Fārābī, 2019.

18. Al-Sibā'ī, Muṣṭafa. *al-Sīrah al-Nabawīyyah: Durūs wa 'Ibar.* Beirut: al-Maktab al-Islāmī, 1985.

19. Al-Ṭabarī, Abū Ja'far Muḥammad ibn Jarīr ibn Yazīd. *Tārīkh al-Ṭabarī.* 2nd ed. Cairo: Dār al-Ma'ārif, 1968.

20. Al-Ṭabarī, Abū Ja'far Muḥammad ibn Jarīr ibn Yazīd. *Jāmi' al-Bayān 'an Ta'wīl Āya al-Qur'ān.* Gizzah: Dār Hajar, 2001.

21. Al-Ṭayyib, 'Abdallah. *Majallat Dirāsāt Ifriqīyyah.* International African University, 1998.

22. Al-Tha'ālibī, Abū Manṣūr. *Thimār al-Qulūb fī al-Muḍāf wa al-Mansūb.* Beirut: al-Maktabah al-'Aṣrīyyah, 2003.

23. Al-Wāqidī, Muḥammad ibn 'Umar. *Kitāb al-Maghāzī.* 3rd ed. Beirut: Dār al-'A'lamī, 1989.

24. Al-Ya'qūbī, Abū al-'Abbās. *Tārīkh al-Ya'qūbī.* 1st ed. Najjaf: Manshūrāt al-Maktabah al-Ḥaydarīyyah, 1964.

25.Ibn al-Athīr, ʿAlī ʿIzz al-Dīn Al-Jazarī. *Al-Kāmil fī al-Tārīkh*. Vol. 2. Beirut: Dār al-Kitāb al-ʻArabī, 1997.

26.Ibn Ḥanbal, Aḥmad. *al-Musnad.* Beirut: Mu'assasah al-Risālah, 2001.

27.Ibn Ḥazm, Abū Muḥammad ʿAlī ibn Aḥmad ibn Saʿīd, *Jawāmiʻ al-Sīrah* (Beirut: Dār al-Kutub al-ʻIlmīyyah).

28.Ibn Ḥazm, Abū Muḥammad ʿAlī ibn Aḥmad ibn Saʿīd, *Kitāb al-Muhallā bi'l Āthār*, Volume 4, https://shamela.ws/book/767/1523.

29.Ibn Ḥazm, Abū Muḥammad ʿAlī ibn Aḥmad ibn Saʿīd, *Kitāb al-Muhallā bi'l Āthār*, Volume 11, https://shamela.ws/book/767/4736.

30.Ibn Hishām, ʻAbd al-Malik. *Al-Sīrah al-Nabawīyyah.* Vol. 1. 2nd ed. Cairo: Muṣṭafa al-Bābī al-Ḥalabī, 1955.

31.Ibn Kathīr, Ismāʻīl ibn ʻUmar. *Al-Bidāyah wa al-Nihāyah.* Damascus: Dār al-Fikr, 1986.

32.Ibn Kathīr, Ismāʻīl ibn ʻUmar. *Tafsīr al-Qur'ān al-ʻAẓīm.* Beirut: Dār al-Kutub al-ʻIlmīyyah, 1998.

33.Ibn Manẓūr, Jamāl al-Dīn. *Mukhtaṣar Tārīkh Dimashq.* Vol. 16. Damascus: Dār al-Fikr, 1984.

34.Ibn Saʻd, Abū ʻAbdallah Muḥammad. *Al-Ṭabaqāt al-Kubra.* Beirut: al-Maktabah al-ʻIlmīyyah, 1990.

35.Al-Nās, Ibn Sayyid. *ʻUyūn al-Athar fī Funūn al-Maghāzī wa al-Shamā'il wa al-Siyar.* 2 vols. Beirut: Dār al-Qalam, 1993.

36.Ibn Zinjawayh, Ḥamad ibn Mikhlad ibn Qutaybah al-Khurasānī. *Kitāb al-Amwāl.* Riyadh: Markaz al-Malik Fayṣal li al-Buḥuth wa al-Dirāsāt al-Islāmīyyah, 1986.

37.Mahrān, Muḥammad Bayūmī. *Dirāsāt fī Tārīkh al-ʻArab al-Qadīm.*

2nd ed. Vol. 1. Alexandria: Dār al-Ma'rifah al-Jāmi'īyyah, 1968.

38. Mīrghanī, Ja'far. *Awrāq al-Mu'tamar al-Duwalī li al-Islām fī Ifrīqīya.* International African University, 2006.

39. Mu'nis, Ḥusayn. *Tārīkh Quraysh – Dirāsah fī Tārīkh Aṣghar Qabīlah 'Arabīyyah Ja'alahā al-Islām 'A'ẓim Qabīlah fī Tārīkh al-Bashar.* Jeddah: Dār al-Sau'dīyyah, 1988.

40. Rizqallah, Aḥmad Mahdī. *al-Sīrah al-Nabawīyyah fī Daw al-Maṣādir al-Aslīyyah: Dirāsah Taḥlīlīyah.* Riyadh: Markaz Malik Fayṣal li al-Buḥūth wa al-Dirāsāt al-Islāmīyyah, 1992.

41. Shāhīn, 'Abd al-Ṣabbūr. *Tārīkh al-Qur'ān.* 3rd ed. Cairo: Dār al-Nahḍah, 2003.

Non-Arabic Sources

42. Anjum, Ovamir. "The 'Constitution' of Medina: Translation, Commentary, and Meaning Today. *Yaqeen Institute,* 14 January 2022, https://yaqeeninstitute.org/read/paper/the-constitution-of-medina-translation-commentary-and-meaning-today.

43. Anthony, Sean W. *Muhammad and the Empires of Faith: The Making of the Prophet of Islam.* Oakland, California: University of California Press, 2020.

44. Apaydin, Mehmet. *Siyer Kronolojisi.* Istanbul: Kuramar, 2018.

45. Beeston, A. F. L. "Two Bi'r Hima Inscriptions Re-Examined". *Bulletin of the School of Oriental and African Studies* 48, no. 1 (February1985): 42-52.

46. Brown, Jonathan A. C. *Hadith: Muhammad's Legacy in the Medieval*

and Modern World. Oxford: Oneworld, 2009.

47.Crone, Patricia and Michael Cook. *Hagarism: The Making of the Islamic World.* Cambridge: Cambridge University Press, 1977.

48.Daniel, Norman. *Islam and the West: The Making of an Image.* Oxford: Oneworld, 1993.

49.Donner, Fred M. *Muhammad and the Believers: At the Origins of Islam.* Cambridge, Massachusetts: Harvard University Press, 2010.

50.*Encyclopædia Iranica*, online edition, New York, 1996-, https://www.iranicaonline.org/pages/citing-iranica.

51.Faizer, Rizwi, ed. *The Life of Muḥammad: Al-Wāqidī's Kitāb al-Maghāzī.* Translated by Rizwi Faizer, Amal Ismail and AbdulKader Tayob. London and New York: Routledge, 2011.

52.Görke, Andreas. "Prospects and limits in the study of the historical Muḥammad". In *The Transmission and Dynamics of the Textual Sources of Islam: Essays in Honour of Harald Motzki,* edited by Nicolet Boekhoff van der Voort, Kees Versteegh, and Joas Wagemakers, 135-151. Leiden and Boston: Brill, 2011.

53.Görke, Andreas and Gregor Schoeler. "Reconstructing the earliest *sīra* texts: The Hiǧra in the corpus of 'Urwa b. al-Zubayr". *Der Islam* 82, no. 2 (2005): 209-220.

54.Görke, Andreas and Gregor Schoeler, *The Earliest Writings on the Life of Muhammad: The 'Urwa Corpus and the Non-Muslim Sources*. Berlin: Gerlach Press, 2024.

55.Görke, Andreas, Harald Motzki and Gregor Schoeler. "First Century Sources for the Life of Muḥammad? A Debate". *Der Islam* 89, no. 2 (2012): 2-59.

56.Guillaume, Alfred. *The Life of Muhammad: A Translation of Ibn Isḥāq's Sīrat Rasūl Allāh.* Oxford: Oxford University Press, 1955.

57.Haykal, Muhammad Husayn. *The Life of Muhammad.* Translated by Isma'il Ragi A. al Faruqi. Oak Brook, USA: American Trust Publications, 1976.

58.Hourani, George Fadlo. *Arab Seafaring in the Indian Ocean.* Princeton: Princeton University Press, 1951.

59.Ibn Rāshid, Ma'mar. *The Expeditions: An Early Biography of Muḥammad.* Edited and translated by Sean W. Anthony. New York and London: New York University Press, 2014.

60.Kaegi, Walter, E. *Heraclius: Emperor of Byzantium.* Cambridge: Cambridge University Press, 2003.

61.Lings, Martin. *Muhammad: His Life Based on the Earliest Sources.* Cambridge: The Islamic Texts Society, 1983.

62.Motzki, Harald, ed. *The Biography of Muḥammad: The Issue of the Sources.* Leiden: Brill, 2000.

63.Nevo, Yehuda D. and Judith Koren. *Crossroads to Islam: The Origins of the Arab Religion and the Arab State.* Amherst: Prometheus Books, 2003.

64.Powers, David S. *Muhammad is Not the Father of Any of Your Men: The Making of the Last Prophet.* Philadelphia: University of Pennsylvania Press, 2009.

65.Procopius Caesariensis. *History of the Wars.* Vol. 1. Translated by H. B. Dewing. Cambridge: Harvard University Press, 1914.

66.Salahi, Adil. *Muhammad: Man and Prophet.* Leicestershire: The Islamic Foundation, 2002.

67.Schoeler, Gregor. *The Biography of Muḥammad: Nature and Authenticity.* Translated by Uwe Vagelpohl, edited by James

E. Montgomery. London and New York: Routledge, 2011.

68. *The Glory of Kings.* Translated by Miguel F. Brooks. Asmara: The Red Sea Press, 2002.

69. Tolan, John. *Saracens: Islam in the Medieval European Imagination.* New York: Columbia University Press, 2002.

70. *Quran.com,* https://quran.com/.

71. Walker, Joel Thomas. *The Legend of Mar Qardagh: Narrative and Christian Heroism in Late Antiquity Iraq.* California: University of California Press, 2006.

Wadah Khanfar

Author

Wadah Khanfar is the President of Al Sharq Forum and the President and Co-founder of the Common Action Forum. He was the Director General of the Al Jazeera Network from 2003 to 2011. He started his career as a journalist in 1997, serving as a foreign correspondent in many countries including South Africa, Afghanistan and Iraq. As a public intellectual, he has addressed leading universities, political and media think tanks. This is his first book.

Aslam Farouk-Alli

Translator

Aslam Farouk-Alli completed a M.Soc.Sci at the University of Cape Town and lectured part-time in the faculties of religion, language and literature and historical studies. He also holds an MA in Arabic Translation from the University of South Africa (UNISA). He left the academy to pursue a career as a diplomat in the South African Civil Service. He is the author of numerous articles and this is his third Arabic monograph translation into English.

www.ingramcontent.com/pod-product-compliance
Lightning Source LLC
Chambersburg PA
CBHW071727270326
41928CB00013B/2587
9781788711036